To John and Pam,

This will give you an idea about how I spend many of my Saturday afternoons now that my kids are out of the house (that is, when I'm not watching the Spartans or Bulldogs!)

All the best and Go Green!

Mel Davisk

INTERNATIONAL TRADE WITH
EQUILIBRIUM UNEMPLOYMENT

INTERNATIONAL TRADE WITH EQUILIBRIUM UNEMPLOYMENT

CARL DAVIDSON
AND
STEVEN J. MATUSZ

PRINCETON UNIVERSITY PRESS

PRINCETON AND OXFORD

Published by Princeton University Press, 41 William Street, Princeton, New Jersey 08540

In the United Kingdom: Princeton University Press, 6 Oxford Street, Woodstock, Oxfordshire OX20 1TW

Library of Congress Cataloging-in-Publication Data

Davidson, Carl, 1957-
   International trade with equilibrium unemployment / Carl Davidson and Steven J. Matusz.
      p. cm.
   Includes bibliographical references and index.
   ISBN 978-0-691-12559-6 (hardback : alk. paper)
   1. International trade.   2. Unemployment.   I. Matusz, Steven J. (Steven Joseph), 1956-   II. Title.
   HF1379.D385 2009
   331.13'72—dc22

                          2009021744

British Library Cataloging-in-Publication Data is available

This book has been composed in Sabon
Printed on acid-free paper. ∞
press.princeton.edu
Printed in the United States of America
10 9 8 7 6 5 4 3 2 1

To Natalie and Marie-France,
who have been there for us all along;
and for Maggie, Jaime, Isabel, and Evan,
who came along during the process and
provided us with all the enjoyable
distractions we could ask for

CONTENTS

PREFACE

This book has been in the works for some time—maybe not formally, but certainly in my mind. It all began back in 1980 when I was in my second year of graduate school at the University of Wisconsin, simultaneously taking graduate courses in international economics, advanced macroeconomics, and advanced microeconomics. International trade was an experiment—I knew almost nothing about the field other than that it relied heavily on models of general equilibrium. I was taking the advanced theory courses for two reasons. In my first-year course in macroeconomics (taught by Ken Burdett) I had been introduced to fascinating new models of unemployment that were in their developing stages. I was particularly taken with search theory, since I found the story of job creation compelling. Firms would post vacancies and announce wages and workers would search for the best job while weighing the costs and benefits of additional search; this just seemed like the right way to insert unemployment into a general equilibrium model. And, with Michael Rothschild teaching the advanced micro course, I knew that I would pick up a healthy dose of search theory there as well. The other reason for taking advanced micro was that microtheory had been my favorite first-year course. I loved the rigor and the elegance of the theory and the theorem-proof nature of the course suited me well—it was mathematics applied to questions of immediate practical importance.

I had heard good things about Bob Baldwin's course in international economics, and it fulfilled most of my expectations. I enjoyed both the geometric exposition of the models and the theorem-proof nature of the basic theory. The course had all of the appealing elements of my first-year courses in microeconomics coupled with questions that I found more interesting than those addressed in my other courses. The determinants of the pattern of trade and the links between trade and factor rewards seemed to me to be of enormous practical importance, and they were topics that were being debated on a daily basis in the political arena. Unfortunately, the public discourse seemed completely disconnected from what I was hearing in class everyday; this was the one disappointing feature of the course. The public debate about the impact of trade focused almost exclusively on the link between trade and jobs, whereas the models that I was being taught in class, the ones used to prove all of the fundamental theorems of trade theory, all assumed full employment. It seemed obvious to me that what was needed was an extension of the traditional trade model that allowed for equilibrium unemployment.[1] However, with Ken Burdett leaving Wisconsin at the end of that year, I could not find anyone willing to supervise such a thesis. One faculty member told me that extending general equilibrium models to allow for unemployment was a noble goal but too ambitious for a thesis. Another member told me that while search theory was once an interesting and promising tool, it was now "dead" since all the interesting questions had been answered.[2] In the end, I found another topic in another area (micro–industrial organization) and put my true research agenda on hold.

An unexpected twist of fate that occurred in my first year at Michigan State rekindled my interest in the topic. We were hiring in international economics and a Bill Ethier student from Penn, Steven Matusz, came through and gave a job talk. Reading Steve's job market paper both excited me and filled me with apprehension. He had taken the standard HOS model and extended it to allow for equilibrium unemployment that was generated by incomplete labor contracts.[3] I was excited by the fact that someone else shared my concerns about standard trade models and their assumption of full employment (although I was a bit worried: he was far into his project and I had not yet started on mine). Moreover, Steve had been able to convince Bill Ethier, a leader in the field, that this topic was worthy of a dissertation. We were fortunate enough to hire Steve that year and the two of us began working together shortly after his arrival.

Steve and I have worked diligently on this topic for over twenty years now, at first with Larry Martin and, more recently, with a variety of co-authors including Chris Magee, Doug Nelson, and Andrei Shevchenko. We have watched, mostly from the sidelines, as the field of international economics explored the implications of imperfect competition in the product market in the 1980s (the strategic trade literature), revisited the issue of growth and trade in the early 1990s, developed new models of political economy in the late 1990s, and turned to new models of firm- and plant-level adjustment to trade in this decade, all the while ignoring

[1] Our subsequent research suggests that trade has an ambiguous, though likely small impact on aggregate unemployment. However, modeling equilibrium unemployment can fundamentally change the general equilibrium allocation of resources and opens the door to a slew of questions that cannot even be asked in the context of full-employment models.
[2] This faculty member seemed convinced that the last question that needed to be addressed was the Diamond paradox—how could one develop a model in which (a) consumers searched optimally across firms and (b) firms would find it optimal to offer different equilibrium prices? A number of papers in the late 1970s managed to provide the necessary answers.
[3] This paper was subsequently published as Matusz (1985). The companion paper from his dissertation is Matusz (1986).

(for the most part) the structure of the labor market and any role that it might have in explaining trade-related outcomes. We have been surprised by this for two major reasons. First, there is the aforementioned disconnect between the public discourse over trade policy and the academic focus. If we are going to simply dismiss public concerns about links between trade and jobs, we ought at the very least to provide a rigorous argument for why such concerns are misguided. This cannot be accomplished within a framework that simply assumes full employment and frictionless labor markets.

Second, differences in labor market structures across the United States, Europe, and Japan are significant and well-documented. The implications of these differences for macroeconomic performance and other issues such as firm-level incentives to provide training for workers have been explored in great detail by macroeconomists and labor economists. One might suspect that these differences would also have dramatic implications for the manner in which trade affects resource allocations and factor rewards. And, although some papers have suggested this (most notably Krugman 1995 and Davis 1998), the topic has simply not garnered much attention.

One of the arguments that we have heard put forth to explain the paucity of work on this topic is that general equilibrium models with equilibrium unemployment are just too complex and unwieldy. In this book, we provide a collection of the work on trade and unemployment that we have carried out over the last twenty years. We have tried to organize the papers in a way that provides a coherent message: building such models is not all that difficult and the payoff to doing so is potentially substantial. While the organization of the book is described in detail in the introduction, it is worth noting that before each section we provide a brief summary of the papers contained within that section and the way in which its messages advance our long-range research agenda.

We first contacted Princeton University Press to explore the possibility of publishing our book in July 2004. We had tossed the idea around for at least a couple of years before that. At that time, we held a near monopoly on modeling trade with unemployment, and we had hoped that our book would encourage others join the discussion and develop general equilibrium trade models allowing for incomplete labor markets. We hoped that others would be inspired to use these sorts of models to analyze standard trade issues such as the determinants of trade patterns and the link between trade and factor rewards as well as important and interesting issues that cannot be tackled using full-employment models (e.g., what is the best way to compensate workers displaced from their jobs due to changes in trade policy?). In the time lag between conception and publication, we have been delighted to see strong and steady growth in this line of research. We point to many of these newer papers in our introductory chapter. So our goal is to now add momentum to this emerging research. Ultimately, we would love to see models with equilibrium unemployment as the norm in international economics.

A few years ago we attended a conference in which a young trade economist was asked to talk about future directions for research in international economics. At one point, he told that audience that we tend to write "too many papers" and that we should focus all of our attention on "important papers"—those that either "start a literature" or "end a literature." Although others have occasionally analyzed trade issues in the presence of equilibrium unemployment over the last twenty years (most notably Hian Teck Hoon), this is not a topic that has garnered much attention. Thus, if this book helps to inspire interest in this area, then we will feel that we have played a role in starting a new literature. If, on the other hand, the field continues to rely on models that simply assume away imperfections in the labor market, then those that make it through this book may simply conclude that we have written too many papers.

Carl Davidson – January 2009

I conceived my research agenda during a ninety-minute seminar at the University of Pennsylvania in the spring of 1981. By that time, I had wrapped up all of my required course work and had passed all of my qualifying exams, including the field exam in international economics. I had spent several months reading through issues of the *Journal of International Economics* (which was still quite young at that time) trying to identify a dissertation topic. Then it happened. As I had done many times before, I took my seat in a third-floor classroom in the McNeil Building for the weekly international economics workshop. The speaker that day was Bill Ethier. He presented a model of dumping where one of the key elements was a labor market characterized by implicit contracts.[4] The basic idea was that firms would lay off some workers but pay those who remained employed a wage in excess of the value of their marginal products during periods of slack demand. The outcome of this equilibrium would be perceived as periodic dumping. I could hardly contain myself. I wanted to rush out of the room and start writing my own paper. It only took me another year or so before I figured out how to do that.

I would not have had the insight to model the relationship between trade and unemployment had it not been for series of fortunate events, culminating in Ethier's seminar. The first steps down that road began during the first semester of my graduate program. Bill Ethier taught the first-

---

[4] This paper was subsequently published as Ethier (1982).

semester microeconomics course, and I found his rigorous treatment combined with deep intuition to be quite appealing. I was already leaning toward international trade as a field of study. My early exposure to Bill's teaching sealed the deal. At the same time, the first semester of macroeconomics was team taught by Costas Azariadis and Bob Shiller. Costas's portion of the course consisted of developing micro foundations of macroeconomics, including a heavy dose of implicit contract theory, of which he was a co-originator.[5] I did well enough in that class that I was invited to be the teaching assistant for the first semester of graduate macro during the fall 1980 semester.[6] This time, Costas taught the class alone. So that I might better help in that class, I sat in on the lectures. Having a couple of years of graduate training under my belt, I was able to better absorb the material.

Even with my fortuitous circumstances, I might not have picked up on the idea of studying the relationship between trade and unemployment if not for the fact that I read newspapers, watched TV, and talked regularly with my father (a factory worker). Everyone seemed to know that international trade was harmful because it destroyed American jobs. Being a wise and respectful son, I would usually just smile and nod during discussions with my father, all the while thinking (but not verbalizing) that trade was not about jobs, but it was about efficiency and comparative advantage. It never occurred to me that this was actually a researchable issue.[7] But Bill's seminar opened my eyes. Not only was this a researchable issue, but I had the tools to do it.

Having arrived at Michigan State University in 1983, I was keen to follow the advice given to me by a young assistant professor at Penn. I was told to always write three papers in a given area. Any fewer than that and people would view your knowledge as too shallow, and any more than that and people would view you as being too narrow. Having two papers carved from my dissertation, I intended to write one more on trade and unemployment, and then move on to other topics. But Carl had other ideas. Almost from my first day at MSU, I began collaborating with Carl and Larry Martin, and before long we had written several papers. As each project was nearing a close, I would vow that it would be my last. Unfortunately (or fortunately), each project seemed to lead us toward further interesting questions. My collaboration with Carl and other co-authors

[5] See Azariadis (1975).
[6] The truth is, I was one of two teaching assistants that semester. The other was Russ Cooper, who did all of the heavy lifting. I was given this job as somewhat of a "makeup" for a plum job that I was denied the previous semester because a professor preferred another candidate. But it worked out.
[7] According to one professor at Penn, nothing in trade was really researchable, since "trade is a moribund field."

has now lasted for more than twenty five years. The papers in this book represent the fruits of that collaboration. All things considered, I'm glad I did not stop at three.

Steven J. Matusz – January 2009

REFERENCES

Azariadis, Costas. 1975. Implicit contracts and underemployment equilibria. *Journal of Political Economy* 83(6): 1183–1202.

Davis, Donald. 1998. Does European unemployment prop up American wages? National labor markets and global trade. *American Economic Review* 88(3): 478–94.

Ethier, Wilfred. 1982. Dumping. *Journal of Political Economy* 90(3): 487–506.

Hoon, Hian Teck. 2000. *Trade, Jobs and Wages*. Northampton, MA: Edward Elgar Ltd.

Hoon, Hian Teck. 2001a. Adjustment of wages and equilibrium unemployment in a Ricardian global economy. *Journal of International Economics* 54: 193–209.

Hoon, Hian Teck. 2001b. General-equilibrium implications of international product-market competition for jobs and wages. *Oxford Economic Papers* 53: 138–56.

Krugman, Paul. 1995. Europe jobless, America penniless? *Foreign Policy* 95: 19–34.

Matusz, Steven. 1985. The Heckscher-Ohlin-Samuelson model with implicit contracts. *Quarterly Journal of Economics* 100(4): 1313–29.

Matusz, Steven. 1986. Implicit contracts, unemployment and international trade. *Economic Journal*, June: 307–22.

ACKNOWLEDGMENTS

Scores of friends and colleagues from Michigan State University and elsewhere have encouraged our research program during the past twenty-five years. Their comments and insights have shaped our thinking, sharpened our ideas, and forced us to think more deeply about our work. We are extraordinarily grateful to them for their many insightful observations and unflagging encouragement.

A number of colleagues deserve special mention because of either the depth of their contributions or the extent of their support. Foremost among them are our co-authors. As noted in our introduction to part 3, Chris Magee, now at Bucknell University, was at Michigan State University for the 1997–98 academic year. We had an opportunity to discuss many issues with Chris during that year, with our discussions ultimately culminating in our co-authorship of "Trade, Turnover, and Tithing" (chapter 8). We first met Doug Nelson, currently at Tulane University, when he was an assistant professor at Syracuse University (and we were assistant professors at MSU). Doug's broad and deep knowledge of the literature has made him a valuable resource for us and we are very pleased to have co-authored several papers with him, including "Can Compensation Save Free Trade?" (chapter 12). Andrei Shevchenko, our colleague at Michigan State University, is our most recent co-author. He brings to our program a deep understanding of search and matching models and is our co-author on "Globalization and Firm-Level Adjustment with Imperfect Labor Markets" (chapter 13) and "Outsourcing Peter to Pay Paul: High-Skill Expectations and Low-Skill Wages with Imperfect Labor Markets" (chapter 14).

We owe a particularly large debt to Larry Martin, who was with us at the beginning and continues to be our most valued sounding board for ideas. He is our co-author on the papers that form the foundation of our research agenda (chapters 2–5): "The Structure of Simple General Equilibrium Models with Frictional Unemployment," "Trade and Search-Generated Unemployment," "Multiple Free Trade Equilibria in Micro Models of Unemployment," and "Jobs and Chocolate: Samuelsonian Surpluses in Micro Models of Unemployment." This research agenda might have never gotten off the ground without Larry's input and we will always have fond memories of those hours spent in the bowels of Marshall Hall and Old Botany debating how to proceed with those early papers.

We are also indebted to seminar participants at numerous universities and conferences. We are particularly grateful to Ray Riezman and the

Midwest International Economics Group and to David Greenaway and our colleagues at the Leverhulme Centre for Research on Globalization and Economic Policy at the University of Nottingham for providing us with such excellent forums to showcase our work over the years. We thank the many editors and anonymous referees who conscientiously read and evaluated our work. We are very appreciative of those individuals who provided specific feedback on individual papers, including Jim Albrecht, Mary Amiti, Spiros Bougheas, Scott Bradford, Richard Brecher, Donald Davis, Steve Davis, Richard Disney, Rodney Falvey, Joel Fried, John Giles, Holger Gorg, Gene Grossman, Steven Haider, Daniel Hamermesh, James Harrigan, Peter Howitt, David Hummels, Andrew John, Ron Jones, Carsten Kowalczyk, Udo Kreickemeier, Steve Magee, Keith Maskus, John McLaren, John Moore, Nina Pavcnik, Tom Prusa, Peter Schmidt, Robert Staiger, Alan Stockman, Vitor Trindade, James Tybout, Richard Upward, Katharine Wakelin, Ping Wang, Jay Wilson, Peter Wright, Jeffrey Wooldridge, Randall Wright, and Susan Zhu.

Finally, we are grateful to the three anonymous reviewers of this book along with the staff at Princeton University Press, particularly Peter Dougherty and Seth Ditchik, for their faith in us and the support that they have given to this project.

CREDITS

"The structure of simple general equilibrium models with frictional unemployment" was authored with Lawrence Martin and first appeared in the *Journal of Political Economy*, December 1988, pp. 1267–93, © The University of Chicago.

The following papers were originally published in the *Journal of International Economics*, © Elsevier B.V.: "Multiple free trade equilibria in micro models of unemployment," authored with Lawrence Martin, published August 1991, pp. 157–69; "Trade with search-generated unemployment," also authored with Lawrence Martin, published August 1999, pp. 271–99; "Trade, turnover and tithing," authored with Christopher Magee, published May 2005, pp. 157–76; "Can compensation save free trade?" authored with Douglas Nelson, published March 2007, pp. 167–86; and "Globalization and firm-level adjustment with imperfect labor markets," authored with Andrei Shevchenko, published July 2008, pp. 295–309.

"Jobs and chocolate: Samuelsonian surpluses in dynamic models of unemployment" authored with Lawrence Martin, was published in the *Review of Economic Studies*, © The Review of Economic Studies Limited, April 1994, pp. 173–92.

The following papers were initially published in the *Review of International Economics*, © Blackwell Publishing Limited. "An overlapping-generations model of escape clause protection," November 2004, pp. 749–68; "Trade and turnover: Theory and evidence," published November 2005, pp. 861–80; and "Long-run lunacy, short-run sanity: A simple model of trade with labor market turnover," May 2006, pp. 261–76.

"Trade liberalization and compensation" originally appeared in August 2006, pp. 723–48, the *International Economic Review*, © Blackwell Publishing Limited.

"Outsourcing Peter to pay Paul: High-skill expectations and low-skill wages," authored with Andrei Shevchenko, was initially published in *Macroeconomic Dynamics*, © Cambridge University Press, September 2008, pp. 463–79.

Finally, "Should policy makers be concerned about adjustment costs?" was originally published in *The Political Economy of Trade, Aid and Foreign Investment*, a volume edited by Devashish Mitra and Arvind Panagariya in honor of Edward Tower, © Emerald Publishing.

Small editorial changes were made to Chapter 2 (as described in the introduction to part 1) and notation was changed for consistency in parts 1 and 2. Other than that, these articles appear in their originally published form.

INTERNATIONAL TRADE WITH
EQUILIBRIUM UNEMPLOYMENT

Chapter 1

OUR MOTIVATION

In 1992 H. Ross Perot ran as an independent candidate for the presidency of the United States. Two of his major campaign issues were the size of the national debt and a promise to block the passage of the North America Free Trade Agreement (NAFTA) in response to fears that this would lead to large job losses for American workers. Perhaps the most well-known phrase from this campaign was tied to his prediction that the passage of NAFTA would result in a "giant sucking sound" as jobs headed south for Mexico where wages were significantly below those paid in the United States. Playing off of such fears, Perot garnered roughly 19% of the popular vote, making him the second most successful third-party presidential candidate over the past hundred years.[1]

Perot is not the only politician to argue that there is a strong link between international trade and jobs. In fact, we would argue that this is the norm. Almost every public debate about trade policy seems to focus on how job creation and job destruction will be affected. The two sides always seem to agree on what the central issue is—trade and jobs—they just disagree about the likely impact of openness on employment. Those who favor freer trade argue that one of its primary benefits is that openness expands our export markets and therefore creates new jobs. In contrast, those that favor trade restrictions worry that liberalization allows countries to shift production to lower wage countries, thereby destroying domestic jobs.

Most academic economists specializing in international economics view both of these arguments as fundamentally flawed. The standard view seems to be that overall employment is largely independent of trade policy and that the primary impact of trade on workers comes through

[1] Teddy Roosevelt was the most successful third-party candidate over the past 100 years, collecting over 27% of the popular vote and 88 electoral votes in 1912. Since then, Perot was the most successful third-party presidential candidate in terms of the popular vote, but he failed to carry a single state and therefore won zero votes in the Electoral College. In terms of the Electoral College, the most successful candidate since 1912 was George Wallace, who won five states and forty six electoral votes in 1968. Wallace was popular only in the South, however, and won only 13.5% of the popular vote.

the changes in their wages. Given this firm belief that trade does not affect aggregate employment, the profession has tended to rely almost exclusively on full-employment models to investigate the link between trade and worker welfare.

Since the early 1980s, we have argued that this reliance on full-employment modeling, by its very nature, misses the point and that it is time to extend conventional trade models to take into account the market imperfections that lead to equilibrium unemployment. We have made this argument in many articles, but each one taken separately addressed only a small subset of issues. In this book, we bring much of our work together. We believe that the value of this exercise is in highlighting a coherent research agenda that has yielded many new insights and strengthens the case that there awaits much fruitful and important research. In particular, we hope to convince our readers that the modeling techniques required to add unemployment to standard trade models are now available and that significant new insights can be gained from such an extension. Moreover, we emphasize that the development of such models allows for the consideration of important issues that simply cannot be addressed in a full-employment framework.[2]

Our goal in this introductory chapter is to make the case that models built around full employment, while clearly useful in understanding many of the most subtle issues involving international trade, are ill equipped to seriously tackle a variety of critically important trade-related issues, for which a deep understanding demands more textured modeling of the labor market. Whereas many reasons led us to believe this to be the case, we concentrate here on the three that we consider to be most compelling. These three reasons are tied to recent developments in labor economics and macroeconomics as well as the apparent disconnect between the public and academic views of the impact of trade on labor market outcomes. Once we have made our case, we then go on to briefly summarize the contents of the book and provide a rationale for its organization.

Reason 1: A lack of adequate research on trade with unemployment leaves a vacuum to be filled by protectionist pressure.

It is easy to make the case that many noneconomists, including those in position to craft policy, seem absolutely convinced that international

---

[2] A great deal of applied policy analysis is conducted by use of computable general equilibrium (CGE) models such as the Michigan Model of World Production and Trade. However, these models are all constructed under an assumption of full employment. See, for example, Brown, Deardorff, and Stern (2001). As one reviewer for this book notes, equilibrium unemployment has not yet made its way into CGE modeling, and this is an area that could bring great payoffs. See footnote 4 for further views on this issue.

trade is all about the jobs that it creates and/or destroys. We began this chapter by pointing to H. Ross Perot's well-know prediction about the "giant sucking sound" that would occur as American jobs moved to Mexico following the passage of NAFTA. Perot was not in favor of trade liberalization with Mexico and made his prediction in an effort to block NAFTA's passage. Of course, we could have just as easily focused on the statement made by George H. W. Bush when on a 1992 trade-promoting visit to Japan he declared that his trip was all about generating "jobs, jobs, jobs." A few other choice quotes from the NAFTA debate help to underscore the prevalence of this view. Note that in each case, the main focus is on the link between trade and jobs:

> Unfair trade agreements, passed by both Republicans and Democrats, have sent millions of jobs to other countries. We need to stop this hemorrhaging and find ways for American workers to compete in the new market. Russ Feingold (U.S. Senator–Wisconsin, February 2005)

> The Bush Administration and the Congress have to stop ignoring this crisis in international trade. The longer we ignore it, the more American jobs will move overseas. It's just that simple. Byron Dorgan (U.S. Senator–North Dakota, March 2005)

> There is $1.4 billion a day in trade that goes back and forth across the border. That means millions of jobs and livelihoods for families here in Canada and for families in the United States. Paul Cellucci (U.S. Ambassador to Canada, March 2005)

Some have even suggested that NAFTA resulted in an outcome that harmed workers on *both* sides of the border, with Mexican workers losing jobs and suffering wages loses along with their American counterparts:

> Since NAFTA was put in place, Mexico has lost 1.9 million jobs and most Mexicans' real wages have fallen. Stephen Lynch (U.S. Congressman–Massachusetts, May 2005)

And this view of trade is not an American phenomenon; it is true in virtually every part of the world:

> The global economy is a fact. The expansion of world trade—with exports up over 50 percent since 1990—has created millions of new jobs and offered many the chance to move from poverty towards prosperity. . . . [A]bove all . . . more open markets and more trade means growth and new jobs. Tony Blair (Statement to the WTO, 1998)

> [Free trade is] the key to jobs for our people, prosperity and actually to development in the poorest parts of the world. Tony Blair (Statement to Canadian Parliament, 2001)

Finally, we note the seemingly far-fetched suggestion that the link among trade, jobs, and economic growth is so strong that liberalizing trade is an ideal way to fight terrorism:

> Trade creates jobs and lifts people out of poverty. And when that happens, societies stabilize and grow. And there is nothing like a stable society to fight terrorism and strengthen democracy, freedom and rule of law. Dennis Hastert (Speaker of the House, July 2005)

Of course, we could easily fill all the pages of this book with more quotes that would support this contention, but we do not think we have to—we would be surprised if anyone disagrees with us.

Given the chorus of public opinion and statements by politicians of all stripes regarding the links between employment and trade, it might be natural for the academic community to provide guidance to those who wish to become informed and sort out the arguments. After all, better policies are likely to result if they are based on scientific principles rather than a politician's gut instincts. In fact, we heartily agree with the sentiments of the former U.S. Senate Majority Leader Bill Frist, who argued that "sound science must be a basis to governing our trade relations around the globe." So, if we turn to academia, what do we find? We believe that the following two quotes, which we have used repeatedly to motivate interest in our previous work, capture the mainstream view among economists specializing in international economics:

> It should be possible to emphasize to students that the level of employment is a macroeconomic issue ... depending in the long run on the natural rate of unemployment, with microeconomic policies like tariffs having little net effect. Paul Krugman (*American Economic Review*, 1993)

> Economists understand that the effect of protectionist policies is not on the overall employment of domestic resources, but rather on the allocation of resources across productive activities. Michael Mussa (*American Economic Review*, 1993)

The point that Krugman and Mussa are making is a simple one that is generally accepted by macroeconomists: the level of aggregate economic activity is dictated solely by macroeconomic variables such as the money supply. While we understand and respect this view, we also feel that it is a mistake to dismiss the public's concerns about trade and jobs so casually. We have several reasons for this. To begin with, very little direct empirical evidence supports the view that aggregate unemployment is independent of trade policy. Although it is true that a large number of studies have examined the impact of trade on jobs, virtually all of these focus on a specific industry or a set of industries (e.g., manufacturing in the United States), and almost none look at aggregate employment (see chapter 2 of Davidson and Matusz 2004 for a detailed review of the evidence).

Moreover, we would argue that there are good reasons to suspect that trade policy *must* affect the natural rate of unemployment in most economies. This follows from the observation that labor market frictions clearly exist and seem to vary across geographic regions within countries and sectors across economies.[3] Differential frictions suggest different "natural rates" of unemployment that are both region specific and sector specific. By construction, the economywide natural rate of unemployment is a convex combination of these component parts. By reallocating resources across regions and sectors, more liberal trade necessarily changes the weighting scheme and must therefore affect the economywide natural rate of unemployment. For example, the economywide natural rate of unemployment would increase if more liberal trade induced a shift of resources from sectors with relatively low natural rates of unemployment to those with relatively high natural rates.

This point has been made in a number of articles including Davidson, Martin, and Matusz (1987, 1999), Matusz (1985, 1994), and, more recently, Helpman and Itskhoki (2007) and Helpman, Itskhoki, and Redding (2008). In addition, Janiak (2006) recently embedded equilibrium unemployment in a Melitz (2003) model of monopolistic competition and firm heterogeneity and demonstrated that higher trade exposure results in lower aggregate employment. This result is supported by Janiak's subsequent empirical work showing that a one-point increase in the import penetration ratio results in a 14.7-point increase in the job destruction rate without any significant increase in the rate of job creation. Additional empirical work on the link between trade and unemployment can be found in Dutt, Mitra, and Ranjan (2008).

While the overall impact of trade on unemployment is an empirical question, our expectation is that it is likely to be quite small. And this issue has never been the focus of our research (which is why this book is *not* titled *Trade and Unemployment*). This leads to a natural question: If our conjecture is correct and trade has only a small effect on aggregate unemployment, what is the cost of simply using full-employment models to investigate trade issues? Our answer consists of two parts; one is tied to the manner in which our views are perceived by the public and the other deals directly with a substantive research issue.

---

[3] The fact that neither the average duration of unemployment nor the average duration of a vacancy is close to zero firmly establishes the existence of frictions in the labor market. And the enormous literature that has followed the pioneering work of Davis, Haltiwanger, and Schuh (1996) on job creation and job destruction in U.S. manufacturing clearly indicates that these rates vary dramatically across industries and across countries.

It is one thing for scientists to dismiss as irrelevant those who believe the Earth is flat. Virtually everyone can tell the difference between fact and fiction with respect to the shape of our planet. In contrast, issues as fundamental to economists as comparative advantage are not as firmly established among the wider public. By assuming away the connection between trade and unemployment, which many people believe to be both real and important, we make it all too easy for those who push for protectionist measures in the popular press to simply dismiss anything that economists have to say about trade. As an example, consider the following passage from an April 2006 article in the *Monthly Review* by Martin Hart-Landsberg titled "Neoliberalism: Myths and Reality":

> Like all theories, the theory of comparative advantage (and its conclusion) is based on a number of assumptions. Among the most important are:
>
> - There is perfect competition between firms.
> - There is full employment of all factors of production.
> - Labor and capital are perfectly mobile within a country and do not move across national borders.
> - A country's gains from trade are captured by those living in the country and spent locally.
> - A country's external trade is always in balance.
> - Market prices accurately reflect the real (or social) costs of the products produced.
>
> Even a quick consideration of these assumptions reveals that they are extensive and unrealistic. Moreover, if they are not satisfied, there is no basis for accepting the theory's conclusion that free-market policies will promote international well being. For example, the assumption of full employment of all factors of production, including labor, is obviously false. Equally problematic is the theory's implied restructuring process, which assumes that (but never explains how) workers who lose their jobs as a result of free-trade generated imports will quickly find new employment in the expanding export sector of the economy. In reality, workers (and other factors of production) may not be equally productive in alternative uses. Even if we ignore this problem, if their reallocation is not sufficiently fast, the newly liberalized economy will likely suffer an increase in unemployment, leading to a reduction in aggregate demand and perhaps recession. Thus, even if all factors of production eventually become fully employed, it is quite possible that the cost of adjustment would outweigh the alleged efficiency gains from the trade-induced restructuring.

The author's message in this passage is clear: because academics use full-employment models, our results have no credibility. Although we do not agree with this conclusion, we must admit that we are sympathetic to some of the points that are made along the way. For example, while the profession acknowledges the existence of trade-related adjustment costs, little effort has been directed at quantifying them at an aggregate level. In addition, whereas the profession acknowledges that trade harms some agents, we have not spent a great deal of energy trying to figure out the best way to redistribute the gains from trade in order to compensate those who lose (so that a true Pareto improvement can be achieved). There has been some work on these topics, but not nearly as much as one would expect given the prominence these issues command in public discourse. It is not hard to figure out why: these issues cannot be examined in full-employment models, which are the bread and butter of our field.

We want to make it clear that we are not questioning the value of abstraction. Models will always be filled with unrealistic assumptions and the profession will always be vulnerable to criticism like the one provided above. But when it comes to trade issues, assuming away unemployment is, in our minds, especially problematic given the recent evidence that the *personal* cost of worker dislocation may be quite high. For example, Jacobson, LaLonde, and Sullivan (1993a, b) find that the average dislocated worker suffers a loss in lifetime earnings of $80,000, with much of the loss attributed to a lower reemployment wage. And, more recently, Kletzer (2001) reported that the average dislocated worker in her study took a 13% pay cut on his or her new job. These are the kinds of personal costs that often accompany changes in trade policy that appear to be of paramount importance to many in the public domain. And even if the aggregate gains from trade swamp such personal losses, the profession appears heartless and disconnected from the concerns of common citizens when it ignores them.[4] This has led several prominent economists such as Alan Blinder and Dani Rodrik to call on economists to think more deeply

---

[4] Or, at the very least, it makes it easy for critics to paint academic economists as out of touch with the concerns of common citizens. A good example of this comes from Peter Dorman's 2001 Economic Policy Institute Briefing Paper (111) titled "The Free Trade Magic Act" in which he completely dismisses estimates of the gains from liberalization provided by highly respected economists Drusilla Brown, Alan Deardorff, and Robert Stern (2001). Dorman argues that their estimates cannot be trusted since the analysis "depends on five sleights of hand." In particular, he states that "The model is flagrantly disconnected from the real world. It assumes that no one is ever unemployed, trade balances never change, and credit is always available to everyone." He also points out that the model ignores the costs of trade liberalization: "All economic analysis must simplify, but what matters in any debate is the usefulness of the assumptions. Critics and supporters of free trade are trying to determine whether the benefits of liberalization exceed the costs. As mentioned earlier, Brown-Deardorff-Stern assume away all criticisms of globalization." Dorman attempts to underscore this point by pointing out (again) that "They further assume full employment of labor in all countries at all times. Workers who lose jobs in one industry instantaneously find others somewhere else."

about our attitude toward trade policy.[5] One of the major points that we hope to make in this book is that there is no need to continue to rely on full-employment models—the tools are now available to build and analyze general equilibrium models that allow for equilibrium unemployment. Doing so and using these models to analyze standard trade issues will make it far more difficult for our critics to ignore our claims.

More fundamentally, and this is the substantive research issue alluded to above, we will argue that models that take into account the market imperfections that generate equilibrium unemployment are likely to behave in *significantly* different ways than models that assume perfectly competitive frictionless labor markets. In fact, much of our research has been devoted to sorting out how the presence of unemployment changes a number of underlying relationships in general equilibrium open economy settings (which is why we decided on the title *Trade with Unemployment*). For example, in chapters 1 and 2 of this book we show that the link between trade and factor rewards, governed by the Stolper-Samuelson theorem in the full-employment Heckscher-Ohlin-Samuelson (HOS) model, is substantively different when there are frictions in the labor market.

Reason 2: Macroeconomics teaches us that imperfections in the labor market are important.

Do models that account for unemployment behave in approximately the same way as full-employment models? If so, then our reliance on full-employment models is probably judicious and pragmatic—the models probably would yield similar conclusions and full-employment models would be far more tractable. However, if these models differ in fundamental ways, then relying on full-employment models may lead to faulty conclusions and may obscure key insights. If this is the case, then it is important to understand how the models differ.

To address this issue, we start by going back to 1968 when Milton Friedman gave his Presidential Address to the American Economic Association and defined the "natural rate of unemployment" in the following way:

> The "natural rate of unemployment," in other words, is the level that would be ground out by the Walrasian system of general equilibrium equations, provided there is embedded in them the actual structural characteristics of the

[5] See, for example, section III.A of Blinder's 1988 Richard T. Ely Lecture in the *American Economic Review* in which he challenged trade economists to take the issue of unemployment seriously. More recently, see the articles in the *Wall Street Journal* "Job Prospects: Pain from Free Trade Spurs Second Thoughts—Mr. Blinder's Shift Spotlights Warnings of Deeper Downside" and "Politics $ Economics—CAPITAL: As Globalization's Benefits Grow, So Do Its Skeptics" (March 28 and 29, 2007, respectively).

labor and commodity markets, including market imperfections, stochastic variability in demands and supplies, the cost of gathering information about job vacancies and labor availabilities, the costs of mobility, and so on.

Although this is just a conjecture on our part, we believe that by invoking the term "Walrasian system" Friedman meant to imply that a general equilibrium model that included these labor market imperfections would share the key features of a standard Walrasian model—in particular, the equilibrium rate of unemployment would be constrained Pareto efficient. Initial work by Lucas and Prescott (1974) seemed to confirm this view.

At the same time that Friedman was pushing his notion of the natural rate of unemployment and the rational expectations revolution was beginning in macroeconomics, significant changes were under way in microeconomics as well. In particular, following George Stigler's classic papers on the economics of information (Stigler 1961, 1962), an enormous literature on markets with incomplete information began to emerge. For our purposes, the most significant work was related to equilibrium price dispersion. Two key questions needed to be addressed. First, suppose that unemployed workers must search for a job without knowing which firms are offering which wages; what is the optimal search strategy? Second, given that workers search optimally, what would the equilibrium distribution of wages look like? In particular, could a nondegenerate distribution of wages be supported in equilibrium? Determining the equilibrium wage distribution would be a key step in analyzing the efficiency properties of the market outcome and, in particular, the efficiency of the equilibrium rate of unemployment.

Assuming that the worker knows the distribution of wages, the first question was answered by McCall (1965, 1970), who showed that it was optimal for workers to use an optimal stopping rule: searching until finding a wage offer at or above a prespecified level. This prespecified level, the "reservation wage," was the wage that equated the expected benefit from continued search (in the form of a higher wage) with the marginal cost of additional search. The initial answer to the second question was provided by Diamond (1971) and it was disturbing. Diamond showed that if all workers know the distribution of wages, search using a reservation wage rule, and face positive search costs (no matter how small), then the only equilibrium is characterized by all firms offering the monopsony wage. In other words, optimal search by workers eliminates the need to search! This became known as the "Diamond paradox."

The Diamond paradox presents two troubling aspects. The first is the implication that it is impossible to build a model of search-generated unemployment in which workers know the distribution of wages and firms

find it optimal to offer different wages.[6] And if all firms offer the same
wage, all workers simply accept the first job offered them, implying that
no one is unemployed in equilibrium. In the late 1970s and early 1980s,
this aspect of the Diamond paradox was resolved in a number of satisfying ways. Reinganum (1979) pointed out that if firms differ in non-labor
costs, then they will not agree on the monopsony wage, and this is enough
to generate equilibrium wage dispersion. Burdett and Judd (1983) demonstrated that if firms take time before making offers after the initial
contact with the worker (so that a worker might receive a second offer
before having to decide on the first one), then this might also result in a
nontrivial equilibrium distribution of wages.

The second troubling aspect of the Diamond paradox is that it implies
that search costs, no matter how small, can create large inefficiencies—
after all, the result that all firms offer the monopsony wage holds regardless of the number of firms and no matter how small the search costs are
(as long as they are all positive). Thus models that are "close" to perfect
competition may have equilibria that are strikingly noncompetitive.[7]
Moreover, these inefficiencies continue to appear in models such as those
formulated by Reinganum (1979) and Burdett and Judd (1983), which
were designed to explain equilibrium wage dispersion. One lesson learned
from this literature is that it would be an error to simply argue that since
search costs are likely to be small, models that include search-generated
unemployment are likely to produce equilibria that are similar to those in
full-employment models. These early search models predicted quite the
opposite!

[6] Assuming that the workers knew the distribution of wages was necessary for tractability.
As Rothschild showed (1974), if the workers do not know the distribution of wages, the
optimal search strategy becomes almost impossible to characterize except in a small subset
of cases.
[7] The logic that supports this result is simple and compelling. The proof can be divided into
two steps. First, show that in equilibrium all firms must offer the same wage. The second
step is to show that the common wage must be the one that a monopsonist would offer. The
first part can be proven by contradiction. Suppose that all firms do *not* offer the same wage.
Let $\varepsilon > 0$ denote the lowest search cost borne by any worker and let w' denote the highest
wage paid by any firm. Then it is clear that any firm offering w' cannot be maximizing profits since it can lower its wage offer by $\varepsilon/2$ without reducing the size of its labor force. To see
this, note that no worker would reject the lower offer since he or she would have to pay at
least ε to search again and can, at best, increase his or her wage offer by $\varepsilon/2$ by doing so.
The lower wage offer reduces the firm's costs without altering output and thus increases
profits. The conclusion is that no firm will be willing to offer the highest wage—thus all
firms offer the same wage. A similar argument can be used to complete the proof. With all
firms offering the same wage, any single firm can (again) lower its wage by $\varepsilon/2$ without
causing any worker to reject its offer. If the common wage is above the monopsony wage,
profit increases as the wage falls, and all firms choose to reduce their wage. The process
continues until all firms pay the monopsony wage.

As search models evolved and macroeconomists began to embed trading frictions in general equilibrium models, their inefficiencies were highlighted and dissected and their implications explored. Peter Diamond (1981, 1982a, 1982b) and Dale Mortensen (1982) emphasized that models with trading frictions are riddled with externalities, making market failure the expected outcome. For example, consider an economy with multiple sectors in which unemployed workers and firms with vacancies must expend time and effort to find each other. Then, any decision by a worker to seek a job in a particular sector makes it harder for other workers in that sector to find a job (a negative externality) while making it easier for firms in that sector to fill their vacancies (a positive externality). Although the external impact on any given worker or firm may be small, a large number of workers and firms are affected. As a result, equilibrium is likely to be suboptimal, and, since each decision generates both positive and negative externalities, the equilibrium rate of unemployment may be too high or too low.

Diamond (1982b) raised another concern by pointing out that models with unemployment are likely to be characterized by multiple equilibria, primarily due to feedback effects and the important role played by expectations about economic activity. To see this, note that the amount of search effort that workers will be willing to expend will be influenced by the number of job opportunities that they expect to be available. If workers expect firms to create a large number of job opportunities, they will be willing to search hard for those openings. And if workers are searching hard, then firms, knowing that new vacancies will be easy to fill, will be willing to create a large number of job opportunities. Thus optimistic, self-fulfilling expectations on the part of workers can lead to an equilibrium with a high level of employment. However, an equilibrium with a low rate of employment may exist as well. This equilibrium is supported by pessimistic, self-fulfilling expectations in which workers expect it to be hard to find a job and therefore choose a low level of search effort. And with workers unwilling to search hard for jobs, firms expect it to be hard to fill new vacancies and thus they do not create many new job opportunities.[8]

While much of our early work focused on the implications of inefficient outcomes and a possible multiplicity of equilibria, we occasionally ran into some rather strong resistance to our basic message. Some individuals

[8] Multiple equilibria and inefficient equilibrium outcomes are not unique to models with search-generated unemployment. As we discussed at length in Davidson, Martin, and Matusz (1991) and Davidson and Matusz (2004), most models that explain unemployment as the result of labor market imperfections exhibit these two characteristics. For example, this is true of the efficiency wage model (Shapiro and Stiglitz 1984) and the fair-wage model (Akerlof and Yellen 1990).

pointed out that search-generated externalities are hard to measure, so that it is difficult to know just how important they are from a practical standpoint. Similar issues arise with respect to the role of the feedback mechanisms and self-fulfilling expectations that lead to multiple equilibria. We became convinced that if we wanted to persuade economists of the practical aspects of modeling trade with unemployment, we were going to have to hang our hat on results derived in models in which equilibrium is unique and constrained Pareto efficient.

In the mid- to late 1990s we began working with such models and we had little trouble finding concrete examples in which the presence of unemployment significantly altered the underlying structure of the model. For example, in full-employment models the rates at which jobs are created and destroyed play no role in the analysis. This is because with frictionless labor markets worker are always guaranteed that they will find new jobs immediately upon termination. Now, consider a model in which jobs take time and effort to find. In some sectors jobs might be easier to find than in others and some occupations may offer more job security than others. It is not hard to see that turnover rates will now play an important role in workers' occupation choices, as a worker might be willing to trade off a lower wage for greater job security. Lower wages, in turn, translate into lower production costs and hence lower autarkic prices. The implication is that turnover rates may play a role in shaping comparative advantage.

Similar logic suggests that turnover rates should affect the link between trade and wages. If jobs are costly to obtain, a worker will be reluctant to quit even if other sectors offer somewhat higher compensation. This implies that trade frictions make employed factors quasi-fixed and this generates qualitative properties that are characteristic of Ricardo-Viner economies even if the remaining structure of the model is consistent with the Hecksher-Ohlin-Samuelson framework. Thus we conclude that even if equilibrium is unique and constrained efficient, there are strong reasons to suspect that the factors that generate unemployment may affect the links between key variables in general equilibrium settings. As a result, models that take the market imperfections that lead to unemployment into account are likely to behave very differently from their full-employment counterparts. And, as macroeconomists have pointed out, this is likely to be the case even when such imperfections are small.

Reason 3: Labor economics teaches us that the structure of the labor market matters and that the personal costs from worker dislocation are large.

When factor markets are incomplete, labor market institutions become particularly important for determining the manner in which trade shocks are propagated throughout the economy. And a large literature in labor economics documents the tremendous heterogeneity in labor market institutions across countries. For example, labor markets in the United States are relatively flexible. Minimum wage laws apply to only a small fraction of the workforce (see, for example, Brown 1999), and union influence has been weak and on the decline for quite some time now (see, for example, Nickell 1997). In addition, job creation and job destruction rates are high relative to other countries, suggesting a dynamic economy in which jobs turn over frequently even when sectors are not expanding or contracting at the aggregate level (Davis, Haltiwanger, and Schuh 1996).

In contrast, in many European labor markets unions still dominate the wage-setting process, and firms face a considerable amount of government regulation that adds to the cost associated with altering the size of its labor force (see Freeman 1994; Nickell 1997). Moreover, job creation and job destruction rates are often considerably lower than those in the United States, even when the economies appear to be quite similar in other respects.[9] This creates an environment in which wages are relatively flexible in the United States but highly rigid in Europe. This point is not lost on economists. Labor economists and macroeconomists have noted the differences in labor market institutions across countries and have explored their implications for a variety of issues (e.g., macroeconomic performance and the manner in which training costs are covered).

The World Bank has developed an index used to measure the degree of labor market flexibility. Table 1.1, taken from Cunat and Melitz (2006), provides a summary of their findings with countries grouped based on GDP per capita. Higher scores indicate a more flexible labor market. The table indicates differences in labor market flexibility even across countries within the same income group. For example, the United States, Canada, and the United Kingdom all have labor markets that are considerably more flexible than countries such as Spain, Portugal, France, Greece, and Germany, all of which belong to the high-income group.

There is also considerable evidence of a great deal of *within*-country variability in job creation and job destruction rates across sectors. Davis, Haltiwanger, and Schuh (1996) provide the documentation for manufacturing sectors in the United States; the enormous literature that has grown up since their pioneering work provides similar documentation for a large number of other countries.

---

[9] For example, Blanchard and Portugal (2001) show that job flow rates in the United States and Portugal are quite different even though the aggregate unemployment rates in the two economies are very similar.

TABLE 1.1

Low-Income Countries		Middle-Income Countries		High-Income Countries	
Country	*Flexibility*	*Country*	*Flexibility*	*Country*	*Flexibility*
Morocco	30	Mexico	28	Spain	31
Ukraine	36	Brazil	28	France	34
Guinea	41	Paraguay	41	Greece	34
Uzbekistan	42	Venezuela	44	Portugal	42
Indonesia	43	Turkey	45	Germany	45
Peru	45	Belarus	46	Slovenia	47
Algeria	45	Tunisia	46	Argentina	49
Moldova	46	South Africa	48	Italy	50
Egypt	47	Colombia	49	Finland	56
El Salvador	48	Latvia	51	Netherlands	57
Ecuador	49	Estonia	56	Sweden	57
Georgia	51	Thailand	58	Austria	60
India	52	Lithuania	59	Oman	65
Philippines	59	Hungary	60	South Korea	66
Bolivia	60	Iran	60	Israel	67
Dominican Republic	60	Costa Rica	65	Norway	70
Guatemala	60	Poland	66	Ireland	71
Sri Lanka	60	Uruguay	69	Czech Republic	72
Kyrgyzstan	62	Bulgaria	72	Japan	76
Azerbaijan	62	Kazakhstan	73	Belgium	80
Macedonia	62	Russia	73	United Kingdom	80
Syria	63	Fiji	79	Kuwait	80
Armenia	64	Chile	81	Switzerland	83
Jordan	66	Slovakia	90	Australia	83
Honduras	69	Malaysia	97	Denmark	83
China	70			Saudi Arabia	87
Albania	70			New Zealand	93
Lebanon	72			Canada	96
Zimbabwe	76			United States	97
Papua New Guinea	83			Singapore	100
Jamaica	90			Hong Kong	100

Table adapted from Cunat and Melitz (2006). Low-income countries have per captia GDP between $2,000 and $5,000, middle-income countries have per capita GDP between $5,000 and $10,000, and high-income countries have per capita income above $10,000.

It is surprising that the evidence of large cross-country and cross-sector differences in basic labor market structure has not yet had a significant impact on research in international economics, a discipline where other sorts of differences (e.g., in endowments, factor intensities, and technology) are central to so many different analyses. There are, of course, exceptions (e.g., Krugman 1995 or Davis 1998); but by and large the importance of labor market structure and labor market institutions has not, in our opinion, received the attention that it deserves.[10]

Clearly, labor market structure can affect (and be affected by) trade. For example, labor market institutions alter the manner in which factor prices adjust to trade-related shocks. They also have profound implications for the hiring and firing decisions of firms. For example, union contracts may restrict the firm's ability to lay off workers when export demand falls. Well-developed markets for temporary hiring may allow firms to expand employment quickly. Thus it is hard to believe that these institutions play no role in the link between trade and wages.

An additional area in which labor market structure is of importance is in the analysis of adjustment costs. Since trade liberalization triggers a reallocation of resources across sectors, it necessarily implies adjustment. The speed and efficiency with which such adjustment takes place is surely influenced by labor market institutions and government support provided through the welfare state. The standard approach in international economics is to acknowledge that there are costs to adjustment and then to note that they are likely to be small and, since labor market structures are rarely, if ever, discussed, one must presume independent of the institutional setting. In this context, "small" means that adjustment costs are likely to be swamped by the benefits from freer trade, so that it would always be possible (in principle) to compensate those who bear the costs without exhausting the gains from trade. However, this conclusion is really more a matter of faith than the outcome of a serious attempt at empirical measurement or theoretical modeling.

The standard frameworks that have been used to analyze international trade issues are simply not adequate either to measure the size and scope of adjustment costs or to provide us with any insight about the most efficient manner to compensate those harmed by liberalization. Models that ignore the search and training processes undertaken by workers to acquire skills and seek out job prospects cannot be used to measure the costs that dislocated workers face when losing a job due to increased

---

[10] We are delighted to note that this has begun to change recently. Over the past few years several new papers have appeared that deal with trade-related issues in the presence of imperfect labor markets and unemployment. Purely theoretical work includes Hoon (2000, 2001a, b), Kreickmeier and Nelson (2006), Moore and Ranjan (2005), Costinot (2007), Davis and Harrigan (2007), Egger and Kreickemier (2007, 2008), Felbermayr, Prat, and Schmerer (2007), Helpman and Itskhoki (2007), Helpman, Itskhoki, and Redding (2008), Mitra and Ranjan (2007), and Song, Xu, and Sheng (2007). Papers that offer theoretical treatments coupled with empirical analysis include Bradford (2006), Cunat and Melitz (2006), Janiak (2006), and Dutt, Mitra, and Ranjan (2008). However, if one compares this with the attention devoted to the product market in the 1980s and growth and models of political economy in the 1990s, it is still remarkably small.

import competition. While there were some early attempts to pin down these costs (see, for example, Magee 1972 or Baldwin, Mutti, and Richardson 1980), unemployment was always treated in an ad hoc and inadequate manner. This was understandable since, at the time that these papers were written, general equilibrium models with micro-based explanations of unemployment were not yet available. This is no longer the case.

The need to account for adjustment costs has been underscored, as we noted at the outset, by the recent findings cited earlier that quantify the personal costs of worker dislocation: the Jacobson, LaLonde, and Sullivan (1993a, b) finding that that the average loss in lifetime income for dislocated workers is roughly $80,000, and the Kletzer (2001) finding that the average dislocated worker takes roughly a 13% wage reduction to find reemployment. The implication is that even if aggregate adjustment costs are small, the personal costs to individual workers may be high.

Such findings have given considerable ammunition to those in Washington who have been pushing for programs to provide support for dislocated workers (see, for example, Lawrence and Litan 1986; Bailey, Burtless, and Litan 1993; Bailey, Burtless, Litan, and Shapiro 1998; Kletzer and Litan 2001). Offering compensation to workers who lose their jobs due to liberalization can be justified in a number of ways.[11] To begin with, there is a straightforward equity argument: since we choose to liberalize trade, knowing that some workers will be harmed, we should compensate those who lose as long as we can afford to do so. This rationale dovetails nicely with the standard argument made in trade textbooks: since liberalization generates aggregate net benefits, we can always compensate the losers without exhausting the gains from trade. In theory at least, this makes it possible to turn trade liberalization into a true Pareto improvement. Of course, when this argument is made in textbooks or in class, we never point out that such compensation is rarely (if ever) offered by governments. Moreover, even if governments wished to provide compensation, little or no existing research provides direction regarding the design characteristics of an efficient compensation scheme. Should the government offer dislocated workers training subsidies, extended unemployment insurance, wage subsidies, or employment subsidies? Is there some other measure that could or should be used? Each program provides a

[11] In practice, it is likely that many more people become unemployed because of non-trade-related issues such as technological advancement, demographic shifts, and reductions in aggregate demand. We focus on trade-related unemployment because this is a politically sensitive issue. Moreover, U.S. laws already distinguish the reasons for job loss among different groups of workers as when workers must receive certification to be eligible for trade adjustment assistance.

unique set of incentives for workers to accept jobs or switch occupations, and therefore each has different implications for labor market adjustment. Proper analysis of the relative efficiencies of these different labor market programs requires a general equilibrium model in which agents face nontrivial spells of unemployment along with search and training costs. In other words, conventional full-employment trade models are not well suited to tackle important policy questions related to worker dislocation and the associated costs from freer trade.

We hope that by now we have made a convincing case that there are sound reasons to build and analyze general equilibrium models of international trade that allow for equilibrium unemployment. Of course, in order to do so, one must make a choice of how to introduce the market imperfections that generate unemployment. In most of our research, we have chosen to work with search models in which unemployment comes about due to a lack of information about job opportunities and worker availability. These information problems make it necessary for unemployed workers to search across firms for a vacancy and for firms to recruit unemployed workers. We have chosen to work in this framework because of our belief in its intuitive appeal. The very idea that time and effort are needed for unemployed workers and firms with vacancies to find each other just feels right to us. In addition, this is the one modern approach to unemployment that has been held up to serious empirical scrutiny. The matching function, which determines the rate of job creation and the equilibrium rate of unemployment, has been estimated and its features have been pinned down (for a survey of the evidence see Petrongolo and Pissarides 2001). This makes it possible to quantify models and use them for serious policy analysis.

There are a variety of other ways to introduce unemployment. One could rely on efficiency wages (Shapiro and Stiglitz 1984) or fair wage considerations (Akerlof and Yellin 1990), models of insider-outsider conflict (Lindbeck and Snower 1989), minimum wages, union influence, or a host of other labor market imperfections. We have argued elsewhere (Davidson and Matusz 2004) that, at least for some results, the approach used does not matter since similar results emerge from all of these frameworks. However, the extent to which this is true remains an open question—one we hope that others will take up in the future.[12]

---

[12] Of course we are aware that some work on trade and unemployment has already been carried out in these alternative settings. For work on trade and unemployment with efficiency wages see Copeland (1989), Brecher (1992), Matusz (1994, 1996, 1998), Hoon (2000, 2001a, b), and Davis and Harrigan (2007). For work on trade and unemployment with fair wages see Kreickemeier and Nelson (2006) or Egger and Kreickemeier (2007, 2008). For work on trade and unemployment with minimum wages see Brecher (1974) or Davis (1998).

A Roadmap of the Book

We have divided our book into five parts. Part 1 contains articles that demonstrate how standard versions of the Heckscher-Ohlin-Samuelson (HOS) and Ricardian trade models can be extended to allow for search-generated unemployment. The industry is considered the appropriate unit of measure in these models, with all firms within an industry being identical. We therefore refer to this part as "new insights from old trade theory." We begin in chapter 2, where we embed labor market frictions into the standard 2×2 HOS model of trade and show how the structure of the model is altered by the presence of equilibrium unemployment. We make use of the well-known "hat calculus" of Jones (1965) to emphasize how the model can be manipulated to look quite similar to the conventional HOS model. This highlights the subtle changes that are introduced when labor market imperfections are taken into account.

The equilibrium characterized in chapter 2 is not efficient because of the presence of externalities due to the manner in which we model the search process. By adjusting the model slightly so that equilibrium is always constrained Pareto efficient, we demonstrate in chapter 3 that labor frictions alter general equilibrium relationships in fundamental ways even when equilibrium is unique and efficient.

As we noted above, one of the goals of our research agenda is to develop models that are rich enough in labor market detail to allow for an analysis of programs aimed at the lowering the costs of adjustment associated with globalization. Such models must allow for nontrivial spells of unemployment and they are also inherently dynamic. These features raise complications that trade economists have not had to deal with much in the past. The three papers in part 2 (which is titled "complications") highlight some of these issues. In particular, the first two papers in this section are devoted to showing that the presence of equilibrium unemployment can generate problems that are usually absent from full-employment models. In chapter 4 we illustrate how labor market imperfections can result in multiple free trade equilibria, whereas in chapter 5 we demonstrate that the presence of unemployment makes welfare analysis in dynamic models considerably more complicated than it would be in the absence of labor market frictions. The reason for this is that changes in employment transfer income across generations, giving rise to social surpluses that have important implications for trade policy.[13] In chapter 6 we emphasize that when carrying out policy analysis in dynamic models,

---

[13] These surpluses are similar to the ones generated by the social planner in Samuelson's original overlapping generations model (Samuelson 1958). See chapter 5 for details.

serious mistakes can arise if one ignores the adjustment path (by relying on a comparison of steady states).

Part 3 of the book consists of two empirical contributions designed to test two of the predictions of the models developed in chapter 3. In particular, chapter 7 presents evidence that the structure of the labor market can influence trade patterns in a manner consistent with the model's predictions, whereas chapter 8 explores the issue of whether labor market frictions alter the link between trade and wages as predicted.

The chapters contained in part 4 are devoted to policy analysis with a particular emphasis on issues that cannot be addressed in full-employment models. We begin in chapter 9 where we present a simple general equilibrium model with turnover in an effort to see how taking search and training costs into account might alter the calculation of the costs of adjustment. Chapters 10 and 11 deal with policy issues related to adjustments costs. In chapter 10 we show how the gradual implementation of new trade policies can be optimal when labor markets exhibit congestion externalities. Chapter 11 compares different labor policies designed to compensate workers who are harmed by trade liberalization and chapter 12 examines the issue of whether coupling trade policy with compensation makes free trade easier to achieve politically.

In the final part of the book, we show how trade frictions can be included in the "new trade models" that have been inspired by empirical studies of firm- and plant-level adjustment to trade. One of the most important features of the new trade models is heterogeneity across firms, usually in terms of productivity or technology choice. In chapters 13 and 14 we develop models with labor market frictions in which workers are also heterogeneous in terms of their skill sets. In chapter 13, we show how the types of employment relationships that workers are willing to enter into can be altered by changes in openness and that this can provide new explanations for many of the empirical regularities that inspired the new trade theory. In particular, we show that changes in openness affect the type of worker-firm matches that can and do take place in equilibrium. We also show that this can explain changes in firm-level decisions to export as well as how openness impacts measures of productivity at the firm and industry levels. In chapter 14, we use the same framework to investigate the implications of the outsourcing of high-skill jobs for the wage distribution.

The model in chapter 13 yields some strong predictions about the link among openness, productivity (both within-firm and industrywide measures), and wage inequality. In the past, researchers would have had little or no hope of testing these predictions due to lack of sufficiently disaggregated data. However, recently a number of matched worker-firm data sets have emerged that will allow for a detailed analysis of labor market adjustment to changes in openness. These data sets make it possible to test our theories, and, perhaps more important, they also allow for a new set of stylized facts about the manner in which labor market outcomes are altered by changes in trade policy and trade costs. For example, we should be able to examine the hiring and firing practices of firms engaged in trade and compare them with those firms that sell all of their output domestically. It should also be possible to examine how industry-level wage distributions are altered when trade liberalization occurs. We should also be able to gain a deeper understanding of how openness affects workers since such rich data sets should provide us with new micro-level insights into the incidence of worker dislocation, the manner in which openness affects the job search process, the pattern of worker turnover across industries, and the manner in which the gains and losses from freer trade are distributed across firms and their workers within industries. That is, it should now be possible to look at labor market adjustment to globalization as closely as the profession has examined firm- and plant-level adjustment.[14]

REFERENCES

Akerlof, G., Yellen, J. 1990. The fair-wage effort hypothesis and unemployment. *Quarterly Journal of Economics* 105(2): 255–83.

Attanasio, O., Goldberg, P., Pavcnik, N. 2004. Trade reforms and wage inequality in Colombia. *Journal of Development Economics* 74(2): 331–66.

Bailey, M., Burtless, G., Litan, R. 1993. *Growth with Equity*. Washington, DC: Brookings Institution.

Bailey, M., Burtless, G., Litan, R., Shapiro, R. 1998. *Globaphobia: Confronting Fears about Open Trade*. Washington, DC: Brookings Institution.

Baldwin, R., Mutti, J., Richardson, D. 1980. Welfare effects on the United States of a significant multilateral tariff reduction. *Journal of International Economics* 10(3): 405–23.

Blanchard, O., Portugal, P. 2001. What hides behind an unemployment rate: Comparing Portuguese and U.S. labor markets. *American Economic Review* 91(1): 187–207.

Blinder, A. 1988. The challenge of high unemployment. *American Economic Review* 78(2): 1–15.

---

[14] Again, there is recent strong evidence that such a literature is starting to emerge. Papers that focus on labor market reallocation in response to liberalization include Currie and Harrison (1997), Revenga (1997), Harrison and Hanson (1999), Topalova (2004), Pavcnik et al. (2004), Attanasio, Goldberg, and Pavcnik (2004), Warcziag and Seddon-Wallack (2004), Cuñat and Guadalupe (2006), and Guadalupe (2007). For papers that use matched worker-firm data to analyze such issues the recent contributions of Filho, Menezes, and Muendler (2007), Muendler (2007), and chapter 5 of Silva (2007).

Bradford, S. 2006. Protection and unemployment. *Journal of International Economics* 69(2): 257–71.

Brecher, R. 1974. Minimum wage rates and the pure theory of international trade. *Quarterly Journal of Economics* 88(1): 98–116.

Brecher, R. 1992. An efficiency wage model with explicit monitoring: Unemployment and welfare in an open economy. *Journal of International Economics* 32(1–2): 179–91.

Brown, C. 1999. Minimum wages, employment, and the distribution of income. *Handbook of Labor Economics,* vol. 3, eds. Orley Ashenfelter and David Card. New York: Elsevier: 2101–63.

Brown, D., Deardorff, A., Stern, R. 2001. CGE modeling and analysis of multilateral and regional negotiating options. Discussion Papers Series, Department of Economics, Tufts University.

Burdett, K., Judd, K. 1983. Equilibrium price dispersion. *Econometrica* 51(4): 955–69.

Copeland, B. 1989. Efficiency wages in a Ricardian model of international trade. *Journal of International Economics* 27(3–4): 221–44.

Costinot, A. 2007. Jobs, jobs, jobs: A new perspective on protectionism? University of California–San Diego Working Paper.

Cuñat, V., Guadalupe, M. 2006. Globalization and the provision of incentives inside the firm: The effect of foreign competition. Columbia University Working Paper.

Cuñat, A., Melitz, M. 2006. Volatility, labor market flexibility, and the pattern of comparative advantage. Harvard University Working Paper.

Currie, J., Harrison, A. 1997. Trade reform and labor market adjustment in Morocco. *Journal of Labor Economics* 15(3): S44–71.

Davidson, C., Martin, L., Matusz, S. 1987. Search, unemployment and the production of jobs. *Economic Journal* 97(388): 857–76.

Davidson, C., Martin, L., Matusz, S. 1988. The structure of simple general equilibrium models with frictional unemployment. *Journal of Political Economy* 96(6): 1267–93.

Davidson, C., Martin, L., Matusz, S. 1991. Multiple free trade equilibria in micro models of unemployment. *Journal of International Economics* 31(1–2): 157–69.

Davidson, C., Matusz, S. 2004. *International Trade and Labor Markets: Theory, Evidence and Policy Implications.* Kalamazoo, MI: W.E. Upjohn Institute for Employment Research.

Davis, D. 1998. Does European unemployment prop up American wages? National labor markets and global trade. *American Economic Review* 88(3): 478–94.

Davis, D., Harrigan, J. 2007. Good jobs, bad jobs and trade liberalization. Columbia University Working Paper.

Davis, S., Haltiwanger, J., Schuh, S. 1996. *Job Creation and Job Destruction.* Cambridge, MA: MIT Press.

Diamond, P. 1971. A model of price adjustment. *Journal of Economic Theory* 32(2): 156–68.

Diamond, P. 1981. Mobility costs, frictional unemployment and efficiency. *Journal of Political Economy* 89(4): 798–812.

Diamond, P. 1982a. Wage determination and efficiency in search equilibrium. *Review of Economic Studies* 49(2): 217–27.

Diamond, P. 1982b. Aggregate demand management in search equilibrium. *Journal of Political Economy* 90(5): 881–94.

Dorman, P. 2001. The free trade magic act. Economic Policy Institute Briefing Paper 111.

Dutt, P., Mitra, D., Ranjan, P. 2008. International trade and unemployment: Theory and cross-national evidence. Syracuse University Working Paper.

Egger, H., Kreickemeier, U. 2007. Firm heterogeneity and labour market effects of trade liberalization. GEP Working Paper, University of Nottingham.

Egger, H., Kreickemeier, U. 2008. Fairness, trade and inequality. GEP Working Paper, University of Nottingham.

Fehr, E., Schmidt, K. 1999. A theory of fairness, competition and cooperation. *Quarterly Journal of Economics* 114(3): 817–68.

Felbermayr, G., Prat, J., Schmerer, H. 2007. Melitz meets Pissarides: Firm heterogeneity, search unemployment and trade liberalization. Working Paper, University of Tubingen.

Filho, N., Menezes, A., Muendler, M. 2007. Labor reallocation in response to trade reform. University of California–San Diego, Working Paper.

Freeman, R. 1994. How labor fares in advanced economies. In R. Freeman (ed.), *Working under Different Rules*. New York: Russell Sage Foundation: 1–28.

Friedman, M. 1968. The role of monetary policy: Presidential address to the American Economic Association. *American Economic Review* 58(1): 1–17.

Guadalupe, M. 2007. Product market competition, returns to skill and wage inequality. *Journal of Labor Economics* 95(3): 439–74.

Harrison, A., Hanson, G. 1999. Who gains from trade reform? Some remaining puzzles. *Journal of Development Economics* 59(1): 125–54.

Hart-Landsberg, M. 2006. Neoliberalism: Myths and reality. *Monthly Review* 57(11).

Helpman, E., Itskhoki, O. 2007. Labor market rigidities, trade and unemployment. Harvard University Working Paper.

Helpman, E., Itskhoki, O., Redding, S. 2008. Inequality and unemployment in a global economy. Harvard University Working Paper.

Hoon, H. 2000. *Trade, Jobs and Wages*. Northampton, MA: Edward Elgar Ltd.

Hoon, H. 2001a. Adjustment of wages and equilibrium unemployment in a Ricardian global economy. *Journal of International Economics* 54(1): 193–209.

Hoon, H. 2001b. General-equilibrium implications of international product-market competition for jobs and wages. *Oxford Economic Papers* 53(1): 138–56.

Jacobson, L., LaLonde, R., Sullivan, D. 1993a. Earnings losses of displaced workers. *American Economic Review*, 83(4): 685–709.

Jacobson, L., LaLonde, R., Sullivan, D. 1993b. *The Costs of Worker Dislocation*. Kalamazoo, MI: W.E. Upjohn Institute for Employment Research.

Janiak, A. 2006. Does trade liberalization lead to unemployment? Theory and some evidence. ECARES, Universite Libre de Bruxelles Working Paper.

Jones, R. 1965. The structure of simple general equilibrium models. *Journal of Political Economy* 73(6): 557–72.

Kletzer, L. 2001. *Job Loss from Imports: Measuring the Costs.* Washington, DC: Peterson Institute for International Economics.

Kletzer, L., Litan, R. 2001. A prescription to relieve worker anxiety. Policy Brief No. 73. Washington, DC: Brookings Institution.

Kreickemeier, U., Nelson, D. 2006. Fair wages, unemployment and technological change in a global economy. *Journal of International Economics* 70(2): 451–69.

Krugman, P. 1993. What do undergraduates need to know about trade? *American Economic Review* 83(2): 23–26.

Krugman, P. 1995. Europe jobless, America penniless? *Foreign Policy* 95: 19–34.

Lawrence, R., Litan, R. 1986. *Saving Free Trade: A Pragmatic Approach.* Washington, DC: Brookings Institution.

Lindbeck, A., Snower, D. 1989. *The Insider-Outsider Theory of Employment and Unemployment.* Cambridge, MA: MIT Press.

Lucas, R., Prescott, E. 1974. Equilibrium search and unemployment. *Journal of Economic Theory* 7(2): 188–209.

Magee, S. 1972. The welfare effects of restriction on U.S. trade. *Brookings Papers on Economic Activity* 3: 645–701.

Matusz, S. 1985. The Heckscher-Ohlin-Samuelson model with implicit contracts. *Quarterly Journal of Economics* 100(4): 1313–29.

Matusz, Steven J. 1993. Calibrating the employment effects of trade. *Review of International Economics* 6: 592–603.

Matusz, S. 1994. International trade policy in a model of unemployment and wage differentials. *Canadian Journal of Economics* 27(4): 939–49.

Matusz, Steven J. 1996. International trade. the division of labor, and unemployment. *International Economic Review* 37: 71–84.

McCall, J. 1965. The economics of information and optimal stopping rules. *Journal of Business* 38(3): 300–17.

McCall, J. 1970. The economics of information and job search. *Quarterly Journal of Economics* 84(1): 113–26.

Melitz, M. 2003. The impact of trade on intra-industry reallocations and aggregate industry productivity. *Econometrica* 71: 1695–1725.

Mitra, D., Ranjan, P. 2007. Offshoring and unemployment. Syracuse University Working Paper.

Moore, M., Ranjan, P. 2005. Globalisation and skill-biased technological change: Implications for unemployment and wage inequality. *Economic Journal* 115(503): 391–422.

Mortensen, D. 1982. Property rights and efficiency in mating, racing and related games. *American Economic Review* 72(5): 768–79.

Muendler, M. 2007. Trade and workforce changeover in Brazil. University of California–San Diego, Working Paper.

Mussa, M. 1993. Making the practical case for freer trade. *American Economic Review* 83(2): 372–76.

Nickell, S. 1997. Unemployment and labor market rigidities: Europe versus North America. *Journal of Economic Perspectives* 11(3): 55–74.

Pavcnik, N., Blom, A., Goldberg, P., Schady, N. 2004. Trade policy and industry wage structure: Evidence from Brazil. *World Bank Economic Review* 18(3): 319–44.

Petrongolo, B., Pissarides, C. 2001. Looking into the black box: A survey of the matching function. *Journal of Economic Literature* 39(2): 390–431.

Reinganum, J. 1979. A simple model of equilibrium price dispersion. *Journal of Political Economy* 87(4): 851–58.

Revenga, A. 1997. Employment and wage effects of liberalization: The case of Mexican manufacturing. *Journal of Labor Economics* 15(3): S20–43.

Rothschild, M. 1974. Searching for the lowest price when the distribution of prices is unknown. *Journal of Political Economy* 82(4): 689–711.

Samuelson, P. 1958. An exact consumption-loan model of interest with or without the social contrivance of money. *Journal of Political Economy* 66(5): 467–82.

Shapiro, C., Stiglitz, J. 1984. Equilibrium unemployment as a worker discipline device. *American Economic Review* 74(3): 433–44.

Silva, J. 2007. Globalization and labor market adjustment: The role of human capital. Ph.D. dissertation, University of Nottingham.

Song, L., Xu, X., Sheng, Y. 2007. A generalized Heckscher-Ohlin-Samuelson model with search unemployment. Australian National University Working Paper.

Stigler, G. 1961. The economics of information. *Journal of Political Economy* 69(3): 213–25.

Stigler, G. 1962. Information in the labor market. *Journal of Political Economy* 70(5): 94–105.

Topalova, P. 2004. Trade liberalization and firm productivity: The case of India. IMF Working Paper.

Wacziarg, R., Seddon-Wallack, J. 2004. Trade liberalization and intersectoral labor movements. *Journal of International Economics* 64(2): 411–39.

NEW INSIGHTS FROM "OLD" TRADE THEORY

INTRODUCTION TO PART 1

We begin our book with two articles that focus on extending conventional general equilibrium models of international trade to allow for unemployment. Here, the term "conventional" is meant to refer to the Hechscher-Ohlin-Samuelson (HOS) and Ricardian models that dominated the field until quite recently. We have little to say in these papers about how trade affects the equilibrium rate of unemployment—in fact, when we have taken up this issue at all, it has always been in response to requests by editors and/or referees. As we noted in the introduction, this is because we view it as an empirical issue. Rather, in this set of papers we are more concerned with the way in which the labor market imperfections that generate unemployment force us to alter our predictions about the manner in which changes in trade patterns and/or trade policies affect equilibrium outcomes. Thus the emphasis in all of these articles is the same: how does the presence of equilibrium unemployment alter the fundamental general equilibrium relationships that dictate the manner in which trade shocks are filtered through the economy?

Our first attempt to address this issue is presented in chapter 2. In this paper, which appeared in the *Journal of Political Economy* in 1988, we analyzed a standard $2 \times 2 \times 2$ HOS model in which frictions in the labor market result in equilibrium unemployment. We felt that this was the most natural starting place for our research agenda, since this model dominated modern trade theory through the early 1980s. We also wanted the paper to look somewhat familiar to trade theorists, so we adopted the Jones (1965) "hat calculus" approach. It was (and still is) our belief that if you want people in the field to read your work, you have to make it as easy as possible for them to comprehend it. This is best accomplished by working in a context that they know well and by trying to make clear how your new twist alters what they already know. Thus we made every effort to beat our model until it looked as much like the standard $2 \times 2 \times 2$ model as possible. In particular, two relationships govern many of the results that come from the $2 \times 2 \times 2$ HOS model. The first links relative commodity prices and relative factor rewards and is derived by differentiating the product market clearing conditions. The second links relative factor rewards and relative output levels and is derived by differentiating the factor market clearing conditions. The former relationship is used to prove the Stolper-Samuelson theorem, whereas the latter can be used to prove the Rybczynski theorem. Combining the two relationships allows one to derive a "relative supply curve" which gives combinations of relative commodity prices and relative output levels that are consistent with equilibrium on the supply side of the economy. Combining the relative supply curve with information about preferences allows one to solve for autarkic prices and, with additional information about world prices, make predictions about the pattern of trade.

In our *JPE* paper we extended the conventional model by assuming that in one sector of the economy time and effort are needed for unemployed workers and firms with vacancies to find each other. Unemployed agents must commit to a sector at the beginning of each period, basing their decision on expected lifetime income (thus all agents are risk neutral). This implies that in a diversified equilibrium, agents must sort themselves such that those that are unemployed and seeking a job in the search sector expect to earn as much over their lifetime as those who accept immediate jobs in the sector with the frictionless factor markets.

Agents who choose to seek employment in the search sector realize that they will spend their lives cycling between periods of employment and unemployment. When an unemployed worker finds a firm with a vacancy, a match is created, a partnership is established, and the firm starts producing output. On the other hand, workers who are unable to find a match in a given period remain unemployed and must continue to seek out employment opportunities. Since trading frictions generate monopoly power, wages in the search sector are negotiated once a partnership is established. Thus there are two key differences between our model and the standard HOS model: frictions create equilibrium unemployment and also lead to wage-setting power in one sector of the economy. Our analysis focuses on how these two features alter the two fundamental relationships that define the structure of the HOS model.

The first key insight that emerges is that in the presence of equilibrium unemployment, the manner in which factor intensities and unit input requirements are measured must be altered: for the search sector, these measures must now take into account the idle factors of production. Once these adjustments are made, we show that our model yields a prediction about the relationship between relative factor prices and relative output levels that is qualitatively identical to the one that comes out of the HOS model.

The next difference between the two models lies in the relationship between relative factor prices and relative output prices. In the HOS model, this relationship is obtained by differentiating the zero-profit conditions. In a frictionless world, the wage rate and rental rate for capital, along with unit input requirements, determine unit production costs, which must equal the price of any good that is actually produced. Things change in the presence of search-generated unemployment. Since search is costly, workers who find jobs will not quit unless there are large shocks to the economy—in fact, the best way to think about this is that trading frictions in factor markets make employed factors quasi-fixed. The implication of this is that when there are small shocks to the economy, it is the unemployed factors of production that move across sectors to restore equilibrium. We show that because of this feature, when the product market clearing conditions are derived, the expected returns to the *unemployed* factors emerge as part of the equation. Differentiating these equations then allows one to derive an extended Stolper-Samuelson theorem. This theorem states that if the wage bargaining in the search sector results in an efficient allocation of resources, then the expected lifetime return to the *unemployed* factors of production will be governed by conventional Stolper-Samuelson forces. Thus if a tariff is instituted in a relatively labor-intensive industry, all *unemployed* labor will benefit while all *idle* capital will be harmed (in terms of expected lifetime income and profit).[1] The reasoning is much like the logic behind the standard Stolper-Samuelson theorem. An increase in the price of a good will draw unemployed factors toward that sector. If the growing sector is more labor intensive than the sector that is shrinking, the bargaining power of workers will rise while the bargaining power of the firm that rents capital and posts a vacancy will fall. Consequently, the return to searching labor will increase while the return to idle capital will fall.

As mentioned above, there is an important qualifier for the extended Stolper-Samuelson theorem: it holds only if wage bargaining is efficient. At the time that we began work on this paper, economists were still sorting out the externalities that were inherent in search models and their implications. In particular, Peter Diamond (1982) had shown that when workers and firms bargain over wages (as in our model), equilibrium is almost always inefficient. Thus in our paper we paid a great deal of attention to how externalities inherent in the search process can alter the relationship between relative output prices and relative factor prices. In fact, we made this the primary focus of our paper and in doing so failed to highlight the extended Stolper-Samuelson theorem appropriately (an issue we tried to correct in our 1999 paper in the *Journal of International Economics*). Looking back, we wish that either we had placed only a small amount of emphasis on the externalities or that we had set up the

---

[1] This result was not highlighted in the published version of our paper. However, as we point out in the newly added section 4.4, this result follows directly from equations (28) and (13) (the equilibrium indifference condition). However, as we discuss below, it is important to note that this theorem holds only if bargaining is efficient (which implies that $\Sigma = 0$).

model slightly differently. In a working paper that was circulating around the time that we were working on our paper, Arthur Hosios had derived the condition that would have to be met for wage bargaining to result in an efficient allocation of resources (this paper became Hosios 1990a). We cannot remember whether we were aware of Hosios's result at the time we published our paper. However, if we had been, it would have been wise to have assumed that this condition was met. If we had done so, then we could have focused all of our attention on the extended Stolper-Samuelson theorem. Instead, we followed Diamond's approach and used the symmetric Nash bargaining solution to determine wages. This made it far too easy to dismiss our paper as yet another paper that focused on controversial search-generated externalities.[2]

The analysis in our 1988 paper was somewhat incomplete, since we did not describe how changes in trade patterns or trade policy would affect the return to *employed* factors. This issue is addressed in the article in chapter 3, which appeared in the *Journal of International Economics* in 1999. We show that search costs create an attachment to a sector that makes employed factors much like the specific factors in the Ricardo-Viner model. Because time and effort are needed for jobless workers and firms with vacancies to find each other, once a match is created both parties are reluctant to sever ties unless they are convinced that they can earn significantly more by searching for another production opportunity elsewhere in the economy. It follows that small changes in prices will not cause employed factors to switch sectors. The implication is that the reward earned by employed factors will be tied to the overall success of the sector. If the export sector is growing, this will tend to increase the reward to labor and capital employed in that sector.

But at some point all productive partnerships break up for one reason or another. When that happens, the firm must recruit a replacement for the lost employee and the worker must search for a new job. Thus the

---

[2] A second regret is related to the manner in which we applied Jones's hat calculus technique. Our model was inherently dynamic and we chose to focus on steady states. Thus when we differentiated the market clearing conditions while continuing to assume that steady-state conditions were satisfied, we were essentially comparing across steady states. At one time, such an approach would have been warranted because solving for the dynamic adjustment path across equilibria and taking the adjustment path into account was far too difficult. However, in 1980 Diamond developed a simple technique that allows one to carry out true comparative dynamics without solving explicitly for the adjustment path. In retrospect, we should have used Diamond's approach. In an excellent paper that followed ours two years later, Hosios (1990b) carried out an analysis quite similar to ours in an almost identical model under the assumption of efficient bargaining. By also making use of the Diamond technique, he was able to avoid these two complications. It is worth noting that his results were qualitatively identical to ours.

expected lifetime income for employed factors includes what those factors expect to earn while idle. We have already argued that this portion of expected lifetime income varies according to the Stolper-Samuelson theorem. It follows that the overall returns to *employed* factors include both Stolper-Samuelson and Ricardo-Viner forces. Moreover, the force that dominates depends upon the turnover rates in the industry. If jobs are difficult to find or last a long time, the attachment generated by the search costs will be strong and the Ricardo-Viner forces will dominate. In contrast, if turnover is high, the attachment will be weak and the Stolper-Samuelson forces will dominate. This is a testable hypothesis which we take to the data in chapter 8.

A second topic that we deal with in chapter 3 is the influence of labor market structure on comparative advantage. As we emphasized in the introduction, substantial evidence indicates that job creation and job destruction rates vary considerably across countries and across industries. We argue that such differences can play a role in shaping trade patterns. The basic idea is straightforward. When agents cycle between periods of employment and unemployment, the amount of time spent in each state is a function of the sector-specific turnover rates. The implication is that the employment process (and, for firms, the job creation process) will be risky and agents will take this risk into account when choosing an occupation (or, for firms, a sector to compete in). Firms attempting to hire workers in riskier industries will be forced to offer higher compensation in order to entice workers to search for their vacancy. These higher wages push up autarkic prices and make it less likely that this good will be exported in an open economy. In chapter 3 we explain this link in detail and then in chapter 7 we test our model's prediction using data on sector-specific turnover rates and trade data.

These two articles demonstrate that new insights about the sources of comparative advantage and the link between trade and factor rewards emerge when one allows for equilibrium unemployment. In both cases, it is job creation and job destruction rates that play key roles. And it is worth emphasizing that in both cases, these predictions do not depend on the presence of search-generated externalities or the possibility of multiple equilibria.

REFERENCES

Diamond, P. 1980. An alternative to steady-state comparisons. *Economics Letters* 5(1): 7–9.

Diamond, P. 1982. Wage determination and efficiency in search equilibrium. *Review of Economic Studies* 49(2): 217–27.

Hosios, A. 1990a. On the efficiency of matching and related models of search and unemployment. *Review of Economic Studies* 57(2): 279–98.

Hosios, A. 1990b. Factor market search and the structure of simple general equilibrium models. *Journal of Political Economy* 98(2): 325–51.

Jones, R. 1965. The structure of simple general equilibrium models. *Journal of Political Economy* 73(6): 557–72.

Chapter 2

THE STRUCTURE OF SIMPLE GENERAL EQUILIBRIUM MODELS WITH FRICTIONAL UNEMPLOYMENT

CARL DAVIDSON, LAWRENCE MARTIN, AND STEVEN MATUSZ

1. INTRODUCTION

Because of its simple structure and intuitive appeal, the two-sector general equilibrium Walrasian model has served "as the workhorse for most of the developments in the pure theory of international trade" (Jones 1965, p. 557). This model has also been used extensively in most of the other applied fields of economics. In his seminal article "The Structure of Simple General Equilibrium Models," Jones contributed to our understanding of this model by exposing its basic structure in a manner that allowed him to unify the many approaches that had been developed in different applied areas. In particular, he examined two key relationships that govern the behavior of the supply side of a competitive economy. The first relationship links factor endowments, factor rewards, and output levels and is derived from the requirement that factor markets clear. The second relationship is between factor rewards and commodity prices and results from the fact that unit production costs must equal output prices in the presence of constant returns to scale. By carefully examining these relationships, it is possible to derive several of the fundamental theorems of international economics (e.g., the Rybczynski and Stolper-Samuelson theorems). In addition, the effects of parametric changes in the economy (e.g., tax rates) can be easily understood by examining how such changes work through these two basic relationships.

While the Walrasian model is exceedingly useful for many types of analysis, one may be reluctant to rely on it to analyze situations in which unemployment is a consideration: factors of production are always fully employed in the full-information, frictionless markets. Since casual observation suggests that the effects of a policy on the unemployment rate and the welfare of the unemployed are often major considerations for policymakers, it is vitally important to augment the Walrasian approach in a way that permits the investigation of these issues. The purpose of this paper is to do just that. In particular, we present and analyze a simple two-sector general equilibrium model that allows for equilibrium unemployment. Our main goal is to understand how our model differs in structure from the model analyzed by Jones (which we refer to as the Jones model).[1] Our analysis indicates that introducing frictional unemployment creates the potential for the structural relationships within the economy to be qualitatively different from the analogous relationships in a frictionless economy.

We model unemployment by assuming that in one sector, factor markets are frictionless so that the duration of unemployment is zero, while in the other sector, idle factors of production must search each other out in order to produce.[2] Factors are mobile across sectors and in equilibrium distribute themselves so that the expected lifetime return is the same in both sectors. The trading frictions in the search sector represent the only difference between our model and the Jones model, and yet we demonstrate that in some cases this leads to an economy with a surprisingly different structure. In particular, we show that the relationship between factor rewards and commodity prices is fundamentally different in an economy with search-generated unemployment. This leads to the possibility of downward-sloping relative supply curves, and, in fact, we demonstrate that such a phenomenon is likely to occur if the search sector is relatively *small*. If, however, the search sector is large enough, the structure of the economy will be qualitatively the same as the structure of the frictionless general equilibrium model.

---

[1] More accurately, we compare our model with the standard two-sector, two-factor model using an approach that closely resembles the approach adopted by Jones in his masterful exposition and synthesis of earlier work. Our reference to the "Jones model" is not intended to imply that Jones was the first to formalize, develop, or use the model.

[2] This approach was originally suggested by Friedman (1968) in his classic paper "The Role of Monetary Policy," in which he defined the natural rate of unemployment as "the level that would be ground out by the Walrasian system of general equilibrium equations, provided there is imbedded in them the actual characteristics of the labor and commodity markets, including market imperfections, stochastic variability in demands and supplies, the cost of gathering information about job vacancies and labor availabilities, the costs of mobility, and so on." This definition has recently been made operational by Diamond in a series of papers (1981, 1982, 1984a, b) in which he models unemployment as the result of problems in coordinating exchange. He accomplishes this by assuming that it takes time and effort for potential trading partners to find each other. Our approach is therefore very similar to Diamond's. However, his purpose in developing these models was to investigate the macroeconomic properties of economies with a natural rate of frictional unemployment, and he was able to do so in a remarkably simple setting: a barter economy with one good and one factor of production. The questions that we wish to address are fundamentally different and require a somewhat more elaborate model.

In the next section, we introduce the model, define equilibrium, and briefly discuss its efficiency properties. Equilibrium is generally *not* efficient, and this is one of the driving forces behind our results.

In section 3, we derive the two fundamental relationships that describe the structure of the model and compare them with their counterparts in the Jones model. In order to gain some insight into the forces behind our results, we devote section 4 to a detailed investigation of the nature of the production process in the search sector. In this section, we demonstrate that the equilibrium factor intensity employed in the search sector is not optimal. Changes in factor prices alter this factor intensity and may enhance or inhibit efficiency. When the search sector is small these efficiency effects are large enough to dominate the traditional mechanism linking commodity and factor prices. As the sector grows in size, this effect shrinks relatively and the economy eventually behaves in a manner similar to a pure Walrasian economy. Some applications of the analysis are discussed in section 5, and concluding remarks are offered in section 6.

2. THE MODEL

2.1 Endowments, Production Technology, and Preferences

Our economy consists of two sectors (X and Y) and two factors of production (L and K). Agents are born either as workers (and hence supply labor, L) or entrepreneurs (and hence supply capital, K) and each agent is endowed with one (indivisible) unit of his or her factor in each period. These factors are supplied inelastically in the factor markets in order to earn income. Each agent is finitely lived, although the age of an agent at death is a random variable. The probability that any individual of either type dies in any given period is time invariant and equal to d, which also equals the birth rate for both types of agents. All agents are risk neutral.

We assume that the production function corresponding to good Y is twice continuously differentiable and characterized by constant returns to scale:

$$Y = Y(L_y, K_y) \tag{1}$$

where I_y is the amount of factor I used in the production of Y ($I = L, K$).

Finally, we assume that the production of one unit of X requires exactly one unit of each factor. We refer to a pairing of a worker and an entrepreneur as a "match" and note that, given our assumption about X sector production, the number of matches in any given period is given by X.

2.2 The Search Process

Factors in sector Y are immediately hired in full-information, competitive auction markets, while agents who seek matches in sector X must search each other out. If a type-i agent in sector X fails to locate an agent of the opposite type, she remains idle (unemployed) for that period. An agent in this sector engages in search at the start of every period in which she is unemployed. Matches survive as long as both agents live. On the death of either partner, the survivor again engages in search.[3]

We assume that the number of new matches created every period, M, is a function of L_s and K_s, the numbers of agents of each type who begin the period searching. This function is characterized by constant returns to scale, positive marginal products, and symmetry such that $M(L_s, K_s) = M(K_s, L_s)$.[4] In this case, the per-period probability that a type i searcher finds a match can be written as $e_i(s)$, where s denotes the proportion of searchers who are of type L. Our assumptions about the search technology imply that $e'_L(s) < 0 < e'_K(s)$ and that $e_i(s) = e_j(1-s)$ for $j \neq i$.[5]

2.3 Factor Returns

Since sector-Y markets are frictionless and competitive, all factors in this sector are always employed and earn the value of their marginal product. If we let w_y denote the wage paid to a worker in this sector, use r_y to denote

---

[3] Consistent with the bulk of the literature in this area, deaths are used to capture the role of exogenous separations in factor markets (see, e.g., Diamond 1981, 1982; Mortensen 1982; Pissarides 1984).

[4] Empirical support for the assumption of constant returns to scale is provided by Nickell (1979). The implications of increasing returns to scale in the search technology are discussed at length in Diamond (1984b). The substance of our results does not depend on the symmetry assumption. In fact, in note 16 we show how our results can be generalized to situations in which the matching function is not symmetric.

[5] We first note that e_i, the probability that a randomly chosen type i searcher becomes matched, is equal to M/I_s, where $M \leq \min(L_s, K_s)$. Dividing the numerator and denominator by the total number of searchers ($L_s + K_s$) permits us to express e_i solely as a function of s, the proportion of searchers who are workers; i.e., $s = L_s/(L_s + K_s)$. Next, symmetry follows because

$$e_L(s) = \frac{M(s, 1-s)}{s} = \frac{M(1-s, s)}{s} = e_K(1-s)$$

Moreover,

$$e'_L(s) = \frac{M_1 s - M_2 s - M}{s^2} = -\frac{M_2}{s^2} < 0$$

where the numeric subscript refers to partial differentiation and the last equality follows from the assumption of constant returns to scale. Finally, we note that constant returns to scale in the matching technology implies $e_L(s)/e_K(s) = (1-s)/s$ for all s.

the rental rate paid to entrepreneurs in sector Y, and use P_y to denote the price of good Y, then this condition is expressed as

$$P_y Y_i = w_y \quad \text{and} \quad P_y Y_i = r_y \tag{2}$$

where Y_i is the partial derivative of $Y(\ )$ with respect to factor i (for $i = L$, K). Letting V_{iy} denote the expected lifetime income to factor i employed in sector Y, we have

$$V_{LY} = \frac{w_y}{d} \quad \text{and} \quad V_{KY} = \frac{r_y}{d} \tag{3}$$

We assume that the proceeds from the sale of a unit of X are divided between the two matched agents who produced it according to the Nash cooperative bargaining solution so that the surplus created by the match is evenly split.[6] For future use, we let α_i denote the share of the proceeds that go to the factor i and use P_x to denote the price of X.

To describe the solution to the bargaining problem formally, let V_{is} denote the expected lifetime income to a type i factor currently searching in sector X and V_{ie} the expected lifetime income to a type i factor currently employed (i.e., matched) in sector X. Then, under the assumption that unemployed factors earn no income,[7]

$$V_{is} = e_i(s)V_{ie} + \left[1 - e_i(s)\right](1-d)V_{is} \tag{4}$$

$$V_{ie} = \alpha_i P_x + (1-d)^2 V_{ie} + d(1-d)V_{is} \quad \text{for } i = L, K \tag{5}$$

In (4), $[1 - e_i(s)](1-d)$ represents the probability of failing to find a match but surviving to search again next period. In (5), $(1-d)^2$ represents the probability that both partners survive the period so that they begin the next period still matched and $d(1-d)$ represents the probability that the type j agent dies and the type i agent survives (in which case the type i agent must begin searching again). Solving (4) and (5) for V_{is} and V_{ie} we obtain

$$V_{is} = \frac{e_i \alpha_i P_x}{d\left[1 - \eta(1 - e_i)\right]} \tag{6}$$

---

[6] This assumption is consistent with a bargaining process in which the agents exchange sharing rules until one agent makes an offer that is acceptable to her partner, and the time it takes to make counteroffers is arbitrarily close to zero. See the work of Binmore (1982), McLennan (1982), Rubinstein (1982), and Rubinstein and Wolinsky (1985).

[7] This assumption is made to keep the algebra as simple as possible; it is not essential for any of our results.

$$V_{ie} = \frac{\left[1-(1-d)(1-e_i)\right]\alpha_i P_x}{d\left[1-\eta(1-e_i)\right]} \quad \text{for } i = L,K \tag{7}$$

where the argument of e_i has been suppressed and we have defined $\eta = (1-d)^2$.

We are now in a position to describe how α_i is determined. As previously indicated, the Nash bargaining solution evenly divides the surplus created by the match. The surplus is the excess of expected lifetime income if matched over the next-best alternative, namely, waiting a period and searching again. The surplus generated for a type i agent is

$$V_{ie} - (1-d)V_{is} = \frac{\alpha_i P_x}{1-\eta(1-e_i)} \quad \text{for } i = L,K \tag{8}$$

Equating $V_{Le} - (1-d)V_{Ls}$ with $V_{Ke} - (1-d)V_{Ks}$ and solving for α_L, we obtain

$$\alpha_L = \frac{1-\eta(1-e_L)}{2-\eta(2-e_L-e_K)} \tag{9}$$

When output prices and the mix of searchers are given, this value of α_L solves the Nash cooperative bargaining problem. Of course, $\alpha_K = 1 - \alpha_L$.

2.4 Equilibrium

In any steady-state equilibrium, the number of type i agents who enter sector X through birth must equal the number who exit the sector because of death. In addition, the number of searchers of each type and the number of matches must be time invariant. If we let β_i denote the proportion of newly born type i agents who choose to seek matches in sector X, I_0 the number of type i agents $(I = L, K)$, and I_s the number of type i searchers remaining after the matching process for the period has ended, then these conditions imply

$$(X + I_s)\, d = \beta_i I_0 d \quad \text{for } I = L, K \tag{10}$$

$$X = \eta X + d(1-d)e_i X + \beta_i I_0 e_i d + I_s(1-d)e_i \quad \text{for } I = L, K \tag{11}$$

In (10), $I_0 d$ is the number of newly born type i agents and $(X + I_s)d$ is the number of type i sector X agents who die each period. If this condition holds, the sector sizes remain constant over time. In (11), ηX is the number of matches that survive from the previous period; $\beta_i I_0 e_i d$ is the number of new entrants who immediately find partners in sector X; $d(1 - d)e_iX$ is the number of type i agents who survived, had partners who died, and immediately found new matches; and $I_s(1 - d)e_i$ is the number of type i searchers who survived and found partners. These last three terms represent all type i agents who begin period t as searchers but end the period matched.[8] The sum of all four terms on the right-hand side yields the number of matches at time t, which must equal the number at time $t - 1$, given on the left-hand side of (11). If this condition holds, the number of matches and the number and mixture of searchers will be time invariant.

In addition to these steady-state conditions, a diversified production equilibrium for this economy is characterized by (a) zero profits in sector Y, (b) indifference between sectors for both types of agents, and (c) zero excess demand for each factor in sector Y.[9]

The zero-profit condition for sector Y is given by

$$P_y = a_{Ly}w_y + a_{Ky}r_y \tag{12}$$

where a_{iy} denotes the unit input requirement for factor i in sector Y.

For a type i agent to be indifferent between sectors, the expected lifetime return to seeking employment in either sector must be the same. More exactly, since an agent cannot choose *employment* in sector X (she can choose only to search), the second equilibrium condition is given by

$$V_{iy} = V_{is} \quad \text{for } i = L, K \tag{13}$$

The final equilibrium condition is met when supply of a factor equals demand:

$$I_0 = I_y + I_s + X \quad \text{for } i = L, K \tag{14}$$

This completes the description of the model. We emphasize that the only difference between this and the Jones model is that search is required to find employment in sector X. If we set $e_i(s) = 1$ for both i and for all s, the model would reduce to the standard model with Leontief technology in sector X.

---

[8] In computing s, it is crucial to distinguish the number of agents who begin the period as searchers from I_s, the number who remain searching after the completion of the matching process.

[9] We should point out that regardless of relative output prices, specialization in good Y is always a production equilibrium. This follows from the fact that if everyone in the economy except one agent seeks employment in sector Y, it will be impossible for that agent to produce in sector X. Thus that agent will take a job in sector Y regardless of the relative product prices.

2.5 Efficiency

Diamond (1982) and others have shown that when search is required to find trading opportunities, externalities are generated that lead to inefficiencies. In the context of the model presented here, it can be demonstrated that in equilibrium the search sector is too small and its factor intensity is too asymmetric (see Davidson, Martin, and Matusz 1987). The reason for this is that whenever a match occurs, *each* of the two partners enjoys an increase in expected lifetime income measured by $V_{ie} - V_{is}$ for $i = L, K$. However, when an agent contemplates entering sector X, she ignores the increase in her partner's expected income that will be generated by every partnership that she enters. Agents therefore ignore a positive externality associated with entering this sector so that it is too small in equilibrium. Moreover, the externalities are not of equal magnitude. If the majority of searchers are type i agents, then, in general, the type j agents ignore a larger external effect than their type i counterparts. Sector X then becomes too i-intensive. Making sector X more j-intensive moves the economy toward the production possibilities frontier as the economy utilizes the search technology more efficiently. As we demonstrate in section 4, it is this externality that, when sector X is relatively small, leads the economy to behave in a fundamentally different manner than a frictionless economy.

3. Hat Calculus

In this section, we derive the equations of change that relate the prices of factors and goods to output quantities.[10] For convenience, we introduce the following additional notation: $I_x = X + I_s$, the total number of type-i agents in sector X; $l_h = L_h/K_h$ = the L-intensity of sector h; θ_{ih} = the value share of factor i in industry h (e.g., $\theta_{Ly} = w_y a_{Ly}/P_y$; $\theta_{Lx} = \alpha_L$); $\theta \equiv \theta_{Lx} - \theta_{Ly} = \theta_{Ky} - \theta_{Kx} = \alpha_L - \theta_{Ly}$; $\lambda_{ih} = I_h/I_0$ = the physical share of factor i in industry h; $\lambda \equiv \lambda_{Lx} - \lambda_{Kx} = \lambda_{Ky} - \lambda_{Ly}$; σ_h = the elasticity of substitution in sector h; $\phi_i = e_i'(s)s/e_i(s)$ = the elasticity of e_i; and $\phi \equiv \phi_L - \phi_K < 0$.

We begin with a brief review of the key equations of the Jones model and an explanation of how these relationships are altered by the introduction of trading frictions. There are six key equations in the Jones model: two factor-market-clearing conditions, two zero-profit conditions,

---

[10] Our comparative static exercises are actually comparisons across steady states. When evaluating the effect of a change in a parameter, we ignore the period of convergence to the new steady state. To take into account this period of convergence, the analysis would have to be modified along the lines of Diamond (1980).

and two cost minimization conditions.[11] In the present context, sector Y is modeled in the standard way, consisting of perfectly competitive profit-maximizing firms with constant returns to scale technology. In addition, factor markets in sector Y are frictionless. Therefore, the zero-profit and cost minimization conditions for this sector are unchanged (eqs. 12 and 2, respectively). The factor-market-clearing conditions (eq. 14) are also unchanged provided that factor usage in sector X is taken to include both matched and unmatched factors. Any differences in the models must therefore be the result of differences in the sector X zero-profit and cost minimization conditions.

The analogue of the sector X zero-profit condition can be derived from (13), the equation that states that agents must be indifferent between sectors in equilibrium. We obtain (see result A1 of the appendix)

$$P_x = a_{Lx} w_y + a_{Kx} r_y \tag{15}$$

By examining (13) in some detail, we can provide an intuitive interpretation of (15).[12] In the appendix we demonstrate that (13) may be written as $\alpha_L P_x = a_{Lx} w_y$ and $\alpha_K P_x = a_{Kx} r_y$ where $a_{ix} = (I_s + X)/X$ for $i = L, K$. Define $\pi_{ix} \equiv 1/a_{ix}$ so that π_{ix} represents the probability that a sector X, type-i factor will be matched at the end of the period (note that $\pi_{ix} \neq e_i(s)$ since the latter represents the probability that a factor, initially unmatched, will find a match during the period). Next, define $w_x \equiv \alpha_L P_x$ and $r_x \equiv \alpha_K P_x$ so that w_x and r_x are the factor rewards earned in sector X by matched workers and entrepreneurs, respectively. Then (13) states that, in equilibrium, arbitrage by factors across sectors requires the certain return in sector Y to equal the (unconditional) expected return in sector X: $w_y = \pi_{Lx} w_x + (1 - \pi_{Lx}) \cdot 0$ and $r_y = \pi_{Kx} r_x + (1 - \pi_{Kx}) \cdot 0$. Equation (15) is obtained by solving for w_x and r_x and then summing w_x and r_x.

Finally, we turn to the analogue of the cost minimization condition for sector X. In the standard model, firms choose their mix of inputs to minimize unit production cost. In our model, however, the factor intensity in the search sector is governed not by a cost minimization condition, but by the steady-state conditions (10) and (11). From these equations we obtain

$$a_{ix} = \frac{1 - \eta(1 - e_i)}{e_i} \quad \text{for } i = L, K \tag{16}$$

[11] Jones actually begins his analysis at a more fundamental level, explicitly pointing out the dependence of the input requirements on factor prices. The six equations that we describe can be derived from his slightly larger system.

[12] We would like to thank an anonymous referee for this interpretation.

In section 2 we noted that the equilibrium factor intensities in our model
are not optimal. Therefore, the value of a_{ix} in (16) is not the value that
minimizes the cost of producing a given amount of X. As we will see
below, this is the driving force behind our results.

We are now in a position to derive the equations of change. We first
develop the relationship between factor rewards and output quantities by
rewriting (14), the factor-market-clearing condition, as

$$I_0 = a_{ix}X + a_{iy}Y \quad \text{for } i = L, K \tag{17}$$

Logarithmic differentiation of this condition yields

$$\hat{I}_0 = \lambda_{ix}\hat{X} + \lambda_{iy}\hat{Y} + \lambda_{ix}\hat{a}_{ix} + \lambda_{iy}\hat{a}_{iy} \tag{18}$$

where the circumflex denotes the proportionate change in a variable.

We use the equilibrium conditions to express $\hat{a}_{ih}$ as a function of the
changes in sector Y factor prices. We begin by differentiating (16) to
obtain

$$\hat{a}_{ix} = -\frac{\phi_i(1-\eta)\hat{s}}{1-\eta(1-e_i)} \tag{19}$$

Next, we can use (3), (6), (9), and (13) to solve for the equilibrium wages
as a function of s. Doing so, we obtain $w_y/r_y = e_L/e_K$.[13] Differentiation
yields

$$\hat{s} = \frac{\hat{w}_y - \hat{r}_y}{\phi} \tag{20}$$

Substitution of (20) into (19) yields $\hat{a}_{ix}$ as a function of $\hat{w}_y - \hat{r}_y$.

Similarly, cost minimization in sector Y implies

$$\hat{a}_{Ly} = -\theta_{Ky}\sigma_y(\hat{w}_y - \hat{r}_y) \quad \text{and} \quad \hat{a}_{Ky} = -\theta_{Ly}\sigma_y(\hat{r}_y - \hat{w}_y) \tag{21}$$

---

[13] The relationship states that relative sector-Y factor rewards equal relative ex-ante employment probabilities for those initially unemployed. The latter ratio depends on the relative proportions of factors among the unemployed. This dependence makes sense in that
unemployment in sector X is the relevant alternative for employed sector-Y agents. On the
other hand, relative sector-X factor rewards (for matched agents) equal the ratio of unconditional probabilities of employment: $w_x/r_x = \pi_{Lx}/\pi_{Kx} = l_x$. In this case, the latter ratio is the
sectoral factor intensity, including the employed and the unemployed agents. The reason for
this is that sector-X factor rewards are the result of a bargaining process. In this process, the
factor that is more abundant in the sector negotiates from a weaker position because if the
match were to dissolve, she would have a more difficult time finding a new partner.

Finally, substituting (19)–(21) into (18) and setting $\hat{I}_0 = 0$ yields

$$\lambda_{Lx}\hat{X} + \lambda_{Ly}\hat{Y} = (\hat{w}_y - \hat{r}_y)(q_L + \lambda_{Ly}\theta_{Ky}\sigma_y) \tag{22}$$

$$\lambda_{Kx}\hat{X} + \lambda_{Ky}\hat{Y} = (\hat{w}_y - \hat{r}_y)(q_K - \lambda_{Ky}\theta_{Ly}\sigma_y) \tag{23}$$

where $q_i = \lambda_{ix}\phi_i(1 - \eta)/\phi[1 - \eta(1 - e_i)]$ for $i = L, K$.

The relationship between factor rewards and output quantities is now found by subtracting (23) from (22). The resulting expression is

$$\lambda(\hat{X} - \hat{Y}) = (\hat{w}_y - \hat{r}_y)(q_L - q_K + t_y\sigma_y) \tag{24}$$

where $t_h = \theta_{Kh}\lambda_{Lh} + \theta_{Lh}\lambda_{Kh} > 0$ for $h = X, Y$.

Compare (24) with the result implied by equations (1b) and (2b) of Jones (1965), reported here (with obvious changes of notation) as

$$\lambda(\hat{X} - \hat{Y}) = (\hat{w} - \hat{r})(t_x\sigma_x + t_y\sigma_y) \tag{25}$$

Because there are no factor market frictions in the Jones analysis, w and r denote the payments to the two factors regardless of sector.

By inspection, the only difference between (24) and (25) is that $q_L - q_K$ replaces $t_x\sigma_x$. However, $q_L > 0$ and $q_K < 0$. Therefore, $q_L - q_K > 0$, and it follows that the mechanism linking output levels to factor rewards in our model is qualitatively identical to the mechanism at work in the standard two-sector general equilibrium model. In both cases, the qualitative effect of a change in relative outputs on relative factor returns depends on the relative *physical* factor intensities of the sectors (i.e., the sign of λ).

We now turn to the derivation of the equation that relates commodity and factor prices in our model. Totally differentiating (15), the sector-X pricing equation, and using (19) and (20), we obtain

$$\hat{P}_x = \theta_{Lx}\hat{w}_y + \theta_{Kx}\hat{r}_y - (\hat{w}_y - \hat{r}_y)\Sigma \tag{26}$$

where $\theta_{ix} = \alpha_i$ (for $i = L, K$) and $\Sigma = (\phi_L + \phi_K)(1 - \eta)/\phi[2 - \eta(2 - e_L - e_K)]$.

Similarly, we differentiate (12) to obtain an expression for $\hat{P}_y$:

$$\hat{P}_y = \theta_{Ly}\hat{w}_y + \theta_{Ky}\hat{r}_y \tag{27}$$

Finally, subtracting (27) from (26) provides the link between factor prices and product prices when factor markets exhibit frictional unemployment:

$$\hat{P}_x = \hat{P}_y = (\theta - \Sigma)(\hat{w}_y - \hat{r}_y) \tag{28}$$

Now, from (3b) and (4b) of Jones (1965), we can derive

$$\hat{P}_x - \hat{P}_y = \theta(\hat{w} - \hat{r}) \tag{29}$$

Comparing (28) with (29), we see that the link between commodity and factor prices in our model is fundamentally different from that in the standard model. In the latter, the qualitative effect of a change in commodity prices on factor returns depends on the relative *value* factor intensities (i.e., the sign of θ). As we show below, the Σ term in (28) complicates this link in a manner that has significant implications for the shape of the relative supply curve (i.e., the supply-side relationship between X/Y and P_x/P_y).

In a frictionless, nondistorted world, increases in the relative price of X *always* cause the supply of X to rise and the supply of Y to fall. This is seen by combining (25) and (29) to yield

$$\hat{X} - \hat{Y} = (\hat{P}_x - \hat{P}_y)\frac{t_x\sigma_x + t_y\sigma_y}{\lambda\theta} \tag{30}$$

In an economy with no distortions or frictions, the two measures of factor intensity (in terms of value and physical quantities) have the same sign so that $\lambda\theta > 0$. Thus the relative supply curve is always upward sloping.

Combining (24) and (28), we can see the fundamental difference caused by factor market frictions:

$$\hat{X} - \hat{Y} = (\hat{P}_x - \hat{P}_y)\frac{q_L - q_K + t_y\sigma_y}{\lambda(\theta - \Sigma)} \tag{31}$$

It is now clear that the relative supply curve need not be upward sloping. Even if we could demonstrate that $\lambda\theta > 0$ (which need not be the case since the equilibrium is distorted), it would still be possible to have $\lambda(\theta - \Sigma) < 0$ and hence a downward-sloping relative supply curve. In the next section, we demonstrate that our economy is quite regular in the sense that when supply is downward sloping, sector X must be relatively small. In addition, by examining the sector X production process in detail, we are able to expose the forces at work that may lead to such perverse supply responses.

4. INTERPRETATION

We noted in section 2.5 that the search sector is generally too asymmetric. This production inefficiency is the source of the potentially perverse supply response derived in section 3. To see this, note that the fundamental difference between our search model and the standard general equilibrium model is the relationship between commodity and factor prices. When factor prices increase, there are two effects: commodity prices must rise as well if the firms are to continue to break even; in addition, firms will economize on the factor whose *relative* price has risen. In the standard model, this second effect is zero by the envelope theorem. The introduction of factor market frictions causes this effect to be nonzero and to be important since the original equilibrium factor intensities are not optimal. An increase in w/r causes P_x/P_y to rise in the standard model if sector X is relatively L-intensive. With frictions, this effect may be offset if the new production technique adopted in sector X is more efficient, allowing P_x/P_y to actually fall. The purpose of this section is to determine the circumstances under which this might occur.

4.1 Equilibrium Factor Intensities

We begin by describing how the equilibrium physical factor intensities are determined and how they respond to changes in commodity prices. This is accomplished by focusing on the zero-profit condition for sector Y and the condition that guarantees indifference of agents across sectors.

Figure 2.1 is analogous to a factor price frontier. The YY' curve represents combinations of w_y and r_y that are consistent with zero profits in sector Y. Formally, this curve is implicitly defined by (12), where a_{Ly} and a_{Ky} minimize the cost of producing one unit of Y. Its slope is the physical factor intensity of the sector, $-l_y$.

Points along VV' represent combinations of w_y and r_y consistent with equal expected lifetime incomes across sectors for both types of agents. Points above (below) VV' generate higher expected lifetime income in sector Y (X). To derive this curve, substitute the value of α_L given in (9) into (6) and then equate V_{is} and V_{iy} (see eq. 3). We then obtain

$$w_y = \frac{e_L P_x}{2 - \eta(2 - e_L - e_K)} \quad \text{and} \quad r_y = \frac{e_K P_x}{2 - \eta(2 - e_L - e_K)} \qquad (32)$$

Given product prices and the proportion of searchers who are workers (and thus e_i), (32) describes one point on VV'. As s increases, w_y/r_y falls, and there is a movement up VV' to the left. We show in result A2 of the

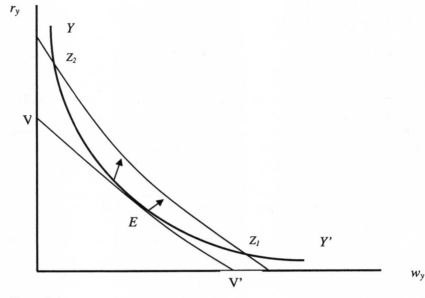

Figure 2.1.

appendix that the slope of VV' is $e_k [2(1 - \eta)\phi_k - \eta e_L \phi]/e_L[2(1 - \eta)\phi_L + \eta e_K \phi] < 0$.

Since both equilibrium conditions are satisfied at E, this wage vector is consistent with diversified production. However, at all other points along YEY', sector Y is able to offer high enough factor rewards to draw all agents away from sector X and still break even. Therefore, except at E, production is specialized to good Y (see note 9).

An increase in P_x (with P_y held constant) makes sector X more attractive and causes VV' to shift to the right. This curve now intersects YY' twice.[14] Both points of intersection represent a wage vector consistent with diversified production; yet one point (Z_1) represents an increase in w_y/r_y, while the other point (Z_2) signifies a decrease. Moreover, s falls (rises) as we move to Z_1 (Z_2) since w_y/r_y and s are inversely related.

Once factor prices in sector Y have been determined, we can derive the physical factor intensities. In sector Y, cost minimization requires $Y_L/Y_K = w_y/r_y$. This equation defines l_y for any given vector of factor

[14] Since VV' does not necessarily possess any nice curvature properties, there may be more than one point of tangency with YY' and more than two intersections when P rises. We restrict attention to the simplest case in this paper.

SIMPLE GENERAL EQUILIBRIUM MODELS   47

prices. Therefore, an increase in P_x causes l_y to decrease at Z_1 and to increase at Z_2.

Next, from (16), $l_x = [1 - \eta(1 - e_L)]e_K/[1 - \eta(1 - e_K)]e_L$, which is increasing in s (result A3 of the appendix). This implies that an increase in P_x causes l_x to fall at Z_1 and to rise at Z_2. We conclude that increasing P_x causes both sectors to economize on labor (capital) if we are at Z_1 (Z_2).

4.2 Output Responses

The response of output to changes in relative commodity prices can be determined with the aid of figure 2.2. Suppose that the initial relative price (P) is such that there is a unique factor price vector for sector Y consistent with diversified production (E in figure 2.1). Suppose further that for any factor price vector sector X is physically more L-intensive than sector Y. The factor intensities at E are depicted in figure 2.2. Finally, suppose that the economy's factor endowment is represented by l, which lies in the diversification cone.[15] We begin by noting that a drop in the relative price of X causes the economy to specialize in the production of Y. This follows since the fall in P causes VV' to shift down so that it does not intersect or touch YY'. In this situation, all firms produce Y since they can easily afford to pay the factor prices necessary to attract sector X agents. Therefore, P is the lowest relative price consistent with diversified production.

Now, suppose that P rises. This leads to two possible vectors of factor prices for sector Y. If Z_1 represents the new equilibrium, both sectors become more K-intensive, causing the diversification cone to rotate counterclockwise. This implies that the demand for capital increases while the supply remains the same. To bring the demand for capital back into line, production must shift to the L-intensive good. Thus the production of X relative to Y rises.

This is not the case, however, if the new factor prices are given by Z_2. In this case, as P rises both sectors become more L-intensive. Equilibrium in the factor markets therefore requires expansion of the sector that is relatively K-intensive. Thus the production of X falls as its relative price rises. Had we assumed that sector X was K-intensive, the result would have been reversed, with the type Z_1 equilibria leading to the perverse supply responses.

[15] It is, of course, possible that l lies outside of the diversification cone when we are at E. If $l > l_x > l_y$ when VV' and YY' are just tangent, the economy is specialized to the production of good X. Increasing the relative price of good X will ultimately result in diversified production but with a negatively sloped relative supply curve throughout. If $l > l_y > l_x$ when VV' and YY' are just tangent, the economy is specialized to the production of Y. Increasing the relative price of good X will ultimately result in diversified production and a positively sloped supply curve throughout.

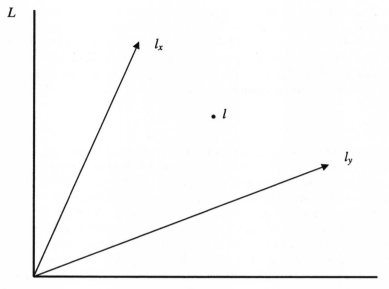

Figure 2.2.

We are now in a position to relate this discussion to the algebra of section 3. At E of figure 2.1, YY' and VV' are tangent. If we equate the slopes derived above and use the fact that in equilibrium $e_K/e_L = r_y/w_y$, we can show that at E, $\Sigma = \theta$ (result A4 of the appendix). In fact, whenever VV' is steeper (flatter) than YY', it can be shown that $\Sigma < (>) \theta$. Therefore, if sector X is L-intensive ($\lambda > 0$), then the type Z_1 equilibria are well behaved since $\lambda(\theta - \Sigma) > 0$. At Z_2, on the other hand, $\lambda(\theta - \Sigma) < 0$, implying that the supply response is perverse.

4.3 Search Sector Production Functions

To gain further insight into the forces behind our results, we devote this subsection to an analysis of the sector X production process. We do so because the fact that production in this sector is not technologically efficient leads to the downward-sloping portion of the supply curve.

The total number of type i agents in this sector at the end of the matching process is $I_x = a_{ix}X$. Substitution from (16) yields

$$X = \frac{I_x e_i}{1 - \eta(1 - e_i)} \qquad \text{for } i = L, K \tag{33}$$

By varying s, we can obtain all combinations of L_x and K_x that produce X units of the search sector good. That is, we can obtain the search sector isoquant. By solving the L_x expression for s, substituting into the K_x expression, and differentiating, we can obtain the slope of this isoquant. Straightforward calculations yield $dK_x/dL_x = e_L\phi_K/e_K\phi_L < 0$. To guarantee that the isoquants are convex, we assume that $e_i''(s) < 0$.

Production efficiency requires that agents be distributed across sectors such that the marginal rates of technical substitution are the same in each sector. The slope of the sector Y isoquant is given by $-(Y_L/Y_K)$. Therefore, production efficiency requires that

$$\Omega = \frac{Y_L}{Y_K} + \frac{e_L\phi_K}{e_K\phi_L} = 0 \qquad (34)$$

This condition will be met by the market only if, in equilibrium, the search sector is perfectly symmetric $(s = \frac{1}{2})$.[16] To see this, note that we have already shown that in equilibrium $Y_L/Y_K = w_y/r_y = e_L/e_K$. The first equality follows from cost minimization in sector Y while the second follows from the agent indifference condition. Substituting into (34) yields

$$\Omega^e = \frac{e_L}{e_K} + \frac{e_L\phi_K}{e_K\phi_L} \qquad (35)$$

where the superscript e denotes that we are evaluating the term at equilibrium values. Since the search technology is symmetric, $\Omega^e = 0$ if and only if $s = \frac{1}{2}$. If $s \neq \frac{1}{2}$, then it is always possible to increase the production of Y while holding X constant by making sector X more symmetric (see Davidson et al. 1987 for details).

To see why this is important, return to figure 2.1. Note that as P_x rises, s falls in a type-Z_1 equilibrium and rises in a type Z_2 equilibrium. Unless s is $\frac{1}{2}$ at point E, this implies that increases in P_x enhance the efficiency of sector X production in one type of equilibrium and hamper it in the other.

Suppose, for example, that sector X is physically more L-intensive for all factor price vectors so that there are no factor intensity reversals. When this is true, s must be greater than $\frac{1}{2}$ at E (result A5 in the appendix). Now suppose that we move to Z_1. As we do so, P_x/P_y and w_y/r_y both rise as in the traditional model. The increase in w_y/r_y causes P_x to

[16] The result that the optimal value of s is $\frac{1}{2}$ is an artifact of the assumption of symmetry in the matching function. If we let s^* denote the value of s that solves (34)—that is, $\phi_L(s^*) + \phi_K(s^*) = 0$—then it can be shown that, in general, s^* is unique. Our results easily generalize to nonsymmetric matching functions if we then define "too asymmetric" to mean "too far from s^*." In addition, throughout the remainder of the text, phrases such as "s moves toward $\frac{1}{2}$" would need to be replaced by "s moves toward s^*."

rise relative to P_y since X is relatively L-intensive. This traditional effect is captured by θ. At the same time, however, s falls and approaches ½, which implies that X is being produced more efficiently. This effect, captured by Σ, puts downward pressure on P_x/P_y. At Z_1 we know from above that the traditional effect outweighs the efficiency effect (since $\theta > \Sigma$). Hence, the mechanism linking movements in relative commodity prices and factor prices is qualitatively identical to the mechanism at work in the two-sector Walrasian model.

Now suppose that we move from point E to Z_2. As we do so, P_x/P_y rises and w_y/r_y falls. The reduction in relative factor prices puts downward pressure on the relative price of good X since it is relatively L-intensive. As before, this traditional effect is captured by the θ term in (31). However, as we move toward Z_2, s rises and moves further from ½. This implies that X is being produced less efficiently and puts upward pressure on P_x. This effect is captured by Σ, and at Z_2 it is this effect that dominates. Therefore, commodity and factor prices are no longer linked in the traditional manner, and it is this result that leads to the perverse supply responses. Again, had we assumed that X was relatively K-intensive (i.e., $\lambda < 0$) for all factor prices, then a similar argument could have been used to show that the perverse supply responses occur at type Z_1 equilibria.

It is worth noting that the perverse supply responses occur when the search sector is relatively *small*. It is as if the efficiency effect is subject to diminishing returns as the sector grows. Thus Σ dominates θ only when sector X is small. This is somewhat surprising since the only difference between this model and the Walrasian model is the inclusion of the trading frictions in one sector. One would therefore expect that if this sector were small, the model would continue to possess properties similar to those in the standard model. However, this is not the case.[17]

4.4. Efficient Bargaining and an Extended Stolper-Samuelson Theorem

Up to this point we have emphasized that the inefficiencies caused by search-generated externalities alter the general equilibrium relationship

---

[17] It is well known that perverse supply responses can occur when factor markets are distorted (see, e.g., Jones 1971, Magee 1976). Since the search sector production process in our economy is distorted, one might suspect that our results are caused by a factor market distortion. However, this is not the case. With only factor market distortions, reversal of the physical and value measures of factor intensity is both a necessary and a sufficient condition for generating perverse supply responses; this is simply not the case when frictions are introduced. In our working paper, we demonstrated that at E, the point at which the perverse supply responses begin, $\lambda\theta > 0$. For elaboration on this point see Davidson, Martin, and Matusz (1986).

between factor rewards and output prices. Of course, the manner in which these externalities affect equilibrium depends upon the way in which factor rewards are determined. We have assumed that the partners split the surplus created by the match as would be dictated by the Nash bargaining solution. We would argue that there are good reasons to follow this approach, given the wage-setting power generated by trading frictions and the noncooperative foundations for the Nash bargaining solution (McLennan 1982, Rubinstein 1982). However, it is useful to ask what would happen if the trading frictions were present *without* the distortions caused by the search-generated externalities. This could be accomplished by assuming efficient bargaining (à la Hosios 1990), which would imply that the equilibrium factor intensity of the search sector would be optimal.

The answer to this question follows directly from (28) and (29). With efficient bargaining, $\Sigma = 0$. A comparison of (28) and (29) then reveals that the link between output prices and sector Y factor rewards is identical to the link in the standard competitive model. Furthermore, since unemployed workers sort themselves such that the expected return from X sector search equals the return from Y sector employment (see eqs. 3 and 13), (28) tells us that there is an extension of the Stolper-Samuelson theorem in the presence of trading frictions. This theorem links changes in relative output prices to the relative returns to *searching (or unemployed)* factors of production. Thus if a tariff is instituted in a relatively labor-intensive industry, all *unemployed* labor will benefit while all *idle* capital will be harmed (in terms of expected lifetime income and profit). The reasoning is much like the logic behind the standard Stolper-Samuelson theorem. An increase in the price of a good will draw unemployed factors toward that sector. If the growing sector is more labor-intensive than the sector that is shrinking, the bargaining power of workers will rise while the bargaining power of the firm that rents capital and posts a vacancy will fall. Consequently, the return to searching labor will increase while the return to idle capital will fall. In retrospect, this should not be all that surprising; after all, in the presence of trading frictions when there are small shocks to the economy, it is the unemployed factors of production that move across sectors to restore equilibrium.

5. Applications

The formulation and analysis of a general equilibrium model with frictional unemployment serve two purposes. First, because we have been able to exposit the model in a familiar framework, one can easily examine a host of traditional issues in a framework that is somewhat more secure against the charge of unrealism to which any standard, full-employment Walrasian model is subject. It seems appropriate to address such questions within a model as similar as possible to those that economists have used in the past, for in this way one facilitates comparison with existing work and builds on earlier understanding. Second, by expanding the standard model in this manner we can examine questions that bear directly on issues surrounding unemployment. The examples below illustrate the usefulness of this framework.

5.1 Tax Incidence

In this subsection, we consider the impact of a partial factor tax on the earnings of labor in sector X. Let $T_{Lx} = 1 + t_{Lx}$, where t_{Lx} denotes the proportional tax rate. We assume that our economy is originally tax free and that all tax revenue is refunded in a lump-sum fashion to consumers.

The first step in the analysis is to add a demand side to the model. For simplicity, we assume that preferences are homothetic. In this case, it is well known that the demand side is represented by

$$\hat{X} - \hat{Y} = -\sigma_d(\hat{P}_x - \hat{P}_y) \tag{36}$$

where σ_d represents the elasticity of substitution in consumption.

Incorporating the partial factor tax into the supply side of our model yields the following basic equations (see result A6 in the appendix):

$$\lambda(\hat{X} - \hat{Y}) = (\hat{w}_y - \hat{r}_y)(q_L - q_K + t_y\sigma_y) - (q_L - q_K)\hat{T}_{Lx} \tag{37}$$

$$\hat{P}_x - \hat{P}_y = (\theta - \Sigma)(\hat{w}_y - \hat{r}_y) + (\alpha_L - \Sigma)\hat{T}_{Lx} \tag{38}$$

The algebraic expression for the incidence of T_{Lx} is

$$\sigma(\hat{w}_y - \hat{r}_y) = \left[-(q_L - q_K) - \sigma_d\lambda\alpha_L + \Sigma\lambda\sigma_d \right]\hat{T}_{Lx} \tag{39}$$

where $\sigma \equiv \lambda(\theta - \Sigma)\sigma_d + (q_L - q_K + t_y\sigma_y)$ corresponds to Jones's aggregate elasticity of substitution. We assume an adjustment process that directs factors to move between sectors in order to equalize returns. With this assumption, σ must be positive in order to guarantee local stability.

The incidence expression in (39) has three terms on the right-hand side. The first two are the usual factor substitution and output effects, but the last term captures the effect of the tax on relative factor prices through changes in the efficiency of the search process. This effect depends on the sign of $\Sigma\lambda$, which in turn depends on both the physical

TABLE 2.1

	$s > \frac{1}{2}$	$s < \frac{1}{2}$
$\lambda > 0$	$\lambda\Sigma > 0$	$\lambda\Sigma < 0$
$\lambda < 0$	$\lambda\Sigma < 0$	$\lambda\Sigma > 0$

factor intensities and s, the mix of searchers. To see this, note that from the definition of Σ we have sign (Σ) = sign$(s - \frac{1}{2})$. The possibilities are summarized in table 2.1.

Regardless of the factor intensities, the initial impact of the tax causes sector X to contract. If sector X is relatively L-intensive ($\lambda > 0$), it contracts by adopting more L-intensive techniques, thereby increasing s. This increase in s enhances search efficiency only if the original s is less than $\frac{1}{2}$. If this is the case, the improved efficiency puts downward pressure on P_x/P_y, and the resulting exit of factors further augments the relative decline in returns to the factor intensively employed in the sector. Consequently, w_y falls further relative to r_y in this case. If, on the other hand, s initially exceeds $\frac{1}{2}$, the contraction of sector X is offset by the decline in search efficiency. The case in which sector X is K-intensive is analogous.

In addition to its impact on factor prices in sector Y, the factor tax can also be expected to change the ratio of expected lifetime income if currently matched to that if currently searching. From (6), (7), and (9) we have

$$\frac{V_{ie}}{V_{is}} = \frac{1 - (1-d)(1-e_i)}{e_i} \quad \text{for } i = L, K \tag{40}$$

Differentiation of (40) yields

$$\hat{V}_{ie} - \hat{V}_{is} = \left(\frac{\phi_i d}{e_i}\right)s \tag{41}$$

The effect of the tax on the relative welfare of the employed depends solely on its effect on the composition of the searchers. For example, if the tax increases s, searching workers have a more difficult time finding a match, and thus the relative welfare of their employed counterparts rises.

Intuitively, the tax affects s in two ways. First, it causes sector X to contract. If X is relatively L-intensive, it must become more K-intensive as it contracts so that the conditions in (14) continue to hold. As X becomes more K-intensive, s falls. In addition to this output effect, there is a substitution effect since sector X becomes relatively less attractive to workers. In this case, the substitution effect reinforces the output effect, and s falls. If sector X is relatively K-intensive, the output effect would be reversed and would tend to offset the substitution effect.[18]

5.2 The Protection of Jobs

Calls for protection of domestic production against foreign competition are strongest when economic opportunities are lowest among a segment of the population. Wages and unemployment rates are two dimensions of these economic opportunities, and the question arises as to the effectiveness of, for example, tariff barriers in improving wages and reducing unemployment rates.

To address the consequences of protection, assume that sector X is relatively L-intensive, that the initial equilibrium is stable, and that X is imported. Now impose a small tariff that increases the relative domestic price of X. The first issue is the effect on the relative well-being of the protected factor, labor, measured as V_{Ls}/V_{Ks}, which in equilibrium equals relative factor rewards. In essence, this is the standard Stolper-Samuelson discussion extended to the case of friction-ridden factor markets.

We can see from (28) that the impact of a change in relative prices on relative factor rewards depends on the sign of $(\theta - \Sigma)$, which (because $\lambda > 0$) has the same sign as the slope of the relative supply curve. Thus if the initial equilibrium is on the upward-sloping portion of the relative supply curve (where $\theta > \Sigma$), small tariffs enhance the relative well-being of unemployed labor. On the other hand, $\theta > \Sigma$, which occurs only when sector X is relatively small, implies a decline in the relative return to the protected factor. In general, the Stolper-Samuelson relationship depends on the mechanism linking relative product and relative factor prices. Along the downward-sloping part of the relative supply curve this relationship does not correspond to that implied by relative factor intensities.

In addition to its influence on factor rewards, the tariff also affects the rate of unemployment, $\mu = (L_s + K_s)/(L_0 + K_0)$. From (10) and (11), we obtain

$$\mu = (1 - \eta)\left[\left(\frac{1 - e_L}{e_L}\right) + \left(\frac{1 - e_K}{e_K}\right)\right]\frac{X}{L_0 + K_0} \qquad (42)$$

---

[18] Using (41) and result A6, we obtain $\sigma\hat{s} = (1/\phi)(-\lambda\sigma_d\theta_{Ly} + t_y\sigma_y)\hat{T}_{Lx}$. The first term in parentheses on the right-hand side represents the output effect, while the second term reflects the substitution effect.

Logarithmic differentiation of (42) reveals that

$$\hat{\mu} = -\left(\frac{e_K \phi_L + e_L \phi_K}{e_L + e_K - 2e_L e_K}\right)\hat{s} + \hat{X} \qquad (43)$$

The coefficient of $\hat{s}$ in (43) is monotonically increasing in s. Furthermore, the coefficient is negative, zero, or positive as s is less than, equal to, or greater than ½. Therefore, the unemployment rate varies inversely with the symmetry of sector X and directly with its size. There are two opposing effects on the unemployment rate. First, as s moves toward ½, the sector grows more symmetric and unemployment per unit of X declines. On the other hand, the sector itself increases in size, bringing more unemployment. We derive the effect of any tariff by noting that it shifts VV' away from the origin in figure 2.1. If the initial equilibrium is Z_1 (the relative supply slopes upward), then sector X expands and s falls. If, in free trade, $s <$ ½, then unemployment rises unambiguously. Extension to the case involving Z_2 and $s >$ ½ is straightforward.

6. Conclusion

There is no doubt that over the years the use of the simple two-sector general equilibrium model has led to many valuable insights. Notwithstanding its wide applicability, many issues require the development of new models. For example, Diamond's general equilibrium search models (1984a, b) provide us with a framework in which to consider traditional macroeconomic questions (e.g., the neutrality of money and the effects of government policies on business cycles) in a microeconomic framework. Our intent in this paper is to reconcile these new models with the existing body of literature concerning simple general equilibrium models. This approach facilitates comparison and discerns how much of the earlier intuition is preserved. This gives us some idea as to what extent our analyses and conclusions need to be modified. Toward this end, we have provided a model that is very much in the spirit of the simple two-sector general equilibrium model yet allows for frictional unemployment. We then analyzed its structure in a manner that encourages comparison with Jones (1965). We demonstrated that while much of the structure remains, the addition of frictions in the labor market alters the basic relationship linking factor and commodity prices. This new relationship admits the possibility of downward-sloping relative supply curves, especially when the search sector is small. We then used our model to reexamine two old questions: the incidence of taxation and the effects of protection. We demonstrated that our synthesis can yield new insights in each case.

Appendix

Result A1

Begin by using (3), (6), (13), and (16) to obtain

$$\alpha_L P_x = \left[\frac{1-\eta(1-e_L)}{e_L}\right] w_y = a_{Lx} w_y \text{ and } \alpha_K P_x = \left[\frac{1-\eta(1-e_K)}{e_K}\right] r_y = a_{Kx} r_y$$

Now sum $\alpha_L P_x$ and $\alpha_K P_x$ to obtain (15).

Result A2

Two equations define the VV' curve: $V_{iy} = V_{is}$ for $i = L, K$. From (6) and (3) these equations imply

$$w_y = \frac{e_L P_x}{2 - \eta(2 - e_L - e_K)} \text{ and } r_y = \frac{e_K P_x}{2 - \eta(2 - e_L - e_K)}$$

Using the w_y expression we could, in principle, solve for s as a function of w_y. Substituting this function into the r_y expression then yields the VV' curve. Define $G(r_y, s(w_y))$ to be the equation for VV'. Totally differentiating G we obtain

$$\frac{dr_y}{dw_y} = -\frac{(\partial G/\partial s)(\partial s/\partial w_y)}{\partial G/\partial r_y}$$

Now use the implicit function theorem to obtain $\partial s / \partial w_y$ from the w_y expression above and substitute to obtain

$$\frac{dr_y}{dw_y} = \frac{e_K' \left[2(1-\eta) + e_L \eta\right] - e_L' e_K \eta}{e_L' \left[2(1-\eta) + e_K \eta\right] - e_K' e_L \eta}$$

Straightforward algebra can now be used to obtain the desired expression.

Result A3

We wish to show that l_x is an increasing function of s. We have

$$l_x = \frac{\left[1-\eta(1-e_L)\right]/e_L}{\left[1-\eta(1-e_K)\right]/e_K}$$

The derivative of the numerator of this expression is

$$\frac{\eta e_L' e_L - [1 - \eta(1 - e_L)]e_L'}{e_L^2} = -\frac{e_L'(1-\eta)}{e_L^2} > 0$$

By symmetry, the denominator is decreasing in s. Therefore, l_x is increasing in s.

Result A4

We wish to show that, at point E, $\Sigma = \theta$.

At point E the slope of YY' is $-ly = -(a_{Ly}/a_{Ky})$ and the slope of VV' is $e_K[2(1 - \eta)\phi_K - \eta e_L\phi]/e_L[2(1 - \eta)\phi_L + \eta e_K\phi]$. Equate these values, multiply both sides of the equation by e_L/e_K, and substitute w_y/r_y for e_L/e_K to obtain

$$-\frac{\theta_{Ly}}{1-\theta_{Ly}} = \frac{2(1-\eta)\phi_K - \eta e_L\phi}{2(1-\eta)\phi_L + \eta e_K\phi}$$

Solving for θ_{Ly} yields

$$\theta_{Ly} = \frac{e_L\eta\phi - 2(1-\eta)\phi_K}{\phi[2 - \eta(2 - e_L - e_K)]}$$

Now $\theta = \alpha_L - \theta_{Ly}$ and α_L is given in (9). Combining the two yields Σ.

Result A5

We wish to demonstrate that $s > \frac{1}{2}$ at point E if and only if $\lambda > 0$. Now begin by noting that $\text{sign}(\lambda) = \text{sign}(l_x - l_y)$, where l_x is given in result A3 and, at point E, $-l_y$ is equal to the slope of the VV' curve, which is given in result A4. Substituting these values and subtracting yields

$$\text{sign}(\lambda) = \text{sign}\left[-(\phi_L + \phi_K)\right]$$

To sign $\phi_L + \phi_K$, simply use our assumption that $e_i''(s) < 0$. Finally, note that by symmetry of the search technology, $\phi_L + \phi_K = 0$ when $s = \frac{1}{2}$.

Result A6

We define T_{ix} such that the net income of a matched agent is $w_x = \alpha_L P_x/(1 - \eta)/T_{Lx}$ for labor or $r_x = \alpha_K P_x/(1 - \eta)/T_{Kx}$ for capitalists.

The expected consumption resulting from a match is $\alpha_i P_x / (1 - \eta) T_{ix}$. Thus, from (4) and (5), we have the surplus due to a match:

$$\frac{\alpha_i P_x}{(1 - \eta) T_{ix}} - \frac{(1 - d)(1 - d - \eta)}{1 - \eta} V_{is}$$

Since only labor income is taxed ($T_{Kx} = 0$), the Nash bargaining solution does not split the surplus evenly. The solution requires maximization of the product of the surpluses. The first-order conditions to this problem imply $\alpha_L / (1 - \alpha_L) = [1 - \eta(1 - e_L)] / [1 - \eta(1 - e_K)]$. Substituting into (13) and dividing the equation for $i = L$ by that for $i = K$ yields $e_L / e_K = w_y T_{Lx} / r_y$. Differentiating, we obtain $\phi \hat{s} = \hat{w}_y - \hat{r}_y + \hat{T}_{Lx}$ Repeating the derivations in (21)–(29) yields (37) and (38).

References

Binmore, K. 1982. Perfect equilibria in bargaining models. Working Paper 8258, London School of Economics.

Davidson, C., Martin, L., Matusz, S. 1986. The structure of simple general equilibrium models with frictional unemployment. Working Paper 8604, Michigan State University.

Davidson, C., Martin, L., Matusz, S. 1987. Search, unemployment, and the production of jobs. *Economic Journal* 97(388): 857–76.

Diamond, P. 1980. An alternative to steady state comparisons. *Economic Letters* 5(1): 7–9.

Diamond, P. 1981. Unemployment and vacancies in steady state growth. Manuscript. Cambridge: Massachusetts Institute of Technology.

Diamond, P. 1982. Wage determination and efficiency in search equilibrium. *Review of Economic Studies* 49(2): 217–27.

Diamond, P. 1984a. Money in search equilibrium. *Econometrica* 52(1): 1–20.

Diamond, P. 1984b. *A Search-Equilibrium Approach to the Micro Foundations of Macroeconomics: The Wicksell Lectures.* Cambridge, MA: MIT Press.

Friedman, M. 1968. The role of monetary policy. *American Economic Review* 58(1): 1–17.

Hosios, A. 1990. On the efficiency of matching and related models of search and unemployment. *Review of Economic Studies* 57(2): 279–98.

Jones, R. 1965. The structure of simple general equilibrium models. *Journal of Political Economy* 73(6): 557–72.

Jones, R. 1971. Distortions in factor markets and the general equilibrium model of production. *Journal of Political Economy* 79(3): 437–59.

Magee, S. 1976. *International Trade and Distortions in Factor Markets.* New York: Marcel Dekker.

McLennan, A. 1982. A non-cooperative definition of two-person bargaining. Working Paper 8303, University of Toronto.

Mortensen, D. 1982. The matching process as a non-cooperative bargaining game. In *The Economics of Information and Uncertainty*, edited by John J. McCall. Chicago: University of Chicago Press (for NBER).

Nickell, S. 1979. Estimating the probability of leaving employment. *Econometrica* 47(5): 1249–66.

Pissarides, C. 1984. Efficient job rejection. *Economic Journal* 94(376a): 97–108; Supplement.

Rubinstein, A. 1982. Perfect equilibrium in a bargaining model. *Econometrica* 50(1): 97–109.

Rubinstein, A., Wolinsky, A. 1985. Equilibrium in a market with sequential bargaining. *Econometrica* 53(5): 1133–50.

Chapter 3

TRADE AND SEARCH-GENERATED UNEMPLOYMENT

CARL DAVIDSON, LAWRENCE MARTIN, AND STEVEN MATUSZ

1. INTRODUCTION

The vast majority of public debate concerning trade policy centers on the impact of trade on employment. Those opposed to free trade argue that lower production costs and fewer regulations in other countries allow foreign firms to outcompete domestic producers. This, they argue, results in less domestic output and fewer domestic jobs. On the other hand, proponents of free trade argue that free trade expands our export markets, resulting in a greater demand for our products, greater domestic production, and more jobs.

The vast majority of economists view both of these arguments as misguided and fundamentally incorrect. In fact, the debate about trade policy among economists almost always ignores the impact of trade on employment. There are at least two reasons for this dichotomy. First, most international trade economists view trade as a microeconomic issue that focuses on the distribution of resources within an economic environment while they view unemployment as a macroeconomic concern related to the overall level of economic activity and other aggregate measures of economic performance.[1] Second, the field of international trade has been, since inception, predominately a micro-based theoretical field relying on insights from mathematical models to draw conclusions about the impact of trade policies on real-world economies. Since, until recently, economists have been unable to produce convincing microeconomic models of unemployment, trade economists have largely ignored the role

---

[1] See, for example, the articles of Krugman (1993) and Mussa (1993) in the *American Economic Review* in which they argue that "it should be possible to emphasize to students that the level of employment is a macroeconomic issue . . . depending in the long run on the natural rate of unemployment, with microeconomic policies like tariffs having little net effect" (Krugman), and that "economists . . . understand that the effect of protectionist policies is not on the overall employment of domestic resources, but rather on the allocation of resources across productive activities" (Mussa).

SEARCH-GENERATED UNEMPLOYMENT 61

of unemployment in the debate about trade policy.[2] In fact, the mainstream view among economists is that trade has little, if any, impact on unemployment. This is true in spite of the fact that there is little evidence to support or contradict this view. Almost all models of trade, and certainly those that have served as the area's workhorses, are full-employment models. In addition, although there is some empirical work on the impact of trade on employment in particular sectors of an economy, there is very little empirical work on the aggregate employment effects of trade policies (see Baldwin 1995 for a recent survey).

Recently, the obstacles to the development of trade models with unemployment have slowly been removed. Over the past 20 years economists have made great progress in developing micro-based models of unemployment. In these models, the frictions that obstruct labor market clearing are explicitly modeled and the rate of unemployment arises endogenously as an equilibrium outcome. These theories include, but are not restricted to, efficiency wages, search, implicit contracts, and insider-outsider models of the labor market (for a review, see Davidson 1990). Since the equilibrium unemployment rate generated in these models is generally intertwined with the equilibrium allocation of resources, anything that results in resource reallocation (e.g., trade policy) must affect the rate of unemployment and its composition across sectors of the economy. As a result, some economists have begun to emphasize the importance of generalizing the analysis of international trade to include considerations of unemployment (see, for example, the Ely Lecture of Blinder (1988) in the *American Economic Review*).

Extending standard trade models to allow for equilibrium unemployment is important for at least two reasons. First, there is the issue of whether trade creates net job opportunities. While we provide some preliminary answers to this question in this paper, we view this as largely an empirical question. Second, and we believe more important, there is the issue of whether or not results obtained in traditional, full-employment trade models extend to settings in which unemployment is carefully modeled. This issue is particularly important for those results that have not held up well to empirical scrutiny.

The purpose of this paper is to use a simple general equilibrium model of international trade that includes an equilibrium rate of unemployment to address these two issues. That is, our goal is to try to determine the

---

[2] Of course, there are some exceptions. In particular, in the 1970s there were several attempts to investigate the impact of trade policy on economies with imperfect labor markets. This literature, known primarily as the "labor-market distortions literature," eventually fell out of favor due to the inability of the authors to draw general conclusions (see, for example, Magee, 1976). This failure was largely a result of inadequate micro-based models of unemployment.

extent to which some of the classic results of trade theory must be modified when unemployment is a concern. In addition, we show that some questions that cannot be addressed in full employment models can be answered in our simple framework.

The plan of the paper is as follows. In the next section, we introduce a simple general equilibrium search model of trade between two countries. In this model, it takes time for unemployed factors to find each other and start a productive partnership. While searching for a partner both factors are unemployed. In section 3 we determine the pattern of trade and show that the traditional list of the determinants of comparative advantage must be broadened to include features of the labor market (i.e., turnover rates) when unemployment is present. In section 4 we investigate the link between trade and the distribution of income. We show that there is an extended Stolper-Samuelson theorem that describes the impact of trade on *searching* factors. The impact on *employed* factors is more complicated, including Stolper-Samuelson forces as well as those at work in a traditional specific-factors model.

While sections 3 and 4 deal with issues that have been addressed previously in full-employment models, section 5 deals with an issue that full-employment models cannot handle—the impact of trade on the unemployed. Our main finding is that when a relatively capital-abundant large country begins to trade with a small, relatively labor-abundant country, unemployed workers in the large country unambiguously suffer welfare losses. In addition, we find that such trade increases the aggregate unemployment rate in the large country. We close the paper in section 6 where we discuss the generality of our results and suggest future avenues for research.

2. THE MODEL

2.1 The Basic Structure

We consider a continuous time model of a world consisting of two countries, Home and Foreign, with all foreign country variables designated by an asterisk. Each economy consists of two sectors (X and Y) and two types of agents, workers and entrepreneurs. Each infinitely lived worker is endowed at each instant with one (indivisible) unit of leisure that is sold as labor (L). Each infinitely lived entrepreneur is endowed at each instant with one (indivisible) unit of capital (K) that is rented for production. At each instant, workers are either employed or unemployed and capital is either active or idle. Both factors are assumed to be mobile across sectors and thus when unemployed (idle), workers (capital) must choose a sector in which to seek a job (rental opportunity).[3] We use I_{sh} to represent the number of type-i factors searching in sector h and I_{eh} to denote the number of type-i factors employed in that sector ($i = L, K$; $h = X, Y$). Therefore, $I_h = I_{sh} + I_{eh}$ is the number of type-i factors attached to sector h at any point in time and $I_0 = I_x + I_y$ is the number of type-i factors in the economy.

In order to focus on the implications of factor market frictions, we assume that both countries have the same factor endowments and that the production technology, shared by both countries, is the same in both sectors. In each sector, it takes one unit of each factor to produce a unit of output. Accordingly, an unemployed worker is searching for an entrepreneur with idle capital. Once that capital is found, a match is created that lasts until an exogenous shock causes the partners to separate. Upon separation, both partners must reenter the factor market in search of a new match. In order to allow the duration of a match to vary across sectors and countries, we assume that the break-up rate is both sector and country specific with b_h denoting the break-up rate in sector h. The production technology implies that the output produced in a sector is equal to the number of agents of each type employed (matched):

$$h = L_{eh} = K_{eh} \quad \text{for } h = X, Y \tag{1}$$

We also assume that in one sector matches might be relatively harder to find. We use e_h^i to denote the arrival rate of employment prospects for a type-i factor searching in sector h, and assume that

$$e_h^l = (1 - s_h)E_h \quad \text{for } h = X, Y \tag{2}$$
$$e_h^k = s_h E_h$$

where $E_h > 0$ is a constant and s_h denotes the proportion of the sector-h unemployment pool that is made up of labor (i.e., $s_h = L_{sh}/(L_{sh} + K_{sh})$).[4]

---

[3] This is not to say that we require factors to commit to a sector. In fact, they may switch sectors at any time. However, at any instant a worker (or capitalist) can only search in one sector. Therefore, although unemployed individuals may feel no particular attachment to either sector, at any point in time their search decision identifies the sector to which they belong.

[4] In earlier work (Davidson, Martin, and Matusz 1987) we examined the implications of a more general search technology for a closed economy. We use this linear form, which is a special case of a constant returns to scale matching technology, so that we may focus on the implications of differential turnover rates across national and international labor markets with as few distractions as possible. Empirical support for the assumption of constant returns to scale can be found in Pissarides (1990). The importance of this assumption for an open economy is discussed in footnote 7 below.

From (2), it becomes more difficult for an unemployed worker to find a match as the labor intensity of the searching population increases. In addition, as this labor intensity increases it becomes easier for an entrepreneur with idle capital to find a match. In (2), the constant term E_h can be interpreted as an index of aggregate arrival rates or employment probabilities in sector h.[5] In what follows, we shall sometimes use e_h^i to represent the arrival rate, and sometimes use the specific functional form, depending upon which is more notationally convenient.

Finally, although we assume that search is required to find employment, product markets are assumed to be frictionless and competitive.

2.2 Factor Returns

Our risk-neutral searching agents seek matches in the sector that offers the highest expected lifetime utility. Agents can expect to spend a fraction of their lifetime searching (unemployed or idle) and a fraction matched. No agent receives income while searching. When employed, each partner earns a share of the revenue generated by the sale of the output they produce. We denote the share of revenue obtained by a type-i partner in sector h by a_h^i and use P_h to denote the unit price of good h. Therefore, a type-i sector-h partner earns $a_h^i P_h$. Of course, $a_h^i + a_h^k = 1$.

We are now in a position to derive the expected lifetime utility for a typical agent. Let V_{sh}^i denote the expected lifetime utility for a sector-h type-i searcher and V_{eh}^i the expected lifetime utility for a sector-h type-i agent who is currently matched. For a type-i searcher we have the asset value equation

$$\rho V_{sh}^i = e_h^i (V_{eh}^i - V_{sh}^i) \tag{3}$$

where ρ is the discount rate. In (3) the term $(V_{eh}^i - V_{sh}^i)$ represents the capital gain that would be earned if the agent became matched. This term is weighted by the probability of the capital gain occurring given that the agent is currently searching.

Similarly, the asset value equation for an agent who is currently matched can be expressed as

$$\rho V_{eh}^i = a_h^i P_h - b_h (V_{eh}^i - V_{sh}^i) \tag{4}$$

---

[5] Over a small period of time (Δ_t), the probability of success for a type-i agent who is looking for a job in sector h can be approximated as $e_h^i \Delta_t$. The mean probability of employment for sector h searchers is then $s_h e_h^k \Delta_t + (1 - s_h) e_h^i \Delta_t$. Substituting from (2) allows us to show that the probability that a searcher finds a job in sector X relative to the probability for finding a job in sector Y equals E_x / E_y.

The first term on the right-hand side of (4) represents the instantaneous utility of an agent who is currently matched while the second term represents the capital loss that accompanies sudden separation of the partners. As before, the latter term is weighted by the probability of the capital loss occurring.

Equations (3) and (4) can be solved to obtain

$$\rho V_{sh}^i = e_h^i a_h^i P_h / \Delta_{ih} \tag{5}$$

$$\rho V_{eh}^i = (\rho + e_h^i) a_h^i P_h / \Delta_{ih} \tag{6}$$

where $\Delta_{ih} = \rho + b_h + e_h^i$.

To complete the description of our model we must explain how the revenue shares are determined. For most of our results, it does not matter what assumption we make at this point. The exception can be found in the section on the impact of trade on income distribution. We therefore delay a detailed discussion of this issue until then. The assumption that we use, which is common in the search literature,[6] is that the revenue shares are determined by the Nash cooperative bargaining solution. This solution evenly splits the surplus created by the match. Whenever a match occurs, the expected lifetime utility for the type-i partner rises from V_{sh}^i to V_{eh}^i. Therefore, the total surplus generated by a match is $(V_{eh}^l - V_{sh}^l) + (V_{eh}^k - V_{sh}^k)$. Splitting the surplus evenly yields

$$a_h^i = \Delta_{ih} / \{2(\rho + b_h) + E_h\} \tag{7}$$

Note that increasing e_h^i improves the bargaining position of a type-i agent and increases her share.

2.3 Autarkic Equilibrium

We close this section with the description of the autarkic equilibrium. In this paper, we focus only on steady-state equilibria. To ensure that the composition of each sector is stationary over time, we need to guarantee that the flows into and out of employment are balanced for each type of agent in each sector. In other words, the number of matches that are dissolved by separation must equal the number of new matches that are created. This condition is given by

[6] See, for example, Diamond (1982), Mortensen (1982), or Pissarides (1990).

$$b_h I_{eh} = e_h^i I_{sh} \quad \text{for } h = X, Y \text{ and } i = L, K \tag{8}$$

On the left-hand side we have the number of matches that dissolve due to the exogenous break-up rate. The right-hand side represents the number of new matches formed by factor i in sector h.

In addition to the steady-state conditions represented by (8), an equilibrium for this economy is characterized by utility maximization by all agents and zero excess demand in both product markets. Individual utility maximization requires that mobile factors search for matches in the sector that offers the highest expected lifetime utility. If both goods are to be produced in equilibrium, mobile factors must distribute themselves such that the expected lifetime return from search is equal across sectors; or, if factor i is mobile it must be the case that

$$V_{sx}^i = V_{sy}^i \tag{9}$$

If we substitute (7) into (5) to obtain V_{sh}^i, we then find that factor i earns the same expected lifetime utility from searching in either sector if

$$e_x^i P / [2(\rho + b_x) + E_x] = e_y^i / [2(\rho + b_y) + E_y] \tag{10}$$

where $P \equiv P_x / P_y$.

Equation (10) is the fundamental equilibrium condition in our model. For both goods to be produced (10) must hold for all mobile factors in the economy. Otherwise, one sector—say, for example, sector X—will offer searchers a higher expected lifetime reward and will attract all such searchers to that sector. Over time, as the established matches in sector Y break up, the newly separated factors will switch sectors and start looking for sector-X matches. Eventually, production of Y will cease.

To complete our background discussion of the autarkic equilibrium, we must now discuss product market demand. Utility maximization requires workers to purchase the optimal mix of goods for consumption purposes. Individuals are not allowed to save and goods cannot be stored. We assume that all agents have the same homothetic utility function. As such, relative demands for the two goods are independent of the distribution of income, the economy's factor mix, as well as the level of unemployment. Given these assumptions about preferences, the relative demand for (X/Y) is simply a function of relative prices (P_x/P_y).

We are now in a position to characterize the autarkic equilibrium. Since labor and capital are mobile, (10) must hold for both factors. We can then use (10) to prove the following result.

Lemma 1. *The equilibrium composition of the searching population is independent of the sector. That is, $s_x = s_y = s$.*

Proof. Dividing the indifference condition for labor by that for capital reveals that $e_x^l/e_x^k = e_y^l/e_y^k$. Substitution from (2) then yields the desired result. #

We can solve (10) to find the relative output price that would cause all factors to be indifferent when choosing a sector in which to search for a match. Upon doing so, we obtain the following result.

Lemma 2. *There exists a unique value of P (denoted as $\bar{P}$) consistent with the factor indifference condition. Furthermore, $\bar{P}$ depends only on exogenous variables. In particular, $\bar{P}$ is independent of s, the fraction of all searchers who are workers.*

Proof. We first rearrange (10) to yield

$$\bar{P} = \frac{2(\rho + b_x) + E_x}{2(\rho + b_y) + E_y} \frac{e_y^i}{e_x^i} \tag{11}$$

From (2) and Lemma 1, $e_y^i/e_x^i = E_y/E_x$. Therefore, $\bar{P}$ is independent of endogenous variables. #

If $P > \bar{P}$, sector X offers searchers a higher expected lifetime utility than they could expect to receive in sector Y. In this case, only X is produced. If $P < \bar{P}$, the reverse is true, with the economy specialized in the production of Y. Based on this reasoning, we can infer that the economy's relative supply curve is horizontal at $\bar{P}$, as shown in figure 3.1.[7]

Given our assumptions about preferences, we can also draw the relative demand curve in figure 3.1 to determine equilibrium relative outputs. As figure 3.1 and Lemma 2 make clear, our model with unemployment has a decidedly Ricardian nature. The job dissolution and job creation

---

[7] If we had assumed a more general matching technology (such as e_h^i is not linear in s), the right-hand side of (11) would depend on s. As such, changes in s would result in changes in P and the relative supply curve would not be horizontal. In fact, we demonstrated in Davidson, Martin, and Matusz (1991) that there exists the possibility of U-shaped relative supply curves when only one sector is characterized by unemployment. By choosing this search technology we are able to focus clearly on the impact of differences in the search technology as a basis for comparative advantage. In particular, this form of the search technology assures that differences in relative factor endowments have no independent role in determining the pattern of trade.

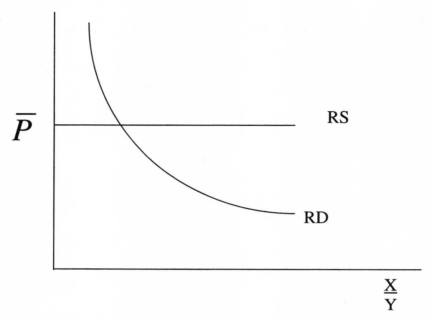

Figure 3.1. Autarkic equilibrium.

technologies determine the (unique) relative price that is consistent with a diversified supply-side equilibrium and then preferences determine the relative outputs. This is summarized in Proposition 1.

Proposition 1. *Autarkic equilibrium exists and is unique.*

3. COMPARATIVE ADVANTAGE

We now turn to the determinants of the pattern of trade. In standard trade models the primary determinants of comparative advantage are production technologies and endowments. We have removed these factors from consideration by assuming that they are identical across countries. Therefore, the only factors that could cause international trade in our model are tied to the structure of the labor markets.

How would we expect the structure of the labor market to matter for trade patterns? In our model, it is clear that labor market turnover rates influence the autarkic prices that are required to induce factors to search for matches in a sector. If sector-h jobs are easy to find (E_h is high) or long lasting (b_h low), then the compensation needed to attract factors to that sector (P_h) is relatively low.

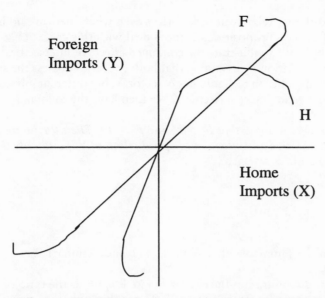

Figure 3.2. Offer curve depicting a trading equilibrium for a small home country.

Things get more complicated when turnover rates vary across countries but *not* across sectors. Suppose, for example, that one country has a more efficient search technology in all sectors. Which good would this country be likely to export? Alternatively, suppose that one country has a more "dynamic" labor market in that the flows into *and* out of employment are higher in that country than in the labor market of their trading partner. How will this affect the pattern of trade?

We begin by noting that from the analysis of autarkic equilibrium, our model possesses Ricardian properties. From Lemma 2, the autarkic relative supply curve is horizontal at a relative price that is determined strictly by parameters associated with the job search and job dissolution technologies. As such, the offer curves of the two countries appear as in figure 3.2. The linear portion of the offer curves have slopes of $\bar{P}$ and $\bar{P}^*$. As drawn, the home country has the comparative advantage in Y. We have also drawn figure 3.2 such that the home country is "small," in the sense that differential shifts of its offer curve due to policy changes have no effect on its terms of trade.

As noted above, there are two ways in which the search technology can contribute to systematic differences in relative autarkic prices. First, parameters that vary across sectors might also vary across countries. Proposition 2 summarizes the determinants of comparative advantage in this case. Second, it is possible that intercountry variation in parameters leads to different relative autarky prices even when there are no intersectoral differences. Propositions 3 and 4 deal with this case.

For simplicity, we illustrate the combined effects of intersectoral and intercountry variation by assuming that both countries possess the same job search/job dissolution technologies in sector X, but different job search/job dissolution technologies in sector Y. We then have the following result.

Proposition 2. *Assume that $b_x = b_x^*$ and $E_x = E_x^*$. Then the home country has a comparative advantage in the production of Y if and only if the following relation is satisfied:*

$$\frac{\rho + b_y}{E_y} < \frac{\rho + b_y^*}{E_y^*} \tag{12}$$

Proof: Follows immediately from (2), (11), and Lemma 1. #

For low discount rates the expression $(\rho + b_h)/E_h$ is the ratio of the factor market turnover rates in sector h. To see this, note that since b_h is the break-up rate, $1/b_h$ is the expected duration of a job in sector h. In addition, since E_h is the average rate at which jobs are found in sector h (see footnote 5), the inverse is the average duration of unemployment.

The inequality in (12) is valid if, all else equal, the expected job duration in sector Y is higher in the home country than in the foreign country, or if the expected duration of unemployment in sector Y is lower in the home country than in a foreign country. In either case, searching for a Y-sector job in the home country is more attractive than comparable job search in the foreign country, so, compared with their foreign counterparts, home factors need less compensation to induce them into sector Y.

Comparative advantage can also derive from intercountry differences in parameters that do not vary across sectors. Suppose, for example, that $E_x = E_y = E, E_x^* = E_y^* = E^*$, and $E \neq E^*$. Further assume that the break-up rates differ between sectors, but not between countries. We then have

Lemma 3. *Suppose that there are intercountry but not intersectoral differences in aggregate search efficiency and that there are intersectoral but not intercountry differences in break-up rates. Then the country with the more efficient search technology (i.e., higher value of E) has a comparative advantage in the good produced in the sector with the high break-up rate.*

The proof of this lemma follows the same logic as the proof of Proposition 2 and is therefore omitted. Intuitively, the sector with the higher break-up rate requires a higher price to compensate workers. This follows since job acquisition rates are the same in both sectors. The higher the average rate of job acquisition (i.e., the larger the value of E), the smaller the amount of compensation needed to induce factors to enter the sector. In the limit, as E rises and the duration of unemployment goes to zero, any finite differences in the sector-specific break-up rates will be swamped by the fact that new employment is always obtained instantly, so relative price tends toward unity.

Although Lemma 3 links cross-country differences in search technologies to the pattern of trade, it does not link the pattern of trade directly to unemployment rates. The following lemma, along with Lemma 3, allows us to do just that.

Lemma 4. *Suppose that there are no intersectoral differences in aggregate search efficiency and that there are intersectoral differences in break-up rates. Then the sector with the high break-up rate is also the sector with the high unemployment rate and vacancy rate. That is, if $E_x = E_y$ then $b_x > b_y \leftrightarrow \mu_x \geq \mu_y \leftrightarrow v_x \geq v_y$ where $\mu_h = L_{sh}/(L_{sh} + H)$ is the sector h unemployment rate and $v_h = K_{sh}/(K_{sh} + H)$ is the sector h vacancy rate for $h = X, Y$.*

Proof. Recognizing that $L_{eh} = K_{eh} = H$, we can use the steady-state conditions in (8) to show that $\mu_h = b_h/[b_h + (1-s)E]$ and $v_h = b_h/[b_h + sE]$.[8] It follows that if $b_x > b_y$ then $\mu_x > \mu_y$ and $v_x > v_y$. Thus, the high-unemployment sector is also the high-vacancy sector. #

Combining Lemmas 3 and 4, we arrive at the following result.

Proposition 3. *The country with the more efficient search technology has a comparative advantage in the good produced in the high-unemployment/high-vacancy sector.*

Proposition 3 links differences in search technologies across countries to the pattern of trade and tells us that, with all else equal, the country with a more efficient matching process will have a comparative advantage in the high-unemployment/high-vacancy good.[9] As we discuss below, there is reason to believe that the U.S. labor market is characterized by a

[8] Note that these results make use of Lemma 1, which states that $s_x = s_y = s$.
[9] Note that Proposition 3 links the pattern of trade to differences in search technologies using sectoral unemployment and vacancy rates evaluated in the *autarkic* equilibrium. Thus, it appears at first that to test Proposition 3 we would need to know autarkic unemployment and vacancy rates. However, since s does not vary across sectors (Lemma 1), the ranking of sectors in terms of unemployment and vacancy rates does not change when trade is allowed—that is, there are no unemployment rate or vacancy rate reversals caused by trade. Thus, free trade rates are sufficient to test Proposition 3.

more efficient matching process than either Europe or Japan. However, there is also evidence to suggest that break-up rates may be higher in the United States than elsewhere (see below). In other words, the United States has a more dynamic labor market than Europe and Japan in that flows into *and* out of unemployment are both higher in the United States. Thus, before discussing the practical implications of our results, we provide one last result.

Proposition 4. *Suppose that $E_x = E_y = E$, $E_x^* = E_y^* = E^*$, and that $E = \beta E^*$. Suppose further that $b_h = \beta b_h^*$ for $h = X, Y$ and that $\beta > 1$. Then the home country has a comparative advantage in the good produced in the low-unemployment/low-vacancy rate sector.*

Proof. Suppose that $b_x > b_y$ so that Y is the low-unemployment/low-vacancy rate sector. Then, since

$$\bar{P} = \frac{2(\rho + b_x) + E}{2(\rho + b_y) + E}$$

it follows that increasing b_x, b_y, and E by a factor of β increases the autarkic relative price of X. #

According to Proposition 4, if the home country has more turnover in its labor market (through job creation *and* destruction) than the foreign country, then it will have a comparative advantage in the good produced in low-unemployment/low-vacancy sector. This result contrasts sharply with Proposition 3 and can best be understood by considering the prospects of an unemployed worker trying to decide where to search for a job.[10] With $E_x = E_y = E$, the expected duration of unemployment is the same in both sectors while with $b_x > b_y$, a job found in sector Y will last longer (on average) than a job found in sector X. Now, consider the income that this worker can expect to earn up to time T where $T = 1/E + 1/b_x$. During the spell of unemployment (which lasts, on average, $1/E$ periods) the worker earns nothing. Once a job is found, it lasts, on average $1/b_h$ periods if it is in sector H. Thus, up to time T the expected income earned by a worker searching in sector X is $a_x^j P_x / b_x$ while the same worker can expect to earn $(T - 1/E) a_y^j P_y / b_y$ if employed in sector Y. Now assume that there is a marginal increase in b_x, b_y, and E with all increasing proportionately. The increase in E shortens the expected duration of unemployment in both sectors. The increase in b_x also shortens the expected duration of a sector-X job, and therefore reduces the amount

---

[10] The argument works equally well for an entrepreneur with idle capital.

of income expected to be earned in that sector up to T. On the other hand, the amount of income expected to be earned in sector Y up to T actually rises—even though the duration of a job is now shorter, employment begins earlier and is not expected to end until after T. It follows that even though there is no change in the relative incomes from the two jobs, income earned in Y is pushed forward in time. With discounting, this time-shifting of income makes sector Y (the low-unemployment/low-vacancy sector) more attractive and allows that sector to offer less compensation to searching factors. As a result, the autarkic relative price of that good falls.

Our results to this point suggest that the structure of the labor market can play a role in determining the pattern of trade with the key features being the job creation and job destruction technologies. Since it takes time and effort for idle factors to meet, the longer it takes to meet in a sector, the higher the compensation must be for factors to seek employment in that sector. Similarly, the longer a partnership lasts in a sector, the lower the compensation can be and still attract workers to that sector. In practical terms, this suggests that labor market turnover costs may play a role in determining comparative advantage. Moreover, in a more elaborate model of unemployment, other turnover costs (e.g., training and recruitment costs) would surely influence equilibrium prices.

Are turnover costs significant enough to matter? Do they vary across sectors and across countries enough to make a significant difference? While a detailed answer to these questions is beyond the scope of this paper, a casual review of the labor economics literature suggests that the answer is probably yes. A review of turnover costs in Hamermesh (1993) indicates that in many sectors the turnover costs incurred by firms trying to fill vacancies are quite high. For example, one large pharmaceutical company estimated the present value of the cost of replacing a worker at roughly twice the worker's annual salary. A second study pegs the cost of replacing a truck driver at slightly less than half of that worker's annual pay. There are, of course, some sectors where these costs are quite low (the lowest of the hiring cost estimates reported by Hamermesh appears to be about three weeks worth of pay).

It is also well known that there are significant differences in the turnover rates across countries. The average duration of a job is much higher in Europe and Japan than it is in the United States—in a typical month in 1988 about 2% of Americans became unemployed while in Europe and Japan the rate was much lower at 0.4% (Freeman 1994). In addition, workers find reemployment much more rapidly in the United States than they do in Europe—for example, in 1988 almost half (46%) of all Americans who were unemployed in a given month were no longer unemployed in the next month, while in Europe the rate of reemployment was only

5% (Freeman 1994). Labor economists conclude that U.S. labor markets are much more flexible than their European counterparts. They have recognized for quite some time now that this difference in flexibility has important implications for a variety of issues including job training and macroeconomic performance (see, for example, Layard, Nickell, and Jackman 1991). It is not at all hard to imagine that there are important implications for the pattern of trade as well.

4. Trade and the Distribution of Income

One of the most debated issues concerning trade policy both publicly and in the profession is the impact of trade on the distribution of income. This has been a particularly hot topic recently with public debate about the welfare implications of NAFTA and the Uruguay round of GATT and debate within the profession as to whether or not international trade has played a significant role in the recent dramatic changes in the distribution of income in the United States.[11]

If we turn to the textbook explanations of how trade affects income distribution there are two competing theories. In the traditional full-employment two-factor two-good Heckscher-Ohlin model the impact of trade on income distribution is summarized by the Stolper-Samuelson theorem. This theorem states that protecting an industry increases the real return to the factor that is used relatively intensively in that sector and lowers the real return to the other factor. In contrast, the traditional full-employment Ricardo-Viner model predicts that free trade benefits the factor specific to the export sector, harms the factor specific to the import sector, and has an ambiguous impact on the welfare of the mobile factor.

In this section we ask whether the insights from the Heckscher-Ohlin (HO) model generalize to models with unemployment.[12] This is one question concerning trade and unemployment that has recently received some serious attention in the literature. Two papers, Davidson, Martin, and Matusz (1988) and Hosios (1990), both provide partial answers to this question in an HO setting. Thus, we begin this section by summarizing their findings. We then extend their results to provide a more complete picture of the link between welfare and trade in a Heckscher-Ohlin setting with unemployment.

---

[11] See, for example, the articles on income inequality and trade in the Summer 1995 *Journal of Economic Perspectives*.

[12] For the link between trade and income distribution in the Ricardo-Viner model, see Davidson (1997).

While the analyses offered in Davidson, Martin, and Matusz (1988) and Hosios (1990) are very similar, for our purposes, there is one key difference—the manner in which the surplus is split once a partnership is formed. In our earlier article, we followed the search literature tradition in using the Nash cooperative bargaining solution with splits the surplus created by a match evenly between the partners. As is well known (see, for example, Diamond 1982) this sharing rule leads to suboptimal equilibria. In fact, we showed in our paper that with this sharing rule the factor mix attracted to each sector will not, in general, be optimal. Hosios, on the other hand, assumed efficient bargaining so that the factor mix attracted to each sector would, in fact, maximize the value of steady-state output.

To see why this matters, consider the standard Stolper-Samuelson argument. In the Heckscher-Ohlin model of trade the cost of producing a unit of output equals the price of that output, or

$$P_h = a_{lh} w_l + a_{kh} w_k \tag{13}$$

where a_{ih} is the cost minimizing amount of factor i used to produce one unit of good h and w_i is the payment to factor i. Totally differentiating this expression for each sector, translating the terms into percentage changes and then subtracting across sectors leads to the familiar expression

$$(\hat{P}_x - \hat{P}_y) = \theta^*(\hat{w}_l - \hat{w}_k) \tag{14}$$

where θ^* ranks the sectors in terms of their value factor intensities ($\theta^* > 0$ implies that the X sector is relatively labor intensive in value terms) and a circumflex above a variable represents a percentage change in that variable. Thus, an increase in P_x/P_y leads to an increase in w_l/w_k. This argument leads directly to the Stolper-Samuelson theorem. However, it is important to note that in deriving (14) it is necessary to make use of the fact that, due to cost minimization, $w_l da_{lh} + w_k da_{kh} = 0$. That is, since factors are chosen to minimize the cost of producing output, small changes in the factor mix result in only second-order changes in the cost of production.

Now, turn to models with unemployment. Hosios shows that in a model quite similar to ours in which both factors are mobile an expression similar to (13) holds. In particular, he shows that

$$P_h = a_{lh} \rho V_{sh}^l + a_{kh} \rho V_{sh}^k \tag{15}$$

where $a_{ih} = (I_{eh} + I_{sh})/h$ measures the total number of type-i workers attached to sector h (both employed *and* searching) per unit of output.

Totally differentiating (15) and following the same procedure outlined above, Hosios derives an extension of the Stolper-Samuelson theorem for models with unemployment. This theorem states that if a sector is protected, the steady-state real return to the unemployed factor used relatively intensively in that sector rises and the steady-state real return to the other factor falls. However, in calculating factor intensities those who are searching in each sector must be included in the calculations. Moreover, the theorem tells us how the steady-state returns to searching factors are affected (i.e., V_{sh}^i). It says nothing of the impact of protection on the steady-state return to employed factors (i.e., V_{eh}^i). We return to this issue below and extend Hosios's analysis to see how the steady-state returns to employed factors are affected by trade.

In deriving this extended Stolper-Samuelson theorem Hosios makes use of the fact that the equilibrium factor intensities in his sectors are optimal [and, thus, $\rho V_{sh}^l (da_{lh}) + \rho V_{sh}^k (da_{kh}) = 0$]. This follows from his assumption of efficient bargaining. In our article (Davidson, Martin, and Matusz 1988) we showed that with the bargaining shares determined by the Nash cooperative bargaining solution the Stolper-Samuelson theorem could be overturned since changes in the (inefficient) factor mix exert a second impact on steady-state factor rewards that may swamp the Stolper-Samuelson effects. It follows that the impact of trade on the distribution of income depends crucially on whether sectoral factor mixes are efficient.

Which assumption concerning bargaining is most realistic? While the answer to this question is beyond the scope of this paper there are a few comments that can be made. First, there is a solid noncooperative foundation for the Nash cooperative bargaining solution in that it has been shown to be the equilibrium outcome of a well defined, sensible bargaining process (e.g., Binmore, Rubinstein, and Wolinsky 1986). We know of no similar noncooperative foundation for efficient bargaining. On the other hand, we know of no empirical evidence that search externalities cause significant inefficiencies in factor mixes. Although such externalities are easy to analyze theoretically, it is extremely difficult, if not impossible, to measure them. Our own view is that it is unlikely that factor intensities are indeed optimal; but, it is also unlikely that changes in those factor intensities could generate secondary effects strong enough to overturn the extended Stolper-Samuelson theorem described above.

Now, as noted above, the extended Stolper-Samuelson theorem of Hosios (1990) holds for *searching* factors—it says nothing about how trade affects the steady-state welfare of employed factors. However, it is straightforward to generalize his results to employed factors. To see this, let $P^{\%}$ denote the price index that is used to turn nominal values into real values. Then, from (5)–(7) we have

$$\frac{\rho V_{eh}^i}{P^\%} = \frac{\rho V_{sh}^i}{P^\%} + \frac{\rho}{2(\rho + b_h) + E_h} \frac{P_h}{P^\%} \tag{16}$$

As (16) makes clear, the impact of trade on the steady-state return to employed factors is determined by two forces. The first term on the right-hand side of (16) is the steady-state return to searching factors and, as we have seen above, changes in this term are governed by Stolper-Samuelson forces. The second term on the right-hand side of (16) rises for factors employed in the export sector and falls for those employed in the import sector. This term captures the benefit (loss) to employed factors for being fortunate (unfortunate) enough to be already matched in the sector that benefits (suffers) from free trade.

It follows that if a factor is employed *and* used intensively in the export sector, then it gains from trade. If a factor is employed *and* used intensively in the import sector, then it is harmed by free trade. The impact on the other two types of employed factors is ambiguous. A factor that is employed in the export sector but used relatively intensively in the import sector gains from being matched in the export sector but suffers from the Stolper-Samuelson forces. A factor that is employed in the import sector but used relatively intensively in the export sector gains from the Stolper-Samuelson effects but suffers from being matched in the import sector. Thus, we have

Proposition 5. *If bargaining between matched factors is efficient, then the steady-state real return to searching factors varies according to the Stolper-Samuelson theorem. For matched factors it is somewhat more complicated. For the factor that is used relatively intensively in the export (import) sector, its steady-state real return varies according to the Stolper-Samuelson theorem if it is matched in the export (import) sector. The effect of trade on the steady-state real return to the remaining matched factors is ambiguous.*

The intuition behind Proposition 5 is that when time and effort are required to find employment, an existing job creates a sectoral attachment since employed agents are reluctant to quit their jobs in order to search for new employment elsewhere. Matched factors in this model are therefore analogous to the immobile factors in a Ricardo-Viner model. By contrast, unemployed factors have no attachments to any sector and are therefore completely mobile. As a result, the gains and loses from trade that accrue to *searching* factors are precisely what would be found in a Heckscher-Ohlin model. On the other hand, the impact of trade on *employed* factors combines specific-factor effects (through sectoral attachments) with Heckscher-Ohlin effects (since they will someday become unemployed again). It is clear from (16) that the specific-factor effects are more likely to be dominant if employed factors have strong attachments to their sector. This occurs when b_h and E_h are low so that jobs are long lasting and difficult to find.

This proposition has implications for the empirical literature that has attempted to distinguish between the predictions of the Stolper-Samuelson theorem and the Ricardo-Viner model. Magee (1980) tested the predictions of these two theories by examining whether labor and capital within a given industry tended to oppose each other on the issue of protection for that industry. One of the implications of the Stolper-Samuelson theorem is that a factor's position with respect to free trade does not depend on the sector in which it is employed—all that matters is whether the factor is relatively scarce or abundant. Thus, different factors employed in the same industry should oppose each other on this issue. The Ricardo-Viner model suggests just the opposite. By examining the positions taken by labor and capital in 27 industries during their Congressional testimony with respect to the Trade Reform Act of 1973, Magee finds strong evidence that factors within an industry tend to be on the same side of the protection/free trade argument.[13] Of the 27 industries studied, 15 are clearly consistent with the Ricardo-Viner model, three others lean heavily in that direction, six are ambiguous, and only two are consistent with the Stolper-Samuelson theorem. He concludes that this test, along with the results of two others, support the Ricardo-Viner model at the expense of the Stolper-Samuelson theorem.

Our results indicate that distinguishing between these two models is not quite so easy—when search is required to find a job a sectoral attachment is created by employment that muddles the distinction between these two theories. Industries in which job attachments are strong (i.e., the duration of a job and the duration of unemployment are both relatively long) should behave more like the Ricardo-Viner model since employment creates a strong tie to the industry and makes employed factors behave as if they were specific to the industry. In contrast, if jobs are relatively transitory or easy to find in an industry, then job attachments will be weak and industry behavior is more likely to be consistent with the Stolper-Samuelson theorem. Although a careful empirical analysis of this claim is beyond the scope of this paper, a quick look at some preliminary data suggests that this might be an avenue worth pursuing. In table 1 we list the expected duration of a job in 12 of the industries that Magee considered. These are the only industries for which we could find labor market turnover data at

[13] Magee actually provides data on 33 industries. However, for six of the industries the data is incomplete.

TABLE 3.1
Expected Duration of a Job in 12 of the Industries Considered by
Magee (1980)

Industry	SIC Code	Data Consistent With	Average Job Duration (months)
Plastics	2821	Ricardo-Viner	119.05
Paper	26	Ricardo-Viner	64.94
Machine tools	3541	Ambiguous	60.98
Machinery	35	Ricardo-Viner	58.14
Textiles	22	Ricardo-Viner	54.95
Aviation	3720	Ricardo-Viner	54.35
Electrical	36	Ambiguous	53.19
Bearings	3562	Ricardo-Viner (weakly)	47.17
Stone	32	Ricardo-Viner	46.73
Rubber	30	Ambiguous	44.25
Trucks	3713	Ricardo-Viner	38.76
Apparel	23	Ricardo-Viner	35.46
Leather	31	Ricardo-Viner	34.25
Tobacco	21	Stolper-Samuelson	33.33

Note: Average job duration is the inverse of average monthly involuntary separations
(per 100 workers). Data on involuntary separations (total separations less quits) is taken
from *Employment and Earnings* (United States Government Printing Office, 1970, 1971,
1972, 1973, 1974).

the same Standard Industrial Classification (SIC) level that Magee reports
in his table 3.1. These expected durations were based upon the average
monthly rate of involuntary separation (total separations less quits) in
each industry over the period 1969–73 (the data is taken from the March
issue of *Earnings and Employment* for each year). Expected job duration
is then the inverse of this separation rate. Table 1 lists the industries according to expected job duration with the industry with the longest duration listed first. Note that the only industry consistent with the Stolper-
Samuelson theorem (tobacco) also turns out to be the industry with the
weakest job attachment![14,15]

[14] In terms of our model, table 1 reports data on $1/b_h$. Unfortunately, since data on industry-
specific average durations of unemployment are not available, we could not derive estimates
of E_h.
[15] We were unable to find involuntary separation rates for petroleum, the other industry
consistent with the Stolper-Samuelson theorem in Magee's table 1, at the same SIC level as
Magee (2911). However, we were able to find data at a different SIC level (291) that indicates relatively strong job attachment in that sector, contrary to what our model predicts.

5. TRADE AND THE UNEMPLOYED

The most heated debates concerning trade and unemployment typically arise during discussions about trade agreements between developed countries and their less developed counterparts. Arguments that reduced trade barriers would lead to job losses in the United States were central in the debate leading up to the establishment of NAFTA. In fact, careful scrutiny of the debate preceding the vote on NAFTA in the U.S. House of Representatives and the U.S. Senate reveals that of the 141 anti-NAFTA statements made, 112 were of the form "NAFTA will destroy jobs" while of the 219 pro-NAFTA statements made, 199 were of the form "NAFTA will create jobs."[16] Similar fears and discussions can be found in Europe where there is concern about the admission of Turkey to the EC and in Asia where Japan risks increases in unemployment if it were to reduce trade barriers with its industrializing neighbors.

While traditional full-employment models cannot directly address such issues, our model with unemployment offers an ideal setting to begin an examination of these concerns.[17] Thus, in this section, we investigate the impact of free trade on unemployment and the steady-state welfare of the unemployed when a large, relatively capital-abundant country trades with a small, less developed, relatively labor-abundant neighbor. We assume that the large country has a more efficient labor market in the sense that it has a lower aggregate unemployment rate than its trading partner (these assumptions are made precise below).

We consider the impact of free trade between these countries in two steps. We begin by considering the impact of trade in goods, holding factor allocations fixed. We then move on to investigate the consequences of an integrated capital market for the flow of capital that such trade may induce and the ultimate impact of such flows on unemployment.

To capture the essence of the situation, we assume that the break-up rates are identical in the two countries, but differ across sectors, and that the large country has a more efficient search technology. This leaves us with a setting similar to the one used to derive Propositions 3 and 4 in section 3—we have $b_x = b_x^* > b_y = b_y^*$ and $E_x = E_y = E > E^* = E_x^* = E_y^*$. This implies that sector X is the high-unemployment sector and that the home country (which we take to be the large country) has the more efficient search technology. We also assume that after trade is liberalized, the small country ends up specialized while the large country remains diversified.

---

[16] These data were collected by Robert Baldwin and Christopher Magee while preparing Baldwin and Magee (1997) and were reported to us by Magee.

[17] For a different approach to these issues see Davidson, Martin, and Matusz (1988) and Matusz (1996).

Thus, from Lemma 2, free trade between these two countries does not affect the relative price level in the large country.

From Proposition 3 we know that in this setting the large country has a comparative advantage in the high-unemployment good and will therefore export X. The small country will specialize in Y. Thus, in the large country free trade results in an increase in X/Y produced. To determine the impact on unemployment and the steady-state welfare of the unemployed in the large country, we differentiate the steady-state conditions in (8) to obtain

$$\lambda^*(\hat{X} - \hat{Y}) = -D\hat{s} \tag{17}$$

where $\lambda^* \equiv (\lambda_{lx} - \lambda_{kx})$, $\lambda_{ih} \equiv I_h/I$, $D \equiv [s/(1 - s)]\{(\lambda_{lx}/a_{lx}) + (\lambda_{ly}/a_{ly})\} + \{(\lambda_{kx}/a_{kx}) + (\lambda_{ky}/a_{ky})\} > 0$, and $a_{ih} = I_h/H$ (as in section 4) for $i = l, k$ and $h = X, Y$. Equation (17) shows that the impact of this trade-induced change in production on s depends on the relative factor intensity of the export sector. To be consistent with our description of this situation at the beginning of this section, we assume that the export sector is relatively capital intensive—that is, $\lambda^* < 0$. This implies that trade leads to an increase in s (the fraction of the searching population that is made up of unemployed workers).

The consequences for unemployment can be determined by expressing the country's aggregate unemployment rate (μ) as a weighted average of the sectoral unemployment rates (μ_x and μ_y):

$$\mu = \lambda_{lx}\mu_x + \lambda_{ly}\mu_y$$

As we demonstrated above $\mu_h = [b_h/(1 - s)E]$ is increasing in s. Thus, since $\mu_x > \mu_y$, the aggregate unemployment rate rises with s and free trade increases the unemployment rate in the large country.

Finally, (5) and (7) confirm that the increase in s lowers the steady-state welfare of all unemployed workers in the large country while increasing the steady-state welfare of all idle capital. We summarize these findings in Proposition 6.

Proposition 6. *Trade between a small country and a capital-abundant large country with a relatively more efficient search technology increases the aggregate unemployment rate in the large country, reduces the steady-state welfare of all unemployed workers in the large country, and raises the steady-state welfare of all idle capital in the large country.*

The second step in our analysis is to investigate the implications of such trade for capital flows when capital is mobile across countries. As we argued above, the fear of job destruction is often an important element of the discussion surrounding trade agreements, but this fear is often linked to the possibility of large foreign investment flows that could accompany liberalization. If capital flows freely between the two countries, its expected returns will be equalized in equilibrium. The relevant measure of expected returns, however, is the return to idle capital (V_{sh}^{k}) Suppose then that we begin with the free trade equilibrium in which capital is *not* mobile across international boundaries and then allow capital to move. In which direction will it flow? It will flow from the large country to the small country if (V_{sy}^{k}) is relatively higher in the small country or, from (5) and (7), if (note that we need only to consider capital's expected return from searching in sector Y since the small country specializes in Y)

$$sE/[2(\rho + b_y) + E] < s^*E^*/[2(\rho + b_y) + E^*]$$

The fact that $E > E^*$ tends to discourage capital outflow from the large country, since its factor markets are relatively more efficient at matching unemployed workers with idle capital. On the other hand, the fact that $s^* > s$ encourages capital to flow to the small country. Thus, if the small country is sufficiently more labor abundant than the large country, capital outflow is possible.

It follows that in our model there are two opposing forces that determine the flow of capital when trade is liberalized. In the small country a large ready pool of unemployed workers leads to short durations of vacant job openings and higher profits. On the other hand, working against this is a more efficient factor market in the large country that produces a relatively large number of new jobs given a fixed number of idle factors (with all else equal). (Note that one additional feature that is usually assumed to work *against* capital outflows from the large country is missing from our analysis—we have assumed that matched labor is equally productive in both countries. If labor in the small country is less productive, it becomes even more unlikely that capital will flow toward the small country.)

If capital does flow out of the large country, the impact on unemployment is obvious—as idle capital leaves, s rises and, as we demonstrated above, such an increase in s raises unemployment in the large country and makes unemployed workers worse off in the steady-state equilibrium.

6. DISCUSSION

In this paper we have argued that trade economists should begin to seriously consider environments in which unemployment is carefully modeled.

We have introduced such a model, derived several results, and compared those results to similar ones derived in full-employment models. We have argued that some traditional results are probably too narrow (the determinants of comparative advantage) and that some results do not generalize to models with unemployment (the link between trade and income distribution for *employed* factors). We have also shown that in some important cases results do generalize (there is an extended Stolper-Samuelson theorem that links trade to the distribution of income for *searching* factors) and that our model allows us to address some issues that traditional models cannot handle (the impact of trade on the welfare of the unemployed and the impact of trade on unemployment).

In deriving our results we have made several important modeling decisions and it is natural to ask just how robust our results are with respect to these choices. For example, we have modeled unemployment as the outcome of a search process. How would our results differ if we had used another model of unemployment? We have also used a specific search technology and assumed that all factors are mobile across sectors. Would our results generalize to a more complex setting? In this section we explain the rationale behind our modeling choices and discuss how our results would be altered if these assumptions were dropped. We then close the paper by suggesting some future avenues for research.

6.1 Generality

Our model yields clean, sharp predictions about the links between labor market characteristics and trade due to its Ricardian nature. This feature of our model can be traced to two assumptions—the specific search technology that we used (with employment probabilities linear in s) and the assumption that both factors are mobile. The combination of these two assumptions results in Lemma 1, which states that the equilibrium factor intensity of the searching population is the same in both sectors. Without Lemma 1 the economy's relative supply curve would not be horizontal and the model would be more complex. In Davidson, Martin, and Matusz (1987) we demonstrated that with a different search technology the complications that arise in deriving equilibrium are due to externalities that are inherent in the search process. Thus, if we were to use a different search technology, our model would indeed become much more complicated. However, our goal in this paper is to argue that models that include unemployment may behave very differently from full-employment models *regardless of whether or not equilibrium is efficient*. That is, we do not want our results to depend on the presence of hard to measure search externalities or search-generated inefficiencies. Although we find such arguments interesting, they have been dealt with elsewhere by a number of authors including us.[18] This is precisely why we chose to use a linear search technology—it allows us to focus on the implications of labor market frictions for trade with few distractions.

An alternative way to investigate the robustness of our results with respect to the Ricardian nature of our model is to drop the assumption that both factors are mobile. For example, if we assume that capital is sector-specific, Lemma 1 will not hold and the relative supply curve will be upward sloping. While autarkic equilibrium is still unique, it is natural to ask if our other results generalize to such a setting. In a recent working paper, Davidson (1997) provides the answer to this question by showing how our propositions must be modified when capital is sector-specific. We briefly review his findings here to show that while Lemma 1 simplifies our analysis greatly, it does not lead to any fragile results.

Propositions 2–4 describe the role that labor market turnover rates can play in determining the pattern of trade. The proofs of each of these propositions make use of Lemma 1, which no longer holds when capital is sector-specific. This introduces two new complications in the link between the structure of factor markets and the pattern of trade. First, changes in factor market parameters (e.g., turnover rates) may alter factor intensities, which may have feedback effects on autarkic prices. Second, with capital sector-specific and factor intensities varying across sectors, the high-unemployment sector may no longer be the high-vacancy sector. While this second complication affects only Propositions 3 and 4, the first has implications for all three. Nevertheless, variants of Propositions 2–4 do hold in a specific-factors setting. Below we offer a detailed discussion of how Proposition 2 is altered followed by a somewhat more terse description of the impact on Propositions 3–5. The interested reader is referred to Davidson (1997) for details.

Proposition 2 states that a lower break-up rate or a higher job-acquisition rate in a sector makes it more likely that a country will have a comparative advantage in that sector's good. This is because a lower break-up rate or a higher job-acquisition rate makes the sector more attractive and reduces the level of compensation that must be offered to factors to satisfy the factor indifference condition. In other words, these changes in the factor market parameters lower the autarkic relative price for that good.

Identical forces are at work in a specific-factor setting, although changes in the factor market parameters now have additional affects as they alter sectoral factor intensities. Suppose, for example, the E_x increases. The immediate impact of this change is that the X sector becomes more attractive and searching labor begins to relocate to this sector. This increases (X/Y), shifting the relative supply curve to the right, and lowers the autarkic

---

[18] See, for example, Davidson et al. (1987, 1988, 1991).

relative price of X. However, this is not the only impact of the increase in E_x. Since E_x is now higher, more X-sector matches are created each instant. Since each match consists of one worker and one entrepreneur, these new X-sector matches remove an equal number of workers and entrepreneurs from the pool of X-sector unemployed, leaving the remaining pool more asymmetric. If $s_x < \frac{1}{2}$, the reduction in s_x makes the X sector even more attractive for labor (since it becomes easier for labor to find an X-sector match) and more unemployed labor moves to sector X. In this case, the change in s_x leaders to a further increase in (X/Y) and a further reduction in P. However, if $s_x > \frac{1}{2}$, making the X sector more asymmetric makes it harder for workers to find an X-sector match and, as the sector becomes more asymmetric, unemployed workers may flow back toward sector Y. This secondary effect lowers (X/Y) and may swamp the direct effect (which increases X/Y), leading to an increase in P. This perverse outcome is more likely to happen if E_x is large so that the increase in E_x has a large impact on s_x. It follows that Proposition 2 will generalize to a specific-factors setting if $s_x < \frac{1}{2}$ or if $s_x > \frac{1}{2}$ and E_x is not too large.

Changes in the break-up rate alter autarkic prices in similar ways—an increase in b_h makes sector h less attractive for labor and makes sector h's unemployment pool more symmetric (since break-ups release an equal amount of labor and capital back into the unemployment pool). It follows that an increase in the h-sector break-up rate raises the autarkic relative price of good h unless $s_h > \frac{1}{2}$ and E_h is sufficiently high.

Turn next to Proposition 3. This proposition holds in a Heckscher-Ohlin setting since if $E_x = E_y = E$ and if $b_x > b_y$, then an increase in E lowers P—thus, if a country's matching process becomes more efficient, the autarkic relative price of the good produced in the high-unemployment/high-vacancy sector falls. Two complications arise in trying to extend this result to a specific-factors setting. First, as with Proposition 2, changes in E alter the equilibrium factor intensities in the two sectors and this can cause feedback effects that dominate the direct effects of the change in E on X/Y. Second, since capital is sector-specific, the high-unemployment sector may no longer be the high-vacancy sector. In fact, since capital cannot move in response to changing incentives, the increase in E has a bigger impact on the sector with the highest vacancy rate (which may not be the high-unemployment sector). Proposition 3 therefore generalizes provided that (a) it is stated in terms of vacancy rates and (b) the feedback effects from changes in factor intensities do not swamp the direct effects from the changes in E.

As for our Proposition 4, the only modification that is required for its generalization is that, since the low-unemployment and low-vacancy sectors may no longer be the same, it must now be stated in terms of vacancy rates. This is due to the fact that the changes in the factor mixes brought about by the changes in the turnover rates generate forces that work in the same direction as those that lead to Proposition 4.

Finally, consider Proposition 5, which links trade to the distribution of income. As we showed above, in generalizing the forces at work in a full-employment Heckscher-Ohlin model to a setting with unemployment, the only complication that arises is that employment creates an attachment to a sector that makes employed factors somewhat immobile. Thus, it should not be surprising that in a specific-factors setting the impact of trade on income distribution is exactly the same whether there is full employment or search-generated unemployment.

In summary, all of our results generalize when Lemma 1 fails to hold, although it is necessary, in some cases, to put qualifications on them.

The other special feature of our model is the manner in which we introduce unemployment. We have chosen to model unemployment as the outcome of a search process for two reasons. First, we find the notion of unemployment arising due to trade frictions intuitively appealing. To us it seems natural to model the labor market as a market characterized by informational asymmetries that make it difficult for unemployed workers and firms with vacancies to find each other. Second, in our opinion, search theory is the only modern theory of unemployment that has been subjected to and withstood serious empirical scrutiny. It appears that minimum wages cannot explain a significant amount of adult unemployment.[19] Efficiency wage models depend upon a link between unemployment and wages which is difficult, if not impossible, to pin down empirically.[20] On the other hand, the primitive feature of most search models is the matching function that links the number of new matches created to the number of searching factors on each side of the market. This matching function has been estimated by a number of authors and by now we have a fairly good understanding of its characteristics.[21] In addition, search theory has been shown to be consistent with a fairly large number of stylized facts of both labor markets and business cycles (Mortensen and Pissarides 1994).

Nevertheless, it would be useful to know if results similar to ours would hold in alternative models of unemployment. It seems clear that labor market turnover rates would emerge as a determinant of comparative advantage in any model of international trade with unemployment.

---

[19] See, for example, Brown, Gilroy, and Kohen (1982).

[20] There have been a number of attempts to determine whether or not interindustry wage data are consistent with the predictions of efficiency wage models (for a detailed survey see Katz 1986). We are skeptical of this work for reasons that are carefully laid out in Topel (1989).

[21] See, for example, Blanchard and Diamond (1989), Chirinko (1982), and Pissarides (1990).

In an efficiency wage model of international trade the average durations of unemployment and employment would play key roles in determining the efficiency wage, which would in turn affect autarkic prices. In an insider/outsider model of unemployment these turnover rates would determine the relative strength of insiders over outsiders and would therefore affect equilibrium outcomes. Thus, it seems clear that the essence of Propositions 2–4—that turnover rates matter for the pattern of trade—generalizes, although the specific nature of the link may be different in other settings.

Another insight that would surely carry over to other models of international trade with unemployment is the result that a job creates an attachment to a sector that makes employed factors similar to the immobile factors in a Ricardo-Viner model. This should be true in any model in which factors must incur costs to find employment. Thus, even if all factors are mobile, the returns to employed factors will depend, in part, on the fate of the sector in which they are employed. Whether or not there exists an extended Stolper-Samuelson theorem for searching factors in other models with unemployment remains an open question.

6.2 What Next?

We are not unique in suggesting that the labor market could have important implications for international trade. In fact, several recent papers have stressed this very point. For example, it is well documented that over the past 15 years there have been significant changes in the distribution of income in the United States and in unemployment in Europe. Some have argued that these changes can be traced, at least in part, to changes in international trade (see, for example, the articles in the Summer 1995 volume of the *Journal of Economic Perspectives*). Krugman (1995) has argued that the two regions have responded to these changes in very different manners due to the different structures of their labor markets. The United States with its relatively competitive labor market, has seen the real wages of low-skilled workers decline while in Europe, where real wages are far more rigid, there has been a significant increase in unemployment among low-skilled workers. Similar arguments can be found in recent papers by Davis (1996a, b) and Bloom, Davis, and Evans (1996). This paper builds upon this developing theme by stressing the importance of modeling the factors that underlie the natural rate of unemployment.

There are several possible avenues for future research that are suggested by our results. First, although we have argued that turnover costs *might* play a role in determining the pattern of trade, a careful empirical analysis is required to test this view. Since turnover rates by industry are

available, such a test is certainly feasible. Second, a more rigorous extension of the test of the Stolper-Samuelson theorem of Magee (1980) that
takes into account the strength of sectoral attachment for factors is clearly
in order. This would require finding more complete data on separation
rates (for Magee's remaining 15 industries) and finding data that could be
used to determine industrywide expected durations of unemployment. In
addition, an analysis similar to Magee's could also be carried out for the
1987/8 Trade and Competitiveness Act, since industry-specific data on
labor market turnover is more complete for the 1980s than it was for the
late 1960s.

There are two obvious theoretical extensions of our work as well. It is
by now well known that unemployment comes through very strongly in
virtually all work on the political economy of protection. It comes through
in time-series and cross-section analyses of levels of protection, in cross-
section analyses of the incidence of administered protection, and in cross-
section analyses of congressional voting on protection.[22] Yet, as far as we
know, there is not a single theoretical model of the political economy of
trade policy that includes unemployment.[23] The results that we report in
section 4 that link trade to the preferences of searching factors provide
the framework upon which such a model could be built.

Finally, the analysis offered in this paper has focused on steady states.
That is, we have ignored the transition path that leads the economy to the
new steady state after a shock has occurred. Yet, there can be no doubt
that there are significant private losses associated with trade shocks as the
economy adjusts to its new steady state. Trade policies that alleviate or
exacerbate such losses could be analyzed in an extension of our model
that takes non-steady-state behavior into account.

REFERENCES

Baldwin, R. 1976. The political economy of postwar US trade policy. Bulletin 4,
    Center for the Study of Financial Institutions, Graduate School of Business Ad-
    ministration, NYU.
Baldwin, R. 1995. The effect of trade and foreign direct investment on employ-
    ment and relative wages. NBER Working Paper No. 5037.
Baldwin, R., Magee, C. 1997. Is trade policy for sale? Congressional voting on
    recent trade bills. Working Paper. Michigan State University.
Binmore, K., Rubinstein, A., Wolinsky, A. 1986. The Nash bargaining solution in
    economic modeling. *Rand Journal of Economics* 17(2): 176–88.

---

[22] See, for example, Baldwin (1976), Coughlin (1985), Magee (1987), Magee and Young
(1987), McCarthur and Marks (1989), and Takacs (1981).
[23] We thank Doug Nelson for this observation.

Blanchard, O., Diamond, P. 1989. The Beveridge curve. *Brookings Papers on Economic Activity* 20(1): 1–76.

Blinder, A. 1988. The challenge of high unemployment. *American Economic Review* 78(2): 1–15.

Bloom, D., Davis, D., Evans, C. 1996. Economics of labor in a global economy. Working Paper, Harvard University.

Brown, C., Gilroy, C., Kohen, A. 1982. The effect of the minimum wage on employment and unemployment. *Journal of Economic Literature* 20(2): 487–528.

Chirinko, R. 1982. An empirical investigation of the returns to search. *American Economic Review* 72(3): 498–501.

Coughlin, C. 1985. Domestic content legislation: House voting and the economic theory of regulation. *Economic Inquiry* 23(3): 437–48.

Davidson, C. 1990. *Recent Developments in the Theory of Involuntary Unemployment.* W.E. Upjohn Institute for Employment Research, Kalamazoo.

Davidson, C. 1997. A specific factors model with unemployment. Working Paper, Michigan State University.

Davidson, C., Martin, L., Matusz, S. 1987. Search, unemployment, and the production of jobs. *Economic Journal* 97(388): 857–76.

Davidson, C., Martin, L., Matusz, S. 1988. The structure of simple general equilibrium models with frictional unemployment. *Journal of Political Economy* 96(6): 1267–93.

Davidson, C., Martin, L., Matusz, S. 1991. Multiple free trade equilibria in micro models of unemployment. *Journal of International Economics* 31(1-2): 157–69.

Davis, D. 1996a. Does European unemployment prop up American wages? Working Paper, Harvard University.

Davis, D. 1996b. Technology, unemployment, and relative wages in a global economy. NBER Working Paper No. 5636.

Diamond, P. 1982. Wage determination and efficiency in search equilibrium. *Review of Economic Studies* 49(2): 217–28.

Freeman, R. 1994. How labor fares in advanced economies. In: Freeman, R. B. (Ed.), *Working under Different Rules*, Russell Sage Foundation, New York.

Hamermesh, D. 1993. *Labor Demand.* Princeton University Press, Princeton.

Hosios, A. 1990. Factor market search and the structure of simple general equilibrium models. *Journal of Political Economy* 98(2): 325–55.

Katz, L. 1986. Efficiency wage theories: A partial evaluation. In *NBER Macroeconomics Annual 1986*. MIT Press, Cambridge, MA.

Krugman, P. R. 1993. What do undergraduates need to know about trade? *American Economic Review* 83: 23–26.

Krugman, P. 1995. Growing world trade: Causes and consequences. Working Paper, Stanford University.

Layard, R., Nickell, S., Jackman, R. 1991. *Unemployment: Macroeconomic Performance and the Labor Market.* Oxford University Press, Oxford.

Magee, S. 1976. *International Trade and Distortions in Factor Markets.* Dekker, New York.

Magee, S. 1980. Three simple tests of the Stolper-Samuelson theorem. In: Oppenheimer, P. (Ed.), *Issues in International Economics: Essays in Honor of Harry Johnson.* Oriel, London.

Magee, S. 1987. The political-economy of US protectionism. In: Giersch H. (Ed.), *Free Trade and the World Economy: Towards an Opening of Markets.* Westview Press, Boulder.

Magee, S. Young, L. 1987. Endogenous protection in the United States, 1900–1984. In: Stern, R., (Ed.), *US Trade Policies in a Changing World Economy.* MIT Press, Cambridge.

Matusz, S. 1996. International trade, the division of labor, and unemployment. *International Economic Review* 37(1): 71–84.

McCarthur, J., Marks, S. 1989. Empirical analysis of the determinants of protection: A survey and some new results. In: Odell, J., Willett, T. (Eds.), *International Trade Policies: Gain from Exchange Between Economics and Political Science.* University of Michigan Press, Ann Arbor.

Mortensen, D. 1982. The matching process as a non-cooperative bargaining game. In: McCall, J.J. (Ed.), *The Economics of Information and Uncertainty.* University of Chicago Press, Chicago.

Mortensen, D., Pissarides, C. 1994. Job creation and job destruction in the theory of unemployment. *Review of Economic Studies* 61(3): 397–415.

Mussa, M. 1993. Making the practical case for freer trade. *American Economic Review* 83(2): 372–76.

Pissarides, C. 1990. *Equilibrium Unemployment Theory.* Basil Blackwell, Oxford.

Takacs, W. 1981. Pressures for protection: An empirical analysis. *Economic Inquiry* 19: 687–93.

Topel, R., 1989. Comment on industry rents: Evidence and implications, by L. Katz and L. Summers. In *NBER Microeconomics Annual 1989.* MIT Press, Cambridge.

United States Government Printing Office. 1970. Employment and Earnings.
United States Government Printing Office. 1971. Employment and Earnings.
United States Government Printing Office. 1972. Employment and Earnings.
United States Government Printing Office. 1973. Employment and Earnings.
United States Government Printing Office. 1974. Employment and Earnings.

PART 2

COMPLICATIONS

INTRODUCTION TO PART 2

In part 1, we highlighted results that would hold in general equilibrium models of trade with search-generated unemployment when equilibrium is constrained Pareto efficient. In the articles in part 2 we take a different approach. Here, we emphasize the role that labor market externalities can play in open economies and explore some welfare complications that arise in dynamic models with unemployment.

The article in chapter 4, which appeared in the *Journal of International Economics* in 1991, demonstrates that in certain situations, labor market externalities can lead to problems when attempting to predict trade patterns. The basic result builds upon the analysis of the suboptimal equilibria presented in chapter 2. In that model, we showed that search-generated externalities can cause nonmonotonicities in the relationship between relative commodity prices and relative factor rewards. Such nonmonotonicities generally lead to a relative supply curve that has both upward- and downward-sloping portions. Although this can lead to multiple autarkic equilibria, our emphasis in chapter 4 is on the problems that can arise in a small open economy. In fact, we assume throughout that the two countries are identical and that autarkic equilibrium is unique. Nonetheless, we show the existence of multiple stable free trade equilibria. Moreover, we show that in such a setting there is no necessary link between relative opportunity costs and trade patterns. While our primary focus is on search-generated unemployment, we argue that the analysis also applies to situations where unemployment is generated by minimum wages, efficiency wages, or implicit contracts. Thus these problems are generic to almost any economy that is characterized by equilibrium unemployment, regardless of the source.

Many important issues related to trade and labor market outcomes are inherently dynamic. Prime examples of this would be an analysis of the adjustment costs associated with trade liberalization and/or an analysis of alternative labor market policies aimed at compensating workers harmed by globalization. It should also be obvious that a careful analysis of both of these issues requires a framework that allows for nontrivial spells of unemployment. In chapter 5 we point out that complications that arise in most dynamic models with unemployment are absent from full-employment models; therefore, one must be careful when carrying out welfare analyses in dynamic models with imperfect labor markets. We show that these complications stem from the fact that in an overlapping-generations model with imperfect labor markets, changes in employment facilitate the transfer of income across generations.

Intuitively, workers who have already secured jobs can expect to earn more income in the future than those who are currently unemployed—that is, current employment carries with it a claim on future income. In an overlapping-generations model with unemployment, all current jobs are held by mature members of the current generation, while all newborn agents start life unemployed. Thus, at any point in time, the current cohort of mature agents has a greater claim on future income than the cohort of newborn agents. Moreover, the size of this claim is increasing in steady-state employment. We show that when employment is at the level that maximizes the value of net output, a marginal increase in employment transfers income from future generations to the current generation (by increasing their claim on future income) and makes the current generation better off. In addition, we show that this transfer does not harm future generations—although members of each future generation give up income when they are young, they receive compensation for this when they mature, find jobs, and secure a greater claim on future income.

This result has several important policy implications. For example, this implies that the allocation that maximizes the value of net output is (potentially) *Pareto dominated* by another allocation that is characterized by a lower level of equilibrium unemployment. It immediately follows that the government can increase welfare above its free trade level by instituting policies aimed at lowering the natural rate of unemployment. Another direct consequence of these intergenerational transfers is that in the free trade equilibrium some types of jobs add more to social welfare than others. Thus as the government lowers unemployment it should do so by targeting employment in certain well-defined sectors. As a result, this model provides some justification for claims in the popular press that some jobs are "good jobs" that may be worth protecting.

In chapter 6 we turn to a different issue: the importance of transitional dynamics for policy analysis. We had mixed feelings about including this chapter in the book. On the one hand, we feel that for almost all issues related to trade and the labor market, transitional dynamics are essential. We explicitly make this point later in the book, particularly in chapters 9 and 11 where we deal with adjustment costs and compare schemes aimed at compensating workers who are harmed by trade liberalization. In this chapter we argue against comparative steady-state analysis and point out some mistakes that can arise when the adjustment path is ignored. As will be evident to the readers, we had great fun writing this paper (which appeared in the *Review of International Economics* in

2006) and one should keep in mind that many passages are meant to be read with your tongue planted firmly in your cheek. Our reluctance to include this chapter stems from the fact that many astute readers will notice that much of our own analysis (including the analysis presented in chapters 2 and 3) relies on a comparisons across steady states. The reason for this is that although the profession has developed many new micro-based models of unemployment, the models tend to be tractable only when one focuses on steady states. We return to this issue and discuss it at greater length in the introduction to section 4 of this book.

Chapter 4

MULTIPLE FREE TRADE EQUILIBRIA IN MICRO

MODELS OF UNEMPLOYMENT

CARL DAVIDSON, LAWRENCE MARTIN, AND STEVEN MATUSZ

1. INTRODUCTION

Neoclassical trade theory predicts that the pattern of trade will be linked to autarkic differences in relative opportunity costs. These differences are often attributed to unequal factor endowments across countries, but may also result from variations in technologies, tastes, or other factors. However, if countries are identical and if autarkic equilibrium is unique, the pretrade opportunity costs will be the same in all countries, and there will be no basis for trade. The purpose of this paper is to demonstrate that when the standard, competitive, frictionless international trade model is extended to allow for unemployment, the simple link between relative opportunity costs and the pattern of trade may no longer hold. We illustrate this by examining the properties of a simple two-sector, two-factor, two-country model with unemployment. For concreteness, we focus on an example where the two countries are identical and show that there are forces present that create multiple free trade equilibria. One equilibrium that always exists mimics the autarkic equilibrium and involves no trade. However, additional *asymmetric* equilibria may also exist. In these latter equilibria the countries attain different levels of economic welfare and unemployment despite the fact that they are ex ante identical. Therefore, the presence of unemployment may create a strategic environment in which countries attempt to use trade policies to influence the type of equilibrium achieved in world markets. While we focus on the case of two identical countries, a corollary to the analysis is that there may exist equilibria involving little or no trade between countries that are very different from one another. This is a point to which we return in our concluding remarks.

Our analysis is facilitated by the use of a few simple diagrams, the most important of which is the relative supply curve. We present a reduced-form search model in section 2 to illustrate the properties of the relative supply curve in an economy with frictional unemployment, and argue that our framework is general enough to embrace labor markets characterized by several other forms of unemployment. In section 3 we use the relative supply curve to illustrate the multiplicity of trading equilibria. We discuss the welfare consequences of trade in section 4. We conclude with a discussion of some of the implications of the multiplicity problems for the way we view international trade theory and commercial policy.

2. DERIVING RELATIVE SUPPLY

2.1 A Model with Search Unemployment

In a two-good (X and Y) world, an economy's relative supply curve shows how the supply of X relative to the supply of Y changes as the relative price of X changes. As we will show, the relative supply curve can be a powerful tool to illustrate an economy's behavior and to describe equilibrium in world trade. In the standard Heckscher-Ohlin-Samuelson (HOS) framework, an economy's relative supply curve is upward sloping, as long as there exist possibilities to substitute production of X and Y. If substitution possibilities do not exist, the relative supply curve is vertical when factors are fully employed, and horizontal at the prices that lead to unemployed factors.

The purpose of this section is to illustrate that the addition of unemployment can cause the relative supply curve to be U-shaped (horizontal, if unemployment stems from minimum wage laws), and it is this property that leads to multiple trading equilibria. We choose to conduct our analysis within the context of a reduced-form search model that is based on Davidson, Martin, and Matusz (DMM) (1988). We argue, however, that the same results apply in a variety of other settings as well.

Consider a standard HOS model with the following twists. The two factors of production (L and K) are supplied by two different types of finitely lived agents (workers and entrepreneurs, respectively). Production of X requires one unit of each factor, but it takes time for an unemployed worker to find an entrepreneur with idle capital. Once the agents find each other, they form a "match," producing one unit of output per period as long as they both live. The proceeds generated by the sale of output are divided between the matched partners according to the Nash noncooperative bargaining solution. If one agent dies, the other must commence the search for a new production opportunity. Sector-Y factors, traded in auction markets, are paid their marginal product.

Two conditions that are necessary for diversified production are that the expected lifetime utility for a type-i searcher equals the expected lifetime utility of a type-i agent earning income in sector Y, and sector-Y profit is driven to zero. The expected lifetime utility of an agent who chooses to search depends on the relative price of $X(P)$, the death rate (denoted by d, assumed independent of type, and equal to the birth rate), and the composition of the searching population. The composition of the searching population is measured by s, the fraction of searchers who are workers (as opposed to entrepreneurs). The expected lifetime utility of an agent earning income in sector Y depends only on the real factor rewards and the death rate.

For a searcher, an increase in P implies higher income once a partner is found, but an increase in d means less time to enjoy that income. Therefore, expected lifetime utility depends positively on P and negatively on d. We have indicated elsewhere (e.g., DDM 1998) that the expected lifetime utility of a searching worker depends negatively on s, while that of a searching entrepreneur depends positively on s. In particular, as s increases, it becomes increasingly difficult for an unemployed worker to find a match, while it becomes easier for an entrepreneur with idle capital to find a match. Furthermore, once a match is found, agents in the minority are in a stronger bargaining position since their outside option (looking for another match) is relatively more attractive. Both influences enhance the welfare of entrepreneurs at the expense of workers. Assuming that all agents are risk neutral, we can write the expected lifetime utility of a type-i searcher as $I(P)V_{is}(P,s)$, where $I(P)$ is a price index and where dependence on the death rate has been suppressed.

For an agent earning income in sector Y, expected lifetime utility equals the product of the real factor reward and expected lifetime. In particular, the expected lifetime utility for a worker in this sector is $I(P)w_y/d$, where w_y is the sector-Y wage (measured in terms of Y); whereas the expected lifetime utility for an entrepreneur is $I(P)r_y/d$, where r_y is the sector-Y rental rate for capital (measured in terms of Y).

Equating expected lifetime utility earned by searching with the expected lifetime utility earned by working in sector Y yields

$$\frac{w_y}{d} = V_{Ls}(P,s) \text{ and } \frac{r_y}{d} = V_{Ks}(P,s) \tag{1}$$

Taking P as given, (1) is illustrated as the curve VV' in figure 4.1.[1]

Moving northwest along VV' corresponds to higher sector-Y rewards for entrepreneurs and lower sector-Y wages for workers. To compensate searchers, the equilibrium value of s must increase. Since the ratio of

---

[1] As drawn, VV' has a slope of -1, as would be the case if the probability of employment for an unemployed worker (searching entrepreneur) was $1 - s$ (s). Set $e_L = 1 - s$ and $e_K = s$ in (32) of DMM (1988). In general, the curvature properties of VV' depend on the exact way in which employment probabilities depend on s, but the slope of VV' is always negative.

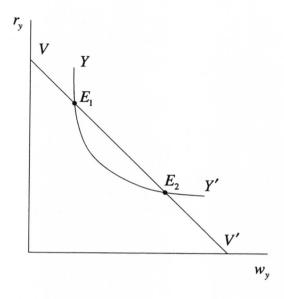

Figure 4.1.

workers to entrepreneurs actually earning income in sector X is always equal to unity, an increase in s implies that the ratio of total workers to total entrepreneurs in sector X increases. The L-intensity of sector X is not measured by the slope of VV', as the sector becomes more L-intensive moving northwestward along VV'.

Diversified production also requires zero profit in sector Y. With Y as numeraire and assuming constant returns to scale, this condition is

$$c(w_y, r_y) = 1 \qquad (2)$$

where $c(\ )$ is the unit cost function. Equation (2) is illustrated by the YY' curve in figure 4.1.

Simultaneous solutions to (1) and (2) are found at E_1 and E_2 in figure 4.1. Both sectors are more L-intensive at E_1 when compared with E_2. Since the L-intensity of sector X is not measured by the slope of VV', it is possible that sector X is relatively L-intensive compared with sector Y even at a point such as E_1 (see DMM 1988). In this situation, both E_1 and E_2 would be consistent with equilibrium supply if at both points the L-intensity of sector X was higher than the economy's endowment of workers relative to entrepreneurs, which in turn was larger than the L-intensity of sector Y.

Consider a change in P. An increase in P yields higher expected lifetime utility for sector-X searchers, implying that sector Y must pay higher factor rewards in order to attract agents. These changes are illustrated by an

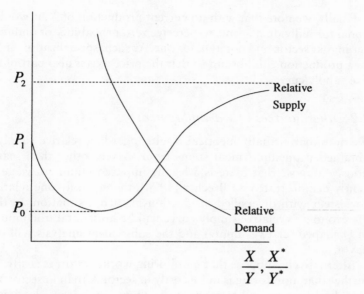

$$\frac{X}{Y}, \frac{X^*}{Y^*}$$

Figure 4.2.

outward shift of the VV' curve. At E_2 in figure 4.1 both sectors become more K-intensive, while both sectors become more L-intensive at E_1. The shifts in intensity imply, in the usual fashion, that the output of X expands and that of Y falls at E_2, with the reverse happening at E_1. Repeating this process for all P allows us to derive the U-shaped relative supply curve in figure 4.2.

Although the forces that generate the perversely shaped region of the relative supply curve have been discussed at length elsewhere (DMM 1988), we provide a brief intuitive explanation here for completeness. Since each agent's decision about where to earn income affects the employment prospects of other agents, there are congestion externalities inherent in the search process. These externalities drive a wedge between the private and social returns to search. Of course, agents make their decision based on the private returns and equilibrium occurs when the private return to search in sector X equals the private return offered by sector Y. Therefore, since the social returns are not equated, the equilibrium factor intensity in sector X (where the factor intensity includes searching factors) is not optimal. Changes in P affect this factor intensity and may enhance or inhibit efficiency in the production of X. When an increase in P makes the production of X more technically efficient (i.e., improves the factor mix), the social cost of producing X may fall as the production of X expands. This results in the downward-sloping portion of relative supply (see DMM 1988 for details).

Finally, we note that with no current production of X, it would be rational for individual agents to perceive zero probability of finding a partner in that sector, and not look for one. As such, specialization in Y would be a production equilibrium so that the price axis is also part of the relative supply curve.

2.2 Other Sources of Unemployment

We note that virtually identical results regarding relative supply can be obtained if unemployment stems from sources other than search frictions.[2] Suppose that there is a legally imposed minimum wage. As elegantly demonstrated by Brecher (1974), there is only one relative price consistent with diversified production in such a situation. In this case, the economy's relative supply curve will be horizontal (the limiting case of U-shaped relative supply) and the subsequent analysis will retain its flavor.

Alternatively, suppose that monitoring worker effort is costly. Suppose further that monitoring is more costly in sector X than in sector Y. In this case, both sectors will raise the wage above the market-clearing level to provide incentives not to shirk, but the wage in sector X will be higher than that in sector Y. In figure 4.1 we can drop the y subscripts on the factor payments and then the VV' curve would represent zero profit in sector X. However, the slope of the VV' curve would not represent the labor intensity in sector X. Again, there would be the possibility for two supply-side equilibria and the resultant U-shaped relative supply curve.[3] Here, the perverse supply response is once again due to nonoptimal factor intensities. The external effects present in an efficiency wage economy are described in detail in Shapiro and Stiglitz (1984).

Finally, the same results would obtain if production of X was characterized by uncertainty, with workers in this sector being offered implicit contracts. Here, the (constant) wage in sector X would exceed that in sector Y to compensate workers for the risk of layoffs.[4] In this setting, the inequality of relative factor prices between sectors leads to unequal marginal products, and the resulting inefficiencies.

The one difference between the search model and the alternative paradigms rests on the fact that specialization to Y is a supply-side equilibrium for all P only for the search framework.

[2] More generally, the relative supply curve can consist of combinations of negatively and positively sloped portions.
[3] Copeland's (1989) model of efficiency wages has a unique equilibrium because each type of job pays the same wage, regardless of sector. Bulow and Summers (1986) have a one-factor efficiency wage model, therefore there can be no distortion of factor intensities.
[4] This possibility was not recognized in Matusz (1985).

3. The Free Trade Equilibria

The full equilibrium is determined by adding preferences, which we assume to be homothetic and identical across individuals and countries. With intersectoral factor mobility, only one set of factor prices can actually emerge in autarky. However, international factor immobility makes it possible for one country to be producing on the upward-sloping part of its relative supply curve (offering factor rewards illustrated by E_2 in figure 4.1) while the other produces on the downward-sloping part of its relative supply curve (offering factor rewards illustrated by E_1 in figure 4.1). We now construct the world relative supply curve to examine these possibilities.

Assume that trade between two *identical* countries is allowed. We use an asterisk to denote the foreign country. To derive the world relative supply curve, we begin by assuming that trade is characterized by factor price equalization, which (given our assumption of identical factor endowments) occurs only when both countries produce the same bundle of goods. As such, the world relative supply curve would coincide with the autarkic relative supply curves. However, international factor immobility implies that countries need not have the same relative factor prices. In general, the world supply curve is a weighted average of the two autarkic supply curves. That is

$$\frac{X^w}{Y^w} = \phi\left[\frac{X}{Y}\right] + (1 - \phi)\left[\frac{X^*}{Y^*}\right] \tag{3}$$

where X^w and Y^w are the world supplies of the two goods, and ϕ is defined as the home country's share of the world production of Y.

The world supply curve is illustrated in figure 4.3, and consists of the autarkic supply curve, augmented by a number of different segments. It is derived by considering all possible combinations of output in the two countries at each relative price.

For relative prices above P_2, there are four possibilities. The first possibility is that both countries specialize in the production of X, so that $X^w/Y^w \to \infty$. Alternatively, both countries might specialize in the production of Y, so that $X^w/Y^w = 0$. Finally, there is the possibility that the home country might specialize in X, while the foreign country specializes in Y, along with the mirror image. In either case, $X^w/Y^w = X_{max}/Y_{max}$, where X_{max} and Y_{max} are the maximum amounts of X and Y that can be produced within a single country.

When the relative price of X falls between P_1 and P_2, there are again four possibilities. In the first case, each country is diversified and factor

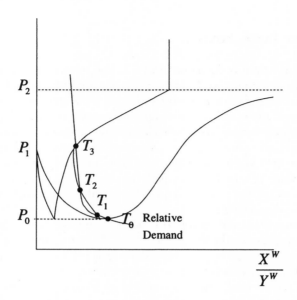

Figure 4.3.

prices correspond to E_2 in figure 4.1. Consequently, $X^w/Y^w = X/Y = X^*/Y^*$, and this portion of the world supply curve corresponds to the upward-sloping part of the autarkic supply curve. The second possibility is that both countries specialize to the production of Y, making the price axis also part of the world supply curve. Finally, one country may specialize to Y, while the other remains diversified, with factor prices corresponding to E_2 in figure 4.1. The roles of the countries may be reversed, but in either case there is an additional portion to the world supply curve, and it corresponds to the weighted average of the price axis and the upward-sloping part of the autarkic supply curve. In particular, if the home country is diversified,

$$\frac{X^w}{Y^w} = \frac{X}{Y + Y_{max}} = \phi\left[\frac{X}{Y}\right]$$

Clearly, this part of the world supply curve is upward sloping.

Between P_0 and P_1, there are nine possibilities. The first three entail both countries pursuing the same course of action. They may both specialize in Y, making the price axis part of the world supply curve. Next, they may be diversified in production, with factor prices corresponding to E_1 in figure 4.1, in which case the world supply curve corresponds to the upward-sloping part of the autarkic supply curves. Two of the remaining combinations have the home country specialized to Y, while the foreign country remains nonspecialized. The difference between these two possibilities is in the factor prices in the foreign country. Alternatively, both countries could remain diversified, but with different factor prices. In this case the world supply curve is a weighted average of the upward- and downward-sloping portions of the autarkic supply curve.[5] The remaining three possibilities are the mirror images of the latter three situations.

Finally, if the relative price of X falls below P_0, both countries specialize in Y, so that the price axis becomes the world supply curve.

Since both countries are assumed to possess identical homothetic preferences, the world demand curve is the same as the autarkic demand curve. The exact number of free trade equilibria depends on the position and shape of the world demand curve. For brevity, we focus on a situation where demand is well behaved, yet there exist seven free trade equilibria.

The world demand curve is drawn in figure 4.3 so that it intersects the world supply curve in four locations, labeled T_0 through T_3. The intersection at T_0 corresponds to a situation where free trade is permitted, but no trade actually takes place. The intersection at T_1 corresponds to two equilibria that are mirror images of one another. In each instance, both countries are diversified with one country producing on the upward-sloping portion of its relative supply curve (thus factor prices correspond to E_2 in figure 4.1), while the other country produces on the downward-sloping portion of its relative supply curve (with factor prices corresponding to E_1 in figure 4.1). Similarly, T_2 corresponds to two mirror-image equilibria, each involving diversified production by both countries. Finally, T_3 corresponds to two mirror-image equilibria where, in each instance, one country is specialized to the production of Y, while the other remains diversified (with factor prices corresponding to E_1 in figure 4.1).

4. SOME WELFARE ASPECTS OF TRADE

There are two comparisons that need to be made in the welfare analysis. First, there is the comparison of home and foreign welfare. Since both countries are identical, but may end up producing different bundles of goods with free trade, the comparison is important. Second, we wish to know if free trade increases welfare. The latter issue is more complex,

[5] This portion of the world supply curve may be either positively or negatively sloped. For brevity, we only consider the case where this portion of the supply curve is negatively sloped. None of the results hinge on this particular configuration.

since it also involves an examination of the effects of a discrete change in relative prices on welfare. We therefore begin by comparing welfare levels between the two countries, taking output prices as given.

Measuring welfare as the sum of expected utilities of all individuals in the economy yields

$$W = I(P)\left[X\{V_{Le} + V_{Ke}\} + L_s V_{Ls} + K_s V_{Ks} + \frac{L_y w_y}{d} + \frac{K_y r_y}{d} \right] \quad (4)$$

where for $I = L, K$, I_s is the number of type-I searchers, I_y is the number of type-I agents earning income in sector Y, and V_{ie} is the expected lifetime income of a type-i worker matched in sector X. The welfare of the foreign country is of the same functional form.

Define I_0 to be the endowment of type-I agents (for $I = L, K$). Then, at each instant, $I_0 = X + I_s + I_y$. Rearranging the terms in (4) and using (1) then yields

$$W = I(P)\left[\frac{w_y L_0 + r_y K_0}{d} + XZ(P,s) \right] \quad (5)$$

where $Z \equiv (V_{Le} - V_{Ls}) + (V_{Ke} - V_{Ks})$. Since the expected utility of an agent matched in sector X is higher than that for a searcher, $Z > 0$. Furthermore, in the structural model from which the reduced form is taken, it can be shown that $w_y L_0 + r_y K_0 = PX + Y$ (see DMM 1988).

According to (5), social welfare equals the real value of expected output, *plus* an additional term. Consider output first. Because the factor market is distorted, factors are not allocated to their highest marginal value product, and the value of output is not maximized. The comparison of home and foreign production, or of free trade versus autarky, involves the comparison of distorted equilibria.

The second term in (5) captures the surplus value of X-sector jobs. In DMM (1990), we demonstrate that this *pure* surplus arises in any setting in which life is finite, jobs are durable, and employed agents consume more than unemployed. (By job durability, we mean that an agent with a job today has a greater probability of employment tomorrow than an otherwise identical unemployed agent.) In particular, the same results would obtain if both death and job durability were incorporated into a model with a legally imposed minimum wage, or in a model with efficiency wages.[6] Briefly, since all agents are born into the world unemployed, while a fraction of the living hold durable jobs, it follows that

---

[6] As implicit contracts are typically modeled, jobs are not durable.

current generations will be overrepresented, relative to future generations, in future employment. Since employed agents consume more than their unemployed counterparts, current generations are overrepresented in future consumption as well. In essence, each job transfers consumption from the future to the present. This is a pure surplus given an infinite future from which to borrow, since each generation receives a similar transfer. The size of the surplus (i.e., the total value of jobs) depends on the number of sector-X matches, the relative price of X, unemployment, and its composition (here summarized by the dependence of Z on s). Jobs will be more valuable, and current job-holders can expect to consume relatively more of future output, when the unemployment rate is higher. This is because future generations will compete for jobs with a larger pool of unemployed.

To gain some idea of the welfare consequences of trade, consider a free trade equilibrium such as T_2 in figure 4.3. Here, each country consumes the same relative quantities of the two goods, but their expected total consumption differs for two reasons. First, the value of output will, in general, differ at E_1 and E_2. Precise comparisons require more information. For example, in figure 4.1, where the slope of VV' is -1 (which would be the case in a search model with employment probabilities equal to s and $1 - s$) expected real income (the first term inside the brackets of (5)) is higher when wages correspond to E_2 if $L_0 > K_0$.

The second issue for comparison is the surplus value of jobs. Clearly, the country producing at E_2 has more high-value jobs than the other country. If Z were independent of s, then this component of welfare clearly would be higher. With $L_0 > K_0$, welfare would be higher at E_2 than at E_1. However, the situation is not as clear if $L_0 < K_0$. In this case, expected real income is higher on the downward-sloping part of the supply curve, but the value of jobs is higher on the upward-sloping part of the supply curve. It may be that the high value of jobs dominates the reduced level of expected income, so that total welfare is still higher on the upward-sloping part of the relative supply curve, but it may also be that welfare is higher on the downward-sloping part of the relative supply curve.

Free trade welfare may be higher or lower than autarkic welfare. The ambiguity stems from two sources. First, the autarkic equilibrium is generally inefficient (DMM 1987). As such, an exogenous change in relative price would result in an increase in the value of output only if production shifted closer to the efficient level. Beyond this ambiguity, there is the issue of jobs. Since jobs have a surplus value, and since that value is proportionate to P, welfare is enhanced by trade if P increases (as it always does in the examples of figure 4.3) and if the output of X increases. If the economy produces less X in the move to free trade, the total surplus value of jobs could fall and this may be sufficient to outweigh any increase in the value of output.

Similarly, the introduction of trade has an ambiguous effect on the overall unemployment rate. Expanding X production increases unemployment (holding sector-specific unemployment constant), but changes in relative prices could shrink the sector-X unemployment rate. In any case, it is straightforward to show that the unemployment rate need not be correlated with social welfare.[7]

5. Conclusion

We have shown that introducing frictional unemployment into the standard factor endowment model with homothetic preferences creates the potential for multiple trading equilibria between identical countries. While illustrated in the context of a reduced-form search model, our result is generally applicable to a variety of different models, including efficiency wage models.

The existence of multiple equilibria compromises our ability to infer trade patterns based upon relative factor endowments. In particular, it becomes difficult to argue that trade should be larger among countries with very different endowments than among countries with similar endowments. While we have not done so in this paper, it is possible to construct an example where two countries with very different factor endowments would have no incentive to trade. These conclusions complement the work of others in explaining the apparent anomaly that most world trade actually does occur among relatively similar countries.

We have suggested that both countries may either gain or lose from free trade (as compared with autarky). Moreover, the welfare levels in the two countries may differ, even though they are identical in all other respects. The difference in welfare levels creates an incentive for the country with the lower welfare to look for ways to move the world to the mirror-image equilibrium, where it would enjoy a higher level of welfare at the expense of its trading partner. This creates a strategic environment between the two countries, and the outcome of that environment is a subject of future research. One possibility might be a trade war that pushes the world to a no-trade equilibrium.

Finally, we have suggested that the introduction of trade may either increase or decrease the economy's unemployment rate. However, the unemployment rate is not an accurate barometer of economic welfare.

---

[7] For a more complete description of the structure of the model and its results, see our working paper.

REFERENCES

Brecher, R. 1974. Minimum wage rates and the pure theory of international trade. *Quarterly Journal of Economics* 88(1): 98–116.

Bulow, J., Summers, L. 1986. A theory of dual labor markets with application to industrial policy, discrimination, and Keynesian unemployment. *Journal of Labor Economics* 4(3): 376–414.

Copeland, B. 1989. Efficiency wages in a Ricardian model of international trade. *Journal of International Economics* 27(3–4): 221–44.

Davidson, C., Martin, L., Matusz, S. 1987. Search, unemployment, and the production of jobs. *Economic Journal* 97(388): 857–76.

Davidson, C., Martin, L., Matusz, S. 1988. The structure of simple general equilibrium models with frictional unemployment. *Journal of Political Economy* 96(6): 1267–93.

Davidson, C., Martin, L., Matusz, S. 1989. Multiple free trade equilibria in a model of frictional unemployment. Manuscript, Michigan State University.

Davidson, C., Martin, L., Matusz, S. 1990. Dynamic welfare and the value of employment in a model of search with finite life. Manuscript, Michigan State University.

Matusz, S. 1985. The Heckscher-Ohlin-Samuelson model with implicit contracts. *Quarterly Journal of Economics* 100(4): 1313–29.

Shapiro, C., Stiglitz, J. 1984. Equilibrium unemployment as a worker discipline device. *American Economic Review* 74(3): 433–44.

Chapter 5

JOBS AND CHOCOLATE: SAMUELSONIAN SURPLUSES IN DYNAMIC MODELS OF UNEMPLOYMENT

CARL DAVIDSON, LAWRENCE MARTIN, AND STEVEN MATUSZ

1. INTRODUCTION

Economics is rife with examples of important results that were derived in static models that may not hold in dynamic settings. One of the most celebrated examples of this phenomenon is Samuelson's (1958) result that in an overlapping-generations framework competitive equilibria are not generally Pareto efficient. In its simplest form, the logic is as follows.[1] Suppose that we have an overlapping-generations economy with zero population growth and no discounting in which agents live for two periods. In each period of life, agents receive an endowment of one unit of nonstorable chocolate. For simplicity, assume that agents view consumption in the two periods as perfect substitutes. Then, it is easy to show that the competitive equilibrium entails each agent consuming his or her endowment in each period—that is, there is no trade. However, if, in every period, each of the young were to give one chocolate to each of the old, then everyone in the first generation would gain without anyone losing. This follows from the fact that the agents in every subsequent generation would receive a transfer when they are old that exactly offsets what they give up when they are young. Therefore, this transfer of chocolate across generations generates a Pareto improvement. Moreover, since the old agents consume more than the value of their endowment while the remaining agents consume output equal to their endowment, this policy creates a social surplus.[2]

---

[1] See, for example, Shell (1971).

[2] This scheme would not work if agents discounted the future since, in that case, agents would require a reward of more than one chocolate when old to offset the loss of one chocolate when young. However, as is well known, the social surplus can be generated in a model with discounting provided that the population grows at a rate that is no less than the discount rate (see, for example, Blanchard and Fischer 1989).

In this paper, we argue that in dynamic models of unemployment in which the employed consume more than the unemployed, workers are finitely lived, and jobs are lasting, such intergenerational transfers arise naturally and have important consequences that have heretofore gone unnoticed. In particular, we show that in the setting described, employment transfers consumption from future generations to those currently alive. This has at least two important implications. First, as a direct result of these transfers, a social surplus exists. As in the Samuelson example, the surplus implies that the current generation can consume more (in expected value terms) than the value of steady-state output, and that the increase does not come at the expense of future generations. However, in contrast to Samuelson's example, this surplus arises naturally in any steady state and does not require outside (government) action to create it.

Second, the existence of these transfers implies that even when resources are allocated such that the value of steady-state output is maximized (call this allocation A), there exists another feasible allocation (A') that Pareto dominates it. This result arises from the fact that at A, the additional transfer created by a small increase in steady-state employment benefits members of the current generation without harming anyone. This occurs because at that level of employment, what each future generation gives to the cohort preceding it exactly equals what it receives from the cohort that follows it. Since the current generation receives a transfer from the unborn while giving up nothing in return, a marginal increase in employment results in a Pareto improvement.

To make these ideas more concrete, consider the following outline of a model of unemployment. In each period, there are L risk-neutral agents who are either employed or unemployed. These workers face a constant per-period probability of death (d) so that life is finite and, upon death, each agent is replaced immediately by a newborn, unemployed worker.[3] Therefore, each period can be divided into three stages. First, the unemployed compete for jobs. Next, output is produced, traded, and consumed. Finally, some jobs break up. This last stage determines each worker's employment status for the beginning of the next period. We say that

---

More generally, when agents discount the future, the *timing* of consumption is just as important as the *amount* of consumption. Joel Fried (1980) illustrates this point in an overlapping-generals model where a technological improvement increases lifetime consumption but may reduce welfare for every generation after the first. The latter result follows since the exogenous shock is constructed in such a way as to shift income from youth to old age. If agents in his model neither discount the future nor experience diminishing marginal utility, they would delay all consumption to their old age. In this case, any innovation that expands output is necessarily welfare improving for all generations.

[3] This corresponds to what Blanchard and Fischer (1989) refer to as a model of "perpetual youth."

"jobs last" as long as some jobs survive across periods so that some workers begin the period with employment already secured.

For simplicity, assume that each job produces one unit of output, so that the number of jobs (X) is equal to total output. Then, in a steady state, if h represents the survival rate of a job, $(1 - h)X$ new jobs must be created each period to replace those that dissolve at the end of the previous period.[4] Finally, let V_E represent the expected lifetime income for a worker who begins the period employed and let V_U denote the expected lifetime income for a worker who begins the period unemployed.

A key result that we demonstrate in the text is that, if all unemployed workers face the same probability of employment, then $V_U = \{X - c(X)\}/Ld$, where $c(X)$ denotes the social cost of producing X. That is, since $1/d$ is the expected lifetime of the representative worker, each *unemployed* worker can expect to earn an equal share of the net output produced during his expected lifetime. For the employed, however, expected lifetime income is given by $V_E = V_U + (V_E - V_U) = \{X - c(x)\}/Ld + (V_E - V_U)$. Each employed worker can expect to earn *more* than his share of the net output produced during the remainder of his (expected) lifetime.

Now, consider the aggregate income earned during the expected lifetime of the representative agent in this economy. The newborn cohort consists of Ld unemployed individuals, each of whom earn V_U. In addition, there are hX workers who begin the period employed. Each of these workers earns V_E. Finally, there are $\{(1 - d)L - hX\}$ agents who were unemployed at the end of the previous period and survived to the current period. Since these individuals begin the period unemployed, they each earn V_U. Adding up the total expected lifetime income of all agents alive at the beginning of the period therefore yields

$$LdV_U + hXV_E + \{(1 - d)L - hX\}V_U = \frac{X - c(X)}{d} + hX(V_E - V_U) \quad (1)$$

In the aggregate, expected lifetime income *exceeds* the value of expected net output, the difference being the social surplus.

To see how this surplus is created consider two steady states characterized by different levels of employment, with $X_1 < X_2$. Although the mechanism at work is more complex, the transfer works roughly in the following manner. Since jobs last and since the employed consume more than the unemployed, a job today carries with it a claim on future output. An increase in steady-state employment therefore increases the current generation's share of future output. This comes at the expense of the newborns,

---

[4] The relationship between d and h will depend on the model. See the models in the text for specific examples.

who now earn a smaller share of output when they are young (they have a harder time finding jobs when they are young since they are crowded out of the labor market by the older workers). However, as the newborns mature and find employment, they will eventually prefer the high-employment economy since they will then possess a greater claim on future output. Therefore, in moving from X_1 to X_2 the unborn sacrifice jobs when they are young in return for jobs when they are old. Whether they prefer the high- or low-employment economy depends on which effect dominates. Since the interests of the unborn are proportional to the value of steady-state output, these effects exactly offset each other at the employment level that maximizes $X - c(X)$.

The two implications follow immediately. First, the existence of intergenerational transfers creates the possibility of a Samuelsonian social surplus. In fact, as (1) indicates, a social surplus exists as long as there is positive employment ($X > 0$), jobs last ($h > 0$), and the employed consume more than the unemployed ($V_E > V_U$). Moreover, although it is not readily apparent from (1), the surplus would not appear if agents lived forever. After all, the surplus is created by borrowing from the infinite future and, if agents live forever, they would simply be borrowing from themselves (we prove this claim in appendix A). Second, the transfer of consumption forward that is brought about by a marginal increase in employment above the level that maximizes $(X - c(X))$ benefits the current generation without harming the newborns (or future cohorts)—the social surplus is increased at no one's expense.[5] To compare our result to Samuelson's, it is as if the young are transferring jobs (rather than chocolates) to the old.[6]

We make these arguments precise in the remainder of the paper, proceeding in two steps. First, we introduce a simple model of a competitive

[5] This argument is informal and incomplete for the following reason. Let X^* denote the output level at which $X - c(X)$ is maximized. Then, provided that $X(V_E - V_U)$ is increasing in X at $X = X^*$, (1) indicates that the current generation receives a first-order gain when X is marginally increased above X^*. This change in output generates only second-order losses for the unborn, but there are an infinite number of unborn cohorts. Therefore, it is necessary to show that all losers can be compensated sufficiently when output is increased. We return to this issue in section 3.3.

[6] Models without discounting and population growth provide the easiest framework in which to expose and explain the forces generating our results. We therefore restrict attention to such models in this paper. As in the Samuelson model (see footnote 2), all of our results generalize (and, in fact are strengthened) when agents discount the future provided that the population grows at a rate that is no less than the discount rate. If the population grows at a positive rate that is less than the discount rate, the flavor of our results generalize (a social surplus still exists in equilibrium), although there are some minor modifications that must be made (A may no longer be Pareto dominated). Since additional issues arise when the growth rate exceeds the discount rate, we explore such models in greater detail in Davidson, Martin, and Matusz (1992).

economy with a fixed-coefficient technology. In this framework, equilibrium unemployment must be accompanied by a zero wage, and this implies that the employed and the unemployed earn the same income. Therefore, in equilibrium, no social surplus exists (in terms of (1), $V_E = V_U$). However, we show that any policy that transfers income from the unemployed to the employed results in a social surplus. In particular, we show that a minimum wage can generate a Pareto improvement. The mechanism at work is exactly the same as the one described above—the minimum wage transfers income across generations and allows the current generation to borrow from the future without harming anyone.

The advantage of the minimum wage model is its simplicity. Its disadvantages, for our purposes, are that no surplus exists in the laissez-faire equilibrium and that it is not possible to increase employment beyond its equilibrium level (so that it is impossible to show that a marginal increase would result in a Pareto improvement). In sections 3 and 4 we turn to more complex models with a natural rate of unemployment. The unemployment in section 3 is the result of trading frictions while in section 4 it arises due to efficiency wage considerations. In both cases, we show that a social surplus exists for *any* positive level of steady-state employment. We also use the search model to show that the employment level that maximizes the value of net output is Pareto inefficient. Finally, we show that the surplus value from employment drives a wedge between the interests of the current and future generations. In particular, we show that the current generation is likely to prefer policies targeted at expanding employment above the level that would be optimal from the point of view of the unborn.

2. A MINIMUM WAGE ECONOMY

2.1 Assumptions and Equilibrium

In order to illustrate formally the existence and nature of the social surplus attached to employment, we begin with a simple, discrete-time model of a competitive economy that produces one good *(X)* using capital and labor. The structure of the economy is as described in the introduction—each job lasts until either the worker dies or an exogenous shock causes a separation. If we use b to denote the exogenous separation rate, then $h = (1 - d)(1 - b)$.

We assume that each of the economy's L workers is endowed with α units of capital, so that the aggregate endowment of capital is $K = \alpha L$. Production is governed by a fixed-proportions production function of the form

$$X = \min(K_E, L_E) \tag{2}$$

where K_E and L_E represent employed capital and labor. Cost minimization dictates that $K_E = L_E$. Since we are interested in economies characterized by unemployment, we assume that $\alpha < 1$. Given this parameterization, capital will be fully employed but there will exist some unemployed labor in equilibrium. In particular, we have

$$K_E = K \quad \text{and} \quad L_E = \alpha L \tag{3}$$

Once output is produced, it is traded in a perfectly competitive market. This implies that in equilibrium the value of output must equal the cost of production. Since each unit of output is produced using one unit of capital and labor, this condition is expressed as

$$1 = r + w \tag{4}$$

where w is the wage and r is the return to capital. The existence of unemployed labor forces the equilibrium wage to zero, thereby resulting in $r = 1$.

Finally, consider the labor market. At the end of each period, $L_E[d + (1 - d)b]$ vacancies open up as some employed workers die and some employed workers who survive to the next period lose their jobs. Competing for these jobs are the $L_U(1 - d)$ unemployed workers who survive only to lose their jobs, and the $(L_E + L_U)d$ newborns. If we let π represent the steady-state probability of employment and assume that vacancies are filled from a random draw of the unemployed, then we have

$$\pi = \frac{L_E[d + (1-d)b]}{L_E[d + (1-d)b] + L_U} = \frac{\alpha(1-b)}{1 - \alpha b} \tag{5}$$

where the second equality follows from (3) and the fact that $L_U = L - L_E$.

2.2 Expected Lifetime Income

We measure expected income at the beginning of the period—before the vacancies are filled. If we use V_E and V_U to represent the expected lifetime income for employed and unemployed workers in a steady state, respectively, then we have

$$V_E = w + \alpha r + (1 - d)[(1 - b)V_E + bV_U] \tag{6}$$

$$V_U = \pi V_E + (1 - \pi)[\alpha r + (1 - d)V_U] \qquad (7)$$

The derivations of (6) and (7) are straightforward. Consider the prospects of an employed worker. That worker earns $w + ar$ with certainty this period. If he lives until next period and keeps his job, an event that occurs with probability $(1 - d)(1 - b)$, he continues to earn V_E. If he survives but loses his job, an event that occurs with probability $(1 - d)b$, he earns V_U.

The expected income of an unemployed worker is derived in a similar fashion. At the beginning of the period, the worker has a probability π of finding a job, in which case he earns a stream of expected income equal to V_E. If he does not find a job, he earns the return on his capital this period, plus, if he survives to the next period (which occurs with probability $1 - d$), he will begin unemployed and continue to earn V_U. Solving (6) and (7) for V_E and V_U and then using (5) to substitute for π yields

$$V_E = \frac{\alpha r}{d} + \frac{w[\alpha b + d(1 - \alpha b)]}{d(1 - b)} = \frac{\alpha r}{d} + \frac{\alpha w}{d} + \frac{(1 - \alpha)w}{1 - b} \qquad (8)$$

$$V_U = \frac{\alpha(r + w)}{d} \qquad (9)$$

As already noted, in equilibrium $w = 0$ and $r = 1$. Therefore the expected lifetime income of an employed worker equals that of an unemployed worker, with the common value being α/d (the earnings from their capital endowment).

To find conditions under which a social surplus exists, we now sum the expected lifetime incomes of all workers currently alive. Of those alive at the beginning of the period, $(1 - d)(1 - b)L_E$ are employed. Each employed individual has an expected lifetime income of V_E. The remaining $L - (1 - d)(1 - b)L_E$ agents are unemployed, each earning an expected lifetime income of V_U. If V is the aggregate expected income of agents alive at the beginning of the period, then

$$V = (1 - d)(1 - b)L_E V_E + \{L - (1 - d)(1 - b)L_E\}V_U \qquad (10)$$

Substituting from (8) and (9), we can rewrite (10) as

$$V = \frac{rK}{d} + \frac{wL_E}{d} + (1 - d)(1 - b)L_E \frac{w(1 - \alpha)}{1 - b} \qquad (11)$$

The first two terms on the right-hand side of (11) represent the total cost of production multiplied by the expected lifetime of the representative agent. Since the total cost of production must equal the total value of output, these two terms sum to X/d. The social surplus from employment is represented by the last term on the right-hand side of (11). This term can be rewritten so that

$$V = \frac{X}{d} + (1-d)(1-b)L_E(V_E - V_U) \tag{12}$$

Since $h = (1-d)(1-b)$ in this model, (12) is equivalent to (1) in the introduction. It is clear from this expression that as long as $V_E > V_U$ (i.e., the employed expect to earn more than the unemployed), a social surplus exists. However, in equilibrium, $V_E = V_U = \alpha/d$, so the last term on the right-hand side of (12) vanishes. Aggregate expected lifetime income is equivalent to the steady-state level of output multiplied by the expected lifetime of the representative agent. In the next subsection we show that a minimum wage transfers income from the unemployed to the employed, driving a wedge between V_E and V_U and creating a social surplus. In addition, we show that a minimum wage is Pareto improving.

2.3 A Pareto-Improving Minimum Wage

What would be the effect of the government mandating a legally binding minimum wage? Consider any minimum wage $w \in (0,1]$. From (4), the establishment of the minimum wage drives r to $1-w$. Since technology is characterized by fixed proportions, there is no change in K_E or L_E. By extension, there is no change in X. However, V now increases. Substituting these values into (11) (or (12)), we find that V is increasing in w:

$$V(w) = \frac{X}{d} + hL_E \frac{(1-\alpha)w}{1-h} \tag{13}$$

Furthermore, it is easy to show that the expected lifetime income of currently employed workers is strictly higher with the minimum wage when compared with the competitive equilibrium, while that of the currently unemployed is no different than under the competitive equilibrium. Substituting w and $r = 1-w$ into (8) and (9), we have

$$V_E(w) = \frac{w(1-\alpha)}{1-h} + \frac{\alpha}{d} > \frac{\alpha}{d} = V_E(0) \tag{14}$$

$$V_U(w) = \frac{\alpha}{d} = V_U(0) \tag{15}$$

Since the employed gain without harming the unemployed, this policy unambiguously increases welfare.

Intuitively, the minimum wage harms the jobless as long as they remain unemployed, by reducing their return on capital. However, when they eventually do become employed, their wages will be higher. As (15) indicates, a minimum wage between 0 and 1 balances these two opposing forces. Moreover, from (14) the employed always gain from a higher minimum wage. Therefore, any $w < 1$ is (weakly) Pareto dominated by $w = 1$.

Finally, it is possible to obtain a *strict* Pareto improvement relative to the competitive equilibrium by adopting a simple minimum wage/employment tax package. Suppose that the economy is in the laissez-faire equilibrium and that the following policy is proposed—a minimum wage is to be implemented and a small tax of T is to be imposed on anyone holding a job at the end of the first period. No taxes are to be paid by anyone in subsequent periods and the tax revenue is to be used to pay unemployment compensation to jobless agents for future periods. To be precise, measure time such that the proposal is made at the beginning of period $t = 0$. Then, since the tax creates a pool of TL_E, an unemployed agent at the time t can receive an unemployment benefit B_t, where[7]

$$B_t = \frac{sTL_E}{L_U}(1-s)^t \quad s < 1 \tag{16}$$

This policy costs each currently employed worker a small one-time payment of taxes that does not consume the entire expected benefit of the minimum wage and makes all unemployed workers strictly better off, since they now earn $B_t > 0$ when unemployed and the minimum wage when they become employed. Therefore, the proposal would pass unanimously.

2.4 CREATING A SOCIAL SURPLUS

To understand how the minimum wage creates a social surplus, we begin by rewriting V_U, the expected lifetime income of an unemployed worker, as

$$V_U = \frac{\alpha}{d}[r+w] = \frac{\alpha}{d} = \frac{\alpha X}{dK} = \frac{X}{dL} \tag{17}$$

[7] Since this policy does not affect employment, factor allocations, and so on, there is no transition period to consider. Note also that we must assume that X is storable for this proposal to work.

The first equality follows from (9), the second from (4), and the last two make use of the fact that $X = K = \alpha L$. Equation (17) indicates that the unemployed can expect to earn income equal to their share (i.e., $1/L$) of the output produced during their expected lifetime. Moreover, since X is independent of the wage, this remains true regardless of the value of the minimum wage.

Now, consider V_E, the expected lifetime income of an employed worker. We have

$$V_E = V_U + (V_E - V_U) = \frac{X}{Ld} + \frac{w(1 - \alpha)}{1 - h} \tag{18}$$

Since $1 > \alpha$, the employed expect to earn more than their share of the output produced during their expected lifetime. Increasing the minimum wage allows the employed to increase their expected income without lowering the expected earnings of the unemployed. A *pure* social surplus is created.

It is obvious that the minimum wage transfers income from the unemployed to the employed. What is more subtle is that it also transfers income across generations. The reasoning is as follows. Because jobs are lasting, they carry with them a claim on future output. Moreover, since these jobs are held by members of the current generation while all newborns enter the labor market unemployed, the current generation will consume a disproportionate share of future output. As the wage increases, the current generation's share rises at the expense of the newborns, who now earn a smaller return on their capital—there is a transfer of income forward.

As long as the newborns remain unemployed, they are worse off. However, as they age and find employment, the minimum wage allows them to lay claim to a greater share of future output than they would earn in its absence. Therefore, the newborns sacrifice income when they are young (and unemployed) for extra income when they are old (and employed). The loss they suffer when they are young benefits the current generation while the subsequent gain comes at the expense of the cohort that follows them. Equation (17) indicates that the sizes of the intergenerational transfers are equal so that the newborns neither gain nor lose. In addition, since the future is infinite, this holds true for every subsequent generation as well. Just as in the Samuelson consumption-loan model, the current generation gains by borrowing from the infinite future.

There are three features of our model that are crucial to our argument: the overlapping-generations structure, the durability of a job, and the existence of two classes of agents *within* each generation (employed and unemployed) that consume different amounts of output. To see why, consider each feature separately, beginning with the overlapping-generations structure. In appendix A, we extend our model to allow for infinitely lived agents by introducing a discount rate (so that expected lifetime income does not explode). When we do so, (11) becomes

$$V = \frac{1+\rho}{\rho} X \qquad (19)$$

where ρ denotes the subjective discount rate. As (19) indicates, there is no surplus. Intuitively, since the surplus is created by borrowing from the future, without death, agents would be borrowing from themselves and could not gain.

Turn next to the durability of jobs. To demonstrate the importance of this feature, set the break-up rate (b) equal to 1. As (12) clearly indicates, in this case, the minimum wage does not create a surplus. When a job lasts only one period, its holder is no more likely to be employed in the future than his unemployed counterpart. Consequently, employment today does *not* imply an increased claim on future output and a minimum wage does *not* transfer income across generations. With no transfer from the future, expected income cannot exceed the value of output and no surplus can be created.

The last feature concerns the distribution of output. To see why this is important, consider what would happen if, after all vacancies are filled and production takes place, the government were to step in, collect all output, and distribute it evenly across all living agents. The aggregate expected lifetime income for the representative generation would then be

$$\frac{L}{d}\frac{X}{L} = \frac{X}{d}$$

The surplus vanishes! Intuitively, by redistributing income the government is taking away the increased future consumption due to present employment from the current generation and giving it back to the unborn. This transfer from the current to the future obliterates the surplus. Finally, note that by abandoning this policy, the economy can achieve a Pareto improvement. This follows from the fact that those who are currently alive will consume more of the economy's output than those born in the future, while the next generation will receive its compensation as its members find lasting jobs and confer earnings in the more distant future. While the process is stochastic, it should be clear that this policy change increases the expected lifetime consumption of those currently employed without reducing the expected lifetime income of anyone else.

In summary, if the employed and the unemployed consumed the same amount of output, the current generation would not consume a disproportionate share of future output and there would be no transfer of income across generations (as in the laissez-faire equilibrium of this model). In the next two sections we consider models that allow for equilibrium unemployment in the presence of positive wage rates, and we show that no government action is required to create the social surplus.

3. A Simple Search Model

3.1 Overview

Our one-sector, discrete time search model is patterned after the continuous-time models of Mortensen (1982) and Diamond (1982).[8] While it shares the essential features of our minimum wage model, there are a few differences. In particular, unemployed workers must now expend effort searching to find a job and there is no capital.

Production of a unit of X now requires two agents. Accordingly, an unemployed individual must search for another unemployed worker in order to form a partnership. Once a partner is found, a match is created and, as long as it lasts, the partners sell the output they produce and split the proceeds evenly. The output is sold in a perfectly competitive market and we use this consumption good as the numeraire.

Matches last either until one partner dies or until an exogenous shock causes a separation. If a partner dies, the survivor becomes unemployed and begins searching for a new match. If the parties become separated, both must reenter the labor market in search of employment. Therefore, the survival rate for a partnership is given by $h = (1 - d)^2(1 - b)$. That is, the probability that a partnership survives is equal to the joint probability that both partners live and the job does not break up.

We do not allow agents to save, so that all income is spent on the consumption good.[9] Employed workers earn income by producing and selling output, while unemployed workers earn nothing. For simplicity, we assume that each unit of X yields one unit of utility and that utility is separable in consumption and search effort. This implies that expected utility is equal to expected income minus search costs.

---

[8] We have chosen to work in discrete time due to some complexities that arise in continuous-time, overlapping-generations models with search costs. The continuous-time analogue of our model yields exactly the same conclusions as our discrete-time model and is available from the authors upon request.

[9] In appendix B of the working paper precursor to this article (Davidson, Martin, and Matusz 1989), we provide an extension of our model that allows for savings and show that all of our results generalize to such a framework.

Finally, consider the search process. Each searcher can influence the probability of employment by altering search effort. We use e_i to denote the search intensity of agent i and assume that the cost of the search, $c(e_i)$, is increasing and convex with $c(0) = c'(0) = 0$. The search technology is introduced by assuming that the total number of new matches created (M) is an increasing and concave function of aggregate search effort ($E = \Sigma_{i \in s} e_i$ where S denotes the set of searchers) with $M(0) = 0$ and $\lim_{E \to 0} M'(E) = \infty$. In addition, M is bounded above by the cardinality of S. Assuming that all searchers are equally likely to find employment, the probability of any given individual finding a match is given by[10]

$$\pi_i(E) = \frac{2M(E)}{L - 2Xh} \tag{20}$$

Since each match consists of two workers, the numerator is equal to the number of vacancies filled in each period. The denominator equals the total number of searchers at the beginning of the period since hX jobs survive across periods and each job consists of a pair of matched workers.[11]

3.2 Expected Lifetime Utility

If we measure expected lifetime utility at the time that search costs are expended (at the beginning of the period) and if we assume that agents do not discount the future, then we have

$$V_E = \frac{1}{2} + hV_E + (1 - d - h)V_U \tag{21}$$

$$V_U = \pi_i \left\{ \frac{1}{2} + hV_E + (1 - d - h)V_U \right\} + (1 - \pi_i)(1 - d)V_U - c(e_i) \tag{22}$$

For a searcher, the probability of finding immediate employment is π_i, in which case current income is ½. In addition, once matched, the probability that the partnership survives the next period is h (leading to V_E in the future) and the probability that the worker survives but loses his job is $(1 - d - h)$ (leading to V_U in the future). The searcher remains unemployed

[10] The assumption that all agents are equally likely to find a match might seem peculiar in a model in which search effort is endogenous. However, we employ this type of search technology for convenience alone. As should be clear from our analysis, none of our results depend on this particular search technology.
[11] Note that the number of agents who begin the period as searchers, $L - 2Xh$, is not equal to the number who end the period unemployed, $L - 2X$.

and earns no current income with probability $(1 - \pi_i)$. He survives to search again in the next period with probability $(1 - d)$, and this leads to future income of V_U. Search costs are then subtracted to obtain V_U. Similar logic explains (21).

For future reference, we solve (21) and (22) to obtain an expression for the value of employment. Whenever a match occurs, the expected lifetime utility for each partner increases from V_U to V_E so that the total value of a match is $2[V_E - V_U]$. Since all jobless agents are identical, we assume that they all choose the same search effort (e). We therefore omit the subscripts used to denote individual values for the remainder of the paper. Doing so allows us to write the value of a match as

$$2[V_E - V_U] = \frac{1 - \pi + 2c(e)}{1 - h(1 - \pi)} \tag{23}$$

where π is evaluated at $(L - 2Xh)e$. Note that the value of a match is decreasing in π—jobs are most valuable when they are hard to obtain.

3.3 Steady States and the Social Surplus

In a steady state the flows into and out of employment are equal. The number of matches destroyed each period is equal to $(1 - h)X$ while the number of new matches created is M. The steady-state condition is therefore given by

$$M = (1 - h)X \tag{24}$$

We can now combine (20) and (24) to obtain a relationship between X and E that must hold in any symmetric steady state:

$$\pi L = 2X[1 - h(1 - \pi)] \tag{25}$$

In a market equilibrium, each unemployed worker chooses e_i to maximize V_U based on correct conjectures concerning the search effort of all other searchers. We could apply Bellman's principle of optimality and maximize (22) over e_i to obtain this equilibrium expression and close the model. However, in this paper we are not interested in examining the properties of equilibrium. Instead, we wish to show that a social surplus exists in *any* symmetric steady state—that is, for any given value of e. Therefore, we are now ready to move on.

To find conditions under which a social surplus exists, we now sum the expected lifetime utilities of all workers currently alive. At the beginning of any given period, there are $2Xh$ matched individuals while the remainder of the population is unemployed. Therefore, we have

$$V = 2XhV_E + (L - 2Xh)V_U = LV_U + 2Xh[V_E - V_U] \qquad (26)$$

If we solve (21) and (22) for V_E and V_U and then use (25) to substitute for L we obtain

$$V_U = \frac{X - (L - 2Xh)c(e)}{Ld} \qquad (27)$$

which implies

$$V = \frac{X - (L - 2Xh)c(e)}{d} + 2Xh[V_E - V_U] \qquad (28)$$

Equation (28) is analogous to (1) in the introduction and (12) in the previous section. It verifies that the expected lifetime utility of the current generation consists of two components. The first, $[X - (L - 2Xh)c(e)]/d$, is the value of steady-state output produced during the lifetime of a representative agent (net of search costs). The second term, $2Xh[V_E - V_U]$, reflects the increase in expected utility (above what searchers expect to achieve) that can be attributed to the *durable* jobs held in steady state. This term also reflects the surplus value from employment. As indicated by (27), this surplus does not come at the expense of the newborns since they can still expect to earn their share of the output produced during their expected lifetime.[12] In contrast with the model of the previous section, this pure surplus exists for any $X > 0$—no government action is required to produce it.

Like the minimum wage, a durable job transfers income across generations, and it is these transfers that create the surplus. Although the general argument is similar, there are some differences in the details. For example, in the minimum wage model it is the increase in the wage that enlarges the current generation's share of future output. Here, it is the higher level of steady-state employment that does the trick. In addition, in the minimum wage model, any increase in the wage reduces the current income of the newborns as the return to capital falls. However, they make up for this by earning more income in the future when they are employed.

---

[12] Tirole (1985) demonstrates that asset bubbles may appear in the equilibria of growing overlapping-generations economies. That is, the equilibrium value of an asset may be greater than its fundamental value. Since a job in our economy implies an increase in expected future earnings, we could think of each job as an asset. One might then be tempted to think of the surplus value as an asset bubble. However, this is not the case. As Tirole has shown (Proposition 1), for these asset bubbles to appear, the economy must grow at a rate faster than the rate of time preference. Since our economy does not grow (we have fixed factor supplies and constant technology), asset bubbles cannot be supported in equilibrium.

In fact, the gains and losses are always equal so that there is no change in their expected income. Here, if we compare two steady states with different employment levels, the newborns suffer when they are young in the high-employment case because they are crowded out of the labor market by the older workers (there are fewer vacancies). They recoup some of their losses as they age and take on the role of the mature generation since they will then possess a greater claim on future output. Unlike the minimum wage model, these two opposing forces need not be equal.

In determining whether they prefer the low- or high-employment steady state, the newborns compare the losses when they are young to the gains when they are old. Since all newborns begin life unemployed, their interests are reflected by V_U as given in (27). If net output is increasing (decreasing) in X, then the gains in old age dominate (are dominated by) the losses when they are young and the newborns prefer the high-employment (low-employment) steady state. When net output is maximized (call this output level X^*), these two opposing forces offset and a marginal change in employment has only second-order effects on the welfare of the newborns.

The interests of the current generation are reflected in V as given in (28). If employment is such that $X = X^*$ *and* if the surplus value from employment is increasing in X at this output level,[13] then this generation would gain from a marginal increase in employment. This follows from the fact that there would be a first-order increase in the surplus and only a second-order loss in the value of net output. Intuitively, at this level of employment a marginal increase in employment transfers income forward. The current generation receives a transfer from the newborns and they gain. Every other generation transfers income to the generation preceding them when they are young and receives an equal transfer when they are old from the generation succeeding them.

It is tempting to conclude at this point that a marginal increase in employment above the level that maximizes net output would be Pareto improving. After all, there are first-order gains by the current generation and only second-order losses suffered by future generations. However, there are an infinite number of future generations that lose and only one

---

[13] The surplus value from employment is given by $2Xh(V_E - V_U)$. If we use (24) to substitute for M in (20), it is easy to show that π is increasing in X. In addition, we noted that $V_E - V_U$ is decreasing in π. Therefore, as X increases, $(V_E - V_U)$ decreases. This implies that $2Xh(V_E - V_U)$ could be increasing or decreasing in X. We investigated this issue in greater detail in our working paper (Davidson, Martin, and Matusz 1989) and showed that for most empirically relevant values of the parameters, the surplus is increasing in X. Of course, even if $2Xh(V_E - V_U)$ is decreasing in X at X^*, X^* is still Pareto dominated. The only difference is that we would need a marginal decrease in output to obtain the Pareto improvement.

current generation that gains. Therefore, while it is possible to rig policies that are Pareto improving, one needs to be careful in choosing the policy in order to make sure that all losers are compensated sufficiently.[14]

The spartan nature of out model makes it difficult to find simple Pareto-improving policies. However, if we extend the model to allow for a safe asset, then there is a simple policy that always works. All that the government needs to do is tax away half of the current generation's first-order gain, invest the tax revenue in the safe asset, and use the return in each future period to provide the newborns with a payment that dominates the second-order loss. Since the current generation still receives a first-order gain, lump-sum taxation within the generation can be used to ensure that everyone in that cohort is made better off. The result is a Pareto improvement. We provide such an extension in appendix B.

4. EFFICIENCY WAGES

There is nothing special about the search model developed in the previous section. The surplus from employment exists in any dynamic model of unemployment in which $V_E \neq V_U$, jobs are durable, and workers are finitely lived. To illustrate this point, we now demonstrate that the surplus exists in the Shapiro-Stiglitz efficiency wage model once it is modified to allow for finite life.

In the Shapiro-Stiglitz model, utility is given by $w - e$, where w is the wage and e is effort expended on the job by employed workers. Employed workers choose either $e > 0$ (a *fixed* positive level of effort) or $e = 0$. Workers who shirk (choose $e = 0$) earn an expected lifetime *labor* income of V_E^S while the nonshirking workers earn V_E^N. There is an exogenous probability of b that any given worker will be terminated and shirking workers face an additional probability of termination equal to q. Therefore, the expected lifetime labor incomes of shirking and nonshirking workers are given by

$$V_E^S = w + (1 - d)[(b + q)V_U + (1 - b - q)V_E^S] \qquad (29)$$

---

[14] This problem does not arise in models with discounting and population growth if the population grows at a rate greater than the discount rate. The reason for this is as follows. Let n denote the population growth rate and let ρ denote the discount rate. Then, if $n > \rho$, it can be shown that when X increases marginally above X^* the losses the newborn suffer when they are young are smaller than the gains they receive when they are old. Therefore, such an increase in employment generates first-order gains for all cohorts. It follows that X^* is Pareto dominated. It is in this sense that our results are strengthened when $n > \rho$ (see footnote 6).

$$V_E^N = (w - e) + (1 - d)[bV_U + (1 - b)V_E^N] \tag{30}$$

where V_U is the expected lifetime labor income for an unemployed worker. In each equation, expected lifetime labor income is equal to current income plus expected future labor income.

Workers shirk unless $V_E^N \geq V_E^S$. Therefore, the wage satisfies the "no-shirk condition" if

$$w \geq dV_U + \frac{e}{q}\left[q + \frac{1 - h}{1 - d}\right] \tag{31}$$

which must hold in equilibrium. Thus, all workers choose $e > 0$ and $V_E = V_E^N$.

For unemployed workers, expected lifetime labor income is given by

$$V_U = \pi V_E + (1 - \pi)(1 - d)V_U \tag{32}$$

That is, with probability π the worker finds a job and expects to earn V_E, and with probability $(1 - \pi)(1 - d)$ the worker fails to find a job and survives to seek employment again in the next period.

Solving (30) and (32) yields

$$V_E = \frac{(w - e)[d + \pi(1 - d)]}{d[1 - h(1 - \pi)]} \tag{33}$$

$$V_U = \frac{\pi(w - e)}{d[1 - h(1 - \pi)]} \tag{34}$$

where h, the job survival rate, equals $(1 - d)(1 - b)$.

The employment probability, π, is equal to the ratio of job openings $[L_E(1 - h)]$ to job seekers $(L - L_E h)$. Therefore,

$$\pi = \frac{L_E(1 - h)}{L - L_E h} \tag{35}$$

Turn next to the production side of the economy. Assume that there is a single competitive firm that faces a concave production function represented by $F(L_E)$. Since the firm's per-period profit equals $X - wL_E$, the expected lifetime earnings from capital are given by

$$V_K = \frac{X - wL_E}{d} \tag{36}$$

We are now in a position to prove that a social surplus exists in any steady state. Aggregate expected lifetime income for the current generation is given by $V = hL_EV_E + (L - hL_E)V_U + V_K$, while a typical newborn expects to earn V_U from labor and V_K/L from his share of the firm's profits. Substituting from (33)–(36) yields

$$V = \frac{X - eL_E}{d} + hL_E(V_E - V_U), \tag{37}$$

$$V_U + \frac{V_K}{L} = \frac{X - eL_E}{dL} \tag{38}$$

Equation (37) is analogous to (1), (12), and (28). It indicates that the aggregate expected income of the current generation exceeds the output produced during its lifetime. Equation (38) is analogous to (17) and (27) and indicates that each newborn expects to earn an equal share of the net output produced during his expected lifetime. Thus, the current generation's extra consumption does not come at the expense of the unborn—there is a pure surplus.

5. DISCUSSION

In this section, we compare out results to some previous work in the equilibrium unemployment and overlapping-generations literature. In addition, we briefly discuss some of the difficulties involved in determining the optimal policy in this framework.

5.1 Related Work

One of our main results is that the current generation can consume more than the value of the net output produced during its expected lifetime without the extra consumption coming at the expense of future generations. As we noted in the introduction, this is reminiscent of Samuelson's (1958) seminal result that in an overlapping-generations (OLG) framework a surplus could be generated by government programs designed to borrow from future generations. In particular, he showed that transfers to the older generation could be financed by taxing the younger generation with the ultimate repayment postponed to the infinitely distant future. The competitive equilibrium therefore passes up an opportunity to increase the utility of the older generation (at no expense) and is suboptimal.

In that our surplus is also the result of a transfer from the future to the present, these results are similar. However, there are important differences as well. Most important, no surplus is present in the competitive equilibrium in Samuelson's model, while a surplus is always present in our framework (provided that the employed and unemployed expect to earn different lifetime incomes). Moreover, while the surplus is created by an imaginative government policy (e.g., social security financed on a pay-as-you-go basis) in the consumption-loan model, it arises endogenously in models with a natural rate of unemployment. Finally, one of the implications of the surplus in our model is that the interests of current and future generations diverge. While this conflict is also present in most overlapping-generations models, it is due to the fact that the pattern of consumption varies with age and is in no way related to a surplus.

Another result from the OLG literature that is somewhat relevant is due to Blanchard (1985), who showed that in a model with an uncertain length of life, the probability of death drives a wedge between the individual's discount rate and the economy's. He then goes on to show that in a model with capital accumulation this difference in discount rates leads workers to save such that their wealth grows faster than the economy. In our model, a similar result emerges in that the discount factor for individuals is $(1 - d)$, while the explicit interest rate for the economy is zero. In addition, although we do not allow agents to hold physical wealth, it is true that average expected lifetime consumption increases from $[(X - c(X))/Ld]$ at birth to a higher value as members of the cohort age. However, this result is not due to savings behavior; rather it follows from the changing employment status of the representative agent over the life span of the generation.

In comparing our results with those in the literature on unemployment, we simplify matters by focusing on the search and efficiency wage literatures. A common theme in much of this work is that equilibrium is generally inefficient due to externalities inherent in either the search process (e.g., Diamond 1982, 1984; Mortensen 1982; or Pissarides 1984, 1990) or the monitoring process (e.g., Shapiro and Stiglitz 1984). This is often proved by demonstrating that an alternative feasible allocation exists that raises the value of steady-state output. Since almost all of these models are characterized by a single infinitely lived generation, this procedure is entirely appropriate. However, if these models were extended to allow for death, our results indicate that this procedure would no longer be appropriate—the allocation that maximizes steady-state output would be Pareto dominated by another feasible allocation. Two notable models of unemployment that *do* employ an overlapping-generation structure are Albrecht and Axell (1984) and Pissarides (1991). Since both models satisfy the criteria that are needed to generate a social surplus, our analysis suggests that the efficiency analysis carried out in these articles is incomplete.

5.2 Policy

What is the optimal policy in this setting? What policies are likely to be implemented? The answers to these questions are not straightforward. We have argued that policies aimed at maximizing the value of steady-state output are inefficient since they pass up the opportunity to achieve a Pareto improvement. However, it is difficult to say much more without making additional assumptions. Clearly, the policies that will be implemented will depend on the political process in place. Suppose, for example, that we make the reasonable assumptions that only those currently alive are allowed to vote and that the majority rules. Suppose further that we assume that individuals care only about their own expected lifetime incomes and that the employed outnumber the unemployed. Then, since the employed expect to earn V_E, policy will be targeted at increasing V_E. These policies may harm the unemployed, since their interests are represented by V_U. Of course, the fact that the employed and the unemployed have different interests is not a unique feature of our model—this result arises in almost any model of unemployment.

Now, suppose instead that policy is determined by some political leader who wishes to maximize the aggregate expected lifetime income of his constituency (i.e., the current generation). As we have shown above, V, the aggregate expected lifetime income of the current generation, consists of two terms—net output and the surplus value from employment. Therefore, the policy that would be implemented would take into account the social surplus. Such policies may, however, harm the unborn, since their interests lie only in net output. In fact, we have shown elsewhere (Davidson, Martin, and Matusz 1989) that the current generation typically prefers policies aimed at expanding employment beyond the level preferred by the unborn. However, once a cohort is born and matures (so that it takes on the role of the current generation) they will then favor policies that maximize V—in a sense, such policies possess a degree of time consistency. This particular conflict of interest between current and future generation is unique to our model and is the direct result of the surplus value from employment.

Finally, suppose that policy is determined by a social planner who takes into account the interests of all agents—the employed, the unemployed, the living, and the unborn. The result would be an attempt to maximize some weighted sum of the value of net output and the surplus value from employment. Since the interests of the current generation enter into social welfare, *the surplus would matter.*

The matter in which the social surplus affects the optimal policy is beyond the scope of this paper. However, there is one important implication that we would like to point out. There is a substantial and growing literature in labor economics that concerns changes in the sectoral distribution of employment over time and its effect on earnings (see, for examples, the collection of papers in the February 1992 *Quarterly Journal of Economics*). Implicit in this literature is the idea that the sectoral distribution of output plays a role in determining economic welfare. Jobs in some sectors are perceived as "good jobs" (e.g., manufacturing) while others are viewed as "bad jobs" (e.g., minimum wage or low-paying service sector jobs). Recent shifts in employment from good to bad sectors are viewed as detrimental to the U.S. economy and have led some to call for an American industrial policy aimed at encouraging employment in the good sectors. These arguments may be justified when externalities or distortions are present. But, in a competitive labor market, as Bulow and Summers (1986) have observed, "The claims of industrial policy advocates are difficult to understand. Competition equalizes the marginal productivities of all equivalent workers. There is no such thing as a good or a bad industry." In other words, in a nondistorted equilibrium the marginal job in each sector adds the same amount to national income so that a reallocation of employment cannot be beneficial.

This is not the case in our framework. In Davidson, Martin, and Matusz (1991) we present a two-sector version of our search model and show that the surplus value from employment varies across sectors. Durable jobs that are difficult to obtain carry with them a larger social surplus than those that are transient and easy to obtain. This follows from the fact that the difference between what the employed and the unemployed expect to earn in a specific sector is tied to the turnover rates— $(V_E - V_U)$ is increasing the h, the job survival rate, and decreasing the π, the employment probability. Therefore, even if the marginal productivity of labor is equated across sectors, so that the marginal job in each sector contributes the same amount to net output, a reallocation of labor toward the high surplus value sector would increase the expected lifetime income of the current generation (V)—*the sectoral composition of output would matter*! It is important to note that this result does not arise because equilibrium is distorted (as in the efficiency wage model of Bulow and Summers). It arises as a direct result of the social surplus from employment and a difference in turnover rates across sectors. We explore this issue in much greater depth in Davidson, Martin, and Matusz (1991).

APPENDIX A

In order to highlight the importance of death, we modify the basic minimum wage model of section 2 to allow for infinitely lived workers. If workers are assumed to live forever, we need to allow for discounting, otherwise expected utility would be unbounded. We use $\rho > 0$ to represent the discount rate. All other notation and assumptions remain the same as in the text.

The expected incomes of the employed and unemployed are now (the reader is reminded that these values are measured at the beginning of each period)

$$V_E = w + \alpha r + \frac{1}{1+\rho}\{(1-b)V_E + bV_U\} \tag{A.1}$$

$$V_U = \pi V_E + (1-\pi)\left[\alpha r + \frac{1}{1+\rho}V_U\right] \tag{A.2}$$

The probability of finding a job (π) can be obtained from the text by setting $d = 1$ in (5). We obtain

$$\pi = \frac{\alpha b}{1-\alpha + \alpha b} < 1 \tag{A.3}$$

We can now substitute (A.3) into (A.1) and (A.2), and then solve for V_E and V_U. Doing so yields

$$V_E = \frac{1+\rho}{\rho}\left[\frac{\alpha b(1+\rho)+\rho(1-\alpha)}{\alpha b(1+\rho)+(\rho+b)(1-\alpha)}\right]w + \frac{1+\rho}{\rho}\alpha r \tag{A.4}$$

$$V_U = \frac{1+\rho}{\rho}\left[\frac{\alpha b(1+\rho)}{\alpha b(1+\rho)+(\rho+b)(1-\alpha)}\right]w + \frac{1+\rho}{\rho}\alpha r \tag{A.5}$$

By definition, $V = (1-b)L_E V_E + [L - (1-b)L_E]V_U$, where V is aggregate expected income. We can rewrite this expression to highlight the differential expected income due to employment: $V = LV_U + (1-b)L_E(V_E - V_U)$. Using (A.4) and (A.5), along with the fact that $\alpha L = K = L_E$, we have

$$LV_U = \frac{1+\rho}{\rho}(\phi w L_E + rK) \tag{A.6}$$

and

$$(1-b)L_E(V_E - V_U) = \frac{1+\rho}{\rho}(1-\phi)L_E w \qquad (A.7)$$

where

$$\phi = \frac{b(1+\rho)}{\alpha b(1+\rho) + (\rho+b)(1-\alpha)} \leq 1, \qquad \text{equality if } b=1 \qquad (A.8)$$

From (A.6) and (A.7), it is easy to see that

$$V = \frac{1+\rho}{\rho}X \qquad (A.9)$$

and there is no surplus. Furthermore, using the fact that $r = 1 - w$, it is a simple matter to show that V_E is increasing in w, while V_U is decreasing in w. The employed benefit from the implementation of a minimum wage *at the expense* of the unemployed.

APPENDIX B

To demonstrate that a marginal increase in output above X^* can yield a Pareto improvement, we add capital to the search model of section 3. Assume that each matched pair can rent capital from a frictionless market at a per unit price of r, and that the k_i units of capital rented by pair i allows them to produce $f(k_i)$ units of output. Capital does not depreciate (it can be thought of as land). As in our minimum wage model, all living agents own an equal share of the capital with α representing the per capita capital ownership. Finally, we assume that capital can be produced according to the cost function

$$g = g(K) \qquad (B.1)$$

where K is the total capital stock at the beginning of the period.

We consider steady states in which each unemployed worker expends e units of search effort and each matched pair hires (K/X) units of capital. With this modification, we can rewrite (21)–(23) as

$$V_E = \frac{1}{2}\left[f\left(\frac{K}{X}\right) - \frac{K}{X}r\right] + \alpha r + h V_E + (1-d-h)V_U \qquad (B.2)$$

$$V_U = \pi\left[\frac{1}{2}\left(f\left(\frac{K}{X}\right) - \frac{K}{X}r\right) + \alpha r + hV_E + (1 - d - h)V_U\right]$$
$$+ (1 - \pi)(1 - d)V_U - c(e) \tag{B.3}$$

$$2[V_E - V_U] = \frac{(1 - \pi)f(K/X) + 2c(e)}{1 - h(1 - \pi)} \tag{B.4}$$

Solving for V_U we obtain

$$V_U = \frac{Xf(K/X) - (L - 2hX)c(e)}{dL} \tag{B.5}$$

which indicates that a representative newborn still expects to consume an appropriately weighted share of the new output produced during his lifetime. As in the text, let $X^*(K)$ denote the value of X that maximizes this expression given K.

Finally, if we let K_n denote the capital stock at the end of period, then (28), the aggregate expected lifetime of the current generation, becomes

$$V = \frac{Xf(K_n/X) - (L - 2hX)c(e)}{d} + 2hX(V_E - V_U) - [g(K_n) - g(K)] \tag{B.6}$$

The first two terms on the right-hand side reflect the net output produced during an average lifetime and the surplus value from employment. The third term reflects the added cost of any new capital created by the current generation. In a steady state, $K_n = K$, no new capital is created, and no costs are incurred.

We assume that at the beginning of each period the current generation decides whether or not to expand the capital stock. If they decide to do so, they set K_n such that $(\partial V/\partial K_n) = 0$. Let $K^*(X)$ solve this expression given X and let $(K^*, X^*) = (K^*(X^*), X^*(K^*))$.

Now, suppose that the economy is in a steady state with $X = X^*$ and $K = K^*$. Consider the impact of a marginal increase in both X and K. Because the capital lasts forever, this can be seen as an exchange between the current and all future generations. Level sets of V_U and V (as given in (B.5) and (B.6)) are depicted in figure B.1. Since V_U is proportional to net output and since the current generation incurs the cost of increasing K, the slope of the newborns' indifference curve approaches infinity at (K^*, X^*)—that is, if we take the limit as (X, K) approaches (X^*, K^*), we have

$$\frac{\partial V_U(X,K)/\partial K_n}{\partial V_U(X,K)/\partial X} = \infty$$

For the current generation, if we take the limit as (X, K) approaches (X^*, K^*), we have

$$\frac{\partial V(X,K)/\partial K_n}{\partial V(X,K)/\partial X} = 0$$

by the definition of K^*. Therefore, any allocation in the hatched area of figure B.1 benefits both generations (all of these allocations imply greater output). Intuitively, the increase in X creates a first-order gain for the current generation while the increase in K generates only second-order losses. Therefore, the current generation gains. For the newborns, the increase in K generates first-order gains (since they do not incur the cost of increasing K) while the increase in X produces second-order losses. Therefore,

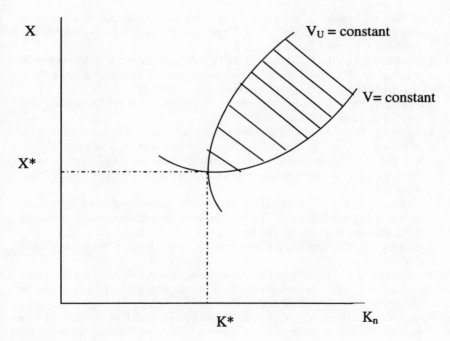

Figure B.1.

the newborns gain as well. This proposal could be implemented by using job subsidies to increase e (and hence X) while taxing the current generation a small amount (so as not to tax away all of their first-order gain). The tax revenue could then be used by the government to purchase the new capital.

References

Albrecht, J., Axell, B. 1984. An equilibrium model of search and unemployment. *Journal of Political Economy* 92(5): 824–40.

Blanchard, O. 1985. Debt, deficits, and finite horizons. *Journal of Political Economy* 93(2): 223–47.

Blanchard, O., Fischer, S. 1989. *Lectures on Macroeconomics.* Cambridge, MA: MIT Press.

Bulow, J., Summers, L. 1986. A theory of dual labor markets with application to industrial policy, discrimination, and Keynesian unemployment. *Journal of Labor Economics,* 4(3): 376–414.

Davidson, C., Martin, L., Matusz, S. 1989. Dynamic welfare and the value of employment in a model of search with finite life. Michigan State University, Working Paper.

Davidson, C., Martin, L., Matusz, S. 1991. A search-theoretic approach to unemployment and international trade: Where have all the good jobs gone? Michigan State University, Working Paper.

Davidson, C., Martin, L., Matusz, S. 1992. Jobs and chocolate II: Samuelsonian surpluses in dynamic models of unemployment with discounting and population growth. Michigan State University, Working Paper.

Diamond, P. 1982. Wage determination and efficiency in search equilibrium. *Review of Economic Studies* 49(2): 217–28.

Diamond, P. 1984. *A Search-Equilibrium Approach to the Micro Foundations of Macroeconomics: The Wicksell Lectures.* Cambridge, MA: MIT Press.

Fried, J. 1980. The intergenerational distribution of the gains from technical change and from international trade. *Canadian Journal of Economics* 13(1): 65–81.

Mortensen, D. 1982. The matching process as a non-cooperative bargaining game. In J. J. McCall (ed.), *The Economics of Information and Uncertainty.* Chicago: University of Chicago Press.

Pissarides, C. 1984. Efficient job rejection. *Economic Journal* 94(396a): 97–108, Supplement.

Pissarides, C. 1990. *Equilibrium Unemployment Theory.* Oxford: Basil Blackwell.

Pissarides, C. 1991. Unemployment fluctuations with different job durations. University of California–Berkeley, Working Paper.

Samuelson, P. 1958. An exact consumption-loan model of interest with or without the social contrivance of money. *Journal of Political Economy* 66: 467–82.

Shapiro, C., Stiglitz, J. 1984. Involuntary unemployment as a worker discipline device. *American Economic Review* 74(3): 433–44.

Shell, K. 1971. Notes on the economics of infinity. *Journal of Political Economy* 79(5): 1002–11.

Tirole, J. 1985. Asset bubbles and overlapping generations. *Econometrica* 53(6): 1071–1100.

Chapter 6

LONG-RUN LUNACY, SHORT-RUN SANITY:

A SIMPLE MODEL OF TRADE WITH

LABOR MARKET TURNOVER

CARL DAVIDSON AND STEVEN J. MATUSZ

> International trade is a long run issue.
> —Paul Krugman (1996)

> But this long run is a misleading guide to current affairs. In the long run we are all dead. Economists set themselves too easy, too useless a task if in tempestuous seasons they can only tell us that when the storm is long past the ocean is flat again.
> —Lord John Maynard Keynes (1923)

> Why aren't we all Keynesians yet?
> —Paul Krugman (1998)

1. INTRODUCTION

The first quote from Paul Krugman represents the widespread view that most important international trade issues can best be understood by focusing on long-run relationships. Many of the assumptions that underlie the most influential model of trade—the Heckshcer-Ohlin-Samuelson (HOS) model—are clearly long-run in nature and it is understood that the model's predictions are intended to describe long-run relationships. Over the years, there have been many attempts to broaden our scope and begin to take the short-run more seriously. The specific-factors (SF) model is one such example. It replaces the HOS assumption of complete factor mobility with another extreme assumption—that some factors can only be employed in certain sectors. By now, the relationship between these two models is well known. Reallocating the mobile factors in the SF model allows one to trace out a short-run production possibilities frontier for each set of assumptions about factor mobility. The long-run production possibilities frontier of the HOS model is the outer envelope of all of the short-run frontiers. Thus, the long-run behavior of the economy is just the natural extension of its short-run behavior.

Viewing production possibilities as a limit on how much can be produced has many virtues, including simplicity of exposition. However, it may be more informative to think of the long run in terms of steady states, turning the long-run production possibilities frontier into a set of sustainable outputs. In this way, it could be possible for an economy in the short run to produce either more or less than the steady-state levels of output, corresponding with unemployment rates that are either lower or higher in the short run than the natural rate of unemployment.

One of our goals in this paper is to capture this richer interplay between the short run and long run without sacrificing the analytic tractability of earlier work. Toward that end, we provide a simple model of international trade with labor market turnover and examine its short- run and long-run behavior. The empirical relevance of labor market turnover has been widely documented over the past decade (Davis, Haltiwanger, and Schuh 1996). Models that account for this phenomenon have become the norm in some subfields in economics, but not in international trade. We have argued elsewhere that the existence of labor market turnover forces us to modify many of the standard theorems in international economics (Davidson, Martin, and Matusz 1988, 1999). In this paper, we argue that its presence makes the relationship between an economy's short-run and long-run behavior more complex than it is in traditional trade models. For example, in the short run, an economy may produce outside of its long-run frontier. In addition, we show that emphasis on long-run relationships is misplaced and can lead one to draw faulty policy conclusions. Focusing on the short-run behavior of the economy restores sanity. The implication is that in the presence of labor market turnover international trade issues can only be understood by focusing on the entire dynamic path of the economy. Long-run relationships should be ignored.

2. THE MODEL

Consider a continuous time model of a small open economy that produces two goods (x and y) with a single factor of production, labor. Workers are infinitely lived, derive utility from consumption, and differ according to ability, with the ability level of worker i denoted by a_i.[1] For simplicity, we assume that a_i is uniformly distributed on $[0,1]$ and that the total measure of consumers is 1.

---

[1] If workers are finitely lived, additional complications arise because changes in employment result in intergenerational transfers. For details, see Davidson, Martin, and Matusz (1994).

The two sectors differ from each other in two ways. First, ability has a stronger influence on productivity in sector x than it does in sector y.[2] To be specific, we assume that a worker employed in sector y produces q_y units of flow output regardless of ability, while a worker employed in sector x with ability a_i produces $q_x a_i$ units of flow output. We assume that workers are paid the value of their marginal product. Thus, if we choose y as the numeraire and use p to denote the world price of x, then a worker with ability a_i earns a wage of q_y if employed in sector y while her sector x wage would be $pq_x a_i$.

The other dimension that differentiates sectors is the degree of job turnover. We again opt for simplicity and assume that there is no turnover in sector y. Workers who choose to seek employment in that sector find jobs immediately and can remain employed there indefinitely. In contrast, workers who wish to obtain jobs in sector x must search for employment and search takes time. In particular, we assume that jobs in this sector are filled stochastically with the rate of job acquisition denoted by λ. It follows that $1/\lambda$ is the expected duration of unemployment in sector x. Once a worker secures a job in this sector, she remains employed until an exogenous shock causes the job to dissolve, forcing her to reenter the search process. The rate at which these jobs break up is denoted by b, so that the expected duration of a job in sector x is $1/b$.[3, 4]

Workers choose their occupation based on expected lifetime income.[5] If we use r to denote the discount rate, then a worker with ability level a_i expects to earn $V_{ey}(a_i) = q_y/r$ over her lifetime if she is employed in sector y.

---

[2] Since labor is the only input, this assumption is necessary to generate diversified production over a wide range of relative prices.

[3] Note that we do not model the source of the turnover. What we have in mind is a model much in the spirit of Mortensen and Pissarides (1994) in which jobs are created when firms enter product markets seeking profits and then are destroyed by random productivity shocks that affect firms' costs. In their model, job acquisition rates are influenced by the tightness of the labor market, which depends on the size of the unemployment pool, the number of vacancies, the search effort by workers and the recruiting effort by firms. Unfortunately, the dynamics of such a model are highly complex, making it impossible to solve explicitly for the transition path across steady states. Our model is an extremely simplistic version of this model—but it captures the elements of the Mortensen and Pissarides framework that are most important for our purpose.

[4] The assumption that search is required to find employment is not essential to our analysis. It could easily be replaced by an assumption that workers must train for employment and that the flow of output produced while training is below the flow produced after training has been completed. All that is required is that there is a labor market state during which output is below its potential level and that there is some randomness in the rates at which workers enter and exit that state.

[5] As we have already noted, all workers live forever in our model, so we are being loose with our use of the term "lifetime." However, it is simpler to use the phrase "lifetime income" rather than the more cumbersome phrase "income discounted over the infinite future."

For sector x, we use $V_{ex}(a_i)$ to denote the expected lifetime income for an employed worker with ability a_i. Analogously $V_{sx}(a_i)$ denotes the expected lifetime income for a worker with ability a_i who is currently searching for a job in sector x. Then, for sector x workers we have the following asset value equations:

$$rV_{sx}(a_i) = 0 + \lambda\left\{V_{ex}(a_i) - V_{sx}(a_i)\right\} + \dot{V}_{sx}(a_i) \tag{1}$$

$$rV_{ex}(a_i) = pq_x a_i - b\left\{V_{ex}(a_i) - V_{sx}(a_i)\right\} + \dot{V}_{ex}(a_i) \tag{2}$$

In each equation, the first term on the right-hand side is current income while the second term is the product of the capital gain (or loss) from changing labor market states and the rate at which such changes take place. For completeness, we include the final term, which is the derivative of the asset value with respect to time. However, in our framework, expected lifetime income depends only on parameters that are time invariant, and therefore these terms equal zero for all time. These equations can be solved to obtain

$$V_{sx}(a_i) = \frac{\lambda}{r+b+\lambda}\frac{pq_x a_i}{r}; \quad V_{ex}(a_i) = \frac{r+\lambda}{r+b+\lambda}\frac{pq_x a_i}{r} \tag{3}$$

Equations (3) have natural interpretations. With our assumptions about the turnover process, each worker expects to spend a fraction of her time employed and a fraction of her time searching. The fraction of time spent employed is $\lambda/(b + \lambda)$. Therefore, the worker's expected lifetime income is a weighted average of what is earned while employed $(pq_x a_i)$ and what is earned while searching (zero). Because of discounting, the weight applied to the current activity is slightly higher than the weight applied to the future activity. As such, searchers place slightly greater weight on their current income of zero than on the positive income that they will earn once employed. Similarly, employed workers place slightly greater weight on their positive income and discount the zero income that they will earn when they become unemployed.

In the market-induced steady-state equilibrium, unemployed workers opt for sector y if $V_{ey}(a_i) > V_{sx}(a_i)$; otherwise, they search for jobs in sector x. We define the *marginal* worker as the one who is just indifferent between taking a job in sector y and searching for a job in sector x. We use a_m to represent the ability level of this worker, where a_m solves $V_{ey}(a_m) = V_{sx}(a_m)$ Using (3) and our value for $V_{ey}(a_i)$ we obtain

$$a_m = \frac{1}{p}\frac{q_y}{q_x}\frac{r+b+\lambda}{\lambda} \tag{4}$$

For the marginal worker, $w_x(a_m) > w_y$. This follows because workers in sector x spend only a fraction of their time employed and earning income, whereas workers in sector y are always employed. Indifference of the marginal worker implies that there has to be a payoff to waiting for a job in sector x. Because of this feature, we shall sometimes refer to sectors x and y as the high-wage and low-wage sectors, respectively.

A diversified production equilibrium exists for a range of prices. That is, $0 < a_m < 1$ as long as the relative price of x is neither too high nor too low. Moreover, all workers with $a_i < a_m$ take jobs in the low-wage sector, while all with $a_i > a_m$ are either searching or employed in the high-wage sector. For future reference, we define a_{ft} as the equilibrium ability value of the marginal worker under free trade. The value of a_{ft} is determined by (4) when the domestic price of x is equal to the world price of x.

Given our assumption that workers earn the value of their marginal products, $w_x(a_m) > w_y$ implies that the value of the *static* marginal product of labor in sector x is higher than that in sector y, suggesting a possible distortion that policy makers might target by means of an industrial policy. However, we demonstrate below that simply comparing the static marginal products of employed workers leads to faulty conclusions.

Define $E_j(t)$ as the mass of workers employed in sector j, and define $S_x(t)$ as the mass of workers searching in sector x at time t. For notational convenience, we define $E_j(\infty)$ and $S_x(\infty)$ as the corresponding steady-state values of these variables. Recalling our assumptions that the mass of workers is equal to 1 and ability is uniformly distributed, we conclude that

$$E_y(\infty) = a_m \tag{5}$$

$$E_y(\infty) + S_x(\infty) = 1 - a_m \tag{6}$$

In addition, in a steady-state equilibrium, the flow into sector-x employment must equal the flow out of employment. Since $\lambda S_x(t)$ searchers find jobs and $b E_x(t)$ workers lose their jobs at each point in time, we must have $\lambda S_x(\infty) = b E_x(\infty)$, so that

$$E_x(\infty) = \frac{\lambda}{b+\lambda}(1 - a_m) \tag{7}$$

$$S_x(\infty) = \frac{b}{b+\lambda}(1 - a_m) \tag{8}$$

Given the equilibrium value of the ability of the marginal worker, we find the steady-state value of flow output (defined as $I(\infty; a_m)$) by integrating across ability:

$$I(\infty; a_m) = \int_0^{a_m} q_y da + \int_{a_m}^1 pq_x a\left(\frac{\lambda}{b+\lambda}\right) da$$

$$= q_y a_m + pq_x\left(\frac{\lambda}{b+\lambda}\right)\left(\frac{1-a_m^2}{2}\right) \tag{9}$$

We use as our measure of social welfare the present discounted value of flow income, $W(a_m)$, where

$$W(a_m) = \int_0^\infty e^{-rt} I(\infty; a_m) dt = \frac{1}{r} I(\infty; a_m) \tag{10}$$

3. LONG-RUN LUNACY

Suppose that a social planner could allocate labor across sectors in a way to maximize the discounted steady-state value of output. That is, suppose that a planner could choose the ability level of the marginal worker to maximize $W(a_m)$ as defined by (10). Substituting (9) into (10), it is a simple matter to deduce that the allocation of labor that maximizes the discounted steady-state value of output is attained when

$$a_p = \frac{1}{p}\frac{q_y}{q_x}\frac{b+\lambda}{\lambda} \tag{11}$$

where we have used the subscript p to indicate that this is the value that the planner would choose to maximize the value of steady-state output. Evaluating (4) and (11) at free trade prices, it is evident that $a_p < a_{ft}$. That is, steady-state income is not maximized under free trade. At the margin, moving some workers from the low-wage sector (where ability is unimportant) to the high-wage sector (where ability is important) increases the value of steady-state output.

Armed with this information, it is easy to imagine a political pundit calling for an industrial policy aimed at expanding the high-wage sector. Many in the policy community have called for such a policy arguing that it is in our interest to protect high-wage jobs and expand sectors where ability is rewarded.[6] If we focus on the long run, it appears that this model provides support for such an argument. Of course, this argument ignores the role played by the short-run transitions between steady states. But if trade is truly a long-run concern, perhaps these short-run costs *should* be ignored. Below, we argue that this is not the case.

[6] See, for example, the writings of Robert Reich or Lester Thurow.

To fix ideas, imagine that this economy is a net importer of good x, so that an industrial policy aimed at expanding this sector is equivalent to an import tariff.[7] What would happen if this economy, initially in the free trade steady-state equilibrium, were to institute a small tariff of size τ on the imports of x? The tariff would make the protected sector more attractive (V_{sx} and V_{ex} would both increase) and some workers would start to switch out of the low-wage sector and search for jobs in the high-wage sector. From (4), the tariff-induced increase in the domestic price of good x generates a new value of a_m. By appropriate choice of τ, it is possible for an industrial policy to target $a_m = a_p$, so that, evaluated at world prices, the tariff maximizes the discounted value of steady-state income. Upon implementation of the tariff, all workers with ability $a_i \in [a_p, a_{ft}]$ immediately quit their low-wage jobs and start to search for jobs in sector x. Since search takes time, aggregate flow income measured at world prices, $I(t; a_p)$, immediately drops and then, as these workers find new jobs, it begins to gradually rise toward its new (higher) steady-state value. A typical time path for $I(t; a_p)$ is depicted in figure 6.1. The discounted value of income in this situation is $W(a_p) = \int e^{-rt} I(t; a_p) dt$. If $W(a_p) > W(a_{ft})$, then the tariff is justified. Otherwise, the short-run adjustment costs required to reach the new steady state exceed any long-run benefits that can be gained by expanding the import-competing sector.

In the next section, we explicitly solve for $I(t; a_p)$ and $W(a_p)$ and show that the adjustment costs are indeed too high to justify the tariff. Yet it is easy to imagine that even with such information available we might still hear calls for import protection. After all, it might be argued, the only thing that makes this policy unattractive is the *short-run* costs. Why not bite the bullet, accept the short-run costs and expand the high-wage sector for the sake of the next generation? We may be worse off for a while, but once we approach the new steady state we will be better off forever after. It is easy to imagine policy wonks carrying the day by peppering such an argument with quotes about the importance of the long run from Paul Krugman and other international trade luminaries.

Suppose now that the economy adopts such a policy and institutes the tariff that maximizes the value of steady-state output. Suppose further that enough time has passed that the economy is now arbitrarily close to the new steady state. Is it now in the economy's interest to stay there or should trade be liberalized? If the tariff is removed, the import-competing high-wage sector becomes less attractive and some workers start switching back to the export sector. If the tariff is removed completely, all workers with $a_i \in [a_p, a_{ft}]$ want to move to the low-wage sector, where jobs are

---

[7] Alternatively, the policy instrument would be an export subsidy if good x is the export good. The qualitative results remain unchanged.

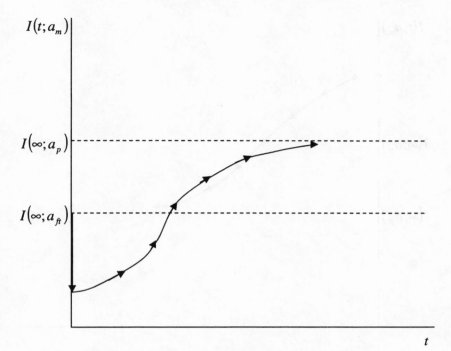

Figure 6.1. Expanding the high-wage sector when initially in free trade.

easy to find and last forever. Workers searching for jobs in the high-wage sector at the time of liberalization make the move immediately while those employed in that sector move after they have lost their job (assuming that after liberalization $V_{ex}(a_i) > V_{ey}$ for all $a_i \in [a_p, a_{ft}]$). Thus, the adjustment is gradual, and if jobs in the import-competing sector are durable, it may take considerable time to approach the free trade steady-state equilibrium.

Aggregate flow income (measured at world prices) during the adjustment to free trade is depicted in figure 6.2. Since searchers produce no output, flow income jumps up immediately when they switch sectors, instantly becoming employed in sector y. However, as time passes, the fact that the value of the output produced by these workers is less in the low-wage sector than the value of the output that they would have produced had they remained in the high-wage sector starts to weigh on the economy, and flow income starts to decrease. It continues to fall until it approaches its new (free trade) steady-state value. Liberalization is optimal if the discounted value of aggregate flow income along the adjustment path is greater than what could be earned by remaining in the tariff-distorted

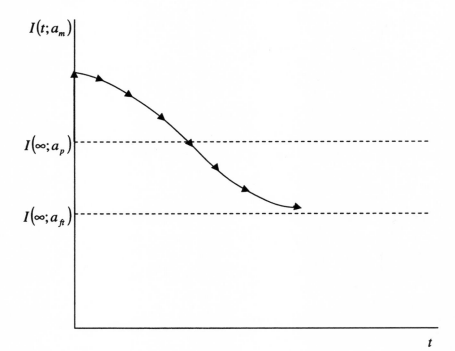

Figure 6.2. Liberalizing trade.

steady state. In the next section, we show that this is indeed the case, so that both arguments in favor of an industrial policy (which are based on *long-run* concerns) are flawed.

4. SHORT-RUN SANITY

One of the advantages of a model as simple as ours is that it is possible to solve for the adjustment path across steady states and take this path into account when making welfare comparisons. Some additional notation will help in this regard. Define a_{m1} as the ability level of the marginal worker in some initial steady state. In this context, $a_{m1} = a_{ft}$ if we are examining movements away from the free trade steady state, and $a_{m1} = a_p$ if we are examining movements away from the tariff-induced steady state. Similarly, define a_{m2} as the ability of the marginal worker after the implementation of the tariff (or after trade liberalization). From our discussion in the previous section, it is clear that the only workers who are induced to switch sectors because of the policy change are those with ability levels between a_{m1} and a_{m2}. We therefore define $ME_j(t; a_{m1}, a_{m2})$ as the mass of workers who move between sectors in response to the policy and are employed in sector j at time t. For example, a policy that causes workers to move from sector x to sector y causes sector-y employment to jump up immediately (as sector-x searchers with ability levels in the critical interval switch sectors), and then it continues to increase gradually as those workers who are employed in sector x move to sector y upon separation. We similarly define $MS_x(t; a_{m1}, a_{m2})$ as the mass of movers who are searching for employment at time t. This measure is zero for all t if the policy change causes the high-wage sector to shrink, since all searchers (within the relevant range of abilities) immediately move to the low-wage sector upon implementation of the policy. However, this measure jumps up and then gradually recedes to its steady-state value for a policy change that makes the high-wage sector more attractive.

We have two cases to consider. First, we consider the case where $a_{m2} = a_{m1} - \Delta$, with $\Delta > 0$. This would be the situation where trade policy protects the high-wage sector, causing it to expand. As we have already noted, $ME_y(t; a_{m1}, a_{m1} - \Delta) = 0$ for all t. We find $ME_x(t; a_{m1}, a_{m1} - \Delta)$ and $MS_x(t; a_{m1}, a_{m1} - \Delta)$ by solving the following system of differential equations:

$$\frac{dME_x(t; a_{m1}, a_{m1} - \Delta)}{dt} = \lambda MS_X(t; a_{m1}, a_{m1} - \Delta)$$
$$- bME_x(t; a_{m1}, a_{m1} - \Delta) \tag{12}$$

$$ME_x(t; a_{m1}, a_{m1} - \Delta) + MS_x(t; a_{m1}, a_{m1} - \Delta) = \Delta \tag{13}$$

Equation (12) notes that the change in sector-x employment equals the difference between the mass of workers who find jobs after searching and the mass of workers who lose their jobs. Equation (13) is an adding up constraint that follows from the fact that all movers are either employed or searching in sector x. Solving this system yields

$$ME_x(t; a_{m1}, a_{m1} - \Delta) = \left(\frac{\lambda}{b + \lambda} - \frac{\lambda}{b + \lambda} e^{-(b+\lambda)t} \right) \Delta \tag{14}$$

$$MS_x(t; a_{m1}, a_{m1} - \Delta) = \left(\frac{b}{b + \lambda} + \frac{\lambda}{b + \lambda} e^{-(b+\lambda)t} \right) \Delta \tag{15}$$

The flow of workers is reversed when a policy change makes the high-wage sector *less* attractive. We can represent this situation by letting $a_{m2} = a_{m1} + \Delta$. Here, $MS_x(t; a_{m1}, a_{m1} + \Delta) = 0$ for all t since all searchers immediately switch to sector y upon implementation of the policy, and all those employed in sector x switch to sector y upon separation. The differential equations describing $ME_j(t; a_{m1}, a_{m1} + \Delta)$ are

$$\frac{dME_x(t; a_{m1}, a_{m1} + \Delta)}{dt} = -bME_x(t; a_{m1}, a_{m1} + \Delta) \tag{16}$$

$$ME_y(t; a_{m1}, a_{m1} + \Delta) + ME_x(t; a_{m1}, a_{m1} + \Delta) = \Delta \tag{17}$$

Using the initial condition $ME_x(0; a_{m1}, a_{m1} + \Delta) = \lambda/(b + \lambda)\Delta$, we solve this system to obtain

$$ME_x(t; a_{m1}, a_{m1} + \Delta) = \frac{\lambda}{\lambda + b} e^{-bt} \Delta \tag{18}$$

$$ME_y(t; a_{m1}, a_{m1} + \Delta) = \left(1 - \frac{\lambda}{\lambda + b} e^{-bt}\right)\Delta \tag{19}$$

Finally, define $G(a_{m1}, a_{m2})$ as the discounted value of the gross increase in output and $L(a_{m1}, a_{m2})$ as the discounted value of the gross loss in output (both measured at world prices) resulting in the move to the new steady state. For example, $G(a_{m1}, a_{m2})$ would correspond to the discounted value of the increase in sector-x output and $L(a_{m1}, a_{m2})$ would correspond to the discounted value of the reduction of sector-y output when the high-wage sector x expands due to import protection ($a_{m1} < a_{m2}$). Using these definitions, a change in policy is welfare improving if $G(a_{m1}, a_{m2}) > L(a_{m1}, a_{m2})$.

Suppose that we start at the free trade steady state and impose a tariff on imports of x, causing this sector to expand. Using our notation, $a_{m1} = a_{ft}$ and $a_{m2} = a_{ft} - \Delta$ with (14) and (15) describing the evolution of employment in each sector. We note also that, evaluated at world prices, the flow value of output lost for each worker exiting the low-wage sector is q_y, while the flow value of output gained by the *average* worker moving into the high-wage sector is $pq_x(a_{ft} - \Delta/2)$ (since a_i is uniformly distributed). Therefore,

$$G(a_{ft}, a_{ft} - \Delta) = \int_0^\infty e^{-rt} ME_x(t; a_{ft}, a_{ft} - \Delta)pq_x\left(a_{ft} - \frac{\Delta}{2}\right)dt \tag{20}$$

$$L(a_{ft}, a_{ft} - \Delta) = \int_0^\infty e^{-rt} q_y \Delta dt \tag{21}$$

Proposition 1. *Expanding the high-wage sector by any amount above its free trade level reduces the net present discounted value of output* *evaluated at world prices. That is, $G(a_{ft}, a_{ft} - \Delta) < L(a_{ft}, a_{ft} - \Delta)$ for all $\Delta > 0$.*

Proof. Substitute (14) into (20) and carry out the integration to obtain

$$
\begin{aligned}
G(a_{ft}, a_{ft} - \Delta) &= \frac{pq_x}{r}\left(a_{ft} - \frac{\Delta}{2}\right)\left(\frac{\lambda}{\lambda + b}\right)\left(1 - \frac{r}{r + \lambda + b}\right)\Delta \\
&< \frac{pq_x a_{ft}}{r}\left(\frac{\lambda}{\lambda + b}\right)\left(1 - \frac{1}{r + \lambda + b}\right)\Delta \\
&= \frac{pq_x a_{ft}}{r}\left(\frac{\lambda}{r + \lambda + b}\right)\Delta = \frac{q_y}{r}\Delta \\
&= L(a_{ft}, a_{ft} - \Delta) \qquad\qquad\qquad \#
\end{aligned}
$$

Proposition 1 shows that expanding the high-wage sector beyond the free trade equilibrium results in a net loss. The short-run costs outweigh the long-run gains.

Suppose, however, that policies have already been implemented to protect the high-wage sector. Or, alternatively, policies to protect that sector are given serious consideration as a way for the current generation (which bears all of the costs) to provide a benefit to future generations (who would appear to reap all of the benefits).[8] Liberalizing trade would result in a decline in the long-run value of instantaneous output. However, this would only occur after an initial burst of activity resulting in a spike in instantaneous output. This follows from the fact that some workers would cease searching for employment in the high-wage sector (where they are not producing anything) and immediately accept employment in the low-wage sector. In this case,

$$
G(a_p, a_p + \Delta) = \int_0^\infty e^{-rt} ME_y(t; a_p, a_p + \Delta)q_y dt \tag{22}
$$

$$
L(a_p, a_p + \Delta) = \int_0^\infty e^{-rt}\left\{\frac{\lambda}{\lambda + b}pq_x\left(a_p + \frac{\Delta}{2}\right)\Delta \right.
$$
$$
\left. - ME_x(t; a_p, a_p + \Delta)pq_y\left(a_p + \frac{\Delta}{2}\right)\right\}dt \tag{23}
$$

---

[8] Of course all individuals are infinitely lived in our model, so our discussion of current and future generations is merely metaphorical in this context.

Equation (23) shows that the discounted loss due to liberalization is the difference between what the movers would have produced had there been no liberalization and what they produce along the adjustment path. In deriving (23), we made use of the fact that the average productivity of the mass of workers who exit sector x is $(a_p + \Delta/2)$.

Liberalization yields discounted net benefits if the short-run gains outweigh the long-run costs. This is indeed the case, as we now demonstrate.

Proposition 2. *Suppose that the high-wage sector is initially protected so that $a_{m1} = a_p < a_{ft}$. Consider a small amount of liberalization such that $a_p < a_{m2} \leqslant a_{ft}$. Then liberalization increases the net discounted value of output (evaluated at world prices) for all values of $\Delta = a_{m2} - a_p$.*

Proof. In this case, workers are moving from the high-wage sector x to the low-wage sector y. Employment evolves according to (18) and (19). Substituting (18) into (23) and carrying out the integration yields

$$
\begin{aligned}
L(a_p, a_p + \Delta) &= \frac{pq_x}{r}\left(a_p + \frac{\Delta}{2}\right)\left(\frac{\lambda}{\lambda + b}\right)\left(1 - \frac{r}{r + b}\right)\Delta \\
&< \frac{pq_x a_{ft}}{r}\left(\frac{\lambda}{\lambda + b}\right)\left(1 - \frac{r}{r + b}\right)\Delta \\
&= \left(\frac{\lambda + r + b}{\lambda}\right)\left(\frac{q_y}{r}\right)\left(\frac{\lambda}{\lambda + b}\right)\left(1 - \frac{r}{r + b}\right)\Delta \\
&= \left(\frac{\lambda + r + b}{\lambda + b}\right)\left(\frac{b}{r + b}\right)\frac{q_y}{r}\Delta \\
&= G(a_p, a_p + \Delta)
\end{aligned}
$$

The last step of the proof follows from substituting (19) into (22) and carrying out the integration. As long as any tariff is in place, further liberalization increases the net discounted value of output. #

Propositions 1 and 2 underscore the importance of the short run. If we look only at long-run outcomes it appears that free trade is suboptimal and that the economy could gain by protecting the high-wage sector. Yet this is not the case—what goes on between the steady states is what matters most and when adjustment costs are taken into account free trade emerges as the optimal policy *regardless of the initial conditions*. This means that in figure 6.1, the up-front loss in income is greater than any long-run benefit from expanding sector x. It also means that in figure 6.2, the short-run increase in income triggered by liberalization swamps any long-run loss from expanding sector y. Of course, this is what the vast majority of economists believe—free trade is always the best option—but when labor market turnover is present we only reach this conclusion when we focus on the short-run behavior of the economy and ignore its long-run properties.

5. INTUITION

We now generalize our model in order to gain a deeper understanding of the relationship between the short and long run. Toward that end, we now assume that both sectors are characterized by job turnover, and that wages in both sectors are increasing in ability. Furthermore, we make no particular assumptions about the distribution of ability other than the normalization that $a_i \in [0,1]$ for all i.

Given these assumptions, unemployed workers must choose a sector in which to search. In an equilibrium with diversified production, the marginal worker is just indifferent between sectors. This means that the marginal level of ability is defined by $V_{sy}(a_m) = V_{sx}(a_m)$, where

$$V_{sj}(a_i) = \frac{\lambda_j}{r + b_j + \lambda_j} \frac{w_j(a_i)}{r} \tag{24}$$

and where our notation follows logically from our earlier discussion. Imagine now that, starting from an initial steady state, we move a small measure of workers into sector j. As in our earlier analysis, moving workers between sectors means changing the identity of the marginal worker from a_m to $a_m + \Delta$, where $\Delta > 0$ if the move is from x to y, and $\Delta < 0$ if the move is in the opposite direction. As before, the discounted gross gain in the value of output in the sector that expands is measured by $G(a_m, a_m + \Delta) = \int_0^\infty e^{-rt} ME_j(a_m, a_m + \Delta)\bar{w}_j dt$, where $\bar{w}_j \equiv \int_{a_m}^{a_m+\Delta} w_j(a)f(a)da$ and where $f(a)$ is the density function of ability. Following Diamond (1980), we define the value of the *dynamic* marginal product of labor as the present discounted value of output that can be obtained by adding an infinitesimal measure of workers to a sector, noting that all workers who enter the sector begin as searchers. Using this definition and (14), the value of the dynamic marginal product of labor in sector x is

$$\lim_{\Delta \to 0} \frac{G_j(a_m, a_m + \Delta)}{\Delta} = \frac{\lambda_j}{r + \lambda_j + b_j} \frac{w_j(a_m)}{r} = V_{sj}(a_m) \tag{25}$$

In equilibrium, these values are equated across sectors. This is no surprise. Forward-looking agents choose the sector that generates the highest discounted value of wages (which reflect output), taking into account expected durations of employment and unemployment. Any movement away from the free trade equilibrium breaks this equality (when evaluated at world prices) and reduces the discounted value of net output.

By contrast, the steady-state value of output is maximized when the steady-state values of the marginal products are equated. The steady-state marginal product for sector j, defined as the increase in the steady-state value of good j given a small increase in the mass of workers in sector j, is

$$\lim_{t \to \infty} \left\{ \lim_{\Delta \to 0} \frac{ME_j}{\Delta} \bar{w}_j \right\} = \frac{\lambda_j}{\lambda_j + b_j} w_j(a_m) \qquad (26)$$

There are only two ways that the steady-state and dynamic marginal products of labor can be simultaneously equated across sectors. The first is if $r = 0$, so that the future is just as important as the present. The second is if $\lambda_x = \lambda_y$ and $b_x = b_y$.

In general, using trade policy to protect the sector with the higher steady-state value of the marginal product of labor results in a higher steady-state value of output but reduces the net discounted value of output. This can only happen if instantaneous output initially falls, which must indeed happen in this case. The negative welfare effects of this policy are clearly seen only by considering the short run.

It is also possible, of course, to fall prey to short-run lunacy. This could happen if a policy were implemented to provide protection to the sector with the lower steady-state marginal product of labor in the hopes of gaining a quick burst of output, delaying the ultimate costs (in the form of lower steady-state output) to the future. For example, returning to the parametric assumptions of section 3, providing protection to sector y (in this case an export subsidy) would cause an immediate expansion in this sector and consequent increase in the value of output. Ultimately, however, the instantaneous value of output must fall as some workers who lose their high-wage jobs take low-wage jobs rather than return to searching in sector x. However, we know that movement away from the free trade equilibrium necessitates a reduction in the net discounted value of output. The short-run gain is not enough to overcome the long-run pain.

6. PRODUCTION POSSIBILITIES VERSUS SUSTAINABLE PRODUCTION

We are certainly not the first to explore the relationship between the short run and long run in the context of a general equilibrium model of trade. Seminal papers by Jones (1971), Mayer (1974), Mussa (1974, 1978), and

Neary (1978) have all enriched our understanding of this connection. We argue here, however, that there is a distinct difference between our approach and the approach taken by others. In the standard approach, exemplified by Mayer (1974), it is assumed that some factor of production (say capital) is immobile in the short run, but then gradually moves between sectors in response to a differential in the rental rate. Ultimately, the allocation of capital reaches its long-run equilibrium when the rental rate (and therefore the marginal product of capital) is the same in both sectors. As Mayer shows, this sort of analysis leads to a long-run production possibilities frontier that is the outer envelope of a family of short-run frontiers, each of which is parameterized by a particular short-run allocation of capital. The key point is that the value output in the short run can never be higher than in the long run. This result is clearly at odds with our formulation.

To illustrate the difference between sustainable production and production possibilities, we return to the specialized model of earlier sections. Define $Q_j(t)$ as the output produced in sector j at time t. Using our earlier notation, $Q_j(\infty) = \lim_{t \to \infty} Q_j(t)$, the steady-state sector-j output. Multiplying steady-state employment by average worker productivity in each sector, sustainable production levels are defined by (27) and (28):

$$Q_x(\infty) = \frac{\lambda}{\lambda + b} \frac{1 - a_m^2}{2} q_x \qquad (27)$$

$$Q_y(\infty) = q_m q_y \qquad (28)$$

Substitution of (27) into (28) shows that the set of outputs that are sustainable in a steady state form a negatively sloped, concave curve, as illustrated in figure 6.3. This is the analogue of the production possibilities curve. However, we have already seen that output in one sector could temporarily exceed (or fall short of) its long-run value.

In figure 6.3, $E_{ft}(\infty)$ and $E_p(\infty)$ represent the free trade and tariff-induced steady states. The straight lines that pass through these points represent world prices.[9] As in the discussion above, figure 6.3 is drawn to show that the value of steady-state output is not maximized at the free trade equilibrium. Rather, the economy would need to move more resources into the high-wage sector to maximize the value of steady-state output. However, implementation of a tariff causes an immediate reduction in the quantity of good y produced, while the quantity of x increases only slowly. The adjustment path lies inside the locus of steady-state production. Measured at

---

[9] In order to avoid clutter, we have not drawn in the line representing domestic relative prices in the case of distorted trade.

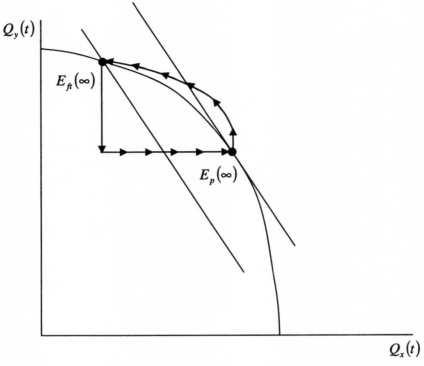

Figure 6.3. Short-run production possibilities and steady-state possibilities.

world prices, the value of output first drops, then expands only gradually, corresponding to figure 6.1.

Starting from the tariff-distorted steady state, removal of the tariff causes an immediate increase in the production of y (with no corresponding reduction in x) as searchers exit sector x, followed by a further gradual increase in y and reduction in x. As with figure 6.2, the value of output expands in the short run, and this is enough to outweigh the lower value of output produced in the steady state.

While we have drawn figure 6.3 based on the version of our model where turnover exists in only one sector, it should be clear that the principles are general. In the special case where turnover parameters are the same in both sectors, adjustment occurs along the steady-state frontier. In this case, the free trade allocation of resources maximizes the steady-state value of output. Implementation of a tariff reduces this value, but the reduction comes only gradually as resources are absorbed in the expanding sector at exactly the same rate as they are released from the contracting sector. The standard full-employment model is a special case, with $b = 0$ and $\lambda = \infty$ in both sectors. That is, once a worker becomes employed, she keeps her job forever (unless she quits), and all jobs are found immediately. A change of policy will, in this case, induce workers to quit one sector and enter the other [this follows since $V_{ej}(a_i) = V_{sj}(a_i) = V(a_i)$ for $j = x,y$] and the transition between one steady state and another is immediate.[10]

7. ON THE LACK OF LUNACY IN MACROECONOMICS

Dynamic models are the norm in macroeconomics, so it is natural to look to this field to see if there are results similar to those we presented in sections 3 and 4. It turns out that there are. In fact, they can be found in the first few chapters of most of the recent graduate-level macro textbooks. These results were not derived recently, as the field began to embrace labor market turnover as a stylized fact that needed to be dealt with. Instead, they were derived over 35 years ago in some of the earliest dynamic models of macroeconomic behavior, those that dealt with capital accumulation and optimal growth.

To review the growth results and relate them to ours, consider a simple infinite horizon one-consumer model of capital accumulation. There is one consumer good (c), which can be produced using capital according to the production function $f(k)$. Once production is complete, the good may be consumed, used to replace depreciated capital, or used to add to the capital stock. It is well known (Phelps 1966) that the capital stock that maximizes steady-state utility satisfies the Golden Rule: $f'(k) = \delta$, where δ denotes capital's depreciation rate. On the other hand, in order to maximize the consumer's discounted utility over her lifetime, capital should be accumulated such that in its steady state it satisfies the Modified Golden Rule: $f'(k) = \delta+r$ (Cass 1965; Koopmans 1965).

The analogy with our results can be understood with the aid of figures 6.1 and 6.2 if we relabel the vertical axis so that we are measuring consumption over time rather than flow income. By definition, steady-state consumption is maximized if the capital stock satisfies the Golden Rule. Then if we let c_G denote the steady-state consumption level in this case, it follows that c_G is equivalent to $I(\infty, a_p)$. In contrast, discounted lifetime utility is maximized when the steady-state capital stock satisfies the Modified Golden Rule. Let c_M denote the consumption level that corresponds

[10] In terms of figure 6.1, output falls immediately to the new steady-state level and remains there forever. In terms of figure 6.2, output immediately increases to the new steady-state level and remains there forever.

to this steady state. Then, since we have shown that free trade is always optimal, c_M is equivalent to $I(\infty, a_{FT})$.

Now, suppose that the consumer is initially in the steady state characterized by c_M. Then it might appear that this consumer could gain by accumulating capital in order to increase steady-state consumption to c_G. After all, once the new steady state is reached, consumption will remain permanently higher forever after. To do so, present consumption must be sacrificed in order to add to the stock of capital. This immediate sacrifice is costly with the reward coming in the future as the larger capital stock eventually allows for increased future consumption. It should be clear that in this case the time path of consumption looks exactly like the time path for flow income in figure 6.1. Moreover, it should also be clear that, just as in our model, such a plan is foolhardy; by the definition of c_M the immediate loss in consumption must be greater than the future gain. In other words, the consumer is better off remaining at c_M.

Turn next to the case in which the consumer is initially in the steady state that satisfies the Golden Rule. Although it was not in this consumer's interest to have accumulated so much capital, now that she has done so, should she remain in this steady state or allow capital to depreciate until steady-state consumption shrinks to c_G? If she remains in the current steady state, then her flow consumption will be higher than it would be in the steady state characterized by c_M. However, if she allows capital to depreciate, she can enjoy higher consumption in the immediate future than she would otherwise. Over time, as the capital stock shrinks, so does consumption until it falls below c_G and begins to approach c_M. Thus, there is a trade-off—the consumer can gain by increasing consumption immediately but at a cost of lower consumption in the future. It should be clear that in this case the time path of consumption is identical to the time path of flow income depicted in figure 6.2. Moreover, by the definition of c_M, it is also clear that the immediate gain in consumption always dominates the future losses so that the consumer gains by allowing capital to depreciate.

While our model does not entail capital accumulation, it is clear that the similarity in the results stems from the fact that both frameworks are dynamic.[11] The basic message is the same in both models—in dynamic settings it is not proper to carry out economic analysis by focusing on the long-run outcomes—the manner in which the economy gets from one steady state to the other is essential. This is well understood in

[11] There are also differences between the results generated by our model and those that are derived in a growth framework. For example, in the presence of discounting, the capital stock that satisfies the Golden Rule is always larger than the capital stock that satisfies the Modified Golden Rule. In our setting, the allocation of labor that maximizes steady-state flow output can be the efficient allocation if the turnover rates do not vary across sectors.

macroeconomics. The Golden Rule and the Modified Golden Rule are introduced right at the beginning of most macro textbooks and the distinction between the two concepts makes it clear that short-run transitions are important. As a result, it is rare to see comparative statics carried out in macroeconomics these days. The field has moved on to embrace the concept of comparative dynamics. This, unfortunately, is not yet the case in international economics where the focus remains on comparative statics and long-run equilibria.

In the previous section, we outlined some of the differences between our approach and those of authors like Jones, Mayer, Mussa, and Neary, who have encouraged the field to take the short run more seriously. It is useful to point out that there are some similarities as well. To begin with, when Mussa (1978) characterized the adjustment path in his model, he showed that under rational expectations the market-induced path maximizes the discounted value of final output. That is, he did not fall prey to long-run lunacy. Second, in the abstract of his paper, Mayer (1974) argued "short-run theory provides a better explanation of factor-owner reactions to trade policies than conventional long-run trade theory." This is the point of our paper—short-run adjustments are just as important (if not more) than the economy's final resting place. And, as international trade theory evolves and begins to account for the short-run costs that must be incurred as economies adjust to trade and technology shocks, it would be useful to keep this in mind.

8. CONCLUSION

Early in our careers a senior colleague warned us that many people read just the introduction and conclusion of papers, figuring that all the essential information is contained in those two sections. Much of the analysis in international trade has followed a similar approach by focusing only on the initial and final equilibria without paying sufficient attention to the manner in which the economy goes from one steady state to another. The purpose of this paper has been to point out that one who just compares long-run steady-state equilibria may be led to draw invalid conclusions. To see how we make this point, you will have to read the intermediate sections of this paper.

REFERENCES

Cass, D. 1965. Optimum growth in an aggregate model of capital accumulation. *Review of Economic Studies*, 32(3): 233–40.

Davidson, C., Martin, L., Matusz, S. 1988. The structure of simple general equilibrium models with frictional unemployment. *Journal of Political Economy* 96(6): 1267–94.

Davidson, C., Martin, L., Matusz, S. 1994. Jobs and chocolate: Samuelsonian surpluses in dynamic models of unemployment. *Review of Economic Studies* 61(1): 173–92.

Davidson, C., Martin, L., Matusz, S. 1999. Trade and search generated unemployment. *Journal of International Economics* 48(2): 271–99.

Davis, S., Haltiwanger, J., Schuh, S. 1996. *Job Creation and Job Destruction.* Cambridge, MA: MIT Press.

Diamond, P. 1980. An alternative to steady-state comparisons. *Economics Letters* 5(1): 7–9.

Jones, R. 1971. A three-factor model in theory, trade and history. In Jagdish Bhagwati, Ronald W. Jones, Robert A. Mundell, and Jaroslav Vanek (eds.), *Trade, Balance of Payments and Growth: Essays in International Economics in Honor of Charles P. Kindleberger.* Amsterdam: North-Holland.

Keynes, J. 1923. *A Tract on Monetary Reform.* London, Macmillan.

Koopmans, T. 1965. On the concept of optimal economic growth. In *The Economic Approach to Development Planning.* Amsterdam: Elsevier.

Krugman, P. 1996. Ricardo's difficult idea. Paper prepared for Manchester Conference on Free Trade, web.mit.edu/krugman/www/ricardo.htm.

Krugman, P. 1998. Why aren't we all Keynesians yet? *Fortune,* August 1998.

Mayer, W. 1974. Short-run and long-run equilibrium for a small open economy. *Journal of Political Economy* 82(5): 955–67.

Mortensen, D. Pissarides, C. 1994. Job creation and job destruction in the theory of unemployment. *Review of Economic Studies* 61(3): 397–415.

Mussa, M. 1974. Tariffs and the distribution of income: The importance of factor specificity, substitutability, and intensity in the short and long run. *Journal of Political Economy* 82(6): 1191–1203.

Mussa, M. 1978. Dynamic adjustment in the Heckscher-Ohlin-Samuelson model. *Journal of Political Economy* 86(5): 775–91.

Neary, J. 1978. Short-run capital specificity and the pure theory of international trade. *Economic Journal* 88(351): 488–510.

Phelps, E. 1966. *Golden Rules of Economic Growth.* New York: W. W. Norton.

PART 3

EMPIRICS

INTRODUCTION TO PART 3

Approximately fifteen years into our research agenda, we began to realize that we could reach a broader audience of nonspecialists if we could have more space than permitted in a single journal article and if we could be a bit more relaxed in our presentation. Thus, looking for a sponsor for a monograph that would pull together the core of our work modeling trade and employment, we approached the Upjohn Institute for Employment Research. Randy Eberts, the director of the institute, was quite interested, but the institute typically sponsored empirical work and Eberts was concerned that our proposed monograph had no empirical component. In responding to this concern, we modified our proposal to include a chapter where we would present data on imports, exports, and industry-specific rates of job turnover in the United States and see if the data was consistent with the theory developed in the early chapters of the monograph. Our look at the data led us to chapter 7 in the current volume.

The theory underlying this empirical analysis suggests that all else equal, industry-specific wages are positively related to industry-specific job break-up rates. Higher wages compensate for shorter average job tenure. In turn, higher wages feed through to higher output prices. Cross-country differences in industry-specific break-up rates then contribute independently to the pattern of comparative advantage. Unfortunately, we had detailed data on break-up rates for only the United States, so we were unable to truly test the model; however, we found a remarkably strong correlation between industry-specific break-up rates and an index of net exports, with lower break-up rates being associated with greater net exports.[1] This correlation appeared in the very first scatter diagrams that we plotted upon receipt of the data, and it remained regardless of how we cleaned the data or controlled for other variables.

This particular chapter has been criticized on two counts. Both criticisms were neatly summarized by an unsympathetic referee who wrote

---

[1] We did, however, have some relatively aggregated Canadian data pertaining to job destruction and were able to use this data to undertake testing that was more tightly tied to the underlying theoretical model. The results, shown at the end of chapter 7, suggest that Canada is more competitive than the United States in sectors where Canadian job destruction is low relative to U.S. job destruction, and the United States is more competitive in sectors when Canadian job destruction is high relative to U.S. job destruction.

that "all the authors have is a correlation that describes a well-known equilibrium phenomenon: in the US, sectors that face a lot of import competition also tend to be more volatile in terms of employment and more prone to net job loss. Since this fact is well established, it is hard to see where the contribution of the paper lies." On the one hand, the referee suggests that we have causality reversed, and on the other hand, that this correlation is well known.

Taking the second criticism first, we searched far and wide for published results that showed similar correlations, and we asked dozens of labor and trade economists for a citation. Many said that this phenomenon was indeed well known, but none could point to a citation. In fact, the only prior research that we uncovered was work by Lori Kletzer (1998a, 1998b, 2000) that provides only very weak evidence of a positive correlation between import penetration and worker displacement, and that of Davis, Haltiwanger, and Schuh (1996, p. 175), who reported "no systematic relationship between the magnitude of gross job flows and exposure to international trade." We stand by our contention that the correlation exists, is strong, and is not widely known.[2]

The second criticism is more difficult to dismiss. While turnover can be an exogenous parameter of a theoretical model, ignoring the issue of endogeneity can be a risky strategy in empirical work and can lead one to falsely attribute causality when the direction is reversed or indeed when none exists. An appropriate empirical strategy would be to instrument for turnover, but we have not yet uncovered any reasonable correlate of turnover that would not also be correlated with trade. We therefore approached the issue of causality by examining the data using a variety of methods. In the end, we are relatively comfortable in our claim that turnover causes trade but admit that our analysis is far from definitive and welcome further research in this area.[3]

Our second foray into empirical implementation of our theory was conceived during the Spring 2001 meetings of the Midwest International Economics Group, hosted that semester by the University of Wisconsin. Christopher Magee presented "Campaign Contributions and Trade Policy: Simple Tests of Stolper-Samuelson," a paper that he had co-authored with Eugene Beaulieu.[4] Listening to his paper, we realized that we could

---

[2] Some research has shown how trade can affect the distribution of employment across sectors. For example, see Grossman (1987) and Revenga (1992, 1997). As we show in chapter 7, this is not equivalent to finding a correlation between job turnover and the pattern of trade.

[3] We suspect that causality runs in both directions. Our suspicion suggests that it might be fruitful to deepen the theory by relating job destruction to the degree of openness or to other shocks related to openness (e.g., movements in the exchange rate).

[4] This paper was published as Beaulieu and Magee (2004).

use the type of data described there to test the insights of Davidson, Martin, and Matusz (1999). In particular, as we showed in that paper (chapter 3 of this volume), factors of production that are employed in sectors with high job break-up rates ought to have diametrically opposed preferences when it comes to trade policy, while those employed in sectors with low break-up rates ought to be in harmony with respect to their positions on trade issues. We realized that we could test this hypothesis by using data on sector-specific job turnover rates combined with data on contributions given by political action committees (PACs) to Congressional representatives and the voting records of those representatives. The hypothesis would be that PACs that represented capital and those that represented labor within the same industry would have indistinguishable patterns of political contributions if their common industry was characterized by low job turnover, but labor PACs would be significantly more protectionist (measured by their pattern of political contributions) than capital PACs when both represented interests in industries characterized by high rates of job turnover. A dual hypothesis emerges where the net export position of a sector does not matter for the pattern of political contributions if the industry is characterized by high turnover, but PACs associated with import-competing industries are likely to be more protectionist than those representing export-oriented industries if job turnover is relatively low. Our results, reproduced as chapter 8 of this volume, lend strong support to these hypotheses.

In reading over chapter 7, we ask the readers to keep in mind that we are primarily theorists, so that the empirical work may seem crude. However, we believe that the data seem to support the predictions of our models. Our hope is that those who have a comparative advantage in undertaking empirical work find our results intriguing enough that they will probe more deeply to check the robustness of our results and to test other aspects of the theory that have yet to be subject to empirical verification.

REFERENCES

Beaulieu, E., Magee, C. 2004. Campaign contributions and trade policy: New tests of Stolper-Samuelson. *Economics and Politics* 16: 163–87.

Davidson, C., Martin, L., Matusz, S. 1999. Trade and search-generated unemployment. *Journal of International Economics* 48: 271–99.

Davis, S., Haltiwanger, J., Schuh, S. 1996. *Job Creation and Destruction*. Cambridge, MA: MIT Press.

Grossman, G. 1987. The employment and wage effects of import competition. *Journal of International Economic Integration* 2(1): 1–23.

Kletzer, L. 1998a. International trade and job loss in U.S. manufacturing, 1979–91. In Susan Collins (ed.), *Imports, Exports, and the American Worker*, Washington, DC: Brookings Institution Press.

Kletzer, L. 1998b. Increasing foreign competition and job insecurity: Are they related? In (P. Voos, (ed.), *Proceedings of the Fiftieth Annual Meeting*. Madison, WI: Industrial Relations Research Association.

Kletzer, L. 2000. Trade and job loss in U.S. manufacturing, 1979–1994. In R. Feenstra, (ed.), *The Impact of International Trade on Wages*. Chicago: University of Chicago Press.

Revenga, A. 1992. Exporting jobs? The impact of international competition on employment and wages. *Quarterly Journal of Economics* 107(1): 255–84.

Revenga, A. 1997. Employment and wage effects of trade liberalization: The case of Mexican manufacturing. *Journal of Labor Economics* 15(3): S20–43.

Chapter 7

TRADE AND TURNOVER:
THEORY AND EVIDENCE

CARL DAVIDSON AND STEVEN J. MATUSZ

1. INTRODUCTION

A view that seems to be commonly held by a significant portion of the public is that international trade generates forces that threaten job security, particularly in the U.S. manufacturing sector. The basic idea is simple and intuitive—a sudden surge of imports in a sector intensifies competition, drives American firms out of business, and destroys American jobs. Of course, international trade could also have a positive effect on labor market outcomes—a sudden increase in the demand for American-made goods could lead to an increase in the number of jobs available as export sectors expand. In either case, changes in the international trading environment create or destroy jobs, leading in turn to worker turnover.[1]

Recently, Carl Davidson, Lawrence Martin, and Steven Matusz (1999) have explored the implications that labor market turnover might have for net exports in a general equilibrium model of trade. In the model that they construct, jobs are continuously created and destroyed at parametrically given rates. In order to attract and retain workers, sectors with above-average rates of job destruction or where jobs are harder than average to find need to compensate searching workers for their risk by paying higher than average wages. Higher wages drive up production costs. By adding a second country, Davidson, Martin, and Matusz (DMM) are able to relate exogenously specified cross-country differences in turnover

---

[1] See also Jagdish Bhagwati and Vivek Dehejia (1994) and Bhagwati (1998), who provide a slightly different theory of how trade affects turnover. According to their theory, dramatic reductions in transportation costs, increases in the speed of communications, and rapidly evolving research have led to a global economy where profit margins are razor thin. Thus, they argue that countries can gain or lose the competitive edge in any particular market almost instantly. In turn, this "kaleidoscopic" comparative advantage creates increased employment volatility as firms that lose their competitive edge exit the market, replaced by new industry leaders.

rates to endogenously determined trade patterns. In particular, holding all else constant, an increase in the rate at which jobs break up in sector i in country C raises the cost of producing that good and erodes the country's comparative advantage in that good (or aggravates its comparative disadvantage). In this view of the world, exogenously given labor market turnover is an independent determinant of comparative advantage.[2]

As we point out below, neither view of the world *necessarily* implies that we would observe a correlation between a country's net exports and labor market turnover. However, both views are at least suggestive of a negative correlation between net exports in a given sector and the rate at which jobs are lost in that sector, with a positive correlation between net exports and the ease with which jobs are found in that sector. Of course, the two theories differ in terms of what they take to be the exogenous cause and the endogenous effect. The two also differ in that the first derives from a partial equilibrium model linking *changes* in trade patterns or volumes to *changes* in employment (and therefore rates of job loss), whereas the second is grounded in a general equilibrium framework describing a steady-state relationship between rates of job turnover and the pattern of trade.

Our purpose in this paper is to more fully articulate the two theories linking trade and turnover and then use data on job turnover, worker turnover, and trade patterns to see if we can find empirical support for either theory. Unlike earlier work that finds only weak evidence of a correlation between job turnover and changes in net exports, we find a very strong negative correlation between rates of job loss and the level of net exports. Moreover, we also look at the connection between job acquisition rates and trade patterns, something that has not (to our knowledge) been explored in the literature. We find some evidence that job acquisition rates are positively correlated with net exports, though the evidence here is not as strong as our evidence on the correlation between net exports and job loss. This may be due to the fact that our measure of job acquisition does not conform as closely to the theoretical concept as does our measure of job loss.[3]

[2] The intuition underlying the Davidson, Martin, and Matusz (DMM) assertion is based on one of the main lessons from general equilibrium trade theory—that comparative advantage is the result of the interaction of intersectoral differences with cross-country differences. In the Ricardian model, comparative advantage arises because labor productivity differs between countries. Comparative advantage in the Heckscher-Ohlin-Samuelson model is the result of cross-sector differences in factor intensities combined with cross-country differences in factor supplies. In the DMM world, it is differences in labor market turnover across industries and countries that drive trade patterns.

[3] Many researchers have studied the way that international competition has shaped the distribution of employment across sectors. See, for example, Gene Grossman (1987) and Ana

In addition to finding these correlations, we attempt to sort out the cause-and-effect relationship. Using a variety of different techniques, we find that the weight of the evidence suggests that it is more likely that turnover causes trade than vice versa.

2. FROM TRADE TO TURNOVER

In a recent series of papers, Lori Kletzer (1998a, b, 2000) finds some weak evidence to support the hypothesis that worker displacement rates are positively correlated with the degree of foreign competition.[4] Before reporting Kletzer's empirical findings, it is useful to describe the conceptual framework that underlies her empirical implementation. This is best done with reference to figure 7.1.

Consider a partial equilibrium model of a single good produced in two countries (the US and a Foreign country) under conditions of perfect competition and increasing marginal cost. The left-hand panel of figure 7.1 represents the US market for this good, while the right-hand panel represents the Foreign market. The US and Foreign demand as well as the US and Foreign supply for this good are taken as exogenous. All quantities and prices are endogenously determined in equilibrium.

As drawn, the US would be a net importer of this good. The equilibrium price of this good can be found by adding the Foreign excess supply curve to the US supply curve and then finding the intersection of the resulting summation with the US demand curve.[5] Assuming that no goods are lost in transit, the quantity of US imports (M_{US}) must equal the quantity of Foreign exports (X_F). The import-penetration ratio for this good can be defined as $m = (M_{US}/Q_{US}^D)$. Suppose now that there is some change in the Foreign market that induces the exogenously specified Foreign supply curve to shift to the right. Examples of such shocks might include technological improvement, reduction in the cost of some important input, or change in government legislation. From figure 7.1, it is evident that this shock will cause (a) a decrease in the world price of the product; (b) an increase in the quantity demanded in the US; (c) a decrease in the quantity supplied in the US; and (d) an increase in the quantity of the good imported by the US from the Foreign country. In turn, (b) and (d)

Revenga (1992, 1997). This is a distinctly different line of research. As we show below, trade can be related to turnover in the labor market even when the cross-sector composition of employment does not change.

[4] Jon Haveman (1998), using a somewhat different empirical methodology, finds similar results.

[5] For simplicity, we abstract from both natural and artificial barriers to trade, so that trade equalizes the equilibrium price across markets.

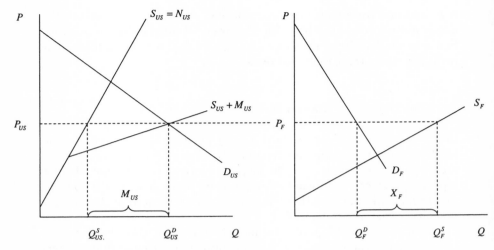

Figure 7.1. Relating domestic import penetration and employment to foreign supply and demand conditions.

combined imply that the shock creates an increase in the import-penetration ratio. Assuming, as is natural, that US employment is positively related to the quantity supplied in the US, the exogenous shock to the Foreign supply curve creates a negative correlation between the endogenously determined import-penetration ratio and US employment and a positive correlation between the endogenously determined world price of the product and the US employment rate.

Kletzer generalizes this comparative static, postulating that shocks occur every time period. She defines the displacement rate (d) as

$$d_t = -\frac{N_t - N_{t-1}}{N_{t-1}} - a_t \qquad (1)$$

where N_t is industry employment in period t and a is the rate of unreplaced attritions (e.g., voluntary quits that are not replaced by new hires).

Based upon this framework and using these definitions, Kletzer tests the hypothesis that $d_{i,t}$ is positively related to $\Delta m_{i,t}$ and negatively related to $\Delta P_{i,t}$, where the subscript i is used to denote an industry and where Δ is the first-difference operator.

There are two fundamental problems with this approach, both of which are acknowledged by Kletzer.[6] The first, as already noted, is that

---

[6] There are some secondary problems as well. For example, there is an implicit assumption that this is the market for a final good. If this is an intermediate good, then stiffer foreign

both $m_{i,t}$ and $P_{i,t}$ are endogenous. It is because of this endogeneity problem that Kletzer is careful about not attributing causality to the results.

The second problem is that the model is also consistent with a *negative* correlation between $d_{i,t}$ and $\Delta m_{i,t}$ and a *positive* correlation between $d_{i,t}$ and $\Delta P_{i,t}$. For example, suppose that there is an exogenous increase in US demand. This creates an unambiguous increase in the equilibrium price of the product, inducing greater US production and employment (less displacement). The import-penetration ratio could increase as well if the Foreign excess supply curve is more elastic than the US supply curve. In this case, there would be a negative correlation between $d_{i,t}$ and $\Delta m_{i,t}$.[7] Alternatively, suppose that there is a negative shock to US supply, causing the aggregate supply of goods to the US market to shift leftward. In this case, the price of the good unambiguously increases, but the quantity produced domestically (and therefore employment) might actually fall, creating a *positive* correlation between $d_{i,t}$ and $\Delta P_{i,t}$. It is not possible to sort out these conflicting relationships in the absence of data relating to both US and Foreign shocks.

With the above model in mind, Kletzer (2000) created a panel combining data from the Displaced Workers Survey with price and quantity data on international trade to test the hypotheses that $d_{i,t}$ is positively related to $\Delta m_{i,t}$ and negatively related to $\Delta P_{i,t}$. To do so, she regressed $d_{i,t}$ on $\Delta m_{i,t}$, $\Delta P_{i,t}$, and a variety of control variables. Of the 15 regressions that use $\Delta m_{i,t}$ as the independent variable of interest, the point estimate of the slope coefficient is positive in all but two cases. In the two cases where the estimated slope coefficient is negative, it is not possible to reject the null hypothesis that the true value is actually zero. Indeed, of the remaining 13 cases, the t-statistic ranges from 0.15 to 3.04, exceeding 1.5 in only 5 instances. Of the 10 regressions where $\Delta P_{i,t}$ was the key independent variable, 1 resulted in a positive point estimate of the slope coefficient, though it was not possible to reject the null hypothesis that the true coefficient is zero. In the remaining nine cases, the t-statistics ranged from 0.30 to 2.10,

---

competition might cost jobs in this sector but increase jobs in the downstream sector where costs fall. If these two "sectors" are narrowly defined so that both fit into the same classification given the data constraints, increased foreign competition would be associated with higher sector-specific employment (lower displacement). In addition, ignoring job acquisitions leads to some curious empirical puzzles. For example, Kletzer identifies some sectors that have persistently high (but relatively stable, or even declining) import-penetration ratios *and* high rates of worker displacement. Assuming that final demand is roughly constant, displacements that are not ultimately replaced ought to lead to a secular decline in domestic output and higher import-penetration ratios.

[7] Even in the event that the import-penetration ratio fell, leading to the hypothesized positive correlation, the underlying chain of cause-and-effect works from the exogenous change in domestic demand to the simultaneously determined displacement rate and import-penetration ratio. This just restates the endogeneity problem.

with only three instances in which the value was larger than 1.5. In summary, Kletzer's results provide only weak evidence that increased international competition is correlated with greater worker displacement.

3. FROM TURNOVER TO TRADE

In contrast to the static, partial equilibrium model that motivates the intuition suggesting that trade shocks cause labor market turnover, DMM developed a dynamic general equilibrium model to show that cross-country and cross-industry differences in labor market turnover can be an independent source of comparative advantage and therefore help shape the equilibrium pattern of trade.

Consider a simplified version of the DMM model where labor is the only input[8] Assume that there are two goods and two countries. Suppose that each worker can produce a single unit of either good regardless of country, so that in the absence of any other considerations there would be no basis for trade. Finally, suppose that in each country workers live forever and alternate between spells of employment and spells of unemployment. In particular, we assume that existing jobs break up and new jobs are acquired according to a Poisson process, where we let b_i^k represent the job break-up rate and e_i^k the job acquisition rate for sector i in country k. We take these parameters as exogenous, though they would clearly be determined in part by optimizing behavior in a more sophisticated model. Because of the implied frictions in the labor market, there will always be some job loss even if a sector is expanding, and there will always be some job gains even if a sector is contracting.[9]

Unemployed workers choose a sector in which to search for a job. Assuming that workers are risk neutral, it is necessarily the case that diversified production necessitates that (appropriately discounted) expected lifetime income must be the same across sectors.[10] This income is a weighted average of the income earned while unemployed (zero) and the income earned while on the job. We assume here that a worker earns the entire value of his marginal product, which is simply P_i. Using V_i to represent the discounted value of lifetime income for an unemployed worker, it is relatively straightforward to show that[11]

[8] The DMM model consists of two factors, allowing for diversified production over a nondegenerate range of prices.

[9] This feature of the model is consistent with the data on gross flows, as suggested by Steven Davis and John Haltiwanger (1992) and Davis, Haltiwanger, and Scott Schuh (1996).

[10] Since workers live forever, we should technically talk about income discounted over the infinite future, but this phrase seems unnecessarily awkward.

[11] See Davidson, Martin, and Matusz (1999) for the derivation.

$$V_i = \left(\frac{e_i}{r + b_i + e_i}\right)\frac{P_i}{r} \qquad (2)$$

where r is the subjective rate of discount. As already noted, diversified production requires $V_1 = V_2$, which from (2) implies that

$$\frac{P_2}{P_1} = \frac{r + b_2 + e_2}{r + b_1 + e_1}\frac{e_1}{e_2} \qquad (3)$$

If P_2 increases relative to P_1, all searchers flow to sector 2 and the economy eventually specializes to the production of good 2. The reverse happens if P_2 falls relative to P_1. We illustrate equilibrium in the absence of trade by reference to the relative supply and relative demand curves in figure 7.2.

In this model, turnover rates are the exogenous shifters of relative supply. If b_2 increases (or e_2 decreases), all else equal, the price of good 2 must increase in order to continue attracting workers to that sector.

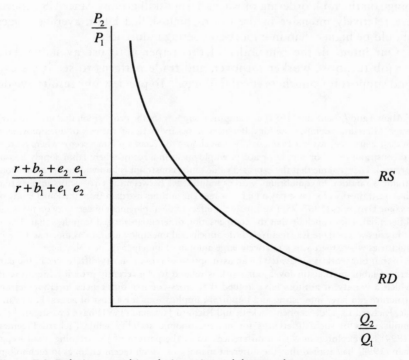

Figure 7.2. Relating autarkic relative price to labor market turnover.

The intuition for this result is akin to that of a compensating wage differential. Holding all other factors constant, sectors that have relatively high break-up rates need to pay higher wages to encourage prospective employees to accept jobs within that sector rather than in a sector where jobs are more secure. Similarly, jobs that are relatively difficult to obtain (that is, where e_i is relatively small) need to offer a wage premium to induce prospective employees to undertake the time and effort needed to obtain a job in that sector rather than another sector where jobs are easier to obtain.[12]

The implication for trade theory is that a country should have a comparative advantage in sectors where the break-up rate is low and/or the job acquisition rate is high relative to the same sector in other countries. This would seem to imply that export industries should be characterized by relatively low wages while import-competing industries should be characterized by high wages. Given the strong evidence to the contrary in the United States, it would appear that this is prima facie evidence against the model. However, this would be a misinterpretation of the model. In particular, each category of labor (skilled, semiskilled, unskilled, and so on) has to be compensated for increased job risk, but this will not impinge on the rank ordering of wages across skill groups. Since US exports are relatively intensive in the use of high-skilled labor, average wages should be higher than in import-competing industries.

Our intent in the remainder of this paper is to use available data on job turnover, worker turnover, and trade patterns to see if we can find support for our theoretical findings.[13] To preview our results, we do

[12] Abowd and Ashenfelter (1981) find empirical support for the proposition that interindustry wage differentials compensate for differences across industries in the risk of unemployment. In their work, they assume that a worker can choose to accept a job in a sector where there is no constraint on labor supply, or accept employment in a sector where labor supply is constrained. They assume that the expected value of the constraint is known, but the actual constraint is random. In equilibrium, worker indifference between the two sectors implies that the constrained sector must pay a higher wage. The authors use data from the Panel Study of Income Dynamics (1967–75) to estimate the effect of unemployment uncertainty on the wage differential. They conclude that the compensating differentials ranged from less than 1% in industries where there was relatively little anticipated unemployment, to as much as 14% in industries where there was a relatively large amount of anticipated unemployment.

[13] In that our work is motivated by an assumption of cross-country differences in the pattern of labor market turnover, our work is related to the recently growing literature in which a variety of authors have argued that cross-country differences in labor market structure can have interesting and important implications for a host of issues. For example, Richard Layard, Stephen Nickell, and Richard Jackman (1991) have investigated the implications of such differences for macroeconomic stability while Richard Freeman (1994) has explored how such differences affect the pattern of job training. Paul Krugman (1994) has argued that the different manner in which recent changes in technology and trade patterns have filtered through economies can be linked to the differences in

indeed find strong evidence that higher rates of job destruction or worker separations are associated with a smaller level of net exports.[14] This correlation emerges from the data even after controlling for other variables that are likely to be associated with the volume and pattern of trade. We also use job creation and worker accessions to create a proxy for the job acquisition rate. While we do find that our proxy for job acquisitions is positively correlated with net trade, the correlation is not as strong as that relating net trade with job destruction or worker separations. As we note in our discussion of the data, our proxy for the job acquisition rate only loosely approximates the theoretical counterpart. By contrast, both the job destruction rate and the job separation rate are reasonably good proxies for the break-up rate that shows up in the theoretical model.[15]

4. THE DATA

As indicated in the introduction, we make use of two distinct sets of data on labor market turnover.[16] The purpose of this section is to describe the

---

their labor market structures. He points out that the United States, with its flexible, high-turnover labor market has been characterized by a dramatic change in the distribution of income while European countries, with their rigid, relatively low-turnover labor markets, have been characterized by a dramatic increase in unemployment among low-skilled workers. Donald Davis (1998) makes a similar point when he shows how countries with downwardly rigid wages may be insulated from trade shocks if their trading partners have flexible labor markets that allow them to absorb such shocks. See also the paper by Olivier Blanchard and Augustin Landier (2001), who relate turnover (a labor market outcome) with French institutional reform undertaken in the 1980s that provided firms with wider leeway in hiring workers under fixed-term contracts (rather than standard contracts of indefinite term). In turn, this has allowed firms more flexibility in terminating workers since firms are permitted to more easily terminate workers who were employed on fixed-term contracts. However, firms are subject to a substantially higher level of firing costs in the event that workers are kept on beyond the duration of the contract. Blanchard and Landier argue on theoretical grounds that this sort of policy could set up perverse incentives for firms to terminate workers on fixed-term contracts even when the quality of the match appears good, thus creating higher turnover. They provide empirical evidence that this has indeed been the case.

[14] Of course, we normalize our trade variables to account for size variation across sectors.

[15] It is perhaps worth noting that we might expect turnover to exert an independent influence on the costs of production, and hence on the pattern of comparative advantage, even in the absence of the general equilibrium effects that were formally modeled in Davidson, Martin, and Matusz (1999). The reason is that turnover itself is costly. Presumably, firms need to expend resources to train newly hired employees and to find and recruit replacements for those who leave. Holding all else constant, higher turnover is more costly.

[16] We are happy to provide all of our data along with the Stata "do file" to anyone wishing to further explore our results.

data and discuss the conceptual fit between the data and the theoretical underpinnings of the general equilibrium model presented in the previous section.[17]

The data underlying the statistical analysis of job creation and destruction undertaken by Davis, Haltiwanger, and Schuh (DHS) is the Longitudinal Research Database (LRD) that was developed by the United States Census Bureau. While the original establishment-level data is not available for public use, DHS have aggregated the data to the sectoral level and made these data freely available for anyone to use.[18]

The LRD combined data from the quinquennial census of manufactures with annual survey data to ascertain, inter alia, establishment-level employment numbers.[19] The survey asks respondents to list the number of employees (both full time and part time) on the payroll as of a specified pay period in March of the designated year. Since the same establishments were surveyed every year, DHS were able to track plant-level employment changes.[20]

To generate job creation and job destruction data for any particular grouping of establishments (for example, by SIC) for year t, DHS first divide the entire set of establishments into three groups. The first group includes all of those establishments that had more employees on the payroll in March of year t than they did in March of year $t - 1$. Call this set of establishments S^+. The second group includes all of those establishments that had fewer employees on the payroll in March of year t than they did in the previous March. The set of establishments in this group is denoted by S^-. Of course the remaining establishments (presumably accounting for only a very small share of overall manufacturing employment) constitute the set of establishments for which there was no change in employment.

Considering only those establishments in the set S^+, DHS define the gross number of new jobs created as the sum of all employment increases

[17] Of course the authoritative (and complete) description of the DHS dataset is provided in the appendix to Davis, Haltiwanger, Schuh (1996).

[18] Recently, Michael Klein, Scott Schuh, and Robert Triest (2003) used the DHS data to examine the impact of exchange rate movements on turnover. Davis, Haltiwanger, and Schuh (1996, p. 175) explicitly looked for a link between turnover and the degree of import penetration or export performance and found "no systematic relationship between the magnitude of gross job flows and exposure to international trade." However, theirs was a very superficial analysis, consisting of a simple cross-tabulation, dividing industries into quintiles (based on import-penetration ratios on the one hand or the share of output devoted to exports on the other), and then reporting the weighted average job destruction and creation rates of four-digit SIC sectors within each quintile. They do not undertake any sort of formalized hypothesis testing.

[19] In this context, an establishment is a plant employing (generally speaking) five or more workers.

[20] Establishments rotated in and out of the sample at five-year intervals.

TRADE AND TURNOVER   175

between year $t - 1$ and year t. To convert this into a job creation *rate*, DHS divide by the average aggregate employment level of all firms in sector S between $t - 1$ and t. That is, if N_{et} represents employment at establishment e in March of year t, and if C_{st} represents the gross number of jobs created in sector S, then

$$C_{s,t} = \sum_{e \in S^+} (N_{e,t} - N_{e,t-1})$$ (4)

$$c_{s,t} = \frac{C_{s,t}}{\frac{1}{2} \sum_{e \in S} (N_{e,t} + N_{e,t-1})}$$ (5)

where the lowercase letter refers to a rate and the uppercase letter refers to a level.

While this job creation variable is certainly very interesting for many purposes, it is not what we have in mind by the job acquisition parameter represented by e_i in the introduction to this paper. The problem is that it does not really tell us how easy or hard it is for an unemployed worker to find a job in a particular sector, nor does it tell us how easy or hard it is for a firm with vacancies to find appropriate employees. Expanding establishments may hire many workers relative to their existing employment base, yet this may only be a small fraction of the workers who are looking for a job in that sector, implying that it is relatively easy for firms to find workers, but difficult for the unemployed to find jobs. Similarly, a small job creation rate could possibly be associated with a small pool of workers looking for employment in that sector, and therefore correspond to relatively easy entrée into the sector, but possibly higher costs of recruiting. Even so, it is possible to use this measure to tease out an expression that has some bearing on the issue at hand.

The supply of new jobs created by firms in sector S relative to the aggregate number of new jobs created by manufacturing firms in all sectors combined provides some sense of the relative magnitude of job creation emanating from sector S. That is, a sector could have a relatively low job creation rate but be responsible for the lion's share of new jobs created in the manufacturing sector if that sector accounts for a relatively large portion of base employment. To calculate our proxy of the job acquisition rate, which we denote by $e_{i,t}$, define $\lambda_{i,t}$ as the share of total manufacturing employment in year t accounted for by sector i. The employment-weighted average job creation rate in year t is then[21]

---

[21] DHS report the annual employment-weighted job creation rates for the United States in table 2.1.

$$c_t = \sum_i \lambda_{i,t} c_{i,t} \tag{6}$$

Furthermore, the share of jobs accounted for by sector j is simply

$$e_{i,t} = \frac{\lambda_{i,t} c_{i,t}}{c_t} \tag{7}$$

We shall refer to $e_{i,t}$ as the job acquisition rate in the remainder of this paper. However, we note here that the measure represented by (7) is not a perfect proxy for the true job acquisition rate, since we know nothing about the pool of workers suited for employment in different sectors. For example, some sectors are intensive in the use of skilled labor; others are intensive in the use of unskilled labor. It may be that e is relatively small for a sector that uses highly skilled labor. However, if the pool of qualified workers is also small, it may not be all that difficult to obtain employment in this sector.

The DHS measure of job destruction is calculated in a manner analogous to the job creation rate. However, this measure is much closer to our concept of the break-up rate, represented by b_i, that is pivotal in our theoretical model. Following the DHS notation, we use the symbol $D_{s,t}$ to represent the gross number of jobs destroyed between period $t - 1$ and period t. Then by definition

$$D_{st} = \sum_{e \in S^-} \left| N_{e,t} - N_{e,t-1} \right| \tag{8}$$

$$d_{s,t} = \frac{D_{s,t}}{\frac{1}{2} \sum_{e \in S} (N_{e,t} + N_{e,t-1})} \tag{9}$$

Because the DHS measure of job destruction is a close approximation of the job break-up parameter in the general equilibrium model, we shall simply let $b_{s,t} = d_{s,t}$.

While the DHS data captures annual changes in the number of jobs at an establishment, the BLS data focuses squarely on worker accessions and separations. Labor market turnover as reported by the United States Bureau of Labor Statistics represents the gross movement of workers into (accessions) and out of (separations) employment at the level of individual establishments. This data was reported in table D-2 of *Employment and Earnings* until 1981, when collection of this data ceased because of budgetary reasons.[22] To see the difference between job flows and worker

---

[22] The BLS data was classified according to 1967 SIC codes prior to 1978, and discontinued after 1981. Note, however, that the 1981 data is reported in the March 1982 issue of *Employment and Earnings*.

flows, note that an establishment might experience a 10% separation rate during the course of the year (due to retirements, quits, or layoffs) at the same time that it has a 10% accession rate (consisting of new hires and rehires). This establishment would end the year with the same number of employees as it had at the beginning of the year, and would therefore not exhibit any job creation or destruction, yet turnover would be substantial. Turnover in the DHS data requires heterogeneity between establishments, while turnover in the BLS data may exist due to heterogeneity of worker experience within establishments.[23]

The BLS measure of job accessions is subject to the same weakness as the DHS measure of job creation is vis-à-vis the match with the theoretical model. Therefore we handle this variable in the same way that we handle the DHS measure of job creation. That is, we construct a proxy for job accession that for each industry is the job accession rate multiplied by the industry's share of manufacturing employment relative to the average accession rate in manufacturing.

Both sets of turnover data are reported at the two-digit and four-digit SIC level (based on the 1972 revision to SIC codes). However, the DHS data encompasses 447 four-digit industries per year, while the BLS data covers only 106 such industries. The DHS data is available for the years 1973–86, while the BLS data is available for the years 1978–81.

In order to look for a correlation between job turnover and trade patterns, we combine the DHS and BLS data sets with data on U.S. trade that was compiled by Robert Feenstra and made available from the National Bureau of Economic Research.[24] To control for a variety of industry-specific characteristics that could be associated with both job destruction and trade patterns, we also use data from the NBER Manufacturing Productivity Database.[25]

5. FIRST IMPRESSIONS

In order to explore the possible connection between labor market turnover and trade patterns, we must first choose a way to measure the degree to which an industry is engaged in international trade. To this end, we represent our measure of net exports in industry i at time t by $T_{i,t}$ and calculate it as

[23] See Davis and Haltiwanger (1998) for a lucid discussion of the differences between worker flows and job flows, along with a description of the available data for each.
[24] See Feenstra (1996, 1997) for a description of the trade data.
[25] This data is maintained by Eric Bartelsman, Randy Becker, and Wayne Gray and is available from the National Bureau of Economic Research. A description of this data is provided in Bartelsman and Gray (1996).

$$T_{i,t} = \frac{E_{i,t} - M_{i,t}}{Q_{i,t} + M_{i,t}} \times 100$$

(10)

where $E_{i,t}$, $M_{i,t}$, and $Q_{i,t}$ represent gross exports, imports, and production attributed to sector i during year t. This measure ranges between $+100$ (if there are no imports and if all output is exported) to -100 (if there is no domestic production and no re-export of imports).[26] The intuition following from the general equilibrium model in section 3 of this paper loosely suggests that the United States should have a comparative advantage in industries with relatively high job acquisition rates and relatively low job destruction rates.[27] Therefore, we might expect to see a positive correlation between our proxy for the job acquisition rate and the trade index, and observe a negative correlation between job destruction rates and the trade index.

Our initial findings are shown in table 7.1. In all regressions, the dependent variable is our measure of normalized net trade. The first four regressions are based upon the DHS turnover data, with the remaining four based upon the BLS turnover data. For controls, we used real capital per worker and the ratio of production workers to total employment, both of which vary by industry and by year.[28] In addition, we use a trade-weighted index of the value of the dollar, which varies by year but not by industry.[29] Since we are only interested in the signs of the turnover variables, we do not report point estimates for any of the remaining control variables or year dummies.

The results reported in table 7.1 indicate a highly significant relationship between job turnover and net trade. As expected, the point estimates for the coefficient on the break-up rate are negative, and those for the coefficients on the proxy for the job acquisition rate are always positive. Moreover, they are estimated with a high degree of precision, as indicated by very low p-values.

---

[26] The qualitative nature of our results are substantially unaffected if instead we were to use either import penetration or exports as a share of output as our dependent variable.

[27] This is only a loose interpretation since what really matters for the pattern of trade is differences in the pattern of job destruction rates *across countries*. Our data only applies to the United States, so we do not have a direct test of this hypothesis. We return to this issue in the conclusion of the paper.

[28] By including these variables, we are in no way attempting to test the factor endowment basis for trade. Indeed, it has been well known at least since Leamer's (1984) work that such regressions are not appropriate tests of that model. Our only intent is to control for some obvious factors that might be correlated with the trade index to see if we can still observe any correlation with respect to job turnover rates.

[29] The exchange rate index is from the *Economic Report of the President* and is the G-10 index.

TABLE 7.1
Baseline Regressions Relating Normalized Net Exports to Labor Market Turnover

Independent Variables	DHS Four-Digit SIC Turnover Data				BLS Four-Digit SIC Turnover Data			
	(1)	(2)	(3)	(4)	(5)	(6)	(7)	(8)
$b_{i,t}$	−0.360	−0.267	−0.415	−0.322	−3.013	−2.205	−3.023	−2.209
	(0.000)	(0.000)	(0.000)	(0.000)	(0.000)	(0.000)	(0.000)	(0.000)
$e_{i,t}$	2.941	1.853	2.872	1.820	2.029	1.690	2.036	1.692
	(0.000)	(0.000)	(0.000)	(0.000)	(0.000)	(0.002)	(0.000)	(0.002)
Controls	No	Yes	No	Yes	No	Yes	No	Yes
Year dummies	No	No	Yes	Yes	No	No	Yes	Yes
R^2	0.0424	0.1300	0.0737	0.1499	0.2360	0.2819	0.2375	0.2827
N	6258	6258	6258	6258	530	530	530	530

The dependent variable is $T_{i,t}$, normalized net exports. Estimated coefficients are in the body of the table, with p-values in parentheses.

In terms of magnitude, the point estimates suggest that the elasticity of the absolute value of the trade index with respect to b ranges from -0.34 to -0.53 based upon the DHS data, and -0.97 to -1.33 when based upon the BLS data. The comparable ranges for the elasticity of the absolute value of T with respect to e are much smaller, ranging from 0.04 to 0.07 when based upon the DHS data, and 0.18 to 0.22 using the BLS data.[30]

While the turnover variables are exogenous in the theoretical formulation of the simple model, it might be reasonable to suppose that they would be endogenous in a more elaborate model.[31] Moreover, there are clearly some important variables missing from our regression analysis, the most obvious being turnover rates in the rest of the world. To the extent that these rates are highly correlated with U.S. turnover rates, we would expect our coefficients to be biased toward zero.[32] In order to handle these issues, it would be desirable to instrument for turnover. The problem in this case is that all known correlates of turnover are also variables that presumably have some impact on trade. We attempt to circumvent this problem by using $b_{i,t-1}$, $b_{i,t-2}$, $e_{i,t-1}$, and $e_{i,t-2}$ to instrument for $b_{i,t}$ and $e_{i,t}$.[33] We report the outcome from the resulting two-stage least-squares regressions in table 7.2. Clearly, the qualitative results are unchanged, with all of the point estimates being of the proper sign and the coefficients being precisely measured. We note also that the magnitudes of the point estimates are larger in these regressions, a result that we might have suspected due to the nature of the unobserved variables.

6. Which Way Does It Go?

As we observed in sections 2 and 3 of this paper, using only U.S. data severely limits our ability to address the issue of causality. In the partial equilibrium model, the relationship between trade and turnover depends upon the origin of the shocks that cause the turnover. In the general

[30] We evaluated all elasticities at the mean value of the data. The mean value of |T| is 8.7 in the DHS data and 8.4 in the BLS data. The mean value of b is 11.1 in the DHS data and 3.7 in the BLS data. The mean value of e is 0.2 in the DHS data and 0.9 in the BLS data.

[31] Even in a more elaborate model, however, one would imagine that some element of turnover would remain exogenous. For example, we typically assume that production technology is exogenous. In the case of turnover, we might assume that there exists a matching technology and that this technology is exogenous, even if the particular point along the function is endogenous.

[32] In the most extreme case, turnover rates would not be an independent source of comparative advantage if industry-specific turnover rates were the same in all countries.

[33] We thank both Richard Disney and an anonymous referee for this suggestion.

TABLE 7.2
Two-Stage Least-Squares Regressions Relating Normalized Net Exports to Turnover

Independent Variables	DHS Four-Digit SIC Turnover Data				BLS Four-Digit SIC Turnover Data			
	(1)	(2)	(3)	(4)	(5)	(6)	(7)	(8)
$b_{i,t}$	-1.678 (0.000)	-1.220 (0.000)	-1.591 (0.000)	-1.278 (0.000)	-3.531 (0.000)	-2.856 (0.000)	-3.535 (0.000)	-2.867 (0.000)
$e_{i,t}$	3.832 (0.000)	2.554 (0.000)	3.814 (0.000)	2.661 (0.000)	2.439 (0.001)	2.136 (0.005)	2.441 (0.001)	2.142 (0.005)
Controls	No	Yes	No	Yes	No	Yes	No	Yes
Year dummies	No	No	Yes	Yes	No	No	Yes	Yes
2SLS	Yes	Yes	Yes	Yes	Yes	Yes	Yes	Yes
N	5364	5364	5364	5364	318	318	318	318

The dependent variable in the second stage regression is $T_{i,t}$, normalized net exports. Estimated coefficients from the second stage are in the body of the table, with p-values in parentheses. One-period and two-period lags of $b_{i,t}$ and $e_{i,t}$ were used as instruments in the first stage.

equilibrium model, the pattern of trade cannot genuinely be predicted without reference to turnover rates in all trading partners, an issue to which we return in the next section of the paper. For now, however, we undertake three separate analyses, the results of which appear to be more consistent with the direction of causality running from turnover to trade, rather than the reverse.

Our first analysis is based on the idea that the general equilibrium model runs off of forward-looking agents doing what is in their own self-interest. Agents base their decisions on long-run characteristics of sectors, not transitory shocks. By contrast, the partial equilibrium model is all about the effect of trade shocks on changes in turnover rates. The implication is that if we regress net trade on average values of turnover ($\bar{b}$ and $\bar{e}$) and their (percent) deviation from the average (Δb and Δe), the point estimates for the coefficients of $\bar{b}$ should be negative and $\bar{e}$ should be positive if the general equilibrium interpretation (turnover causes trade) holds sway, while the point estimates of the coefficients of Δb should be negative and those of Δe positive if the partial equilibrium interpretation (trade causes turnover) is more important.[34]

We report the results of this analysis in table 7.3. The estimated coefficients of $\bar{b}$ and $\bar{e}$ all have the right sign under the general equilibrium interpretation and are precisely measured. The estimated coefficient for Δb is negative, as would be expected under the partial equilibrium interpretation, but standard errors are so large that it is not reasonable to reject the null hypothesis that the true value of the coefficient is zero. The estimates for the coefficient of Δe have the expected sign when the DHS turnover data is used, and they are marginally significant as long as we do not include year dummies. However, the point estimates using the BLS turnover data have the wrong sign. Fortunately, in this case, it is not reasonable to reject the hypothesis that the true coefficient is zero.

Our second approach is closely related to the first. Here, we take advantage of the fact that we have panel data and employ an industry fixed-effects estimation. It is easy to think of unobserved factors that vary by industry, including trade barriers, workforce demographics, geographic dispersion of production facilities, rate of technological change, number of foreign competitors, degree of product differentiation, returns to scale, and so on. Some of these factors are unlikely to change dramatically over a relatively short time, and these are the factors intended to be captured with the fixed-effects approach.

What should we expect of this approach? As we already observed, if the general equilibrium story is correct, implying that forward-looking

---

[34] We thank David Hummels for suggesting this approach.

TABLE 7.3
Average Labor Market Turnover, Deviations from Average, and Trade

Independent Variables	DHS Four-Digit SIC Turnover Data				BLS Four-Digit SIC Turnover Data			
	(1)	(2)	(3)	(4)	(5)	(6)	(7)	(8)
$\bar{b}_i$	−1.393	−1.144	−1.393	−1.126	−3.314	−2.572	−3.314	−2.573
	(0.000)	(0.000)	(0.000)	(0.000)	(0.000)	(0.000)	(0.000)	(0.000)
$\Delta b_{i,t}$	−0.003	−0.001	−0.002	−0.003	−0.003	−0.004	−0.005	−0.006
	(0.332)	(0.789)	(0.574)	(0.310)	(0.917)	(0.905)	(0.884)	(0.855)
$\bar{e}_i$	3.803	2.496	3.803	2.511	2.218	1.906	2.218	1.906
	(0.000)	(0.000)	(0.000)	(0.000)	(0.000)	(0.001)	(0.000)	(0.001)
$\Delta e_{i,t}$	0.007	0.006	0.003	0.004	−0.016	−0.013	−0.014	−0.011
	(0.058)	(0.085)	(0.410)	(0.293)	(0.652)	(0.712)	(0.702)	(0.751)
Controls	No	Yes	No	Yes	No	Yes	No	Yes
Year dummies	No	No	Yes	Yes	No	No	Yes	Yes
R^2	0.1329	0.1818	0.1604	0.1955	0.2591	0.2943	0.2600	0.2948
N	6258	6258	6258	6258	530	530	530	530

The dependent variable is $T_{i,t}$, normalized net exports. Estimated coefficients are in the body of the table, with p-values in parentheses.

agents make decisions based on long-run turnover rates, then temporary deviations of the turnover rates from their long-run averages should not influence trade patterns. By contrast, if the partial equilibrium approach is correct, trade shocks should cause turnover rates to deviate from their long-run averages. The fixed-effects estimation de-trends both the dependent and independent variables, leaving only deviations from the average. Therefore, we would expect that we could not reject the hypothesis of zero effect of turnover on trade if the general equilibrium hypothesis is correct, but we would see statistically significant results with break-up rates having a negative impact and job acquisition rates a positive impact on net exports.

The results of our fixed-effects estimation are shown in table 7.4. In all cases, it is not reasonable to reject the hypothesis that the true coefficient of the job acquisition rate is zero. However, the point estimate for the co-efficient on the break-up rate is negative in all cases and highly significant in three of the four cases based on DHS data. The evidence provided by these regressions is therefore mixed.

Our third approach exploits the intuition that trade shocks in the par-tial equilibrium framework ought to have an asymmetric impact on break-up rates and acquisition rates.[35] In particular, a trade shock that causes an industry to have a high break-up rate should also cause that same industry to have a low acquisition rate, and vice versa. If we only look at industries where both turnover rates are high or where both are low, we ought to find no correlation with trade if the partial equilibrium framework is dominant.

To implement this approach, we created a series of indicator variables that took on a value of 1 if the observation had *both* a low break-up rate *and* a low acquisition rate, *or* a high break-up rate *and* a high acquisition rate. We then interacted these indicator variables with the break-up and acquisition rates. The partial effect of b on T for observations where both b and e are either in the top or bottom 10% of their respective distribu-tions would then be found by summing the estimated coefficients on the relevant interaction terms with the estimated coefficient on b. Our results are reported in tables 7.5 and 7.6.

The key findings are in table 7.6. While the sum of the relevant coeffi-cients is rarely statistically significant when considering the impact of job acquisitions on trade, the sum of the relevant coefficients on job destruc-tion are almost always negative and statistically significant regardless of how far into the tails of the distribution we look. The one exception con-cerns the most extreme values of turnover using the BLS data (where b and e are both in the upper or lower 10 percent of their respective distribution).

---

[35] We thank John McLaren for suggesting this insight.

TABLE 7.4
Regressions Controlling for Sector-Specific Fixed Effects

Independent Variables	DHS Four-Digit SIC Turnover Data				BLS Four-Digit SIC Turnover Data			
	(1)	(2)	(3)	(4)	(5)	(6)	(7)	(8)
$b_{i,t}$	−0.053	−0.011	−0.036	−0.040	−0.069	−0.278	−0.050	−0.301
	(0.000)	(0.261)	(0.000)	(0.000)	(0.674)	(0.124)	(0.763)	(0.110)
$e_{i,t}$	0.343	0.649	0.524	0.617	−0.870	−0.762	−0.894	−0.750
	(0.486)	(0.156)	(0.228)	(0.156)	(0.199)	(0.259)	(0.183)	(0.266)
Controls	No	Yes	No	Yes	No	Yes	No	Yes
Year dummies	No	No	Yes	Yes	No	No	Yes	Yes
Sector fixed Effects	Yes	Yes	Yes	Yes	Yes	Yes	Yes	Yes
R^2	0.0422	0.0238	0.0375	0.0057	0.0086	0.0061	0.0058	0.0025
N	6258	6258	6258	6258	530	530	530	530

The dependent variable is $T_{i,t}$, normalized net exports. Estimated coefficients are in the body of the table, with p-values in parentheses.

TABLE 7.5
Intermediate Regression Results Used in Constructing Table 6

Independent Variables	DHS Four-Digit SIC Turnover Data				BLS Four-Digit SIC Turnover Data			
	(1)	(2)	(3)	(4)	(5)	(6)	(7)	(8)
$b_{i,t}$	-0.378 (0.000)	-0.300 (0.000)	-0.429 (0.000)	-0.347 (0.000)	-3.733 (0.000)	-3.005 (0.000)	-3.758 (0.000)	-3.029 (0.000)
$I(10)_{i,t} \times b_{i,t}$	-0.169 (0.352)	-0.111 (0.523)	-0.106 (0.554)	-0.063 (0.712)	2.346 (0.032)	2.381 (0.026)	2.321 (0.035)	2.374 (0.027)
$I(20)_{i,t} \times b_{i,t}$	0.121 (0.222)	0.171 (0.071)	0.098 (0.317)	0.151 (0.108)	1.431 (0.036)	1.524 (0.024)	1.483 (0.031)	1.547 (0.023)
$I(33)_{i,t} \times b_{i,t}$	0.067 (0.268)	0.058 (0.321)	0.068 (0.260)	0.060 (0.298)	-0.519 (0.359)	-0.747 (0.177)	-0.496 (0.382)	-0.721 (0.194)
$I(50)_{i,t} \times b_{i,t}$	0.037 (0.345)	0.032 (0.392)	0.022 (0.577)	0.021 (0.568)	0.717 (0.081)	0.634 (0.115)	0.744 (0.071)	0.638 (0.114)
$e_{i,t}$	3.273 (0.000)	1.281 (0.038)	3.176 (0.000)	1.266 (0.038)	2.111 (0.005)	1.515 (0.041)	2.182 (0.004)	1.556 (0.037)

	(1)	(2)	(3)	(4)	(5)	(6)	(7)	(8)
$I(10)_{i,t} \times e_{i,t}$	1.813	0.524	−0.002	−0.750	−4.103	−4.402	−3.868	−4.303
	(0.669)	(0.897)	(1.000)	(0.852)	(0.198)	(0.156)	(0.227)	(0.167)
$I(20)_{i,t} \times e_{i,t}$	−1.249	−1.348	−0.953	−0.973	−0.286	−0.406	−0.540	−0.533
	(0.679)	(0.639)	(0.749)	(0.733)	(0.905)	(0.862)	(0.822)	(0.821)
$I(33)_{i,t} \times e_{i,t}$	−0.930	0.255	−0.903	0.244	1.659	2.171	1.674	2.137
	(0.631)	(0.890)	(0.636)	(0.894)	(0.443)	(0.303)	(0.440)	(0.312)
$I(50)_{i,t} \times e_{i,t}$	−1.118	0.221	−0.824	0.316	−3.454	−2.869	−3.606	−2.920
	(0.376)	(0.855)	(0.508)	(0.792)	(0.036)	(0.076)	(0.030)	(0.072)
Controls	No	Yes	No	Yes	No	Yes	No	Yes
Year dummies	No	No	Yes	Yes	No	No	Yes	Yes
R^2	0.0442	0.0893	0.0355	0.1527	0.3086	0.3502	0.3119	0.3512
N	6258	3080	3080	6258	530	530	530	530

The dependent variable is $T_{i,t}$, normalized net exports. Estimated coefficients are in the body of the table, with p-values in parentheses. The variable $I(z)_{i,t}$ equals 1 if $b_{i,t}$ and $e_{i,t}$ both lie in the lower or upper $z\%$ of their respective distributions, zero otherwise.

TABLE 7.6
High (Low) Job Destruction Combined with High (Low) Job Creation and Net Exports

Coefficients	DHS Four-Digit SIC Turnover Data				BLS Four-Digit SIC Turnover Data			
	(1)	(2)	(3)	(4)	(5)	(6)	(7)	(8)
β_{100}	−0.378 (0.000)	−0.300 (0.000)	−0.429 (0.000)	−0.347 (0.000)	−3.733 (0.000)	−3.005 (0.000)	−3.758 (0.000)	−3.029 (0.000)
$\beta_{100} + \beta_{50}$	−0.341 (0.000)	−0.268 (0.000)	−0.407 (0.000)	−0.326 (0.000)	−3.005 (0.000)	−2.371 (0.000)	−3.014 (0.000)	−2.391 (0.000)
$\beta_{100} + \beta_{50} + \beta_{33}$	−0.274 (0.000)	−0.211 (0.000)	−0.34 (0.000)	−0.266 (0.000)	−3.524 (0.000)	−3.118 (0.000)	−3.51 (0.000)	−3.112 (0.000)
$\beta_{100} + \beta_{50} + \beta_{33} + \beta_{20}$	−0.153 (0.087)	−0.04 (0.642)	−0.242 (0.067)	−0.115 (0.177)	−2.093 (0.002)	−1.594 (0.004)	−2.027 (0.000)	−1.565 (0.005)
$\beta_{100} + \beta_{50} + \beta_{33} + \beta_{20} + \beta_{10}$	−0.322 (0.047)	−0.15 (0.330)	−0.347 (0.029)	−0.178 (0.243)	0.242 (0.795)	0.787 (0.410)	0.294 (0.674)	0.809 (0.399)

γ_{100}	3.273	1.281	3.176	1.266	2.111	1.515	2.182	1.556
	(0.000)	(0.038)	(0.000)	(0.038)	(0.005)	(0.041)	(0.004)	(0.037)
$\gamma_{100} + \gamma_{50}$	5.086	1.805	2.352	4.426	-1.343	-1.354	-1.424	-1.365
	(0.054)	(0.160)	(0.033)	(0.136)	(0.373)	(0.358)	(0.347)	(0.356)
$\gamma_{100} + \gamma_{50} + \gamma_{33}$	3.837	0.457	1.449	4.67	0.316	0.816	0.25	0.772
	(0.437)	(0.244)	(0.353)	(0.222)	(0.839)	(0.595)	(0.873)	(0.616)
$\gamma_{100} + \gamma_{50} + \gamma_{33} + \gamma_{20}$	2.907	0.712	0.496	3.697	0.03	0.41	-0.29	0.239
	(0.993)	(0.867)	(0.845)	(0.725)	(0.987)	(0.815)	(0.873)	(0.893)
$\gamma_{100} + \gamma_{50} + \gamma_{33} + \gamma_{20} + \gamma_{10}$	1.789	0.933	0.494	0.103	-4.072	-3.991	-4.158	-4.063
	(0.597)	(0.772)	(0.882)	(0.974)	(0.122)	(0.119)	(0.115)	(0.114)
Controls	No	Yes	No	Yes	No	Yes	No	Yes
Year dummies	No	No	Yes	Yes	No	No	Yes	Yes
R^2	0.0442	0.0893	0.0355	0.1527	0.3086	0.3502	0.3119	0.3512
N	6258	3080	3080	6258	530	530	530	530

The dependent variable is $T_{i,t}$, normalized net exports. The sum of estimated coefficients are in the body of the table, with p-values in parentheses. The coefficient β_{100} is the coefficient of $b_{i,t}$, β_{10} is the coefficient of $I(10)_{i,t} \times b_{i,t}$, and so on. Analogously, γ_{100} is the coefficient of $e_{i,t}$, and so on.

In this latter case, we cannot reject the hypothesis that there is no effect of turnover on trade.

7. ADDITIONAL EVIDENCE

The three tests discussed in the previous section are informative, but certainly not conclusive. An airtight test of either the partial equilibrium or the general equilibrium model absolutely requires data from multiple countries. In the case of the partial equilibrium model, we get the expected correlations between import penetration or import prices and worker displacement only if shocks originate in the Foreign country, which is an implicitly maintained assumption of the analysis.[36] In the case of the general equilibrium model, comparative advantage depends on differences between countries. Suppose, for example, that sector 1 has a higher break-up rate than sector 2 in all countries. Since *some* country has to be a net exporter of good 1, there has to be at least one country that has a comparative advantage in the high turnover good, and data for that country would show a *positive* correlation between net exports and the break-up rate. We could add another assumption to the general equilibrium model to allow us to infer that for the United States the correlation is negative (as observed in the data), but we would be subject to the charge of ex-post theorizing.[37]

Fortunately, we can start to address this issue head on. In their cross-country comparison of job turnover, Baldwin, Dunne, and Haltiwanger (1998) report average job creation and job destruction rates over the period 1994–92 for 19 two-digit SIC industries in the United States and Canada.[38] We can combine this data with data on bilateral trade between the United States and Canada to more closely approximate a true test of the underlying theory. Roughly speaking, the theory suggests that U.S. exports to Canada should be highest in industries where U.S. job destruction rates are lowest relative to Canadian job destruction rates.[39] More specifically, we define the index

---

[36] Of course, if the shocks originate in the Foreign country, then analysis of the Foreign data ought to show the opposite correlations between import share and worker displacement.

[37] For example, if the rank order of break-up rates is the same in all countries, but the dispersion is higher in the United States, then (abstracting from differences in acquisition rates) it is easy to show that the United States will have the comparative advantage in industries characterized by the lowest break-up rates.

[38] The data is reported in their table 7.2. The reason that there are only 19 industries is that they combine industries 38 (instruments) and 39 (miscellaneous products). They note in a footnote that there are slight discrepancies in industry definitions across countries.

[39] Without appropriate data to weight values of job creation, it is not possible to construct a proxy for job acquisition and therefore we cannot use a comparison of U.S. and Canadian job creation data in our analysis.

$$TC_{it} = \frac{EC_{it} - MC_{it}}{X_{it} + M_{it}} \times 100 \qquad (11)$$

where for industry i in year t, EC_{it} represents U.S. exports to Canada and MC_{it} represents U.S. imports from Canada. This is simply net exports to Canada normalized by the total amount of trade (between the United States and all countries) associated with industry i in year t. The theory suggests that this index should be negatively correlated with the ratio of the industry-specific averages of U.S. job destruction relative to Canadian job destruction rates.

We regressed TC_{it} against the ratio of job destruction rates for 19 two-digit SIC industries for the years 1974–94, providing a total of 399 observations. As is evident from figure 7.3, there is indeed a negative relationship between (normalized) net exports from the United States to Canada and the ratio of job destruction rates. The estimated slope coefficient in this figure is highly statistically significant, with a p-value of 0.000 and the regression line fits the data well as suggested by $R^2 = 0.30$. While this result is certainly based on a very limited data set, we find it encouraging that it is consistent with our prior beliefs.

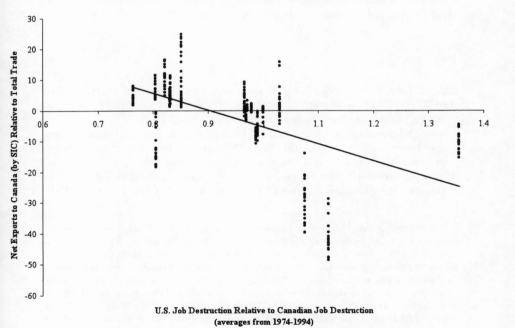

Figure 7.3. Correlating U.S.-Canada trade with cross-country differences in labor market tunover.

8. Conclusion

There are sound theoretical reasons to believe that labor market turnover is linked to international trade, though competing theories offer different mechanisms. In point of fact, these theories are not mutually exclusive, and a more encompassing model that nests the two would likely suggest that external shocks impinge on domestic labor market turnover while cross-country differences in the fundamental determinants of labor market turnover contribute to the determination of the pattern of comparative advantage.

The evidence that we report in this paper, based on two different sources of data for labor market turnover, points to a very strong negative correlation between net exports and rates of job loss. There is also some evidence that job acquisition rates are positively correlated with net exports, but that evidence is weaker, perhaps due to the relatively imperfect measure that we have for job acquisition rates.

Taken in its entirety, we believe that the evidence presented in this paper provides sufficient grounds to encourage further research using alternative data and a sample of different countries to determine the pervasiveness and robustness of this empirical finding.[40]

References

Abowd, John, Patrick Corbel, and Francis Kramarz. 1999. "The Entry and Exit of Workers and the Growth of Employment: An Analysis of French Establishments," *Review of Economics and Statistics* 81(2): 170–87.

Abowd, John and Orley Ashenfelter. 1981. "Anticipated Unemployment, Temporary Layoffs, and Compensating Wage Differentials. In S. Rosen (ed.), *Studies in Labor Markets*. Chicago: University of Chicago Press.

Albaek, Karsten and Bent Sorensen. 1998. "Worker Flows and Job Flows in Danish Manufacturing, 1980–91," *Economic Journal* 108(451): 1750–71.

---

[40] In a separate paper, written with Christopher Magee, we find empirical support for another result implied by the structural model presented in our 1999 paper. Namely, we show theoretically that the impact of trade on the welfare of factors of production that are employed in a particular sector depends on the rates of labor market turnover associated with that sector. At one extreme, with no turnover, the model behaves identically to a Ricardo-Viner specific-factors model. At the other extreme, with infinite turnover, the model behaves identically to a Heckscher-Ohlin model with Stolper-Samuelson effects. More generally, the impact of trade on worker welfare is a weighted average of the two effects, with the relative weight given to each determined by the degree of turnover. We find substantial support for this relationship using data on political contributions to Congress, Congressional voting patterns, and job destruction. See Magee, Davidson, and Matusz (2003).

Baldwin, John, Timothy Dunne, and John Haltiwanger. 1998. "A Comparison of Job Creation and Job Destruction in Canada and the United States," *The Review of Economics and Statistics* 80(3): 347–56.

Baldwin, Robert and Christopher Magee. 2000. *Congressional Trade Votes: From NAFTA Approval to Fast-Track Defeat.* Washington, DC: Institute for International Economics.

Bartelsman, Eric J. and Wayne Gray. 1996. "The NBER Manufacturing Productivity Database," NBER Technical Working Paper 205.

Bhagwati, Jagdish. 1998. *A Stream of Windows: Unsettling Reflections on Trade, Immigration, and Democracy.* Cambridge: MIT Press.

Bhagwati, Jagdish and Vivek Dehejia. 1994. "Freer trade and wages of the unskilled—Is Marx striking again?" In J. Bhagwati and M. H. Kosters (eds.), *Trade and Wages: Leveling Wages Down?* Washington, DC: AEI Press.

Bilsen, Valentijn and Jozef Konings. 1998. "Job Creation, Job Destruction, and Growth of Newly Established, Privatized, and State-Owned Enterprises in Transition Economies: Survey Evidence from Bulgaria, Hungary, and Romania," *Journal of Comparative Economics* 26(3): 429–45.

Blanchard, Olivier and Augustin Landier. 2001. "The Perverse Effects of Partial Labor Market Reform: Fixed Duration Contracts in France," NBER Working Paper 8219.

Blanchflower, David and Simon Burgess. 1996. "Job Creation and Job Destruction in Great Britain in the 1980's," *Industrial and Labor Relations Review* 50(1): 17–38.

Borland, Jeff. 1996. "Job Creation and Job Destruction in the Manufacturing Industry in Australia," *Economic Record* 72(216): 46–62.

Chow, Clement, Michael Fung, and Ngo Hang Yue. 1999. "Job Turnover in China: A Case Study of Shanghai's Manufacturing Enterprises," *Industrial Relations* 38(4): 482–503.

Davidson, Carl, Lawrence Martin, and Steven Matusz. 1999. "Trade and Search Generated Unemployment," *Journal of International Economics* 48(2): 271–99.

Davis, Donald. 1998. "Does European Unemployment Prop Up American Wages? National Labor Markets and Global Trade," *American Economic Review* 88(3): 478–94.

Davis, Steven and John Haltiwanger. 1992. "Gross Job Creation, Gross Job Destruction, and Employment Reallocation" *Quarterly Journal of Economics* 107(3): 819–63.

Davis, Steven and John Haltiwanger. 1998. "Measuring Gross Worker and Job Flows." In John Haltiwanger, Marilyn Manser, and Robert Topel (eds.), *Labor Statistics Measurement Issues.* Chicago: University of Chicago Press.

Davis, Steven, John Haltiwanger, and Scott Schuh. 1996. *Job Creation and Destruction.* Cambridge, MA: MIT Press.

Feenstra, Robert C. 1996. "US Imports, 1972–1994: Data and Concordances," NBER Working Paper 5515.

Feenstra, Robert C. 1997. "US Exports, 1972–1994, with State Exports and Other US Data," NBER Working Paper 5990.

Freeman, Richard. 1994. "How Labor Fares in Advanced Economies." In Richard Freeman (ed.), *Working under Different Rules*. New York: Russell Sage Foundation.

Genda, Yuji. 1998. "Job Creation and Destruction in Japan, 1991–1995," *Journal of the Japanese and International Economies* 12(1): 1–23.

Grossman, Gene. 1987. "The Employment and Wage Effects of Import Competition," *Journal of International Economic Integration* 2(1): 1–23.

Haveman, Jon D. 1998. "The Influence of Changing Trade Patterns on Displacements of Labor," *The International Trade Journal* 12(2): 259–92.

Klein, Michael W., Scott Schuh, and Robert K. Triest. 2003. "Job Creation, Job Destruction, and the Real Exchange Rate," *Journal of International Economics* 59: 239–65.

Kletzer, Lori. 1998a. "International Trade and Job Loss in US Manufacturing, 1979–91," In Susan Collins (ed.), *Imports, Exports, and the American Worker*. Washington, DC: Brookings Institution.

Kletzer, Lori. 1998b. "Increasing Foreign Competition and Job Insecurity: Are They Related?" In Paula Voos (ed.), *Proceedings of the Fiftieth Annual Meeting*. Madison, WI: Industrial Relations Research Association.

Kletzer, Lori. 2000. "Trade and Job Loss in US Manufacturing, 1979–1994," In Robert Feenstra (ed.), *The Impact of International Trade on Wages*. Chicago: University of Chicago Press.

Krugman, Paul. 1994. "Europe Jobless, America Penniless?" *Foreign Policy* 95: 19–34.

Layard, Richard, Stephen Nickell, and Richard Jackman. 1991. *Unemployment: Macroeconomic Performance and the Labour Market*. Oxford: Oxford University Press.

Leamer, Edward E. 1984. *Sources of International Comparative Advantage: Theory and Evidence*. Boston: MIT Press.

Ljungqvist, Lars and Thomas Sargent. 1998. "The European Unemployment Dilemma," *Journal of Political Economy* 106(3): 514–50.

Magee, Christopher, Carl Davidson, and Steven Matusz. 2003. "Trade, Turnover, and Tithing," GEP Research Paper 2003-38, University of Nottingham.

Revenga, Ana. 1992. "Exporting Jobs? The Impact of International Competition on Employment and Wages," *Quarterly Journal of Economics* 107(1): 255–84.

Revenga, Ana. 1997. "Employment and Wage Effects of Trade Liberalization: The Case of Mexican Manufacturing," *Journal of Labor Economics* 15(3): S20–43.

Chapter 8

TRADE, TURNOVER, AND TITHING

CHRISTOPHER S. P. MAGEE, CARL DAVIDSON,
AND STEVEN J. MATUSZ

1. INTRODUCTION

One of the main themes of international economics is that trade relationships have profound implications for the domestic distribution of income. While there is no question that a change in trade policy creates winners and losers, the identity of the winners and losers largely depends on the degree to which factors of production can move between sectors. The two polar extremes are embodied in the Heckscher-Ohlin-Samuelson (HOS) model, where factors are assumed to be perfectly mobile between sectors, and the Ricardo-Viner (RV) model (a.k.a. specific-factors model), where some factors of production are assumed to be completely immobile. One of the fundamental results of the HOS model is the Stolper-Samuelson theorem, which demonstrates that the economy's abundant factor benefits from trade liberalization, even if employed in the declining import-competing sector, and the economy's scarce factor is harmed by trade liberalization, even if employed in the expanding export sector. By contrast, analysis of the Ricardo-Viner model reveals that factors that are trapped in the import-competing sector are harmed by trade reform regardless of relative abundance, while factors fortunate enough to be tied to the export sector benefit.[1]

Attempts to test these two theories have met with limited success. Magee (1980) tested their predictions by exploiting the fact that they have different implications for lobbying activity in the United States. The Stolper-Samuelson theorem predicts that capital, an abundant factor in the United States, should gain from liberalization while low-skilled labor, a scarce factor in the United States, should lose. Consequently, low-skilled labor and capital should have polar opposite views with regard to trade policy even when both are employed in the same industry. On the other hand, if capital and labor are both tied to their sector, then the Ricardo-Viner

---

[1] The welfare impact of trade reform on mobile factors is ambiguous, depending on their preferences.

model predicts that capital and labor groups within each industry should share the same view on trade policy issues. Magee showed that lobbying behavior on the 1973 Trade Reform Act was consistent with the Stolper-Samuelson theorem in only 2 of 21 industries. The Ricardo-Viner model fared much better. In 19 industries labor and capital lobbied for the same type of trade policy. Irwin (1996) also found evidence favoring the predictions of the specific-factors model in the 1923 British election for Parliament, where the main issue was whether or not to adopt tariff protection. He concluded that the main determinants of voting behavior in each district were the industry and occupational characteristic of the county.

Other research has tended to support the Stolper-Samuelson theorem. For example, Rogowski (1987) argues that the theorem can be used to explain the lobbying coalitions that have formed in many developed countries since 1850. Beaulieu (1998, 2000) and Balistreri (1997) find support for HOS in the voting preferences of Canadians with respect to NAFTA, GATT, and the Canada-U.S. Free Trade Agreement of 1989. Scheve and Slaughter (1998) offer similar evidence based on the view of trade policy held by Americans. Finally, Beaulieu and Magee (2001) find that both the industry and the factor that PACs represented influenced the pattern of their contributions to supporters of NAFTA and GATT in the United States. The factor that the group represents appears to be more important than the industry, however, particularly for capital.[2]

The fact that the evidence is so mixed should not be too surprising. These two models embody the two most extreme assumptions that can be made about factor mobility. In reality, factors are quasi-fixed, moving between sectors in response to changes in factor rewards. Recognizing this, a number of authors in the 1970s, most notably Mayer (1974), Mussa (1974, 1978), and Neary (1978), developed models with imperfect factor mobility in which both short-run specific factors and long-run Heckscher-Ohlin labor markets are relevant for worker preferences concerning trade policy. Lobbying behavior then depends on factors that determine which time horizon is most important to each factor in each industry (e.g., time preference and age profile).

Casual observation also suggests that the two models should have difficulty explaining the movement of wages, particularly those of low-wage workers, whose labor market experience bears little resemblance to that

---

[2] Beaulieu and Magee (2001) argue that since the Magee (1980) and Irwin (1996) studies focus on votes that could have been overturned within a decade, what they are picking up is the voters' short-term concerns. In contrast, the other studies focus more broadly on overall views of trade policy that are likely to be governed by long-run concerns. They conclude, as do Leamer and Levinsohn (1995), that this group of results taken as a whole indicates that the HO model does a good job explaining the link between trade and factor rewards in the long-run while the Ricardo-Viner model is more appropriate for the short-run.

modeled in the HOS or RV settings. These workers typically cycle between periods of employment and unemployment, often finding it difficult
to obtain new jobs quickly. Moreover, these workers frequently encounter
significant adjustment costs when switching sectors due to search costs,
the costs of retraining, and the nontrivial amount of time they may spend
unemployed. This experience contrasts with a fundamental assumption
embodied in the HOS and RV models that factors are fully employed at
all times. The models developed by Mayer, Mussa, and Neary also maintain the assumption of full employment and ignore the adjustment costs
that come hand-in-hand with resource allocation.[3] Since recent papers by
Jacobson, LaLonde, and Sullivan (1993a, b), Trefler (2001), Kletzer
(2001), and Davidson and Matusz (2001) suggest that these adjustment
costs may be significant, it is important to take them into account when
assessing the link between trade and the distribution of income.

Davidson, Martin, and Matusz (1999, henceforth DMM), building on
the tradition established by Mayer, Mussa, and Neary, recently extended
the HOS model to allow for labor market turnover and showed that
many of the model's canonical results were altered. In their model, labor
and capital are treated as quasi-fixed in the sense that displaced factors
must search for new production opportunities once a job dissolves. Thus
factors face employment risk and the rate at which jobs are created and
destroyed plays a role in determining the allocation of resources. In such
a setting, any change in trade patterns creates unemployment and generates adjustment costs. The result is a more nuanced view of the link
between trade and the distribution of income.

The picture that emerges from the DMM model has features that derive
from both the HOS and RV models. In particular, when labor market
turnover is modeled, the impact of trade liberalization on factor rewards
is made up of a convex combination of Stolper-Samuelson and Ricardo-
Viner forces. Stolper-Samuelson forces dominate in sectors with high
labor market turnover, while the Ricardo-Viner forces dominate in sectors
that are characterized by low turnover. Intuitively, if jobs are difficult to
find but durable once obtained (that is, if turnover is low), then a worker's
attachment to the sector will be strong. In this case, the difficulty of finding reemployment and the durability of current employment creates an
attachment that makes workers act as if they have sector-specific skills.
On the other hand, if a sector is characterized by high turnover in the
sense that jobs are easy to find or do not last long once secured, then the
worker's attachment to that sector will be weak. In this case, the return to

---

[3] An exception is Mussa (1978), in which adjustment costs associated with changing the
stock of capital in a given sector are taken into account. Labor faces no adjustment costs
when switching sectors.

those workers will vary with trade policy as if they were perfectly mobile across sectors. One of the main conclusions of the DMM model is that the link between trade and the distribution of income should be dependent on job turnover, which varies widely across industries.[4]

In this paper, we test the link between industry turnover and trade preferences.[5] We combine data on PAC contributions with the Davis, Haltiwanger, and Schuh (1996) data on job creation and job destruction in U.S. manufacturing industries to examine how the pattern of campaign contributions varies across industries and factors of production. We use the data to undertake nonparametric tests of intuitive propositions that emerge from the Davidson, Martin, and Matusz (1999) model. Consistent with the theory, the empirical work suggests that labor market turnover plays an important role in the determination of lobbying activity aimed at influencing trade policy.

The remainder of the paper divides into three sections. The following section presents a simple model of adjustment to trade liberalization and discusses some intuitive empirical predictions. Section 3 then describes the data while section 4 reveals the empirical links between industry turnover and political preferences. The final section concludes the paper.

2. THE MODEL

Suppose that a trade liberalization agreement raises the returns to producing export goods and lowers the returns to producing import-competing goods. If a factor is permanently attached to its sector, then workers and capital in import-competing industries are harmed by the liberalization and those in exporting industries benefit. If factors are perfectly mobile, on the other hand, then the abundant factor gains while the scarce factor

---

[4] One possible way to view this result is that when the Mayer, Mussa, and Neary approach is extended to allow for employment risk the difference between the short run and long run is blurred and the link between trade and the distribution of income becomes more complex.

[5] Recent empirical work by Goldberg and Maggi (1999) estimates Grossman and Helpman's (1994) theoretical model relating industry characteristics to the cross-industry structure of tariffs. In that analysis, lobbying is an intermediate step in the chain of causation. Our focus is narrower, using observed lobbying activity to infer preferences over trade policies that are held by interest groups. As Mayer (1984) and others have shown, however, different political institutions can lead to very different political behavior for a given set of trade policy preferences. Thus, as Rodrik (1995) emphasizes, political behavior is the endogenous outcome of the interaction between underlying trade policy preferences and existing political institutions. Magee, Davidson, and Matusz (2003) show in a simple political economy model, however, that the pattern of contributions across candidates can reveal the direction of PAC trade preferences under general conditions.

loses, as the Stolper-Samuelson theorem shows. Davidson, Martin, and Matusz (1999) present a general model encompassing these two extreme cases, in which job matches between capital and labor do not last forever and new matches are difficult to find. As job matches are destroyed in import-competing industries in response to liberalization, the dislocated factors begin searching for (and eventually find) new jobs in exporting industries. Job destruction and creation rates of zero result in the specific factor model while a job creation rate approaching infinity generates the model with perfect mobility.

Assuming that the country is capital abundant, the time paths of real wages and returns to capital that emerge from the DMM analysis are illustrated in figure 8.1, in which Π_{td} (Π_{ft}) represents the tariff-distorted (free trade) price index. Liberalization results in an immediate gain for workers and capital owners in exporting industries and a loss for those in import-competing industries. In the long run, liberalization generates an increased return for capital, the abundant factor, and a loss for the scarce factor, labor. The bold line represents the time path of real factor prices for a low turnover industry while the dashed line shows the transition path for a high turnover industry. Intuitively, high turnover industries reach the new equilibrium steady state in a shorter period of time than low turnover industries.

Figure 8.1 reveals that labor initially employed in the import-competing sector (the upper left graph) is harmed by liberalization, while capital initially employed in the export sector (the lower right graph) clearly benefits. In contrast, the impact of liberalization on the real incomes of labor initially employed in the export sector and on capital originally employed in the import-competing sector is ambiguous. At first, labor employed in the export sector is better off since the real wage in this sector increases while losses do not occur until later. The situation is reversed for capital initially employed in the export sector, where the losses are up front and the gains are delayed.

Given a particular discount factor, the net impact on the real incomes of labor groups in exporting industries and capital groups in import-competing industries hinges on how fast the economy reaches the new steady state. Higher turnover rates speed the adjustment to the new steady state, shortening the time that labor initially employed in the export sector enjoys higher real incomes, and reducing the time that capital initially employed in the export sector suffers lower real incomes. For a sufficiently high turnover rate, workers in both import-competing and exporting sectors oppose trade liberalization while capital owners in both sectors support it, as in the Stolper-Samuelson theorem. For a sufficiently low turnover rate, workers and capital owners in import-competing industries oppose liberalization while factors in exporting industries support it.

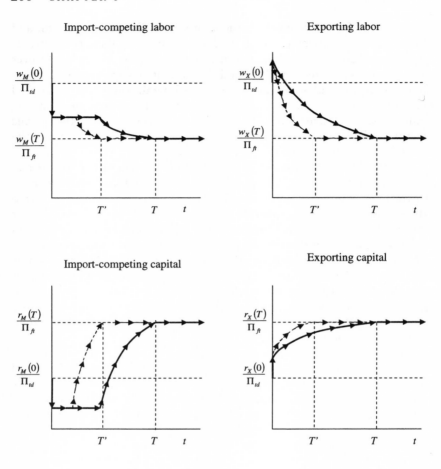

Figure 8.1. Transition paths of real factor prices in response to trade liberalization. Dashed lines represent high turnover industries; bold lines show low turnover industries.

We investigate these predictions empirically in this paper by examining the campaign contributions of political action committees. These PAC contributions reveal interest groups' trade preferences as long as the PAC cares about affecting election outcomes. In that case, interest groups favoring NAFTA give money primarily to candidates expected to vote for trade liberalization while groups against NAFTA give money to likely NAFTA opponents.

3. DATA

Table 8.1 presents the definitions, sources, and means of the variables used in the empirical tests performed in section 4 while table 8.2 provides detail on the number of PACs and average contributions classified by degree of turnover and net trade status.[6] The measure of industry turnover used in this study was compiled by Davis and Haltiwanger (1992) and Davis, Haltiwanger, and Schuh (1996). These authors calculated the change in the number of jobs lost in shrinking establishments (for job destruction) and the change in the number of jobs gained in growing establishments (job creation) relative to the employment base within the industry. The job destruction measure for sector s in time period t is

$$JD_{st} = \sum_{\substack{e \in E_{st} \\ y_{et} < y_{et-1}}} \frac{|y_{et} - y_{et-1}|}{\dfrac{Y_{st} + Y_{st-1}}{2}} \tag{1}$$

where y_{et} is employment in establishment e, Y_{st} is total employment in sector s, and E_{st} is the set of establishments in sector s at time t.[7]

While these data are referenced in the literature as measuring gross job flows, they are in fact measures of the net change in establishment size over one year. Davis and Haltiwanger (1992) discuss several different measures of job turnover based on their data on changes in establishment size. This paper uses the average job destruction rate as defined in (1) between 1988 and 1992 as the measure of industry turnover since the job destruction rate is closely tied to the notion of job security in our model, though we experiment with alternative specifications of turnover discussed in Davis and Haltiwanger in order to explore the robustness of our results.

In order to link political action committees to the industry they represent, we use a data set from the Center for Responsive Politics (CRP) that places 217 manufacturing PACs into groups of four-digit SIC industries. Using descriptions of each company and union available on the Internet, we are able to identify the two-, three-, and four-digit SIC industry affiliations of 202 other corporate and labor PACs that gave money to House members who voted on the bills enacting the NAFTA or Uruguay Round agreements. These political action committees are identified as representing either capital or labor interests based on the Federal Election Commission classification of each PAC as a corporate or labor group. In total, the data set consists of 42 labor and 377 corporate PACs.

---

[6] The data set for this paper is available at http://www.facstaff.bucknell.edu/cmagee/.
[7] The job destruction rate has a value of -2 for plant deaths. Plant births are not incorporated in this measure because it is a measure of job loss, not job gains.

TABLE 8.1
Variable Definitions, Sources, and Summary Statistics

Variable	Definition	Source	Mean	Std. Dev.	Median
Contributions to NAFTA supporters (tables 2, 3, 6, 7)	1991–92 contributions to NAFTA supporters / contributions to NAFTA supporters and opponents	Federal Election Commission	0.60	0.28	0.63
Contributions to GATT supporters (tables 2, 3, 6, 7)	1991–92 contributions to GATT supporters / contributions to GATT supporters and opponents	Federal Election Commission	0.73	0.22	0.75
Contributions to supporters of both (tables 2, 3, 6, 7)	1991–92 contributions to supporters of NAFTA and GATT / contributions to reps voting on both bills	Federal Election Commission	0.51	0.26	0.52
Contributions to NAFTA supporters (tables 4, 5)	1993–94 contributions to NAFTA supporters / contributions to NAFTA supporters and opponents	Federal Election Commission	0.57	0.28	0.49
Contributions to GATT supporters (tables 4, 5)	1993–94 contributions to GATT supporters / contributions to GATT supporters and opponents	Federal Election Commission	0.69	0.25	0.73

Variable	Description	Source			
Contributions to supporters of both (tables 4, 5)	1993–94 contributions to supporters of NAFTA and GATT / contributions to reps voting on both bills	Federal Election Commission	0.46	0.27	0.61
Turnover	Average job destruction rate in industry, 1988–92	Davis, Haltiwanger, Schuh (1996)	8.63	2.62	8.38
Capital	= 1 if PAC is corporate = 0 if labor	Federal Election Commission	0.90	0.30	1
Export industry	= 1 if PAC industry exports is greater than imports over the period 1988–92	NBER Trade Databases	0.46	0.50	1
NAFTA supporter	= 1 if representative voted for NAFTA	Congressional Quarterly Almanac	0.54	0.50	1
GATT supporter	= 1 if representative voted for GATT	Congressional Quarterly Almanac	0.67	0.47	1
Both trade bills supporter	= 1 if representative voted for NAFTA and GATT	Congressional Quarterly Almanac	0.46	0.50	0

TABLE 8.2
Average Contributions from PACs to Representatives

	Capital	Labor	Subtotal
High turnover			
Export	$57,034	$186,699	$65,678
	(70)	(5)	(75)
Import	$22,406	$110,389	$35,538
	(114)	(20)	(134)
Subtotal	$35,580	$125,651	$46,354
	(184)	(25)	(209)
Low turnover			
Export	$29,897	$145,655	$36,764
	(111)	(7)	(118)
Import	$28,794	$82,203	$34,599
	(82)	(10)	(92)
Subtotal	$29,428	$108,330	$35,816
	(193)	(17)	(210)
Grand total	$32,431	$118,640	$41,072
	(377)	(42)	(419)

The numbers of PACs in each cell are in parentheses.
Low turnover PACs are in industries with lower than the median job destruction rate.
High turnover PACs are in industries with greater than the median job destruction rate.
Export industries are those in which net exports are positive on average from 1988 to 1992.
Import-competing industries have negative net exports on average from 1988 to 1992.

Each interest group is classified as representing import-competing or exporting interests based on the net trade position of the PAC's industries of origin. The PAC net export position equals one if the industries' total exports were greater than imports over the period 1988–92, and it equals zero otherwise. Under this definition, the data set includes 226 import-competing interest groups and 193 exporting PACs. The trade flow data used to make these calculations are taken from the NBER U.S. imports and exports data sets (www.nber.org) that are described in Feenstra (1996, 1997).

The Federal Election Commission provides information on the contributions each PAC gives to every candidate in the House of Representatives. In this paper, we examine three different measures of whether the contributions were given primarily to supporters of trade liberalization. These measures are the share of contributions that were given to representatives who voted for NAFTA, the share given to candidates voting to approve the GATT Uruguay Round, and the share given to supporters of both NAFTA and the GATT bills. About 54% of representatives voted for NAFTA, 67% voted for the GATT bill, and 46% voted for both trade bills. Because the literature is divided on the issue of whether contributions are given to help elect favorable candidates or after the Congressional votes the PACs are interested in, we examine contributions both from 1991–92 (the election cycle immediately prior to the trade votes) and from 1993–94, when the votes were being cast.

4. EMPIRICAL EVIDENCE

Table 8.3 provides nonparametric evidence on the predictions of the model described in section 2. In high turnover industries, we should observe a large difference between capital and labor groups in the fraction of contributions given to NAFTA supporters. Low turnover industries should reveal a much smaller difference between capital and labor groups as the Stolper-Samuelson effects are less important. Low turnover industries, however, should reveal a much larger difference between import-competing and exporting PACs in the fraction of contributions given to NAFTA supporters. Table 8.3 presents the fraction of PAC contributions given to Congressional representatives who voted for NAFTA, for GATT, and for both bills. Lobby groups representing the interests of capital owners in low-turnover industries, for example, gave almost 61% of their contributions in 1991–92 to representatives who ultimately voted in favor of NAFTA. The table splits groups into low and high turnover PACs based on whether the turnover rate in the industries represented by the PAC was below or above the median in the data set.

The results in table 8.3 provide strong support for the model's predictions. In high turnover industries, capital groups gave a significantly larger fraction of their contributions to NAFTA supporters, to GATT supporters, and to supporters of both trade bills than did labor groups. In low turnover industries, however, the difference between capital and labor groups in their support for free traders was much smaller and insignificant by all three measures of representatives' trade policy stances.

Table 8.3 also supports the model's prediction that the industry net export position will be important in determining interest group support for trade liberalization only in low turnover industries. In low turnover industries, PACs representing exporting industries gave a significantly greater portion of their contributions to supporters of trade liberalization than did import-competing PACs. In high turnover industries, however,

TABLE 8.3
Fraction of 1991–92 PAC Contributions Given to Free Trade Proponents

	Capital	Labor	Capital–Labor Difference t-Statistic
Low turnover			
NAFTA	0.609	0.531	1.188
GATT	0.728	0.672	1.021
Both	0.515	0.456	0.929
High turnover			
NAFTA	0.636	0.307	5.726***
GATT	0.746	0.635	2.294**
Both	0.543	0.265	5.047***

	Export Industry	Import-Competing Industry	Export–Import-Competing Difference t-Statistic
Low turnover			
NAFTA	0.624	0.577	1.286*
GATT	0.748	0.692	1.867**
Both	0.531	0.484	1.339*
High turnover			
NAFTA	0.586	0.602	−0.381
GATT	0.759	0.718	1.248
Both	0.516	0.506	0.259

Difference in Differences

	High Turnover Capital–Labor Difference	Low Turnover Capital–Labor Difference	High–Low Turnover Difference t-Statistic
NAFTA	0.329	0.079	4.04***
GATT	0.111	0.056	1.07
Both	0.278	0.059	3.70***

	High Turnover Export–Import Difference	Low Turnover Export–Import Difference	High–Low Turnover Difference t-Statistic
NAFTA	−0.016	0.047	−1.60*
GATT	0.042	0.056	−0.45
Both	0.010	0.046	−0.97

Low turnover PACs are in industries with lower than the median job destruction rate. High turnover PACs are in industries with greater than the median job destruction rate. Export industries are those in which net exports are positive on average from 1988 to 1992.

Import-competing industries have negative net exports on average from 1988 to 1992.
*, **, *** Indicate that the means or differences are significantly different at the 10%, 5%, and 1% levels (respectively) in one-sided t-tests.

the difference between import-competing and exporting PACs in their contribution patterns was negligible, as the model predicts.

The hypothesis examined in this paper can be most directly tested using a difference in differences approach. The DMM model prediction is that Stolper-Samuelson forces will be stronger in industries that correspond to the assumption of perfect factor mobility. Thus, the difference between capital and labor groups' support for free trade should be larger among high turnover industries than among low turnover industries. The bottom part of table 8.3 presents this difference in differences comparison. Within high turnover industries, there is a 33 percentage point difference between capital and labor PACs' share of contributions going to NAFTA supporters, while in low turnover industries, this difference is only about 8 percentage points. The t-statistic in the final column reveals that we can reject the null hypothesis that these two differences are equal at the 1% level. The high turnover difference between capital and labor groups' support for free traders is also significantly greater than the low turnover difference using both trade bills as a measure of representatives' support for liberalization.

If specific-factors forces are strongest in low turnover industries, meanwhile, we should observe a larger difference between exporting and import-competing groups' support for free trade in low turnover sectors than in high turnover sectors. The bottom half of table 8.3 reveals some support for this hypothesis. All three difference in differences comparisons have the correct sign, and the export-import gap is significantly greater than zero using NAFTA as a measure of representatives' trade policy stance.

While table 8.3 presents results for combined data on PACs representing capital and labor, there are reasons to expect these groups to behave in different ways. For example, capital income is presumably easier to diversify than labor income and such diversification may dilute the sector-specific interests of capital owners (Feeney and Hillman, 2001).[8] To see if there are any important differences in the behavior of PACs representing the two factors and to make sure that each group independently behaves as the DMM model predicts, table 8.4 splits PACs into four categories: import-competing capital and labor groups and exporting capital and labor groups. The upper half of the table reveals that in low turnover industries, there is no significant difference between capital and labor groups (either in exporting or in import-competing industries) in their support for representatives voting in favor of trade liberalization. Using the GATT vote, however, there is a significant difference between exporting and

---

[8] DMM treat labor and capital turnover symmetrically. While a natural extension of static trade models, this is inconsistent with richer models of capital accumulation such as the putty-clay model of Phelps (1963).

TABLE 8.4
Fraction of 1991–92 PAC Contributions Given to Free Trade Proponents

		Capital	Labor	t-statistic (H_0: fraction given by capital equals fraction by labor)
Low turnover				
Net exporter	NAFTA	0.630	0.524	1.159
	GATT	0.749	0.729	0.262
	Both	0.531	0.518	0.155
Net importer	NAFTA	0.582	0.535	0.472
	GATT	0.699	0.632	0.844
	Both	0.493	0.414	0.860
t-statistic (H_0: fraction given by net exporters equals fraction by net importers)	NAFTA	1.260	−0.083	
	GATT	1.542*	1.723*	
	Both	1.048	1.024	
High turnover				
Net exporter	NAFTA	0.607	0.294	2.507***
	GATT	0.771	0.601	2.079**
	Both	0.535	0.252	2.431***
Net importer	NAFTA	0.653	0.310	5.241***
	GATT	0.731	0.643	1.426*
	Both	0.547	0.268	4.369***
t-statistic (H_0: fraction given by net exporters equals fraction by net importers)	NAFTA	−1.143	−0.106	
	GATT	1.139	−0.375	
	Both	−0.317	−0.136	

Low turnover PACs are in industries with lower than the median job destruction rate.
High turnover PACs are in industries with greater than the median job destruction rate.
Export industries are those in which net exports are positive on average from 1988 to 1992.
Import-competing industries have negative net exports on average from 1988 to 1992.
*, **, *** Indicate that the means are significantly different at the 10%, 5%, and 1% levels (respectively) in one-sided t-tests.

import-competing PACs. Both within capital PACs and within labor unions, exporters gave significantly larger shares of their contributions to representatives voting in favor of the GATT Uruguay Round.

In high turnover industries, the data reveal a very different pattern. In this case there are large and statistically significant differences between capital and labor groups, both within exporting and within import-competing industries. Capital PACs consistently favored free traders for their contributions much more strongly than labor groups did. In contrast, net exporting groups did not concentrate their contributions on free traders more highly than import-competing groups did. These results are again supportive of the idea that high turnover industries conform to the predictions of the free mobility Heckscher-Ohlin model whereas low turnover industries exhibit contribution patterns more consistent with the specific factors model.

In order to provide a robustness check on these results, table 8.5 duplicates table 8.3 using contributions made during 1993–94, when the NAFTA and GATT Uruguay Round bills were being voted on in the Congress. Notice that during this period, capital groups gave significantly larger shares of their money to NAFTA and GATT supporters than did labor groups, in both high- and low turnover industries. As the theory predicts, however, the Stolper-Samuelson forces are stronger in the high turnover industries. The difference between capital and labor in the fraction of their contributions going to free traders is greater within high turnover industries than within low turnover industries by all three measures, significantly so for the NAFTA comparison.

Comparing exporting and import-competing industries, table 8.5 tells the same story as table 8.3. For two of the three measures of representatives' positions on trade policy, low-turnover exporting PACs gave significantly greater fractions of their contributions to free traders than did low turnover import-competing PACs. Among high turnover groups, however, there was no significant difference between import-competing and exporting PACs in their contribution patterns. Although the gap between export and import-competing groups' support for free trade is larger in low turnover industries by all three measures, none of the difference in differences is significantly greater than zero.

Table 8.6 shows that the difference between exporting and import-competing PACs in their 1993–94 contribution patterns comes primarily from within capital groups. Among corporate PACs in low turnover industries, those representing exporters gave significantly greater contributions to free trade supporters (by all three measures) than did those representing import-competing interests. The difference between exporters and import-competing groups is not evident within high turnover industries, however. Examining only labor groups reveals no significant differences in the contribution patterns of exporting and import-competing PACs, for either high or low turnover industries. As in table 8.5, while there are some significant differences between capital and labor groups in low turnover industries, the Stolper-Samuelson forces emerge much more clearly within the high turnover industries.

TABLE 8.5
Fraction of 1993–94 PAC Contributions Given to Free Trade Proponents

	Capital	Labor	Capital–Labor Difference t-Statistic
Low turnover			
NAFTA	0.580	0.461	1.781**
GATT	0.709	0.614	1.630*
Both	0.477	0.291	2.975***
High turnover			
NAFTA	0.599	0.272	4.871***
GATT	0.705	0.539	2.690***
Both	0.495	0.227	4.044***

	Export Industry	Import-Competing Industry	Export–Import-Competing Difference t-Statistic
Low turnover			
NAFTA	0.586	0.550	0.963
GATT	0.738	0.653	2.655***
Both	0.497	0.416	2.322**
High turnover			
NAFTA	0.573	0.556	0.370
GATT	0.717	0.668	1.199
Both	0.501	0.444	1.237

Difference in Differences

	High Turnover Capital–Labor Difference	Low Turnover Capital–Labor Difference	High–Low Turnover Difference t-Statistic
NAFTA	0.327	0.119	3.11***
GATT	0.166	0.095	1.18
Both	0.268	0.186	1.28

	High Turnover Export–Import Difference	Low Turnover Export–Import Difference	High–Low Turnover Difference t-Statistic
NAFTA	0.017	0.036	−0.43
GATT	0.050	0.085	−0.95
Both	0.056	0.081	−0.60

Low-turnover PACs are in industries with lower than the median job destruction rate. High-turnover PACs are in industries with greater than the median job destruction rate. Export industries are those in which net exports are positive on average from 1988 to 1992.

Import-competing industries have negative net exports on average from 1988 to 1992.

*, **, *** Indicate that the means or differences are significantly different at the 10%, 5%, and 1% levels (respectively) in one-sided t-tests.

TABLE 8.6
Fraction of 1993–94 Contributions Given to Free Trade Proponents

		Capital	Labor	t-Statistic (H_0: fraction given by capital equals fraction by labor)
Low turnover industries				
Net exporter	NAFTA	0.601	0.331	2.776***
	GATT	0.739	0.718	0.257
	Both	0.508	0.306	2.098***
Net importer	NAFTA	0.552	0.539	0.133
	GATT	0.667	0.51	1.401*
	Both	0.434	0.282	1.818**
t-statistic (H_0: fraction given by net exporters equals fraction by net importers)	NAFTA	1.320*	−1.150	
	GATT	2.222**	1.143*	
	Both	2.104**	0.158	
High turnover industries				
Net exporter	NAFTA	0.597	0.201	2.890***
	GATT	0.738	0.387	3.143***
	Both	0.523	0.142	2.898***
Net importer	NAFTA	0.601	0.289	3.906***
	GATT	0.683	0.574	1.440*
	Both	0.478	0.247	2.902***
t-statistic (H_0: fraction given by net exporters equals fraction by net importers)	NAFTA	−0.094	−0.460	
	GATT	1.275	−1.350	
	Both	0.988	−0.661	

Low turnover PACs are in industries with lower than the median job destruction rate.
High turnover PACs are in industries with greater than the median job destruction rate.
Export industries are those in which net exports are positive on average from 1988 to 1992.
Import-competing industries have negative net exports on average from 1988 to 1992.
*, **, *** Indicate that the means are significantly different at the 10%, 5%, and 1% levels (respectively) in one-sided t-tests.

Table 8.7 examines the PAC contribution patterns after controlling for industry fixed effects. Since the PACs are defined to the four-digit industry level, there is variation between the turnover rates of different PACs within the same two-digit industry, and it is possible to identify the relationship between turnover and contribution patterns even after removing

TABLE 8.7
Fraction of 1991–92 PAC Contributions Given to Free Trade Proponents, Two-Digit SIC Industry Means Removed

	Capital	Labor	Capital–Labor Difference t-Statistic
Low turnover			
NAFTA	0.010	−0.069	1.213
GATT	0.002	−0.030	0.583
Both	0.006	−0.046	0.823
High turnover			
NAFTA	0.029	−0.240	4.754***
GATT	0.011	−0.076	1.867**
Both	0.024	−0.193	4.147***

	Export Industry	Import Industry	Export–Import-Competing Difference t-Statistic
Low turnover			
NAFTA	0.015	−0.011	0.714
GATT	0.008	−0.012	0.683
Both	0.012	−0.011	0.662
High turnover			
NAFTA	−0.018	0.005	−0.552
GATT	0.018	−0.009	0.865
Both	0.004	−0.006	0.271

Difference in Differences

	High Turnover Capital–Labor Difference	Low Turnover Capital–Labor Difference	High–Low Turnover Difference t-Statistic
NAFTA	0.269	0.079	3.10***
GATT	0.087	0.031	1.11
Both	0.216	0.052	2.82***

	High Turnover Export–Import Difference	Low Turnover Export–Import Difference	High–Low Turnover Difference t-Statistic
NAFTA	−0.022	0.026	−1.25
GATT	0.028	0.020	0.24
Both	0.010	0.023	−0.37

Low turnover PACs are in industries with lower than the median job destruction rate. High-turnover PACs are in industries with greater than the median job destruction rate. Export industries are those in which net exports are positive on average from 1988 to 1992.

Import-competing industries have negative net exports on average from 1988 to 1992.

*, **, *** Indicate that the means or differences are significantly different at the 10%, 5%, and 1% levels (respectively) in one-sided t-tests.

the more aggregate industry effects. The numbers in the table show the average residual from a regression of the fraction of contributions going to free trade supporters on a series of two-digit SIC industry dummy variables. Capital PACs in low turnover industries, for instance, gave about a 1 percentage point greater share of their contributions to NAFTA supporters than the average PAC in those industries, while labor groups gave about a 7 percentage point smaller share. The table shows that controlling for industry means does not alter the result that there is a larger difference between capital and labor group contribution patterns in high turnover industries than in low-turnover industries. On that score, the results are nearly identical to table 8.3. Controlling for industry fixed effects does, however, weaken the result that exporting PACs give significantly greater shares of contributions to free trade supporters in low turnover industries.

Table 8.8 investigates whether differences in support for each political party between capital and labor groups are driving the results. The first three columns of numbers in the table show the fraction of contributions going to free trade supporters among contributions to Republicans only, while the last three columns examine contributions to Democrats only. The results remain quite supportive of the hypothesis presented in this paper. Among contributions to Republicans, capital groups favored free traders more strongly than labor groups did in both high and low turnover industries. The mean difference between the two groups was consistently larger in the high turnover industries, however. Among Democrats, the results are even stronger, with large and statistically significant differences between capital and labor groups' support for free traders in high turnover industries but no significant differences between capital and labor's contribution patterns in low turnover industries.

The hypothesis that low turnover industries will exhibit a more stark difference between exporting and import-competing PACs than high turnover industries is also supported in table 8.8. In low turnover industries, exporters gave significantly greater support to free traders than did import-competing PACs using all three measures among Republican recipients and for the GATT measure among Democrats. In high turnover industries, only the GATT measure among Republicans reveals any significant difference between exporting and import-competing PAC contribution patterns.

Furthermore, the bottom half of table 8.8 reveals that the difference between capital and labor groups' support for free trade is significantly larger among high turnover industries than among low turnover industries for three of the six comparisons: NAFTA within both parties, and both trade bills within Democrats. The other three capital-labor difference in differences comparisons are correctly signed but not significantly greater

TABLE 8.8
Fraction of 1991–92 PAC Contributions Given to Free Trade Proponents, by Party

	Republicans Only			Democrats Only		
	Capital	Labor	Difference t-Statistic	Capital	Labor	Difference t-Statistic
Low turnover						
NAFTA	0.766	0.616	1.992**	0.486	0.459	0.361
GATT	0.749	0.555	2.769***	0.736	0.673	1.005
Both	0.656	0.501	1.979**	0.415	0.425	-0.142
High turnover						
NAFTA	0.812	0.503	4.991***	0.514	0.240	4.068***
GATT	0.758	0.554	3.373***	0.758	0.624	2.438***
Both	0.692	0.462	3.503***	0.452	0.200	3.765***
	Export Industry	Import Industry	Difference t-Statistic	Export Industry	Import Industry	Difference t-Statistic
Low turnover						
NAFTA	0.786	0.710	1.904**	0.482	0.487	-0.121
GATT	0.772	0.680	2.461***	0.752	0.705	1.374*
Both	0.682	0.591	2.195**	0.416	0.415	0.035

High turnover

	Republicans Only			Democrats Only		
	High Turnover	Low Turnover	High–Low Difference t-Statistic	High Turnover	Low Turnover	High–Low Difference t-Statistic
NAFTA	0.766	0.796	−0.775	0.482	0.478	0.081
GATT	0.770	0.720	1.379*	0.746	0.739	0.195
Both	0.681	0.665	0.396	0.409	0.428	−0.398

Difference in Differences

	Republicans Only			Democrats Only		
	High Turnover	Low Turnover	High–Low Difference t-Statistic	High Turnover	Low Turnover	High–Low Difference t-Statistic
	Capital–Labor Difference			Capital–Labor Difference		
NAFTA	0.309	0.150	2.30**	0.273	0.027	3.46***
GATT	0.203	0.194	0.14	0.134	0.063	1.21
Both	0.230	0.155	1.04	0.252	−0.010	3.76***
	Export–Import Difference			Export–Import Difference		
NAFTA	−0.030	0.076	−2.70***	0.004	−0.005	0.20
GATT	0.050	0.092	−1.14	0.007	0.047	−1.10
Both	0.016	0.091	−1.85**	−0.019	0.001	−0.46

Low turnover PACs are in industries with lower than the median job destruction rate.

High turnover PACs are in industries with greater than the median job destruction rate.

Export industries are those in which net exports are positive on average from 1988 to 1992.

Import-competing industries have negative net exports on average from 1988 to 1992.

*, **, *** Indicate that the means or differences are significantly different at the 10%, 5%, and 1% levels (respectively) in one-sided t-tests.

than zero. The gap between export and import-competing groups' support for free trade is significantly larger within low turnover industries than within high turnover industries for the NAFTA and both trade bill comparisons among Republicans.

A brief overview of the results in tables 8.3–8.8 illustrates the support in the data for the hypothesis from DMM examined here. In these tables there are 27 variations of the comparison between the contribution patterns of capital and labor PACs. Among the high turnover industries, capital PACs gave a significantly larger fraction (at the 10% significance level or better) of their contributions to free trade supporters than labor groups did in all 27 comparisons. Among low turnover industries, capital groups gave significantly more money to free traders in only 10 of the 27 comparisons. Examining import-competing and exporting industries provides a different story. Among high turnover industries, exporting PACs never donated a significantly larger fraction of their contributions to free traders than did import-competing PACs. Among low turnover industries, exporting groups gave significantly more support to free traders than import-competing groups in 14 of the 27 comparisons.

We also find broad support for the prediction that the difference between capital and labor groups' support for free traders will be larger in high turnover industries than in low turnover industries. This difference in differences is correctly signed in 26 of the 27 comparisons in tables 8.3–8.8, with 12 significant at the 1% level, 3 at the 5% level, and 1 at the 10% level. The data provide only slightly weaker support for the prediction that low turnover interest groups will demonstrate a larger difference between exporters and import-competing industries in their support for free traders. This difference in differences comparison is correctly signed in 24 of the 27 comparisons, with 8 significant at the 10% level or better (3 of these at the 1% level).

In previous versions of this paper we ran a variety of tests to check the robustness of the results presented in tables 8.3–8.8. For example, using alternative measures of turnover, such as the sum of job creation and job destruction or the minimum of these two variables, yields essentially the same results. We also ran regressions in which representatives' votes were treated as endogenous. These regressions incorporated measures of workers' skill levels in an industry, PAC, candidate, and industry fixed effects and controlled for representatives' party affiliation, committee membership, terms in office, and leadership positions. In each case, the results provided broad support for the hypothesis advanced in this paper. Finally, we also included a measure of the industry capital-labor ratio and interacted this variable with PAC factor and net export variables in order to make sure that the PACs were not reacting to factor intensities. As with the other robustness checks, this did not alter the results presented in tables 8.3–8.8. These alternative tests can be found in Magee, Davidson, and Matusz (2003).[9]

5. CONCLUSION

Goldberg and Maggi (1999) suggest that "factors linked to unemployment may affect protection through channels different than the ones suggested by the (Grossman and Helpman 1994) theory." Goldberg and Maggi speculate that it would be empirically rewarding to incorporate sector-specific unemployment rates into the Grossman-Helpman framework. Davidson, Martin, and Matusz (1999) provide a theoretical basis for linking industry turnover and international trade, and they show that high turnover industries will be ruled by Stolper-Samuelson forces while the specific factors model is more applicable to low turnover industries. This paper empirically examines the hypothesis that industry turnover can be used to divide interest groups into those whose trade preferences should be determined primarily by their factor of production and those whose preferences depend mainly on the industry's net export position. While both short-run specific factors and long-run Heckscher-Ohlin considerations will affect interest group trade preferences, this paper reveals that industry turnover influences the relative importance of these considerations.

We use data on campaign contributions to supporters and opponents of NAFTA and GATT in the U.S. House of Representatives to investigate the link between industry turnover and political groups' trade policy preferences. The empirical results support the predictions in Davidson, Martin, and Matusz (1999) and are quite intuitive. There is strong and robust evidence that the factor (either capital or labor) a PAC represents exerts a very large effect on the share of its contributions flowing to free trade supporters for high turnover industries but has a much smaller impact for low turnover industries. There is also evidence in favor of the hypothesis that the industry net trade position has a large impact on lobbying behavior only in low turnover industries. The empirical results strongly suggest that industry turnover affects the determinants of interest group trade preferences in an intuitive manner.

---

[9] The only exception is the results of the regression in which we interacted capital intensity with PAC factor and net export variables. These results are available from the authors upon request.

REFERENCES

Balistreri, E. 1997. The performance of the Heckscher-Ohlin-Vanek model in predicting policy forces at the individual level. *Canadian Journal of Economics* 30(1), 1–17.

Beaulieu, E. 1998. Factor or Industry Cleavages in Trade Policy? An Empirical Test of the Stolper-Samuelson Theorem. Department of Economics, University of Calgary Discussion Paper Series 98–12.

Beaulieu, E. 2000. The Stolper-Samuelson Theorem Faces Congress. University of Calgary Working Paper.

Beaulieu, E., Magee, C. 2001. Campaign Contributions and Trade Policy: New Tests of Stolper-Samuelson. University of Calgary Working Paper.

Davidson, C., Martin, L., Matusz, S. 1999. Trade and search generated unemployment. *Journal of International Economics* 48(2), 271–99.

Davidson, C., Matusz, S. 2001. On Adjustment Costs. Michigan State University Working Paper.

Davis, S., Haltiwanger, J. 1992. Gross job creation, gross job destruction, and employment reallocation. *Quarterly Journal of Economics* 107(3): 819–63.

Davis, S., Haltiwanger, J., Schuh, S. 1996. *Job Creation and Destruction*. MIT Press, Cambridge.

Feeney, J., Hillman, A. 2001. Trade Liberalization and Asset Markets. SUNY–Albany Working Paper.

Feenstra, R. 1996. NBER Trade Database, Disk 1: U.S. Imports, 1972–1994: Data and Concordances. NBER Working Paper 5515.

Feenstra, R. 1997. NBER Trade Database, Disk 3: U.S. Exports, 1972–1994, with State Exports and Other U.S. Data. NBER Working Paper 5990.

Goldberg, P., Maggi, G. 1999. Protection for sale: An empirical investigation. *The American Economic Review* 89(5): 1135–55.

Grossman, G., Helpman, E. 1994. Protection for Sale. *American Economic Review* 84(4): 833–850.

Irwin, D. 1996. Industry or class cleavages over trade policy? Evidence from the British General Election of 1923. In Feenstra, R., Grossman, G., and Irwin, D. (Eds.), *The Political Economy of Trade Policy: Papers in Honor of Jagdish Bhagwati*. MIT Press: Cambridge, pp. 53–76.

Jacobson, L., LaLonde, R., Sullivan, D. 1993a. *The Costs of Worker Dislocation*. W.E. Upjohn Institute for Employment Research, Kalamazoo, MI.

Jacobson, L., LaLonde, R., Sullivan, D. 1993b. Earnings losses of displaced workers. *American Economic Review* 83(4): 685–709.

Kletzer, L. 2001. *What Are the Costs of Job Loss from Import-Competing Industries?* Institute for International Economics, Washington, DC

Leamer, E., Levinsohn, J. 1995. International trade theory: The evidence. In Grossman, G., Rogoff, K. (Eds.), *Handbook of International Economics*, vol. 3. North-Holland, Amsterdam, pp. 1339–94.

Magee, S. 1980. Three simple tests of the Stolper-Samuelson theorem. In Oppenheimer, P. (Ed.), *Issues in International Economics*. Oriel Press, London, pp. 138–53.

Magee, C., Davidson, C., Matusz, S. 2003. Trade, Turnover, and Tithing. GEP Working Paper 2003/38, University of Nottingham.

Mayer, W. 1974. Short-run and long-run equilibrium for a small open economy. *Journal of Political Economy* 82(5): 820–31.

Mayer, W. 1984. Endogenous tariff formation. *American Economic Review* 74(5): 970–85.

Mussa, M. 1974. Tariffs and the distribution of income: The importance of factor specificity, substitutability and intensity in the short and long run. *Journal of Political Economy* 82(6): 1191–1203.

Mussa, M. 1978. Dynamic adjustment in the Heckscher-Ohlin-Samuelson model. *Journal of Political Economy* 86(5): 775–91.

Neary, P. 1978. Short-run capital specificity and the pure theory of international trade. *Economic Journal* 88(351): 488–510.

Phelps, E. 1963. Substitution, fixed proportions, growth and distribution. *International Economic Review* 4(3): 65–288.

Rodrik, D. 1995. Political economy of trade policy. In Grossman, G., Rogoff, K. (Eds.), *Handbook of International Economics*, vol. 3. North-Holland, Amsterdam, pp. 1457–94.

Rogowski, R. 1987. Political cleavages and changing exposure to trade. *American Political Science Review* 81(4): 1121–37.

Scheve, K., Slaughter, M. 1998. What determines individual trade policy preferences? NBER Working Paper 6531.

Trefler, D. 2001. The Long and the Short of the Canada-U.S. Free Trade Agreement. University of Toronto Working Paper.

PART 4

ADJUSTMENT COSTS AND POLICY ISSUES

INTRODUCTION TO PART 4

Generally, those who discuss trade liberalization acknowledge that there will be winners and losers, and it may even be the case that the losses outweigh the gains in the short run. But it is a matter of faith that the long-run benefits of freer trade dominate any short-run losses, allowing those who win from trade reform to compensate those who lose. Despite abundant empirical evidence that displaced workers suffer significant personal costs, shockingly few attempts have been made to quantify or model the aggregate costs of adjusting to trade liberalization.[1]

As we argue in chapter 6, ignoring short-run adjustments can result in misleading policy conclusions. We address this issue head on in chapter 9, where we explicitly model the adjustment costs of trade liberalization within a framework that captures the nontrivial spells of unemployment that dislocated workers endure in searching for new opportunities as well as possible time and resource costs associated with retraining. Because there are no distortions in our model, adjustment costs are necessarily less than the gains from trade when both are appropriately discounted over the infinite horizon. However, depending on our set of parameter assumptions, these costs can range from a low of 10% to a high of 80% of the gains from trade.

We take a slightly different approach to the issue in chapter 10, where we consider appropriate policies when labor markets are characterized by congestion externalities. We cast the model in an overlapping-generations framework with search-generated unemployment. Using this framework, we map out the adjustment path when the terms of trade unexpectedly improve. We show that the welfare impact is uneven across generations, illustrate the possibility of multiple equilibria, and highlight the way in which a temporary policy (such as escape clause protection) can steer the economy to the equilibrium with the highest welfare.

---

[1] See Jacobson, LaLonde, and Sullivan (1993) or Kletzer (2001) for estimates of the personal cost of dislocation. Magee (1972) was the first to try to quantify the aggregate costs of adjustment. Baldwin, Mutti, and Richardson (1980) also attempted to model and quantify adjustment costs. Most recently, Trefler (2004) empirically measured the adjustment costs borne by Canadian workers and firms subsequent to the adoption of the Canada-U.S. Free Trade Agreement.

In chapter 11, we turn to the important issue of how best to design policies aimed at compensating workers for the losses that they may suffer due to liberalization. While much is known about how to use taxes and subsidies on goods to effectuate a Pareto gain from trade liberalization, such policies have highly demanding informational requirements and are impractical to implement.[2] Our intent in this chapter is to show how simple labor market policies can be used to offset the adjustment costs of liberalization. We consider policies that are widely used in practice as well as policies that have been used sparingly or not at all, but have been suggested as a possible remedy for compensating workers who bear the brunt of adjustment. Extended unemployment compensation and modest retraining subsidies (under the guise of trade adjustment assistance) fall into the former category, while employment subsidies (sometimes referenced as reemployment bonuses) and wage subsidies fall into the latter category.[3] We consider four policies in particular: unemployment compensation, training subsidies, wage subsidies, and employment subsidies. Our framework is well suited to comparing these various policies since we can easily account for equilibrium unemployment and training costs.

In our analysis, we divide those who lose into two categories: displaced workers and those who are trapped in the import-competing sector. Each of the policies that we consider generates its own distortion, so we show which policy generates the smallest distortion given the goal of compensating a particular group of workers. In the context of the model, we show that wage subsidies create the smallest distortion when the goal is to fully compensate displaced workers, and employment subsidies create the smallest distortion when the goal is to fully compensate those who remain trapped in the import-competing sector. We conclude the chapter by arguing that the likely cost of offering compensation is small compared with the aggregate gain from trade.

We close this part of the book with chapter 12, co-authored with Doug Nelson, where we present a political-economy model of trade policy to ask if offering compensation of the form described in chapter 11 makes trade liberalization more likely or less likely. We also ask whether voters will choose the efficient policy (as detailed in chapter 11) if they choose to compensate. The bottom line is that compensation expands the parameter space where a majority would prefer free trade to protected trade. However, a small twist appears in the form of a parameter space where the majority would have preferred free trade to protected trade in

---

[2] See, for example, Dixit and Norman (1980) and Kemp and Wan (1986).
[3] Kletzer and Litan (2001) make the case for wage subsidies while a reemployment bonus program was part of President Clinton's 1996 Workforce Reinvestment Act.

the absence of compensation, and this preference remains when compensation is on the table. The difference is that the ultimate equilibrium will have compensated free trade. The wage subsidy, which is less distorting than the employment subsidy, is chosen as the preferred form of compensation. The distortion due to compensation is minimized by the choice of a wage subsidy but, because it is still positive, the political equilibrium results in lower aggregate welfare than uncompensated liberalization.

References

Baldwin, R., Mutti, J., Richardson, D. 1980. Welfare effects on the United States of a significant multilateral tariff reduction. *Journal of International Economics* 10(3): 405–23.

Dixit, A., Norman, V. 1980. *Theory of International Trade: A Dual General-Equilibrium Approach*. Cambridge: Cambridge University Press.

Jacobsen, L., LaLonde, R., Sullivan, D. 1993. Earnings losses of displaced workers. *American Economic Review* 83(4): 685–709.

Kemp, M., Wan, H. 1986. Gains from trade with and without compensation. *Journal of International Economics* 21(1–2): 99–110.

Kletzer, L. 2001. *What Are the Costs of Job Loss from Import-Competing Industry?* Washington, DC: Institute for International Economics.

Kletzer, L., Litan, R. 2001. A prescription to relieve worker anxiety. Policy Brief No. 73, Brookings Institution.

Magee, S. 1972. The welfare effects of restrictions on U.S. trade. *Brookings Papers on Economic Activity* 3(3): 645–701.

Trefler, D. 2004. The long and the short of the Canada-U.S. Free Trade Agreement. *American Economic Review* 94(4): 870–95.

Chapter 9

SHOULD POLICY MAKERS BE CONCERNED ABOUT ADJUSTMENT COSTS?

CARL DAVIDSON AND STEVEN J. MATUSZ

1. INTRODUCTION

E ven the most strident advocates of free trade would readily admit that it takes time for economies to reap the benefits from trade liberalization. As trade patterns change, some workers lose their jobs and must seek reemployment in expanding sectors. There may be some cases in which these workers need to retool in order to find new jobs. Of course, these workers do not produce any output while they search for reemployment and/or retrain. As a result, during the adjustment process, there may be a period during which welfare falls below its initial level. Policy makers often have a difficult time weighing these short-run adjustment costs against the long-run benefits from freer trade and this has made some countries reluctant to reduce barriers to trade. Growing concern about the importance of the adjustment process in the policy community is evident, as recent studies commissioned by the World Bank (Brahmbhatt 1997) and the WTO (Bacchetta and Jansen 2003) clearly indicate. Beyond concerns for equity, a full understanding of the magnitude and scope of adjustment can inform our views of the political economy of protectionism. In this paper, we investigate the nature of the adjustment process and try and get some handle on the magnitude of the costs involved in order to determine whether such concerns are warranted.

Recent research suggests that the *personal* cost of worker dislocation may be quite high. Jacobson, LaLonde, and Sullivan (1993a, b) find that the average dislocated worker suffers a loss in lifetime earnings of $80,000. Yet, as disturbing as this finding may be, it tells us nothing about the *aggregate* costs of adjustment. It is quite possible for individual workers to lose a great deal while at the same time the economy is suffering only minor aggregate adjustment costs. Nevertheless, those who oppose trade liberalization often point to such personal losses, along with wage losses to those who remain employed in import-competing industries, and ask whether the gains from freer trade are really worth such costs. Academic economists tend to dismiss such concerns by either suggesting that the aggregate costs of adjustment are probably very small compared to the gains from trade or by pointing out that the gains from trade are always large enough that we can fully compensate all those who suffer personal losses without exhausting the gains. Unfortunately, there are problems with both of these arguments. The latter argument ignores the fact that such compensation rarely, if ever, takes place. And the problem with the former argument is that there is almost no solid research on which to base such claims. That is, we know very little about the magnitude and scope of aggregate adjustment costs.

Estimates of aggregate adjustment costs are rare.[1] The two main contributions are Magee (1972) and Baldwin, Mutti, and Richardson (1980), both of which follow a similar approach. First, estimates were made about the number of workers who would lose their jobs due to liberalization. These job losses were then evaluated based on an appropriate measure of the displaced workers' wages. Finally, the authors then assumed that these workers would find reemployment after a length of time determined by estimates of the average duration of unemployment. Both papers conclude that adjustment costs are probably very small when compared to the gains from liberalization. For example, with a 10% discount rate, they both estimate that the short-run costs of adjustment would eat away no more than 5% of the long-run gains from trade.[2]

It is hard to know what to make of these estimates. Neither paper attempts to take into account either the time or resource costs that are involved in the retraining that dislocated workers may be forced to go through. The resource cost of job search is also ignored. Moreover, since the reemployment process is not modeled, it is hard to take into account any displacement that may occur as dislocated workers find reemployment in new sectors. There are other problems as well, but all stem from the same basic issue—since there is no model of the adjustment process underlying these estimates, there may be many general equilibrium spillover effects that are not being captured. This is not intended as a criticism of these papers. At the time that these papers were written, rigorous models that

[1] A number of authors have attempted to measure adjustment costs within specific industries. See, for example, de Melo and Tarr (1990), who focus on the U.S. textile, auto, and steel industries, or Tackas and Winters (1991), who studied the British footwear industry.

[2] In a recent paper Trefler (2001) examined the short-run adjustment costs and long-run efficiency gains from trade liberalization in Canada by quantifying the impact of NAFTA on specific Canadian industries subject to large tariff cuts. He found evidence of substantial short-run adjustment costs—a 15% decline in employment and a 10% decline in output. Balanced against these costs were only moderate productivity gains of about 1% per year. However, Trefler made no attempt to measure the aggregate gains and losses from NAFTA.

explicitly allow for the trade frictions and informational asymmetries that lead to equilibrium unemployment were only in their infancy.[3] It would have been difficult to extend the type of general equilibrium models typically used for trade analysis to allow for equilibrium unemployment and retraining. The empirical approach adopted by these authors was entirely appropriate given the state of the trade literature at that time.

There is another line of research that is relevant for what follows. This research simply assumes that adjustment costs are nontrivial and then examines the implications of this for the optimal time path of liberalization. It has been argued that in order to minimize adjustment costs, trade barriers should be removed gradually (see, for example, Cassing and Ochs 1978; Karp and Paul 1994; Gaisford and Leger 2000; and Davidson and Matusz 2002).[4] The rationale behind this rests on the assumption that as workers flee the import-competing sector and seek jobs in the expanding export sectors, congestion externalities will arise that increase the cost of adjustment. If the government removes trade barriers slowly, it can control the flow of workers, reduce congestion, smooth out the adjustment process, and minimize the social cost of adjustment.

Our goal in this paper is to build on recent advances in the theory of equilibrium unemployment by presenting a simple general equilibrium model of trade that includes unemployment and training. We then use the model to explore the scope and magnitude of adjustment costs relative to the gains from trade. In our model, workers differ in ability and jobs differ in the types of skills they require. Workers sort themselves by choosing occupations based on expected lifetime income. These workers then cycle between periods of employment, unemployment and training with the length of each labor market state determined by the turnover rates in each sector. One of the advantages of the model is that it is simple enough to allow us to solve analytically for the adjustment path between steady states, thereby allowing us to calculate the adjustment costs associated with trade reform. Another advantage is that many of the key parameters (e.g., labor market turnover rates) are observable, so that we can rely on existing data to determine their likely values. However, one of the shortcomings of the model is that there are few existing estimates on which to base assumptions about the resource and time costs associated with training and these values play important roles in our analysis. We therefore solve the model for a wide variety of assumptions about these values and look for conclusions that are robust.

---

[3] We are referring to the literatures on trading frictions (search theory), efficiency wages, and insider/outsider models of the labor market, among others.
[4] For a survey of this literature, see Falvey and Kim (1992). Other recent contributions that do not focus on the role of congestion include Li and Mayer (1996) and Furusawa and Lai (1999).

In developing our model, we purposefully abstract from congestion externalities by assuming that after liberalization, the job acquisition rate in the export sector remains at its preliberalization level. We do so for two reasons. First, our main goal is to show that by including the resource and time costs associated with training and job search we obtain estimates of adjustment costs that are substantially larger than those in the existing literature. In doing so, we want to ensure that our estimates are conservative, and by abstracting from congestion externalities, we are likely to be underestimating the true magnitude of these costs. Moreover, this ensures that our estimates are not driven by a (potentially) controversial assumption about the search process. The second reason that we assume away congestion has to do with the nature of the liberalization process itself. In this paper we are not interested in adding to the literature on the optimal time path of liberalization. As we mentioned above, previous work has shown that when congestion externalities are present, removing trade barriers gradually can lower aggregate adjustment costs. However, in the absence of congestion, there is no reason for gradualism. By assuming away congestion externalities we can keep our analysis simple and focus on the magnitude of the adjustment costs that arise when liberalization is complete and immediate.

Our results are surprising and contrast sharply with the previous literature. First, our model predicts that adjustment will take place relatively quickly, with net output returning to its preliberalization level within 2.5 years. This result, which is partly due to our assumption that postliberalization export sector labor markets are not troubled by congestion, implies that an empirical analysis of adjustment based on yearly data could easily lead to the conclusion that adjustment costs are quite small. However, this is not the case in our model. Even with our most modest assumption concerning training costs we find that their inclusion in the model significantly increases our estimates of aggregate adjustment costs. For example, we find that when we take the time cost of retraining into account the short-run adjustment costs amount to (at least) 10 to 15% of the long-run benefits from liberalization. When the resource costs of retraining are taken into account as well, our estimates jump to 30 to 80% of the long-run gains from freer trade![5] The fact that we obtain these results in a model in which the job acquisition rate in the export sector does not fall after liberalization is particularly noteworthy.

---

[5] It is worth noting that while our conclusion that short-run adjustment costs may be quite high is quite different from those reached by Magee (1972) and Baldwin, Mutti, and Richardson (1980), it is consistent with the basic message of Trefler's (2001) study of the impact of NAFTA on select Canadian industries (see footnote 2).

In the latter part of the paper we turn to a related issue, and ask whether there is any way to know a priori which types of economies are likely to face relatively large adjustment costs. Labor markets and the institutions that govern them vary greatly across the world. Jobs tend to last longer in the United States than they do in Europe and Japan. The average duration of unemployment is relatively short in the United States, while it can be quite long in some European countries. The implication is that all labor market turnover rates tend to be higher in the United States than they are in most European countries. In addition, wages are more flexible in U.S. labor markets than they are in their European counterparts. Consequently, labor economists typically characterize U.S. labor markets as flexible while European labor markets are considered sluggish. One would expect that the flexibility of the labor market would play a key role in determining the relative importance of adjustment costs.

We investigate this issue by determining how the ratio of adjustment costs to the gains from trade varies as turnover rates increase uniformly. In our model, we find, perhaps as expected, that relative adjustment costs are decreasing in the degree of labor market flexibility so that economies with slothful labor markets face higher costs of adjustment than economies with either flexible or sluggish labor markets. However, somewhat surprisingly, we find that the net benefits from trade reform have the same relationship with labor market flexibility so that economies with slothful labor markets have the most to gain from liberalization.

This surprising result has its roots in the manner in which tariffs distort economies with different degrees of labor market flexibility. We find that tariffs distort slothful labor markets more than sluggish ones. The removal of the tariff therefore generates large benefits in such economies; in fact, they are even large enough to swamp the economy's high level of short-run adjustment costs. As a result, economies with the most slothful labor markets gain the most from trade liberalization.

In the conclusion we discuss the appropriate way to view our results. We emphasize that although our estimates of adjustment costs are quite high, this should not be misinterpreted as a warning about the dangers of liberalization. Instead, we argue that economists and politicians should spend more time worrying about the appropriate way to compensate those who bear the burden of these costs and that these policies should be an important component of the liberalization process. We also point out that our results suggest that the cost of new protectionist policies may be substantially higher than previous estimates indicate since newly created barriers to trade generate adjustment costs as well.

2. The Model

2.1 Background

In developing our model, we have several goals in mind. First, we want to use a general equilibrium trade model that is rich enough to capture some essential features of the employment process. In particular, we want a model that explicitly allows for both a training process in which workers acquire the skills required to find a job and a search process that those same workers must go through to find an employer. Second, we want to keep the model simple and tractable in order to be able to solve analytically for the transition path between steady states. This allows us to calculate the adjustment costs associated with trade reform. Third, we want the model to be general enough to allow for cross-country differences in labor market structure so that we may investigate the relationship between labor market flexibility and adjustment costs.

The basic structure of the model is as follows. We have an economy in which workers with differing abilities must choose between two types of jobs—those that do not require many skills and offer low pay and those that require significant training and pay relatively high wages. Jobs in the low-tech sector are easy to find, do not last very long (there is high turnover), and require skills that are job specific. In contrast, high-tech jobs are relatively hard to find, presumably because the matching problem is harder to solve, last longer once employment is secured, and require a combination of job-specific and general skills. We assume that in each sector high-ability workers produce more output than their low-ability counterparts. Under certain assumptions, this implies that in equilibrium workers sort themselves so that high-ability workers train for high-tech jobs while low-ability workers are drawn to the low-tech sector.

We begin by assuming that the low-tech sector is protected by a tariff. This raises the return to training in that sector and causes some workers who should train in the high-tech sector to seek low-tech jobs instead. When the tariff is removed, these workers shift to the high-tech sector. This shift is gradual, however, since these workers will first have to enter the high-tech training process and then search for jobs. In addition, some of the workers who may eventually want to shift sectors may already hold low-tech jobs and since training and search are costly, they may choose to wait until they lose their low-tech jobs before making the switch. As a result, it may take significant time before the economy gets close to the new steady state. In this setting, adjustment costs are measured by comparing what the economy could gain if it could jump immediately to the new steady state with what it actually gains taking into account the costly transition that it experiences in moving to the new steady state.

2.2 Formalizing the Model and Finding the Initial Steady State

We consider a continuous time model of a small open economy consisting of two sectors and a single factor of production, labor. We use a_i to denote worker i's ability level and we assume that a_i is uniformly distributed across $[0, 1]$ with the total measure of workers equaling L. To obtain a job in either sector, workers must first acquire the requisite skills. Training is costly, both in time and in resources. In sector j, workers seeking a job must pay a flow cost of $p_j c_j$ while training, where p_j denotes the price of good j (so that sector-j training costs are measured in units of the sector-j good). The length of the training process is assumed to be random, with sector-j trainees exiting at rate τ_j. This implies that the average length of training in sector j is $1/\tau_j$. Our notion that training is more costly both in time and resources in sector 2, the high-tech sector, is captured by assuming that c_1 and τ_2 are small while c_2 and τ_1 are large (we will be more precise below). We use $L_{jT}(t)$ to denote the measure of workers training in sector j at time t.

After exiting the training process, workers must search for employment.[6] Jobs in the low-tech sector are plentiful, so that jobs are found immediately.[7] In contrast, it takes time to find high-tech jobs and we use e to denote the steady-state job acquisition rate in that sector. It follows that in the initial steady state the average spell of sector-2 unemployment is $1/e$. We use $L_S(t)$ to denote the measure of workers searching for high-tech jobs at time t.

Once a job is found, a type-i sector-j worker produces a flow of $q_j a_i$ units of output as long as she remains employed. Since output is increasing in a_i, higher ability workers produce more than their lower ability counterparts in each sector.[8] This output is sold at p_j and all of the revenue goes to the worker in the form of earned income (so that the sector-j wage earned by a type-i worker is $p_j q_j a_i$). We assume that in a steady state sector-j workers lose their jobs at rate b_j, so that the average duration of a sector-j job is $1/b_j$. Since high-tech jobs are assumed to be more durable

[6] The assumption that the training process takes place before search is not crucial for the analysis. We could assume instead that training takes place after completion of search without altering the nature of our results.

[7] Of course, many low-ability workers face difficulty finding any job whatsoever and therefore face a long expected duration of unemployment whenever they lose their job. We believe that this is largely due to their work history and overall ability level. By assuming that low-tech jobs are plentiful (so that sector-1 employment can be found immediately), we are trying to capture the notion that the *marginal* worker (who has the ability to train for a high-tech job) would be able to find menial employment quite easily if she chooses to do so.

[8] Ability could refer to attributes that the worker is born with, or it could refer to a combination of attributes that are either innate or acquired during the elementary education process.

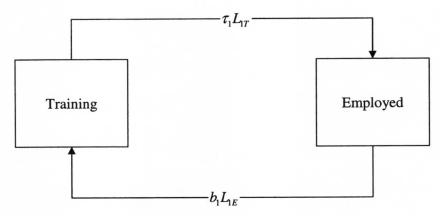

Figure 9.1. Labor market dynamics in sector 1.

than low-tech jobs, it follows that $b_1 > b_2$. The measure of workers employed in sector j at time t is denoted by $L_{jE}(t)$.

Upon separation, a worker must retrain if her skills are job specific. In contrast, if her skills are general, she can immediately begin to search for reemployment. As noted above, we assume that the skills acquired during low-tech training are job specific. We make this assumption because, to us, it seems natural. While training, a store clerk may need to learn the layout of the store in which she is employed, the procedure involved in opening and closing the store, the functioning of a particular type of cash register, and so on; but in gaining this knowledge the worker learns nothing about how to prepare fast food (or perform other low-skill tasks). In contrast, high-tech workers like accountants, managers, and lawyers all must complete college and obtain some postgraduate education. If they lose their job, many of these workers will be able to obtain reemployment in the same field and in doing so they will not be required to go back through school. Moreover, even if these workers choose to change occupation, they will have acquired some general skills along the way that may allow them to land new jobs without acquiring additional skills. The implication is that all unemployed low-tech workers need to retrain in order to find reemployment, while some high-tech workers can move into a new job without having to retrain. To make this precise, we assume that with probability ϕ high-tech workers need not retrain after losing their jobs.

The dynamics of the two labor markets are depicted in figures 9.1 and 9.2. The evolution of the labor markets over time can be described with the aid of these figures. Let $\dot{X}(t)$ denote the growth rate of X at time t.

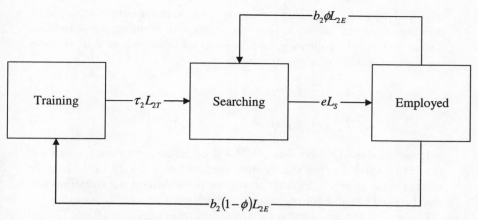

Figure 9.2. Labor market dynamics in sector 2.

These growth rates can be found by comparing the flows into and out of each labor market state. For example, in sector 1, the flow out of training is equal to the measure of workers who complete the training process and take low-tech jobs, $\tau_1 L_{tT}(t)$. The flow into training is equal to the measure of low-tech workers who lose their jobs due to exogenous separation, $b_1 L_{tE}(t)$. It follows that the growth rate of low-tech trainees is given by

$$\dot{L}_{1T}(t) = b_1 L_{1E}(t) - \tau_1 L_{1T}(t) \tag{1}$$

Similar logic can be used to find the growth rates of employment, $\dot{L}_{2E}(t)$, and the unemployment pool in sector 2, $\dot{L}_S(t)$. We have

$$\dot{L}_{2E}(t) = e L_S(t) - b_2 L_{2E}(t) \tag{2}$$

$$\dot{L}_S(t) = \tau_2 L_{2T}(t) + b_2 \phi L_{2E}(t) - e L_S(t) \tag{3}$$

In (2), the flow into high-tech employment consists of searching workers who find employment, $e L_S(t)$, while the flow out is made up of employed high-tech workers who lose their jobs, $b_2 L_{2E}(t)$. In (3), the flow into the pool of searchers is made up of those who complete the high-tech training process, $\tau_2 L_{2T}(t)$, and those workers who lose their high-tech jobs but do not have to retrain because their skills are transferable, $b_2 \phi L_{2E}(t)$. The flow out of unemployment is equal to the measure of high-tech searchers who find jobs, $eL_S(t)$.[9] Finally, in sector 1, workers are either employed or training, while in sector 2, they are employed, training, or searching. Thus, we have the following adding up conditions (where $L_j(t)$ denotes measure of sector-j workers at time t):

$$L_1(t) = L_{1E}(t) + L_{1T}(t) \qquad (4)$$

$$L_2(t) = L_{2E}(t) + L_{2T}(t) + L_S(t) \qquad (5)$$

If we set the left-hand side of (1)–(3) equal to zero, then we can use (1)–(5) to solve for the steady-state measure of workers in each labor market state. In appendix A we show that these differential equations can also be used to solve for the transition path between steady states.

It is important to note that the transition rates (e, b_1, and b_2) in (1)–(3) are set at their steady-state values. There are two reasons for this. First, as we mentioned above, we want to abstract from congestion externalities that might lower e during the transition period by holding e fixed at its steady-state level. Second, as we show below, once liberalization occurs all economically inefficient jobs are immediately destroyed as some low-tech workers quit their jobs and switch sectors. Thus, the job destruction rate increases endogenously but it does so instantaneously and then returns to its steady-state level immediately after. It follows that the increase in job destruction shows up not in the differential equations describing labor market flows, but in the initial conditions that hold once liberalization occurs (L_{2T} jumps up immediately once the tariff is removed).

Of course, in order to solve (1)–(5) we must first explain how to solve for $L_1(t)$ and $L_2(t)$. These values are determined by the behavior of individual workers, who choose their occupations based on the lifetime income that they expect to earn in each sector. When workers initially enter the labor market they have no skills. Thus, their initial choice depends on the relative values of V_{1T} and V_{2T}, which measure the expected lifetime income for workers training in sectors 1 and 2, respectively. If we define V_{2S} as the expected lifetime income for sector-2 workers who are currently searching for a job and use V_{jE} to denote the expected lifetime income for employed workers in sector j, then we have the following asset value equations (with r denoting the discount rate and γ denoting the tariff on good 1):

$$rV_{1T}(t) = -p_1(1 + \gamma)c_1 + \tau_1[V_{1E}(t) - V_{1T}(t)] + \dot{V}_{1T}(t) \qquad (6)$$

---

[9] Similar growth equations for L_{1E} (low-tech employment) and L_{2T} (trainers in sector 2) could also be defined. However, given the adding up conditions in (4) and (5) they would be redundant.

$$rV_{1E}(t) = p_1(1 + \gamma)q_1a_i + b_1[V_{1T}(t) - V_{1E}(t)] + \dot{V}_{1E}(t) \tag{7}$$

$$rV_{2T}(t) = -p_2c_2 + \tau_2[V_{2S}(t) - V_{2T}(t)] + \dot{V}_{2T}(t) \tag{8}$$

$$rV_{2S}(t) = 0 + e[V_{2E}(t) - V_{2S}(t)] + \dot{V}_{2S}(t) \tag{9}$$

$$rV_{2E}(t) = p_2q_2a_i + b_2[\phi V_{2S}(t) + (1 - \phi)V_{2T}(t) - V_{2E}(t)] + \dot{V}_{2E}(t) \tag{10}$$

In (6)–(10), the first term on the right-hand side represents flow income. For employed workers, flow income is equal to the value of the output they produce ($p_jq_ja_i$ for a type-i worker in sector j). Trainees and searching workers earn nothing while unemployed, and trainees must pay training costs while acquiring their skills. Thus, current income for searchers is equal to zero while trainees lose their training costs. The second term on the right-hand side of each equation is the product of the capital gain (or loss) from changing labor market status and the rate at which such changes take place. For example, the flow rate from searching to employment in sector 2 is e while the capital gain associated with employment is $V_{2E} - V_{2S}$. Note that for workers who are employed in the high-tech sector, there are two possibilities when they lose their job. With probability ϕ these workers retain their skills and begin to search for a new job immediately, while with the remaining probability they must retrain before they can seek a new job. The final term on the right-hand side, the $\dot{V}$ term, represents the growth rate of V. This term captures the appreciation (or depreciation) of the asset value over time and it is equal to zero in a steady state.

In order to describe the initial steady-state equilibrium, we now set each $\dot{V}$ term in (6)–(10) equal to zero and solve for the expected lifetime income associated with each labor market state. We obtain (V_{2S} and V_{2E} are omitted since we do not use them in the subsequent analysis)

$$V_{1E} = \frac{p_1(1 + \gamma)\{(r + \tau_1)q_1a_i - b_1c_1\}}{r\Delta_1} \tag{11}$$

$$V_{1T} = \frac{p_1(1 + \gamma)\{\tau_1q_1a_i - (r + b_1)c_1\}}{r\Delta_1} \tag{12}$$

$$V_{2T} = \frac{p_2\{\tau_2eq_2a_i - [(r + b_2)(r + e) - \phi eb_2]c_2\}}{r\Delta_2} \tag{13}$$

where $\Delta_1 = r + b_1 + \tau_1$ and $\Delta_2 = (r + b_2)(r + \tau_2 + e) + e\tau_2 - b_2\phi e$.

Unemployed workers with no skills choose to train in the low-tech sector if $V_{1T} \geq \max \{V_{2T}, 0\}$ and they choose to train in the high-tech sector if $V_{2T} \geq \max \{V_{1T}, 0\}$. Workers with ability levels such that $0 \geq \max \{V_{1T}, V_{2T}\}$ stay out of the labor market since it is too costly for them to train for any job. These workers are effectively shut out of the labor market—there are no jobs available for them to train for since their training costs would exceed any income that they could expect to earn after finding employment.

As for employed and searching workers, we assume that they are free to change occupations, but each time they do so they must start out by retraining. It follows that, in any steady-state equilibrium, these workers never switch sectors. However, changes in parameters or world prices may result in these workers changing occupations if the expected lifetime income associated with training in the other sector exceeds what they expect to earn as a searcher or an employed worker in their current sector.

To complete the characterization of equilibrium we must place some restrictions on our parameters. What we have in mind is a model in which high-ability workers are better suited to produce the high-tech good. It is clear from (12) and (13) that V_{1T} and V_{2T} are linear and increasing in a_i. Moreover, in each sector there is a critical value for a_i, denoted by $\underline{a_j}$, below which $V_{jT}(a_i) < 0$. Workers separate in the desired way if V_{2T} is steeper than V_{1T} at the initial world prices and if $\underline{a_1} < \underline{a_2}$. This is the case if $p_1(r + \tau_1)q_1\Delta_2 < p_2\tau_2 eq_2\Delta_1$ and $(r + b_1)c_1\tau_1 eq_2 < [(r + b_2)(r + e) - \phi eb_2]c_2\tau_1q_1$. With these two assumptions in place, V_{1T} and V_{2T} are as depicted in figure 9.3. Note that the figure includes two new terms, a_L and a_H, with $a_L \equiv \underline{a_1}$ and a_H defined as the ability level for the worker who is just indifferent between training in sector 1 or sector 2, that is, $V_{2T}(a_H) = V_{1T}(a_H)$.

From figure 9.3, it is clear that workers with ability levels below a_L do not enter the labor force. For these workers, the cost of training for any job is too high. Workers with ability levels $a_i \in [a_L, a_H]$ find the low-tech sector more attractive and choose to train in sector 1. It follows that $L_1 = (a_H - a_L)L$. Finally, workers with ability levels above a_H find the high-tech sector relatively more attractive. These workers train for high-tech jobs, so that $L_2 = (1 - a_H)L$.

We can now return to (1)–(5), set the $\dot{L}$ terms equal to zero, and solve for the measure of workers in each labor market in the initial steady state. We obtain (L_S is omitted since it is not used in the subsequent analysis)

$$L_{1T} = \frac{b_1(a_H - a_L)L}{b_1 + \tau_1} \tag{14}$$

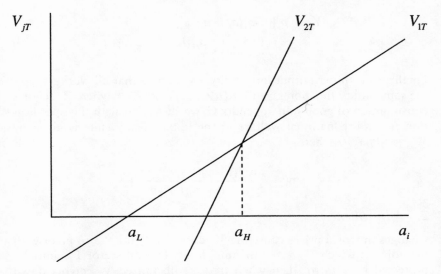

Figure 9.3. The equilibrium allocation of workers.

$$L_{1E} = \frac{\tau_1(a_H - a_L)L}{b_1 + \tau_1} \tag{15}$$

$$L_{2T} = \frac{(1-\phi)eb_2(1-a_H)L}{(e+b_2)\tau_2 + (1-\phi)eb_2}, \tag{16}$$

$$L_{2E} = \frac{\tau_2 e(1-a_H)L}{(e+b_2)\tau_2 + (1-\phi)eb_2}, \tag{17}$$

where, from (12) and (13),

$$a_H = \frac{p_2 c_2 \Delta_1 [(r+b_2)(r+e) - \phi eb_2] - p_1(1+\gamma)c_1\Delta_2(r+b_1)}{p_2\tau_2 eq_2\Delta_1 - p_1(1+\gamma)\tau_1 q_1\Delta_2} \tag{18}$$

$$a_L = \frac{(r+b_1)c_1}{\tau_1 q_1} \tag{19}$$

These values can now be used to determine Y_{SS}, the initial steady-state value of output measured at world prices and net of training costs. Since the average low-tech worker produces ½ $q_1(a_L + a_H)$ units of output while the average high-tech worker produces ½ $q_2(1 + a_H)$ units, we have

$$Y_{SS} = p_1\{0.5q_1(a_L + a_H)L_{1E} - c_1L_{1T}\}$$
$$+ p_2\{0.5q_2(1 + a_H)L_{2E} - c_2L_{2T}\} \tag{20}$$

Finally, to turn net output into utility, we assume that all workers have the same utility function given by $U(Z_1, Z_2) = Z_1^\alpha Z_2^{1-\alpha}$ where Z_j denotes consumption of good j. In appendix C, we show that with this specification for utility, national welfare in the initial steady state is given by $W_{SS} = \eta(\gamma)Y_{SS}/r$ where

$$\eta(\gamma) = \frac{\alpha^\alpha[(1-\alpha)(1+\gamma)]^{1-\alpha}}{\alpha + (1-\alpha)(1+\gamma)}$$

2.3 Adjustment

Changes in world prices cause the V_{jT} curves in figure 9.3 to pivot with the point at which $V_{jT} = 0$ remaining fixed. Thus, if sector 1 is initially protected by a tariff, then when trade is liberalized V_{1T} pivots down causing a_H to fall. If we use a_{FT} to denote the new value of a_H (with the subscript referring to "free trade"), then all workers with ability levels in the interval $[a_{FT}, a_H]$ eventually want to switch from the low-tech to the high-tech sector. Trainees switch immediately while those employed in the low-tech sector must decide whether to quit their jobs and switch sectors immediately or keep their jobs and switch only after losing their jobs. If we use a_Q to denote the ability level of the low-tech worker who is just indifferent between quitting and keeping her job, then it is straightforward to show that $a_Q \in [a_{FT}, a_H]$. Employed workers with $a \in [a_Q, a_H]$ quit immediately and start to train for high-tech jobs while those with $a \in [a_{FT}, a_Q]$ wait and switch after losing their low-tech jobs.

Because of the model's simple structure, it is possible to solve analytically for the transition path between steady states. We begin by noting that all V terms jump immediately to their new steady-state values once trade is liberalized. This is due to the fact that these values depend only on prices, ability, turnover rates, and other parameters that are independent of time (see (11)–(13)). Thus, a_H jumps to its new value immediately as well. The gradual transition to the new steady state occurs in the labor market and involves only those workers with ability levels in the range $[a_{FT}, a_H]$. For these workers, the measures of trainees, searchers, and employed workers change according to the differential equations in (1)–(5). We provide the solution to this system of differential equations in appendix A and show how they can be used to calculate the net output produced by these workers in each sector during the adjustment process. We use $X_j(a_{FT}, a_Q)$ to denote the present discounted value of the net output produced in sector j by workers with $a \in [a_{FT}, a_Q]$ during adjustment and use $X_j (a_Q, a_H)$ to play the same role for those workers with $a \in [a_Q, a_H]$. These values are given by (A.11), (A.12), and (A.15) in appendix A.

Liberalization does not alter the behavior of those workers with $a \leq a_{FT}$ or $a \geq a_H$. The former group remains attached to the low-tech sector whereas the latter group continues to train, search, and work in the high-tech sector. It is possible that as workers flow from the low-tech sector to the high-tech sector, labor market congestion might cause the job acquisition rate in the high-tech sector to fall. If congestion externalities are present, they would increase the cost of adjustment and slow down the transition to the new steady state. However, as we mentioned in the introduction, in order to keep our analysis as simple and tractable as possible, we abstract from this issue by assuming that all workers seeking high-tech jobs continue to find them at the steady-state job acquisition rate of e. This assumption ensures that our estimate of adjustment costs will be on the conservative side. It also implies that for workers with $a \leq a_{FT}$ the measures of workers training and employed in the low-tech sector after liberalization are given by (14) and (15), respectively, with $(a_H - a_L)$ replaced by $(a_{FT} - a_L)$. We use L_{1T}^{FT} and L_{1E}^{FT} to represent these values. Note that for those workers with $a \geq a_H$, the measures of training, searching, and employed in the high-tech sector after liberalization are still given by (16) and (17).

Given the solutions provided in appendix A, we can calculate the value of output net of training costs along the transition path, $Y(t)$. We have

$$Y(t) = p_1\{0.5q_1(a_L + a_{FT})L_{1E}^{FT} - c_1 L_{1T}^{FT}\} + p_2\{0.5q_2(1 + a_H)L_{2E} - c_2 L_{2T}\}$$
$$+ X_1(a_{FT}, a_Q) + X_2(a_{FT}, a_Q) + X_2(a_Q, a_H) \tag{21}$$

To find welfare after liberalization, taking the adjustment path into account, we first transform net output into utility and then integrate over time. Given our specification of utility, we obtain $W_A = \int e^{-rt}\eta(0)Y(t)dt$.

The last step in solving for the cost of adjustment is to compare W_A with the welfare that the economy could achieve if it were able to jump immediately to the new (free trade) steady-state equilibrium (W_{FT}). To find this value, define Y_{FT} as the value of output net of training costs in the new steady-state equilibrium. This value is given by (20) with a_{FT} replacing a_H so that $W_{FT} = \eta(0)Y_{FT}/r$.[10]

Typical time paths for $Y_{SS}, Y(t)$, and Y_{FT} are depicted in figure 9.4. Liberalizing trade increases steady-state net output from its initial value of Y_{SS} to its new free trade value of Y_{FT}. However, to reach the new steady state,

---

[10] Note that we are using the compensating variation to measure the change in welfare due to liberalization.

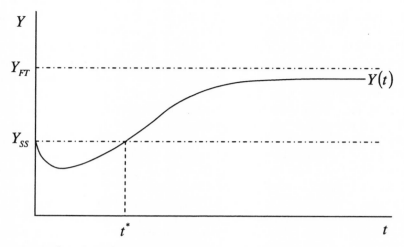

Figure 9.4. The value of output net of training costs over time.

the economy must first go through a costly transition with net output following along the $Y(t)$ path. Note that there is a period of time (up to t^*) during which net output falls below its initial steady-state value. The *potential* gain from trade reform is defined by the properly discounted area below Y_{FT} and above Y_{SS}, or $W_{FT} - W_{SS}$. The *actual* gain is the properly discounted difference between the areas below Y_{SS} and $Y(t)$, or $W_A - W_{SS}$. It follows that aggregate adjustment costs are measured by the appropriately discounted area below Y_{FT} but above $Y(t)$, or $W_{FT} - W_A$.[11] In the next section, we simulate the model, calculate aggregate adjustment costs, and compare them to the potential gains from reform.[12] We do so by focusing on two key variables. The first variable is t^*, which measures the length of time it takes for the economy to get back to its original level of net income (so that t^* solves $Y_{SS} - Y(t^*) = 0$). By looking at t^* we are able to get some sense as to how long it takes the economy to begin to reap the benefits from liberalization. The second variable of interest is R^*, defined as the ratio of aggregate adjustment costs to the potential benefits from trade reform:

$$R^* \equiv \frac{W_{FT} - W_A}{W_{FT} - W_{SS}} \tag{22}$$

[11] This method for calculating adjustment costs was suggested by Neary (1982).
[12] In Davidson and Matusz (2001) we explore other aspects of the adjustment path including the time paths of employment and unemployment during the adjustment period.

2.4 Strengths and Weaknesses of Our Model

At this point, it is useful to highlight some features of our model that we consider strengths as well as some of the weaknesses. Several attractive features are worth emphasizing. First, we have modeled the training and search processes that workers must go through in order to find jobs. This allows us to take into account both the time and resource costs that dislocated workers must incur after losing their jobs. This is a unique and innovative feature of our model and we consider it one of its main strengths. The second important feature is that we have managed to keep the framework relatively simple and tractable. In fact, it is so simple that we can solve explicitly for the transition path between steady states by solving the differential equations in (1)–(5).

Another attractive feature of our model is that many of the key parameters, for example, the labor market turnover rates, are observable. This makes it easy to calibrate the model and find estimates of aggregate adjustment costs for parameter values that have some empirical significance. Moreover, as we emphasized in the introduction, it is well known that labor markets in Europe, the United States, and Japan differ significantly in their structure and that much of the difference has to do with differences in turnover rates. Since it is these turnover rates that drive our analysis, we can easily model the differences in labor market structure across these regions and see how our estimate of adjustment costs relative to the benefits from trade liberalization vary with labor market flexibility.

Finally, there is one other positive feature of our model that we would like to underscore. In appendix B we show that the equilibrium in our model is efficient. This is unusual for search models. It is usually the case that search decisions are rife with externalities. For example, if an unemployed worker chooses to seek a job in a particular sector, this may make it more difficult for other unemployed workers to find a job (that is, there may be congestion externalities). Such externalities typically distort behavior and lead to suboptimal equilibria. This is not the case in our model. In fact, we set up our model with certain features (such as exogenous job acquisition rates) specifically designed to avoid this problem. The reason that we did this is so that we can be sure that when we calculate adjustment costs and compare them to the gains from trade we can be certain that our results do not depend on how trade liberalization affects the distortions created by controversial, hard to measure search-generated externalities.

While there is considerable merit in assuming fixed job acquisition rates, there is also a downside. Agents face changing economic incentives as trade is liberalized. Some workers in the import-competing sector quit and this results in an immediate increase in the job destruction rate. At the same time, since the pool of unemployed workers is swelling in the export sector, the job acquisition rate may fall due to congestion. As mentioned in the introduction, this possibility has been the focus of several papers in which it has been suggested that gradual liberalization may be warranted in order to avoid congestion in export sector labor markets. By treating the job acquisition rate as an exogenously specified parameter, we are ignoring these possibilities and obtaining estimates of adjustment costs that are probably too low.

Another weakness in our analysis concerns the parameters that measure the costs of retraining (c_j and τ_j). Although these parameters play a key role in our analysis, we know very little about their likely values. We handle this problem in two ways. First, since it is unlikely that training costs in the low-tech sector are significant, we set c_1 equal to zero and assume that τ_1 is quite high (so that low-tech training is very brief). Given that we have also assumed that there are no resource costs associated with job search, this is another reason to suspect that our estimates of aggregate adjustment costs are likely to be biased downward. Second, we consider a wide variety of assumptions about the magnitude of high-tech training costs and then try to draw conclusions that are robust across these sets of assumptions.

3. Aggregate Adjustment Costs

The parameters of our model include those that determine the average durations of sector-j training (τ_j), sector-j employment (b_j), and high-tech search (e), those that determine the resource cost of sector-j training (c_j), those that help to determine output per worker in sector j (q_j), the rate of transferability of high-tech skills across jobs (ϕ), the discount rate (r), and the share of income devoted to consumption of good 1 (α). In this section, we choose values for these parameters, solve the model, and provide measures of the aggregate adjustment costs associated with trade reform. We do so under the assumption that the low-tech sector is initially protected by a 5% tariff (thus, $\gamma = 0.05$).

To make certain that we do not discount the future too heavily, we set $r = 0.03$, the lowest discount rate considered by Baldwin, Mutti, and Richardson (1980) and Magee (1972).[13] The average duration of unemployment in the United States can be found in *The 2001 Economic Report*

---

[13] This again biases our result in terms of minimizing the magnitude of adjustment costs, since a low discount rate places relatively little weight on current costs versus the future benefits of reform.

SHOULD POLICY MAKERS BE CONCERNED? 245

of the President (see table B-44). Although this value has fluctuated over the years, it remains fairly stable at about one quarter (or 13 weeks). Our model is consistent with such estimates if we set $e = 4$. Since this value rarely fluctuates by more than a week or two, this is the only value for e that we consider.

For the average duration of employment in the high-tech sector, we turn to the job creation and destruction data of Davis, Haltiwanger, and Schuh (1996), who report that the average annual rate of job destruction in U.S manufacturing during the period 1973–88 was about 10% (this translates into an average job duration of 10 years). There is some variation in this number across years, with the largest rate of job destruction coming in 1975 at 16.5% (implying an average job duration of about 6 years).[14] We therefore assume, for our base case, that an average high-tech job lasts 10 years (which is the case if $b_2 = 0.10$). However, we also solve the model and report results for the case in which high-tech jobs last only six years (which is the case if $b_2 = 0.167$).

It is hard to find data on the average duration of a job in the low-tech sector. We consider these to be transitory, undesirable jobs and although many of these jobs may be found in the manufacturing sector, it is not possible to look at industrywide data and draw conclusions about how long the worst jobs in each industry last. So, we take a different approach. Our low-tech jobs require few skills and little training. These are the types of jobs that many hold while still in school or when they are just starting out in the labor force. If we look at data on the number of jobs held over the lifetime, we find that up to the age of 24 workers hold (roughly) one new job every two years.[15] We therefore consider two cases—one in which low-tech jobs last two years (so that $b_1 = 0.5$) and another in which they last just one year (so that $b_1 = 1.0$). Combining these two cases with the assumptions that we have made about job tenure in the high-tech sector leaves us with four different settings. In the setting with high turnover in both sectors, jobs last a year in the low-tech sector and six years in the high-tech sector. In the setting with low turnover in both sectors, jobs last two years in the low-tech sector and ten years in the high-tech sector. In the other two cases, jobs last either three or ten times as long in the high-tech sector than they do in the low-tech sector. This gives us a wide range of assumptions about labor market turnover.

Turn next to the parameters of the training processes. Since very little is known about the magnitude of training costs we want to be careful not to assume values that seem unreasonably high, and we want to make sure that we consider a wide range of possible values. As we mentioned above,

[14] See table 2.1 on p. 19 in Davis, Haltiwanger, and Schuh (1996).
[15] See table 8.1 on p. 210 in Hamermesh and Rees (1988).

we assume that there are no resource costs associated with low-tech training (i.e., $c_1 = 0$).[16] In addition, we assume that the low-tech training process takes only one week (so that $\tau_1 = 52$). For the high-tech sector, we turn to the limited information that is available on training costs. A review of what is known about turnover costs can be found in Hamermesh (1993), where turnover costs are assumed to include both the costs of recruiting and training the newly hired worker. This literature suggests that such costs may be quite high. For example, a large firm in the pharmaceutical industry estimated that the present value of the cost of replacing one worker amounted to roughly twice that worker's annual salary. Similar, although not quite so dramatic, estimates were obtained for less skilled jobs. One study estimated that the cost of replacing a truck driver amounted to slightly less than half of that worker's annual pay. The lowest estimate of turnover costs reported by Hamermesh appears to be about three weeks worth of salary. Similar estimates can be found in Acemoglou and Pischke's (1999) study of the training process in the German apprentice system. They report estimates of training costs that vary from 6 to 15 months' of the average worker's annual income, depending on the size of the firm. To capture this wide range of estimates, we assume that high-tech training lasts four months ($\tau_2 = 4$) and then we vary the value of c_2. At the low end, we choose c_2 so that training costs for the average worker in the high-tech sector are equal to one month's pay.[17] At the high end, we choose c_2 so that the average high-tech worker's training costs equal 15 months of pay. We also consider two intermediate cases in which training costs equal 5 and 10 months of the worker's annual salary. This gives us a wide range of values for high-tech training costs. Below we look for results that are robust across this range of estimates.[18]

This leaves q_1 and q_2, the productivity parameters in the two sectors, ϕ, which measures how often high-tech workers need to retrain after losing

---

[16] With $c_1 = 0$ we have $a_L = 0$ so that all workers enter the labor market.

[17] High-tech workers pay a flow cost of p_2c_2 while training and training lasts, on average, $1/\tau_2$ periods. Thus, training costs are given by p_2c_2/τ_2. Annual income for the average worker in the high-tech sector is $p_2q_2(a_H + a_L)/2$.

[18] At this point, it is useful to first clarify what we mean by training costs. While acquiring the skills necessary to perform certain tasks, there may be periods during which no production occurs whatsoever (while workers are in school, going through orientation, getting hands-on on-the-job training, and so on). However, there may also be a period during which the worker is producing and yet productivity is below its ultimate level because the worker is still learning about the production process. The output lost during the period of learning-by-doing should also be considered as part of training costs. With this interpretation, it is hard to imagine that our most modest assumptions—that there are no resource cost to training in the low-tech sector, that the low-tech training process takes only one week, and that high-tech training costs amount to only one month's worth of high-tech wages—could be considered excessive.

TABLE 9.1
Aggregate Adjustment Costs as a Fraction of the Gross Benefits from Trade
Reform (R^*)

Training Costs	a_H				t^*
	0.20	0.33	0.50	0.66	
$b_1 = 0.5, b_2 = 0.1$					
1 month	0.42	0.39	0.36	0.34	1.3–1.4
5 months	0.66	0.63	0.57	0.53	1.5–1.8
10 months	0.75	0.74	0.69	0.65	1.7–2.1
15 months	0.78	0.80	0.76	0.72	1.9–2.3
$b_1 = 0.5, b_2 = 0.167$					
1 month	0.42	0.39	0.36	0.34	1.3–1.4
5 months	0.65	0.63	0.58	0.53	1.5–1.9
10 months	0.73	0.74	0.70	0.65	1.8–2.2
15 months	0.76	0.80	0.76	0.72	2.0–2.3
$b_1 = 1, b_2 = 0.1$					
1 month	0.42	0.39	0.36	0.34	1.4–1.5
5 months	0.66	0.63	0.57	0.53	1.8–2.3
10 months	0.75	0.74	0.69	0.65	2.1–2.6
15 months	0.78	0.80	0.76	0.72	2.4–2.7
$b_1 = 1, b_2 = 0.167$					
1 month	0.42	0.39	0.36	0.34	1.4–1.6
5 months	0.65	0.63	0.57	0.53	1.8–2.3
10 months	0.73	0.74	0.70	0.65	2.2–2.6
15 months	0.76	0.80	0.76	0.72	2.4–2.7

their jobs, and α, the parameter in the utility function. Our simulations indicate that our results are quite insensitive with respect to α. Adjustment costs are minimized for $\alpha = \frac{1}{2}$ and rarely vary by more than 0.02 for other values of α. As for ϕ, we have argued that high-tech jobs require both general and job-specific training with much of the training general. The implication is that retraining is not all that common in the high-tech sector, which means that ϕ should be fairly high. In tables 9.1 and 9.2 we provide estimates of the two variables that we are interested in, R^* and t^*, under the assumption that $\phi = 0.8$. However, we also calculated these values assuming that ϕ ranged between 0.5 and 0.9 and found that the values in tables 9.1 and 9.2 were affected only at the third decimal place. Thus, we conclude that our estimates are also largely insensitive to our assumptions about ϕ, provided that this value remains above 0.5.

TABLE 9.2
Aggregate Adjustment Costs as a Fraction of the Gross Benefits from Trade Reform Ignoring the Resource Costs from High-Tech Training (R^*_{GO})

Training Costs	a_H				t^*_{GO}
	0.20	0.33	0.50	0.66	
$b_1 = 0.5, b_2 = 0.1$					
1 month	0.20	0.23	0.24	0.25	1.2–1.3
5 months	0.12	0.16	0.18	0.20	1.0–1.2
10 months	0.08	0.11	0.14	0.16	0.8–1.1
15 months	0.06	0.09	0.11	0.13	0.7–1.1
$b_1 = 0.5, b_2 = 0.167$					
1 month	0.19	0.22	0.23	0.24	1.2
5 months	0.10	0.14	0.17	0.18	0.9–1.2
10 months	0.07	0.10	0.12	0.14	0.7–1.1
15 months	0.05	0.08	0.10	0.12	0.6–1.0
$b_1 = 1, b_2 = 0.1$					
1 month	0.20	0.23	0.24	0.25	1.2–1.3
5 months	0.11	0.16	0.18	0.20	1.1–1.3
10 months	0.08	0.11	0.14	0.16	0.9–1.2
15 months	0.06	0.09	0.12	0.13	0.8–1.2
$b_1 = 1, b_2 = 0.167$					
1 month	0.19	0.22	0.23	0.24	1.2–1.3
5 months	0.10	0.14	0.17	0.18	1.0–1.3
10 months	0.07	0.10	0.12	0.14	0.8–1.2
15 months	0.05	0.08	0.10	0.12	0.6–1.1

For q_1 and q_2 what matters is their relative value. Thus, we set $q_2 = 1.4$ and then vary q_1. As q_1 varies the relative attractiveness of the two sectors changes and thus a_H, which determines the fraction of the workforce that starts out in the low-tech sector, is altered. For completeness, we consider four different values for q_1 for each combination of turnover rates. These are the values that correspond to $a_H = 0.2, 0.33, 0.5$, and 0.66. This gives us a sense as to how our measures of R^* and t^* vary with the size of the sector that is initially protected (sector 1) relative to the size of the sector that is associated with significant training costs (sector 2).

Our estimates of R^* and t^* are reported in table 9.1. They were obtained by assuming that the world prices of the two goods are the same and that the low-tech sector is initially protected by a 5% tariff. Three results stand out. First, our model predicts that adjustment will take place quickly, with output reaching its preliberalization level in about two years. The immediate implication is that if one were to look for evidence of adjustment costs using yearly data, it would appear that such costs are quite low.

Nevertheless, the second result that stands out is that our estimates of adjustment costs are considerably higher than any obtained by Baldwin, Mutti, and Richardson (1980) or Magee (1972). Our lowest estimate in table 9.1 is that adjustment costs eat away about one third of the gains from trade reform. At the other extreme, some estimates are as high as 0.8! Given that we have assumed away search costs and resource costs for low-tech training and abstracted from congestion externalities in the expanding export sector labor markets, these estimates are surprisingly high.

Third, the results with respect to R^* and t^* are remarkably robust across our assumptions about steady state break-up rates—going from high turnover in both sectors to low turnover in both sectors never changes R^* by more than 0.02. Our estimates are also fairly insensitive to our assumptions about the initial size of the low-tech sector. As a_H increases, R^* and t^* tend to fall with the rate of decrease increasing in the magnitude of high-tech training costs.[19] In fact, it is the magnitude of these training costs that clearly matter the most. Not surprisingly, as training costs increase, so do R^* and t^*.

One natural question to ask at this point is whether our results are driven by our assumption that training involves a real resource cost or whether the costs are this high simply because the training and search processes take time and no production occurs while search and training take place. To get some handle on this issue, we introduce two new terms, R^*_{GO} and t^*_{GO}. These terms are defined in exactly the same manner as R^* and t^* with one exception—they measure only gross output (i.e., they ignore the resource cost of training). So, for example, t^*_{GO} measures the amount of time it takes for gross output to get back to its preliberalization level. Our estimates of R^*_{GO} and t^*_{GO} are reported in table 9.2. While our estimates fall significantly, they remain considerably above those found in previous studies. Most of the estimates indicate that when we take into account only the time cost of training, around 15% to 20% of the gains in gross output are lost due to adjustment costs. Moreover, gross output returns to its preliberalization level before net output, making it even harder to find evidence of significant adjustment costs in annual (or even quarterly) data. These estimates are robust across our assumptions

[19] Increasing the initial size of the low-tech sector has two effects on R^*. On the one hand, if the low-tech sector is large, then trade reform will generate large benefits. On the other hand, with a large low-tech sector trade reform will also lead to a great deal of worker reallocation and this will increase adjustment costs.

concerning break-up rates and the initial size of the low-tech sector, but do vary significantly as we change our assumptions about the magnitude of high-tech training costs.

4. Adjustment Costs and Labor Market Flexibility

Tables 9.1 and 9.2 indicate that changes in break-up rates have little influence over our estimates of aggregate adjustment costs. Yet, if we look across the world, it is not only break-up rates that vary but also the rate of job acquisition. In the United States most unemployed workers find re-employment relatively quickly and long-term unemployment is not a significant problem. In contrast, many European economies face serious problems with a large population of workers who have been classified as long-term unemployed. Combining this with the fact that job duration is also longer in Europe leads to the conclusion that labor markets are much more flexible in the United States than they are in Europe. This difference in labor market flexibility has been emphasized by labor economists and macroeconomists studying a variety of issues.[20] In this section, we investigate the implications for aggregate adjustment costs.

To do so, we add a new variable s to our model, which we refer to as speed. We introduce this term by multiplying the turnover rates in the high-tech sector, b_2 and e, by s.[21] As s increases, high-tech jobs become easier to find but they also become less durable. Thus, an economy with a high value for s has a great deal of turnover in the high-tech sector while an economy with a low value for s has a high-tech sector with a long average duration of unemployment and a relatively long expected job tenure. It follows that s measures the flexibility of the labor market with increases in speed associated with more flexible labor markets.[22]

Figure 9.5 shows how R^* varies with s for the case in which there is low turnover in the high-tech sector, high turnover in the low-tech sector, high-tech training costs are equal to five months of the average high-tech worker's income, and one-third of the labor force starts out in sector 1 (i.e., $b_1 = 1.0$, $b_2 = 0.1$, and $a_H = 033$). Qualitatively similar figures

---

[20] See, for example, Freeman (1994) and Layard, Nickell, and Jackman (1991).

[21] Similar results can be obtained by multiplying *all* turnover rates by s so that an increase in s results in higher turnover in both sectors. However, since turnover plays a more prominent role in the high-tech sector, it turns out that changes triggered by changes in the high-tech rates dominate those driven by changes in the low-tech rates. A brief description of this case can be found in Davidson and Matusz (2000).

[22] Note that we do not multiply the turnover rates associated with training by s. It is our view that the length of the training process is determined by the complexity of the job and this is a feature that is linked to technology, not the flexibility of the labor market.

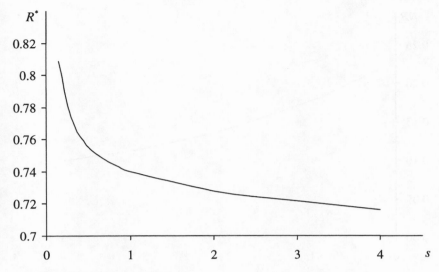

Figure 9.5. R^* as a function of s.

apply for all other parameter values in tables 9.1 and 9.2. As expected, there is a negative relationship between the two measures—increases in labor market flexibility always reduce relative adjustment costs. The implication is that Americans should be less concerned about the costs of adjustment than Europeans and/or the Japanese.

The negative relationship depicted in figure 9.5 suggests that it would be useful to look at how the actual gains from trade (net of adjustment costs) vary with s. To do so, define NB to be the benefit from liberalization net of adjustment costs (as a percentage of initial steady-state welfare):

$$NB \equiv 100 \cdot \left(\frac{W_A - W_{SS}}{W_{SS}} \right) \qquad (23)$$

Figure 9.6 shows how NB varies with s for the parameter values that generate figure 9.5. Surprisingly, as with R^*, the relationship is negative. Even though economies with the least flexible labor markets have the highest adjustment costs, as indicated by high values of R^*, they have the most to gain from liberalization, as indicated by high values of NB.

The surprising outcome depicted in figure 9.6 can be traced to the manner in which the gross benefit from trade varies with speed. The gross benefit from trade reform depends on the amount of workers who switch

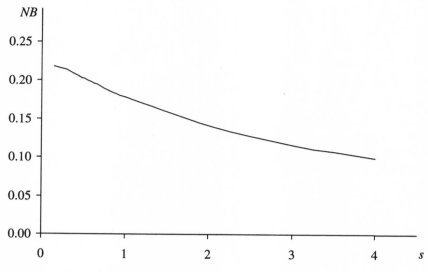

Figure 9.6. *NB* as a function of *s*.

sectors as a result of liberalization. The more workers that switch, the greater the increase in gross output. Figure 9.3 can be used to see how the amount of worker reallocation varies with s. Trade reform lowers the return to training in the low-tech sector, causing the V_{1T} curve to pivot down. The amount of worker reallocation that occurs then depends on the slope of the V_{2T} curve with a flatter curve implying more reallocation. It is straightforward to show that this curve is relatively flat when s is either very low or very high. Intuitively, if $s = 0$, a worker who is currently training has no hope of ever finding a job (since the job acquisition rate is 0) and thus ability, which only affects output while employed, plays no role in determining the value from training. In this case, the V_{2T} curve is horizontal. Increasing s leads to an increase in the fraction of life spent employed and makes ability more important. Thus, when s is low an increase in s causes the V_{2T} curve to become steeper. It follows that trade reform results in a great deal of reallocation when s is very low—thus, when the tariff is removed, large benefits accrue to economies with slothful labor markets. In fact, figure 9.6 reveals that the benefits are so large that they swamp the high costs of adjustments that these economies face.

These results can be viewed one of two ways. On the one hand, there is good news for economies with slothful labor markets—they have much to gain from trade reform, even though they will face high costs of adjustment during the transition to the new steady state. However, the reason that they gain so much is the bad news—in such economies tariffs have large distortionary effects because they cause a great deal of worker reallocation. Removing the tariff therefore generates gross benefits that are large enough to swamp the adjustment costs.

It does, however, take time for the economy with the slothful labor markets to realize these large gains and since turnover is low it may be quite some time before net output returns to its prereform level. For example, for the case reported in table 9.1, while it takes 2 years for the base case economy ($s = 1$) to get net output back to its initial level, it takes an additional 2.5 years for the most stagnant economy (with $s = 0.15$ we find that $t^* = 4.5$). The implication is that although the gains from liberalization may be quite large in such economies, it may be very difficult to find any politician willing to push for such reform.

Recent evidence suggests that one possible way to interpret these results would be to have the United States play the role of the flexible economy, western European countries (e.g., France, Belgium, and the United Kingdom) play the role of the sluggish economies, and countries in eastern Europe (e.g., Estonia, Slovenia, Bulgaria, Hungary, and Romania) play the role of the slothful economies.[23] The case of Estonia is particularly noteworthy. Haltiwanger and Vodopivec (2000) provide evidence that at the time of significant price and trade reforms (in 1989) Estonian labor markets were essentially stagnant. Shortly after instituting these reforms, the Estonian government also began to implement policies aimed at increasing the flexibility of their factor markets. As a result, the economy suffered huge costs in the short run, with real output falling a cumulative 31% between 1991 and 1993. However, the massive reallocation seemed to be nearing completion by 1994 and real output has risen steadily since then. Estonia is largely viewed as a major success story and our results provide some insight as to why it has been so successful. The initial stagnant nature of its factor markets indicated that it had a tremendous amount to gain from reform. In addition, by increasing the flexibility of its labor markets Estonia has been able to realize these gains much quicker than other transition economies.

5. Conclusion

There is no dispute about the fact that workers lose jobs due to changes in trade patterns and that protecting an industry saves jobs. For example,

[23] See Haltiwanger and Vodopivec (2000) for a discussion of job flows in Estonia and Slovenia and Bilsen and Konings (1998) for a discussion of job flows in Bulgaria, Hungary, and Romania.

Hufbauer and Elliott (1994) estimate that eliminating protection in the U.S. apparel industry would cost over 150,000 workers their jobs. It is also well documented that dislocated workers suffer large personal losses with some estimates for the average loss as high as $80,000 in lifetime earnings (Jacobson, LaLonde, and Sullivan 1993a, b). It is therefore not surprising that political leaders are sometimes hesitant about trade reform. Those who lose may lose a great deal and are likely to remember who is at fault when the next election nears. The gains are delayed and are spread out over many so that those who do gain probably gain much less than the few who lose.

Nevertheless, there is probably no other position in economics that has as much widespread support as the belief in the benefits from freer trade. Academic economists typically respond to public concerns about the losses to dislocated workers by explaining that such concerns are misplaced and misguided. This view was summarized and, we feel, appropriately criticized by Baldwin, Mutti, and Richardson (1980) in their article on adjustment costs:

> Economists have sometimes dismissed such adjustment costs with the comment that the displaced factors become reemployed "in the long run." But this is bad economics, since in discounting streams of costs and benefits for welfare calculations, the near-present counts more heavily than "the long-run."

In this paper, we have tried to take a serious look at the possible magnitude of the adjustment costs that are likely to arise from trade reform. The novelty of our approach is that we have modeled the training and search processes that workers must go through in order to find jobs. This allows us to take into account the time and resource costs of retraining and job search. We have tried to be modest in our assumptions concerning these costs. We have assumed away the resource costs associated with job search and low-tech training and assumed that the time costs involved in low-tech training are very small. We have also assumed that workers fleeing the import-competing sector do not encounter congestion when trying to secure reemployment in the export sector. Finally, we have looked at a wide variety of assumptions concerning the cost of training in the high-tech sector.

Our results are surprising. Even with our most modest assumption concerning the cost of high-tech training (that they equal one month of the average high-tech worker's annual earnings), we find that adjustment costs are a significant fraction of the gross benefits from trade reform. Our lowest estimate is that roughly 30% of the gross benefits will be eaten away by adjustment. At the other extreme, we find that when high-tech training is costly (15 months of the average worker's annual salary) as much as 80% of the gross benefits may disappear during the transition period. Even when we focus attention on gross output (so all that matters are the time costs of training and job search) we find that our estimates of adjustment costs are at least twice as high as previous estimates (Magee 1972; Baldwin, Mutti, and Richardson 1980). We also find that the transition period may be quite short, with net output returning to its preliberalization level in 2.5 years or less. We have argued that such quick adjustment may mask the true nature of the adjustment process, perhaps implying that adjustment costs are low when they are, in fact, quite high.

In the latter part of the paper we investigate the relationship between labor market flexibility, the gains from trade reform, and aggregate adjustment costs. It is well documented that turnover rates vary significantly across countries (Freeman 1994). Part of the reason for this is that countries vary in generosity of the social safety nets they provide for the poor and the jobless. Firing costs and generous unemployment insurance programs contribute to long-term unemployment and low turnover throughout Europe (Ljungqvist and Sargent 1998). In addition, the widespread influence of unions in Europe contrasts sharply with their role in the United States, resulting in more rigid wages in European labor markets. Labor economists and macroeconomists have recognized that this difference in labor market structure has important implications for issues such as job training and macroeconomic performance (see, for example, Layard, Nickell, and Jackman 1991). As far as we know, we are the first to investigate the implications for the net gains from trade liberalization.

Again, our main result could not have been anticipated. We find that tariffs create the biggest distortions in economies with slothful labor markets. As a result, when trade is liberalized these economies have the most to gain. This is true in spite of the fact that adjustment costs are high when there is very low turnover. Thus, our analysis indicates that policy makers in economies with slothful labor markets should not be reluctant to reduce barriers to trade, even though their economies are likely to face high adjustment costs.

We close with a word of caution about the interpretation of our results. Although we have argued that adjustment costs are probably higher than previous studies indicate, it is still clear that trade liberalization is the correct path to take—after all, adjustment costs, although high, are always less than the gains from reform. However, what our results do imply is that we should take more seriously the issue of how to compensate those who bear the burden of adjustment and those who lose when trade barriers are removed. In addition, it would be worthwhile to investigate the manner in which various labor market policies affect the speed with which the economy makes the transition to free trade and the manner in which these policies affect the distribution of income during the

transition period. Our results in section 4 indicate that the answers to
these questions will be particularly important for countries with slothful
labor markets.

Finally, there is one other important lesson that can be gleaned from
our analysis—the costs associated with new protectionist measures are
probably higher than previously imagined. Not only do such measures
distort the economy, but our results imply that the cost of moving from
an initial steady state to a new one characterized by higher trade barriers
is quite high. This gives yet another reason to resist protectionist policies.
Moreover, our analysis in section 4 indicates that it is economies with
flexible or slothful labor markets that have the most to lose from new
policies that restrict trade.

APPENDIX A

In this appendix we show how to solve the differential equations in
(1)–(5) and obtain a closed-form solution for the transition path to the
new steady-state equilibrium. As discussed in the text, workers with ability levels in the intervals (a_L, a_{FT}) and $(a_H, 1)$ do not change their behavior
after liberalization. Those in the former interval remain attached to sector 1 while those in the latter interval remain attached to sector 2. It follows that the measure of workers in these intervals that are training or
employed is given by (14)–(17) with the a_H term in (14) and (15) replaced
by a_{FT}.

The remaining workers, those with ability levels in the interval (a_{FT}, a_H),
want to switch from sector 1 to sector 2. Some will do so immediately, either because they are training at the time of liberalization or because they
choose to quit their low-tech job, whereas others opt to keep their low-tech
job and make the switch after that job dissolves. We refer to all of these
workers as the "switchers." To figure out how many switchers are in each
labor market state at time t, we begin by introducing some new notation.
We define $S_T^Q(t)$ as the measure of workers with $a \in [a_{FT}, a_Q]$ who switch
from sector 1 to sector 2 following liberalization and are training in sector
2 at time t. Similarly define $S_S^Q(t)$ as the measure of workers with
$a \in [a_{FT}, a_Q]$ who switch from sector 1 to sector 2 and are searching at time
t and use $S_{E_j}^Q(t)$ to denote the measure of switchers with $a \in [a_{FT}, a_Q]$ who
are employed in sector j at time t. Finally, we define $S_T^H(t), S_S^H(t),$ and $S_{E_j}^H(t)$
analogously for those switchers with $a \in [a_Q, a_H]$.

Since we are using a_Q to denote the ability level of the switcher who is
just indifferent between quitting and not quitting her low-tech job after
liberalization, a_Q is the value of a_i that equates $V_{1T}(a_i)$ with $V_{1E}(a_i)$ after
liberalization (with $V_{1E}(a_i)$ adjusted to take into account the fact that the

worker switches sectors after losing his or her low-tech job) . It follows that all workers with $a \in [a_Q, a_H]$ switch sectors immediately after liberalization, whereas workers with $a \in [a_{FT}, a_Q]$ who are employed when the tariff is removed retain their job until it dissolves. Then, for those switchers with $a \in [a_{FT}, a_Q]$, the system of differential equations can be written as in (A.1)–(A.4):

$$\dot{S}_{E_1}^Q = -b_2 S_{E_1}^Q \tag{A.1}$$

$$\dot{S}_{E_2}^Q = e S_S^Q - b_2 S_{E_2}^Q \tag{A.2}$$

$$\dot{S}_S^Q = b_2 \phi_2 S_{E_2}^Q + \tau_2 S_T^Q - e S_S^Q \tag{A.3}$$

$$(a_Q - a_{FT})L = S_{E_1}^Q + S_{E_2}^Q + S_S^Q + S_T^Q \tag{A.4}$$

where, for notational convenience, we have suppressed the time argument. Equation (A.1) is a simple differential equation, which has the following solution:

$$S_{E_1}^Q(t) = \frac{\tau_1}{\tau_1 + b_1}(a_Q - a_{FT})L e^{-b_1 t} \tag{A.5}$$

In solving (A.1), we make use of the initial condition that

$$S_{E_1}^Q(0) = \frac{\tau_1}{\tau_1 + b_1}(a_Q - a_{FT})L .$$

To solve (A.2)–(A.4), substitute (A.5) into (A.4), solve for S_T^Q in terms of $S_{E_2}^Q$ and S_S^Q, and then substitute the result into (A.3). This leaves us with (A.2) and (A.3), which form a system of two differential equations that can be written in matrix form:

$$\begin{bmatrix} \dot{S}_{E_2}^Q \\ \dot{S}_S^Q \end{bmatrix} = \begin{bmatrix} -b_2 & e \\ b_2\phi_2 - \tau_2 & -(e + \tau_2) \end{bmatrix} \begin{bmatrix} S_{E_2}^Q \\ S_S^Q \end{bmatrix} + \begin{bmatrix} 0 \\ h(t) \end{bmatrix} \tag{A.6}$$

where $h(t) \equiv \tau_2 L(a_Q - a_{FT})\left(1 - \frac{\tau_1}{\tau_1 + b_1}e^{-b_1 t}\right)$. The method for solving a

system of this form can be found in Boyce and DiPrima (1977, pp. 329–31). Using the initial conditions that $S_{E_2}^Q(0) = S_S^Q(0) = 0$, the solutions are

$$S_{E_2}^Q(t) = \frac{e\tau_2(a_Q - a_{FT})L}{\lambda_2 - \lambda_1}\left[\frac{e^{\lambda_2 t}}{\lambda_2} - \frac{e^{\lambda_1 t}}{\lambda_1}\right]$$

$$+ \frac{e\tau_1\tau_2(a_Q - a_{FT})L}{(\tau_1 + b_1)(\lambda_2 - \lambda_1)}\left[\frac{e^{\lambda_1 t}}{\lambda_1 + b_1} - \frac{e^{\lambda_2 t}}{\lambda_2 + b_1}\right]$$

$$- \frac{e\tau_2(a_Q - a_{FT})L}{\lambda_2\lambda_1} - \frac{e\tau_1\tau_2(a_Q - a_{FT})L}{(\tau_1 + b_1)(\lambda_1 + b_1)(\lambda_2 + b_1)}e^{-b_1 t} \quad \text{(A.7)}$$

$$S_S^Q(t) = \frac{\tau_2 b_2(a_Q - a_{FT})L}{\lambda_1\lambda_2}$$

$$+ \frac{\tau_1\tau_2(a_Q - a_{FT})L}{(\tau_1 + b_1)(\lambda_2 - \lambda_1)}\left[\frac{b_2 + \lambda_1}{b_1 + \lambda_1}e^{\lambda_1 t} - \frac{b_2 + \lambda_2}{b_1 + \lambda_2}e^{\lambda_2 t}\right]$$

$$- \frac{\tau_2(a_Q - a_{FT})L}{(\lambda_2 - \lambda_1)}\left[\frac{b_2 + \lambda_1}{\lambda_1}e^{\lambda_1 t} - \frac{b_2 + \lambda_2}{\lambda_2}e^{\lambda_2 t}\right]$$

$$- \frac{\tau_1\tau_2(b_2 - b_1)(a_Q - a_{FT})L}{(\tau_1 + b_1)(\lambda_1 + b_1)(\lambda_2 + b_1)}e^{-b_1 t} \quad \text{(A.8)}$$

where λ_1 and λ_2, the eigenvalues of the coefficient matrix in (A.6), are given by

$$\lambda_1 = \frac{-(b_2 + e + \tau_2) - \sqrt{(b_2 + e + \tau_2)^2 - 4b_2 e(1 - \phi_2)}}{2} \quad \text{(A.9.a)}$$

$$\lambda_1 = \frac{-(b_2 + e + \tau_2) + \sqrt{(b_2 + e + \tau_2)^2 - 4b_2 e(1 - \phi_2)}}{2} \quad \text{(A.9.b)}$$

Finally, the measure of workers with $a \in [a_{FT}, a_Q]$ training in sector 2 at time t is given by

$$S_T^Q(t) = (a_Q - a_{FT})L - S_{E1}^Q(t) - S_{E2}^Q - S_S^Q \quad \text{(A.10)}$$

The discounted present value of the net output produced in each sector by this group of workers is therefore given by

$$X_1(a_{FT}, a_Q) = 0.5(a_{FT} + a_Q)p_1 q_1 \int e^{-rt} S_{E_1}^Q(t)dt \quad \text{(A.11)}$$

$$X_2(a_{FT}, a_Q) = p_2 \int e^{-rt} \{0.5(a_{FT} + a_Q)q_2 S^Q_{E_2}(t) - c_2 S^Q_T(t)\} dt \quad (A.12)$$

For those switchers with $a \in [a_Q, a_H]$, the system of differential equations is given by (A.2)–(A.4) with the Q superscript replaced by H. Equation (A.1) is no longer valid, since all of these switchers quit their jobs. Following the solution method described above yields

$$S^H_{E_2}(t) = (a_H - a_Q)Le\tau_2 \left\{ \frac{1}{\lambda_1\lambda_2} + \frac{1}{\lambda_2 - \lambda_1}\left[\frac{e^{\lambda_2 t}}{\lambda_2} - \frac{e^{\lambda_1 t}}{\lambda_1} \right] \right\} \quad (A.13)$$

$$S^H_S(t) = (a_H - a_Q)$$
$$L\tau_2 \left\{ \frac{b_2}{\lambda_1\lambda_2} + \frac{1}{\lambda_2 - \lambda_1}\left[\frac{b_2 + \lambda_2}{\lambda_2}e^{\lambda_2 t} - \frac{b_2 + \lambda_1}{\lambda_1}e^{\lambda_1 t} \right] \right\} \quad (A.14)$$

and $S^H_T(t) = (a_H - a_{FT})L - S^H_{E_2}(t) - S^H_S(t)$. The discounted present value of the net output produced in sector 2 by this group of workers is therefore given by

$$X_2(a_Q, a_H) = p_2 \int e^{-rt} \{0.5(a_H + a_Q)q_2 S^H_{E_2}(t) - c_2 S^H_T(t)\} dt \quad (A.15)$$

APPENDIX B

In this appendix we show that the laissez-faire equilibrium in our model is efficient. To do so, we calculate the dynamic marginal product of labor in each sector and show that these values are equal in the market equilibrium.

The dynamic marginal product of sector-j labor measures the increase in net output that occurs if the steady state is disturbed by adding an additional worker to that sector, taking into account the adjustment path to the new steady state. To calculate the dynamic marginal products we follow the method developed in Diamond (1980).

We begin by defining $\chi_i(\theta)$ as the present discounted value of output net of training costs produced in sector i when a (small) measure θ of new workers is added to that sector. These workers are assumed to have ability level a_H. Equilibrium is efficient if $\chi_1'(\theta) = \chi_2'(\theta)$.

Start with sector 1. We have[24]

[24] The equation of motion for $\dot\theta^E_1$ is obtained in the following manner. Since search is not required to find employment in sector 1, we have $\dot\theta^E_1 = \tau_1\theta^T_1 - b_1\theta^E_1$. Now, we know that the total measure of trainers (out of the θ) in sector 1 is equal to the difference between θ and the measure of employed workers in that sector. Substituting for θ^T_1 yields the desired result.

$$\chi_1(\theta) \equiv \int_0^\infty e^{-rt} \left\{ a_H q_1 p_1 \theta I(t) - \theta p_1 c_1 \left[1 - I(t) \right] \right\} dt$$

where $\dot{\theta}_1^E = \tau_1 \theta - (\tau_1 + b_1)\theta_1^E$ and $I(t)$ is an indicator function that takes on the value of 1 when the worker is employed and equals zero at all other times. To find $\chi_1'(\theta)$ we start by using the fundamental equation of dynamic programming which states that

$$r\chi_1(\theta) = a_H q_1 p_1 \theta I(t) - \theta p_1 c_1 [1 - I(t)] + \frac{\partial \chi_1}{\partial \theta_1^E} \dot{\theta}_1^E$$

Substituting for $\dot{\theta}_1^E$ from above allows us to write this as

$$r\chi_1(\theta) = a_H q_1 p_1 \theta I(t) - \theta p_1 c_1 [1 - I(t)] + \frac{\partial \chi_1}{\partial \theta_1^E} \{\tau_1 \theta - (\tau_1 + b_1)\theta_1^E\} \quad \text{(B.1)}$$

Differentiating with respect to θ yields

$$r\chi_1'(\theta) = a_H q_1 p_1 I(t) - p_1 c_1 \left\{ 1 - I(t) \right\} + \tau_1 \frac{\partial \chi_1}{\partial \theta_1^E}$$

but $I(0) = 0$, so that at $t = 0$ we have

$$r\chi_1'(\theta) = -p_1 c_1 + \tau_1 \frac{\partial \chi_1}{\partial \theta_1^E} \quad \text{(B.2)}$$

To complete our derivation, we must now calculate $\partial \chi_1 / \partial \theta_1^E$. To do so, we solve (B.1) for $\partial \chi_1 / \partial \theta_1^E$. We obtain

$$\frac{\partial \chi_1}{\partial \theta_1^E} = \frac{r\chi_1 - a_H q_1 p_1 \theta I(t) + \theta p_1 c_1 [1 - I(t)]}{\tau_1 \theta - (\tau_1 + b_1)\theta_1^E}$$

In the initial steady state, the right-hand side of this equation equals $0/0$. Applying l'Hôpital's rule, we have [note that we are differentiating with respect to θ_1^E, which is the same as $\theta I(t)$]

$$\frac{\partial \chi_1}{\partial \theta_1^E} = \frac{r\dfrac{\partial \chi_1}{\partial \theta_1^E} - a_H q_1 p_1 - p_1 c_1}{-(\tau_1 + b_1)}$$

or

$$\frac{\partial \chi_1}{\partial \theta_1^E} = \frac{a_H q_1 p_1 + p_1 c_1}{r + \tau_1 + b_1}$$

We can now substitute this value into (B.2) to obtain the dynamic marginal product of labor in sector 1:

$$r\chi_1'(\theta) = \frac{\tau_1 a_H q_1 p_1 - (r + b_1) p_1 c_1}{r + \tau_1 + b_1} \tag{B.3}$$

Note that this dynamic marginal product equals $rV_{1T}(a_H)$.

We now turn next to sector 2. We have

$$\chi_2(\theta) \equiv \int_0^\infty e^{-rt} \left\{ a_H p_2 q_2 \theta I(t) - c_2 p_2 \theta [1 - I(t) - H(t)] \right\} dt$$

where $\dot{\theta}_2^E = e\theta_2^S - b_2\theta_2^E$, $\dot{\theta}_2^S = \tau_2\theta + (b_2\phi - \tau_2)\theta_2^E - (\tau_2 + e)\theta_2^S$, $I(t)$ is an indicator function that equals 1 when the worker is employed and zero otherwise, and $H(t)$ is an indicator function which equals 1 when the worker is searching and zero otherwise.

As above, we start by applying the fundamental equation of dynamic programming which implies that

$$r\chi_2(\theta) = a_H p_2 q_2 \theta I(t) - c_2 p_2 \theta [1 - I(t) - H(t)] + \frac{\partial \chi_2}{\partial \theta_2^E} \dot{\theta}_2^E + \frac{\partial \chi_2}{\partial \theta_2^S} \dot{\theta}_2^S$$

If we now use the equations of motion to substitute for $\dot{\theta}_2^E$ and $\dot{\theta}_2^S$ and then differentiate with respect to θ, we obtain

$$r\chi_2'(\theta) = a_H p_2 q_2 I(t) - c_2 p_2 [1 - I(t) - H(t)] + \frac{\partial \chi_2}{\partial \theta_2^S} \tau_2$$

But in the initial steady state (at $t = 0$), we know that $I(0) = H(0) = 0$, so that

$$r\chi_2'(\theta) = -c_2 p_2 + \tau_2 \frac{\partial \chi_2}{\partial \theta_2^S} \tag{B.4}$$

The final step requires us to solve for $\partial \chi_2 / \partial \theta_2^S$ and then substitute that value into (B.4). Again following Diamond (1980), we differentiate the fundamental equation of dynamic programming with respect to θ_2^E and θ_2^S. We obtain

$$\begin{bmatrix} \dfrac{\partial \chi_2}{\partial \theta_2^E} \\[3mm] \dfrac{\partial \chi_2}{\partial \theta_2^S} \end{bmatrix} = [(a_H p_2 q_2 + c_2 p_2)\, c_2 p_2] \begin{bmatrix} r + b_2 & -(b_2\phi - \tau_2) \\ -e_2 & (r + \tau_2 + e_2) \end{bmatrix}^{-1}$$

Solving this system of equations for $\partial\chi_2/\partial\theta_2^s$ yields

$$\frac{\partial\chi_2}{\partial\theta_2^s} = \frac{p_2\{a_H q_2 e_2 + c_2(e_2 + r + b_2)\}}{(r + b_2)(r + \tau_2 + e_2) + e_2\tau_2 - e\phi b_2} \tag{B.5}$$

Substituting (B.5) into (B.4) and collecting terms results in

$$r\chi_2'(\theta) = \frac{p_2\{a_H q_2 e - [(r + b_2)(r + e_2) - e_2\phi b_2]c_2\}}{(r + b_2)(r + \tau_2 + e) + e_2\tau_2 - e_2\phi b_2} \tag{B.6}$$

Note that (B.6) is also equal to $rV_{2T}(a_H)$. Thus, since both dynamic marginal products equal the expected lifetime income for a worker training in that sector, and, since workers are allocated so that the expected lifetime income from training is the same in both sectors, the dynamic marginal products are equal in equilibrium. As a result, equilibrium is efficient.

APPENDIX C

In this appendix our goal is to show how to transform our measure of aggregate income in the initial steady state into utility. In particular, we want to show that utility is given by $\eta(\gamma)Y_{SS}$ with $\eta(\gamma) = \dfrac{\alpha^\alpha[(1-\alpha)(1+\gamma)]^{1-\alpha}}{\alpha + (1-\alpha)(1+\gamma)}$.
Given our assumption that the utility function for each consumer is given by $U(Z_1, Z_2) = Z_1^\alpha Z_2^{1-\alpha}$, it follows that the aggregate consumption bundle is given by $Z_1 = \alpha I/(1 + \gamma)$ and $Z_2 = (1 - \alpha)I$ where I is a measure of aggregate income and both world prices have been set to 1. It follows that $Z_2 = \dfrac{(1-\alpha)(1+\gamma)}{\alpha}Z_1$. Now, in the tariff-distorted equilibrium, it must be the case that the value of output equals the value of the consumption bundle when both are evaluated at world prices. The value of output is given by Y_{SS}. It follows that $Z_1 + Z_2 = Y_{SS}$. If we now substitute for Z_2 and solve for Z_1 we obtain $Z_1 = \dfrac{\alpha Y_{SS}}{\alpha + (1-\alpha)(1+\gamma)}$. This implies that $Z_2 = \dfrac{(1-\alpha)Y_{SS}}{\alpha + (1-\alpha)(1+\gamma)}$. Plugging these values into the utility function then yields the desired result.

REFERENCES

Acemoglu, D., Pischke, J. 1999. Beyond Becker: Training in imperfect labor markets. *Economic Journal* 109(453): F112–42.

Bacchetta, M., Jansen, M. 2003. Adjusting to trade liberalization: The role of policy, institutions and WTO disciplines. WTO Special Studies 7.

Baldwin, R., Mutti, J., Richardson, J. D. 1980. Welfare effects on the United States of a significant multilateral tariff reduction. *Journal of International Economics* 10(3): 405–23.

Bilsen, V., Konings, J. 1998. Job creation, job destruction and growth of newly established, privatized and state-owned enterprises in transition economies: Survey evidence from Bulgaria, Hungary, and Romania. *Journal of Comparative Economics* 26(3): 429–45.

Boyce, W., DiPrima, R. 1977. *Elementary Differential Equations and Boundary Value Problems.* John Wiley and Sons, New York.

Brahmbhatt, M. 1997. *Global Economic Prospects and the Developing Countries.* World Bank, Washington, DC.

Cassing, J., Ochs, J. 1978. International trade, factor market distortions, and the optimal dynamic subsidy: Comment. *American Economic Review* 68(5): 950–55.

Davidson, C., Matusz, S. J. 2000. Globalization and labour-market adjustment: How fast and at what cost? *Oxford Review of Economic Policy* 16(3): 42–56.

Davidson, C., Matusz, S. J. 2001. Globalization, employment and income: Analyzing the adjustment process. In Greenaway, D., Upward, R, Wahelin, K. (Eds.), *Trade, Investment, Migration and Labour Market Adjustment.* Macmillan, London: 66–92.

Davidson, C., Matusz, S. J. 2002. An overlapping generations model of escape clause protection. Michigan State University Working Paper.

Davis, S., Haltiwanger, J., Schuh, S. 1996. *Job Creation and Job Destruction.* MIT Press, Cambridge.

De Melo, J., Tarr, D. 1990. Welfare costs of U.S. quotas in textiles, steel and autos. *Review of Economics and Statistics* 72(3): 489–97.

Diamond, P. 1980. An alternative to steady state comparisons. *Economics Letters* 5(1): 7–9.

Falvey, R., Kim, C.D. 1992. Timing and sequencing issues in trade liberalization. *Economic Journal* 102(413): 908–24.

Freeman, R. 1994. How labor fares in advanced economies. In Freeman, R. (Ed.), *Working under Different Rules.* Russell Sage Foundation, New York.

Furusawa, T., Lai, E. 1999. Adjustment costs and gradual trade liberalization. *Journal of International Economics* 49(2): 333–62.

Gaisford, J. D., Leger, L. A. 2000. Terms-of-trade shocks, labor-market adjustment, and safeguard measures. *Review of International Economics* 8(1): 100–12.

Haltiwanger, J., Vodopivec, M. 2000. Gross worker and job flows in a transition economy: An analysis of Estonia. University of Maryland Working Paper.

Hamermesh, D. 1993. *Labor Demand.* Princeton University Press, Princeton.

Hamermesh, D. Rees, A. 1988. *The Economics of Work and Pay*, 4th ed. Harper and Row, New York.

Hufbauer, G., Elliott, K. 1994. *Measuring the Costs of Protection in the United States*. Institute for International Economics, Washington, DC.

Jacobson, L., LaLonde, R., Sullivan, D. 1993a. *The Cost of Worker Dislocation*. W.E. Upjohn Institute for Employment Research, Kalamazoo, MI.

Jacobson, L., LaLonde, R., Sullivan, D. 1993b. Earnings losses of displaced workers. *American Economic Review* 83(4): 685–709.

Karp, L., Paul, T. 1994. Phasing in and phasing out protectionism with costly adjustment of labour. *Economic Journal* 104(427): 1379–92.

Layard, R., Nickell, S., Jackman, R. 1991. *Unemployment: Macroeconomic Performance and the Labor Market*. Oxford University Press, Oxford.

Li, J., Meyer, W. 1996. Age as a determinant of labor's trade policy interests. *Pacific Economic Review* 1(2): 147–68.

Ljungqvist, L., Sargent, T. 1998. The European unemployment dilemma. *Journal of Political Economy* 106(3): 514–50.

Magee, S. 1972. The welfare effects of restrictions on U.S. trade. *Brookings Papers on Economic Activity* 3(3): 645–701.

Neary, P. 1982. Intersectoral capital mobility, wage stickiness, and the case for adjustment assistance. In J. Bhagwati (ed.), *Import Competition and Response*. University of Chicago Press, Chicago.

Tackas, W., Winters, A. 1991. Labour adjustment costs and British footwear protection. *Oxford Economic Papers* 43(3): 479–501.

Trefler, D. 2001. The long and short of the Canadian-U.S. Free Trade Agreement. University of Toronto Working Paper.

Chapter 10

AN OVERLAPPING-GENERATIONS MODEL
OF ESCAPE CLAUSE PROTECTION

CARL DAVIDSON AND STEVEN J. MATUSZ

A Member shall apply safeguard measures only to the extent
necessary to prevent or remedy serious injury and *to facilitate
adjustment*.
— Article 5, Uruguay Round Agreement on Safeguards (emphasis
added)

If the Commission makes an affirmative determination, it
recommends to the President the action that will *facilitate positive
adjustment* by the industry to import competition.
— United States International Trade Commission (1998; emphasis
added)

1. INTRODUCTION

Between January 1974 and January 2002, the United States International Trade Commission (USITC) completed investigations of 73 petitions for import relief filed under the aegis of section 201 of the Trade Act of 1974 (Bishop 2002). This act permits interested parties to petition the USITC for relief from injurious but fair foreign competition. Any relief granted is intended as a temporary measure, providing the industry with time to adjust to changing circumstances.

Of the 73 completed investigations, 40 resulted in affirmative findings by the commission. After forwarding their recommendations to the president of the United States, 24 of these cases resulted in some form of import relief, almost half of which as recommended by the commission, with the remainder being modified by the president.

As the excerpts from the Uruguay Round Agreement on Safeguards and the USITC indicate, safeguard measures are intended, in part, to facilitate adjustment to changes in the international environment. Adjustment typically entails becoming "leaner and meaner" to more effectively compete in the international marketplace. As such, part of "facilitating adjustment" can be viewed as providing time so that resources can be withdrawn from declining industries in an orderly fashion. It has been suggested that the government may also have equity considerations in mind when providing such relief, as this passage from Baldwin (1989) clearly articulates:

> Other authors stressing the income distribution goals of government, like Cheh (1974) and Lavergne (1983), argue that trade policies of governments are motivated by a desire to minimize (or delay) adjustment costs, especially to workers. In examining the Kennedy Round of multilateral trade negotiations, Cheh found a pattern of low tariff cuts in industries with high proportions of elderly workers, declining employment, and rising import penetration ratios.

By providing temporary protection, the government gives young workers time to retrain and make a smooth transition to the growing export sectors while simultaneously softening the blow to the older workers who face bleak reemployment prospects if they try to change their occupation so late in life.

Our goal in this paper is to explore the efficiency consequences of using temporary protection to smooth out the adjustment process following an unexpected, permanent improvement in a country's terms of trade.[1] We assume that the government's primary motivation in providing such relief is twofold. First, it is intended to either reduce or delay the adjustment costs imposed on the young workers who switch occupations as a result of the terms of trade shock. Second, it is intended to lessen the blow to the older workers who find that they regret decisions made earlier in life because they could not anticipate the improvement in the terms of trade. Thus, while the government's primary motives may be equity driven, our goal is to assess the welfare consequences of the government's actions.[2] We do so in the context of a simple overlapping-generations model where

---

[1] Thus, our approach differs, in a fundamental way, from the equity-based explanation of temporary protection offered by Deardorff (1987) and the political economy explanation offered by Sykes (1991). Deardorff bases his explanation on Corden's conservative social welfare function and argues that the government's objective is to prevent a significant fall in real income of a significant sector of the economy. In his setting, safeguard policies "are not intended, as economists more often recommend, to facilitate 'adjustment' in the sense of an orderly transition to a new equilibrium" (p. 24). In contrast, the Sykes approach emphasizes that policy makers may experience a change in political support when the terms of trade change and it is therefore in their interest to respond to this change with newly adopted measures of temporary protection. Our analysis is, in no way, meant to dismiss such alternative explanations of temporary safeguard policies. Instead, our goal is to show that if the government is concerned about adjustment, as has been emphasized by a variety of authors in the past, there may be efficiency as well as equity concerns driving their decisions.

[2] While we are concerned with the efficiency implications of temporary protection, we make no attempt to derive the *optimal* time path. Indeed, as one referee correctly notes, our two-

all newborn agents must decide whether to seek employment in the export sector or the import-competing sector. In making their choice, agents trade off the potentially higher wage that the export sector has to offer with a lower probability of actually finding a job in that sector. Since young agents have a longer time horizon, more young workers than old choose to search for jobs in the export sector. An unexpected improvement in the terms of trade surprises old workers who cannot undo the decisions they made while young. As a result, some old workers who had not planned to search for work in the export sector end up changing their plans, adding to the pool of searchers. As the pool of searchers in the export sector swells, congestion externalities may arise, making it harder to secure employment. This is particularly harmful to old workers since they have less time left to find new jobs than their younger counterparts. By providing temporary protection, the government can stem the tide of searchers, reduce congestion, and make the transition to the new steady state smoother.

We are not the first to examine the broad issue of trade and adjustment costs, nor even the first to examine the more narrowly defined issue of temporary protection and adjustment costs. Several empirical studies, including those by Magee (1972), Baldwin, Mutti, and Richardson (1980), and Trefler (2001) address the size and scope of adjustment costs. Theoretical work by Mayer (1974), Mussa (1974, 1978), Neary (1978), and Davidson and Matusz (2001) emphasizes the importance of taking the adjustment process into account when making welfare judgments. More directly relevant to this paper are the studies by Cassing and Ochs (1978), Lapan (1976, 1978, 1979), Michealy (1986), Mussa (1986), Ray (1979), Karp and Paul (1994, 1998), and Gaisford and Leger (2000) that explore the optimal policy path for liberalization in the presence of adjustment costs.[3] One key insight from this research is that in the absence of factor market distortions, there is no justification on efficiency grounds for gradual liberalization. However, if there are factor market imperfections, then some sort of government intervention, either in the form of temporary protection or some sort of labor market policy, is warranted.[4]

Several of these papers focus on congestion externalities as the source of the factor market distortion. Cassing and Ochs (1978) provide an

---

period overlapping-generations framework precludes any deep analysis of this interesting and important issue.

[3] For an excellent survey of the early work in this literature see Falvey and Kim (1992).

[4] Of course, if factor markets are distorted there are generally policy instruments that are preferable to tariffs. Thus, complete liberalization coupled with temporary labor market policies targeted at the source of the distortions is the optimal policy. It has been pointed out that such policies may be politically infeasible, leaving tariffs as the only way to slow down the adjustment process.

explicit model of the search process and show that the market-induced rate of adjustment is suboptimal when congestion externalities are present. In contrast, Karp and Paul (1994, 1998) and Gaisford and Leger (2000) do not model the source of the externality—they simply assume that the social cost of adjustment exceeds the private cost of adjustment. Both papers then show that government intervention can raise welfare, although Karp and Paul focus on tariff policy while Gaisford and Leger argue that there are always superior policies available.

Our work is similar to Karp and Paul's in that we show that if a change in the terms of trade leads to a temporary enlargement of the pool of searchers and if this creates congestion, then a temporary import tariff that slows down the movement of workers into the export sector might actually increase the value of output (measured at world prices). However, our work is unique in at least three respects. First, by using an overlapping-generations model in which the congestion externalities are carefully modeled we are able to highlight how the unexpected improvement in the terms of trade affects the young and old as well as the current and future generations in fundamentally different ways. We consider this to be important, since, as we noted above, there is empirical evidence that concern about the welfare of older workers plays a role in the government's policy choices. Second, we show that there are conditions under which the congestion externalities in our model lead to multiple steady-state equilibria that can be Pareto ranked. As a result, it is possible that with free trade the change in the terms of trade may push the economy into a new steady state characterized by low job acquisition rates and low output in the export sector. However, if the government intervenes by providing temporary protection to the import-competing sector, the adjustment process may be slowed down enough to steer the economy toward a different steady state that is characterized by higher job acquisition and production rates in the export sector. This leads to the third unique feature of our analysis. In previous work, when the new long-run free trade equilibrium is reached, there are no lasting effects from the period of temporary protection. This need not be the case in our model—temporary protection may lead to a permanent change in the allocation of resources and this permanent change may be welfare enhancing.

We present our model and examine the decision problem faced by workers in the next section. We then solve for the steady-state equilibrium and the transition path between equilibria in section 3, where we also demonstrate how temporary import protection can avert the congestion externality. Since a tariff is distorting, we discuss in section 4 the costs and benefits associated with a temporary tariff, and argue that it will be welfare improving if the magnitude of the minimum tariff necessary to reduce congestion is relatively small. In section 5 we turn to the issue of multiple equilibria and show how a temporary tariff can have a permanent effect on the long-run allocation of resources.

2. AN OVERLAPPING-GENERATIONS MODEL

2.1 Assumptions

We consider an overlapping-generations model where labor is the only factor of production. Workers are indexed by ability a, which is distributed uniformly over [0,1]. Each worker lives for two periods and is replaced by an identical worker upon death. We refer to a generation as "young" or "old" if it contains workers in their first or second period of life, respectively. Correspondingly, we use superscripts y and o to refer to variables that pertain to a given generation at a particular time. We normalize the measure of workers in each generation to 1. Combined with our assumption about the distribution of ability, this means that for any $a^g \in [0,1]$, the measure of workers in generation g with $a < a^g$ is a^g, while the measure with $a > a^g$ is $1 - a^g$.

There are two goods, which we label X (an export good) and M (an import-competing good). Each worker, regardless of ability, can produce one unit of M per period. By contrast, each worker employed in the export sector can produce a units of output per period. With competitive labor markets, constant returns to scale technology, and no other inputs, each employed worker is paid the value of his or her marginal product, which also equals the total value of his or her production.

We assume that the economy is small, choose the export good as numeraire, and define P_t as the exogenously given world price of the import-competing good.

We assume that a worker can always obtain a job in the import-competing sector and keep that job for his or her entire life. By contrast, a worker who wishes to be employed in the export sector must search, and there is some probability the worker will not find a job in that sector. We use π_t to denote the probability of "success" for a worker searching for a job in the export sector at time t, and it is assumed that workers have rational expectations concerning π_t.

While we do not explicitly model the search process, what we have in mind is an underlying model in the spirit of the classic work by Mortensen (1982) and Pissarides (1990) in which firms in the export sector post vacancies while workers search for employment.[5] Workers

---

[5] See also Diamond (1981, 1982, 1984) where the information problems that generate equilibrium unemployment are not explicitly modeled.

know the number of jobs available and the size of the search pool, but they do not know which firms have unfilled vacancies until they visit them. In such settings, a worker who chooses to search for an export sector job makes it harder for the other searchers in that sector to find employment. These congestion externalities distort incentives and lead to suboptimal equilibria. Our focus is on how the government can use temporary protection to improve the efficiency of the adjustment process by controlling the rate at which workers switch sectors. Consistent with previous search theoretic models of unemployment, we are assuming that the government possesses the same information as the workers, and thus cannot eradicate the information problem that generates the equilibrium unemployment.[6]

The main reason that we do not explicitly model the search process is that its exact nature is not important for our purpose—all that matters is that the congestion externalities are present.[7] This can be captured in a simple manner by assuming that the probability of finding a job in the export sector is a decreasing function of the measure of workers searching for export sector jobs, as we do in section 3. Carefully modeling the search process itself would greatly complicate the analysis without providing any additional insight.

2.2 The Worker's Decision Problem

At the start of each period, unemployed workers (including all newborns) must decide whether to accept certain employment in the import-competing sector or search for employment in the export sector. Moreover, each worker who enters the period employed must decide whether to keep his or her job or look for a job in the other sector.[8]

The decision for workers in the old generation is simple. Expected one-period income from searching in the export sector at time t is $\pi_t a$, whereas the certain income of taking a job in the import-competing sector is P_t. Assuming risk-neutrality, workers who are not already employed in the export sector with $a \geq P_t/\pi_t$ will choose to search for a job in that sector, while the remaining workers will choose to work in the import-competing

---

[6] One way that the government could attack the source of the problem directly is through state-run employment agencies. We follow the standard approach in the search literature by assuming that the government does not do so because it would be prohibitively costly to do so.

[7] For recent empirical evidence on the existence and magnitude of congestion externalities in the labor market, see Yashiv (2000).

[8] The only people who have the opportunity to switch jobs are those in the middle of their life, who are just turning old.

sector. We define this critical level of ability as a_t^o and refer to any old worker with this ability as the marginal old worker.[9]

The problem for workers in the young generation is more complicated. Define $V_{St}^y(a)$ as the expected lifetime income of a young worker who searches for a job in the export sector and use $V_{Mt}^y(a)$ to denote the expected lifetime income for a young worker who accepts a job in the import-competing sector.[10] Then

$$V_{St}^y(a) = 2\pi_t a + (1 - \pi_t)\max\{P_{t+1}, \pi_{t+1}a\} \tag{1}$$

$$V_{Mt}^y(a) = P_t + \max\{P_{t+1}, \pi_{t+1}a\} \tag{2}$$

If a young searcher achieves success, she earns a while young, and a when old.[11] If the searcher does not find a job, she has the option of searching again when old, or taking a job in the import-competing sector. Similarly, a worker who accepts a job in the import-competing sector earns P_t while young, and has the option of searching when old.

We define a_t^y as the value of ability that equates (1) and (2) and refer to any young worker with this ability as the marginal young worker. Figures 10.1a and 10.1b illustrate two qualitatively different solutions for a_t^y. In figure 10.1a, some workers who are young at time t will choose to search for a job in the export sector, but if they are not successful, they will return to the import-competing sector when they become old. These workers have ability $a \in (a_t^y, a_{t+1}^o)$. It is in their interest to "test the waters" of the job market. The potential to receive two periods of high wages is worth giving up one period of low wages. But as they near the end of their work life, the potential to receive higher wages no longer offsets the loss of a single period of low wages.

If the marginal young worker depicted in figure 10.1a fails in her search for an export sector job, she will not choose to repeat the search when old. Instead she will choose to accept a job in the import-competing sector. This implies that for this marginal young worker, $\max\{P_{t+1}, \pi_{t+1}a_t^y\} = P_{t+1}$. We can now equate (1) and (2) and solve to obtain

---

[9] Any old worker for whom $a = a_t^o$ will be indifferent between searching for an export sector job and taking a job in the import-competing sector. Without loss of generality, we break the tie in favor of search.

[10] In order to lighten the notation, we assume that the discount rate is zero. This assumption has no substantive bearing on the qualitative features of the model.

[11] Of course, this worker always has the option of quitting her job in the export sector when old and taking a job in the import-competing sector. However, since we are interested in the case in which the economy experiences an unexpected improvement in the terms of trade, the worker will never choose to do so.

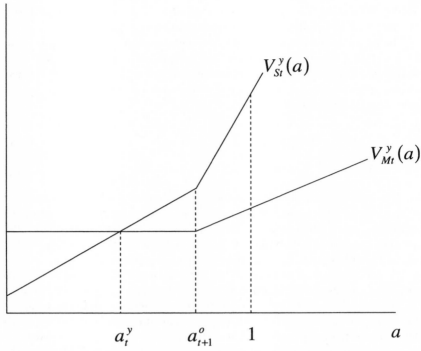

Figure 10.1a. Solving for the marginal young worker: testing the waters.

$$a_t^y = a_t^o \left\{ \frac{1 + \pi_t (P_{t+1}/P_t)}{2} \right\} \tag{3a}$$

The situation depicted in figure 10.1b is different. Fewer workers choose to search when young than when those same workers become old. For these delayed searchers, $\max\{P_{t+1}, \pi_{t+1} a_t^y\} = \pi_{t+1} a_t^y$. Equating (1) and (2) and solving yields

$$a_t^y = a_t^o \left\{ \frac{1}{2 - \pi_{t+1}} \right\} \tag{3b}$$

Alternative assumptions about the parameters underlie the qualitatively different solutions depicted in figures 10.1a and 10.1b. For example, in figure 10.1a it is the case that $a_t^y < a_{t+1}^o$. Using (3a) and our solution for a_t^o, we find that this inequality holds if

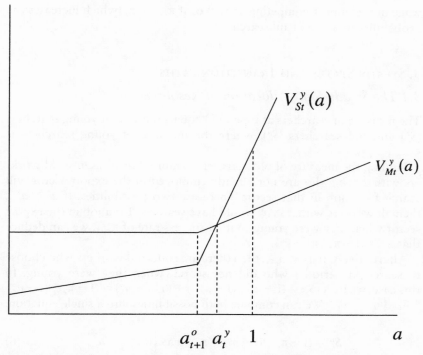

Figure 10.1b. Solving for the marginal young worker: delayed search.

$$\frac{P_t}{\pi_t}\left\{\frac{1+\pi_t(P_{t+1}/P_t)}{2}\right\} < \frac{P_{t+1}}{\pi_{t+1}} \qquad (4)$$

For example, reducing π_{t+1} or P_t or increasing P_{t+1} will lead eventually to the satisfaction of the inequality expressed in (4). All of these partial derivatives are sensible. A reduction in π_{t+1} causes a fall in the expected wage of a worker searching in period $t + 1$, while an increase in P_{t+1} boosts the attractiveness of jobs in the import-competing sector.

Similarly, in figure 10.1b, it is clear that $a_t^y > a_{t+1}^o$. Using (3b) and our solution for a_t^o, this inequality is satisfied if

$$\frac{P_{t+1}}{\pi_{t+1}} < \frac{P_t}{\pi_t}\left\{\frac{1}{2-\pi_{t+1}}\right\} \qquad (5)$$

Since $\pi_{t+1} \leq 1$, delayed search can occur only if the price of the import-competing good falls between periods t and $t + 1$ (which reduces the wage in the import-competing sector) or if $\pi_{t+1} > \pi_t$ (which increases the probability of a successful search).

3. STEADY STATES AND TRANSITION PATHS

3.1 The Steady-State Allocation of Resources

The measure of searchers at time t (S_t) equals the sum of young searchers (S_t^y) and old searchers (S_t^o), where the measure of young searchers is $S_t^y = 1 - a_t^y$.

Finding the measure of old searchers is more difficult. Only old workers with $a \geq a_t^o$ who are not already employed in the export sector will search for a job in that sector. There are two possibilities. If $a_t^o > a_{t-1}^y$, then all workers with $a \geq a_t^o$ would have searched for a job in the export sector when they were young. With a success rate of π_{t-1}, we can deduce that $S_t^o = (1 - \pi_{t-1})(1 - a_t^o)$.

Alternatively, if $a_t^o < a_{t-1}^y$, then there are some old workers who choose to search in period t who did not search when they were young. In this case, we have $S_t^o = (1 - \pi_{t-1})(1 - a_{t-1}^y) + (a_{t-1}^y - a_t^o) = (1 - \pi_{t-1})(1 - a_t^o) + \pi_{t-1}(a_{t-1}^y - a_t^o)$. We can combine both possibilities into a single equation:

$$S_t^o = (1 - \pi_{t-1})(1 - a_t^o) + \pi_{t-1} \max\left\{0, a_{t-1}^y - a_t^o\right\} \tag{6}$$

The second part of (6) can be interpreted as the measure of old searchers who would have gotten a job when young had they searched, and therefore would not be searching when old. Of course, this term is zero if all old searchers also searched when young.

In a steady state, $P_t = P$ and $\pi_t = \pi$ for all t. From our discussion at the end of the last subsection, we can rule out the possibility of delayed search in a steady state. Therefore, all steady states are characterized by figure 10.1a. Let $\bar{S}^y$ and $\bar{S}^o$ denote the steady-state measures of young and old searchers, and define $\bar{S} = \bar{S}^y + \bar{S}^o$. We note that the steady-state measure of searchers in each generation is a function of both P and π. We focus on the relationship between P and the measure of searchers in the remainder of this section, turning to the relationship with π in section 4.

3.2 An Unexpected Improvement in the Terms of Trade

Suppose now that there is a permanent, unexpected improvement in the terms of trade. To help keep track of events, we normalize time by setting $t = 1$ when the terms of trade improve. We can then model a permanent improvement in the terms of trade by assuming that $P_t = P_H$ for $t \leq 0$

and $P_t = P_L$ for $t \geq 1$, where $P_L < P_H$. We begin by investigating how this change in world prices affects worker behavior and the value of output.

Intuitively, the improvement in the terms of trade will push some workers out of the import-competing sector to search for jobs in the export sector. As we noted earlier, it is standard to assume congestion externalities exist so that as the pool of searchers swells the probability that an individual worker will find a job falls. This notion is captured by assuming that π_t is a decreasing function of S_t. While it is natural to think of this function as continuous, doing so complicates our analysis considerably without providing any additional insight.[12] Thus, for illustrative purposes we postulate the following simple form for this function:

$$\pi(S) = \begin{cases} \pi_H & \text{if } S \leq \tilde{S} \\ \\ \pi_L & \text{if } S > \tilde{S} \end{cases} \tag{7}$$

We assume that workers have rational expectations about the time path of π_t. As we show in section 5, there are cases in which there are multiple rational expectations steady-state equilibria. In addition, there may be more than one rational expectations transition path that leads from the initial steady-state equilibrium to the new one. Since we deal with this issue explicitly later in the paper, in this section we focus on the case in which the new steady-state rational expectations equilibrium is unique, as is the transition path that leads to it.

To solve for this equilibrium as well as the transition path, we first specify the workers' expectations regarding the time path for π_t, and then show that these expectations are consistent with equilibrium behavior. The case that we are interested in is the one in which congestion causes the probability of success to temporarily fall from its steady-state value of π_H to π_L immediately after the improvement in the terms of trade. We then want π_t to rise back up to π_H in the next period and remain there forever afterward. That is, we assume that $\pi_t = \pi_H$ for $t \neq 1$ and $\pi_t = \pi_L$ for $t = 1$. This set of beliefs will be rational if $S_1 > \tilde{S} \geq S_t$ for all $t \neq 1$.

The measures of searchers in each of the three periods following the terms of trade shock are depicted in figure 10.2 (the detailed derivations for this figure are provided in the appendix). Since S_t (for $t = 1$–3) is shown as a function of P_L for $P_L \leq P_H$, this figure reveals how the total measure of searchers varies with the degree of improvement in the terms of trade. There are several features worth noting. First, as expected, the measure of

---

[12] In particular, if the probability of success is a continuous function of S_t, we would have to solve a thorny fixed-point problem in order to find equilibrium.

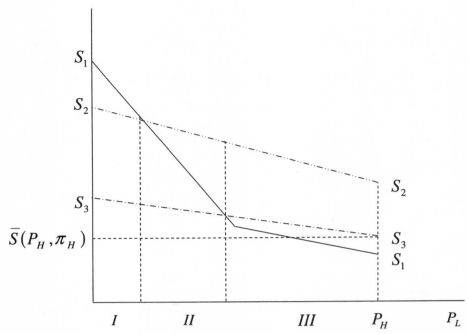

Figure 10.2. The measure of searchers during the transition to the new steady state.

searchers in each period is a decreasing function of P_L since smaller terms of trade improvements cause fewer workers to seek export sector jobs. Second, the curve $S_1 S_1$ is kinked because small deviations of P_L from P_H do not produce regret in old workers. That is, all old workers who search when the price is P_L also searched when they were young. In contrast, large deviations of P_L from P_H induce some old workers to search for the first time. It is this surge of old workers entering the export sector labor market for the first time that can cause the congestion that the government may want to ease. Finally, from figure 10.2 it is evident that there are three ranges for P_L that lead to different patterns for the measures of searchers over time. A rational expectations equilibrium of the type that we are seeking exists for relatively low values of P_L (those in region I).[13] That is, this is the region in which $S_1 > \tilde{S} \geq S_2 \geq S_t$ for $t \geq 3$.[14]

---

[13] As we show in the appendix, region I may not exist is if π_L is sufficiently low. The condition for existence is given in (A.8) of the appendix.

[14] Note that if $S_1 > \tilde{S}$, then it necessarily follows that $S_2 > \tilde{S}$ in range II, and $S_2 > S_3 > \tilde{S}$ in range III. In turn, this would imply that $\pi_2 = \pi_L$ when P_L is in range II, and $\pi_2 = \pi_3 = \pi_L$ if P_L falls within range III. This would contradict our assumption that the workers' expectations concerning π_t are rational.

In region I of figure 10.2 the change in the terms of trade is dramatic and congestion reduces the probability of finding a job in the export sector. In this case, there are important implications for the distribution of income between current members of the young and old generation, as well as between current and future generations. To sort out how the different groups of workers are affected, it is useful to consider the following four questions as they pertain to the old workers at $t = 1$: Does the change in the terms of trade alter their labor market behavior? Do they regret any decisions made when young? Are they harmed by the unexpected change in the terms of trade or do they benefit from it? Is their experience any different from the clones that replace them in the future?

The answers to these four questions are provided in Lemmas 1–4 below. However, before these lemmas can be stated, we need to introduce some new notation: let $\bar{a}^y$ and $\bar{a}^o$ denote the ability level of marginal young and old workers in the initial steady state, respectively, and let a_1^o represent the ability level of the marginal old worker in period 1. In addition, let $\tilde{a}^y$ denote the ability level of marginal young worker at time zero *if the change in the terms of trade could be anticipated.*[15] From our earlier analysis, we know that $\bar{a}^y < \bar{a}^o$. It is also the case that (compared with the actual number of young searchers) more young people would search in period 0 if they anticipated the improvement in the terms of trade. That is, $\tilde{a}^y < \bar{a}_y$. The only question is whether a_1^o is less than or greater than $\tilde{a}^y$. There are two cases to consider. Either $\tilde{a}^y < a_1^o < \bar{a}^y < \bar{a}^o$ or $a_1^o < \tilde{a}^y < \bar{a}^y < \bar{a}^o$, with the particular ordering depending upon the underlying parameters of the model.[16] For brevity, we consider the first case in the text and relegate treatment the second case to the footnotes.

Lemma 1. *When there is an unexpected terms of trade improvement the old workers who change their labor market behavior are the ones with* $a \in [a_1^0, \bar{a}^o]$ *who are not already employed in the export sector. These workers had planned on taking jobs in the import-competing sector but now search for export sector jobs instead.*

Proof. By the definition of $\bar{a}^y$ we know that workers born at $t = 0$ with $a < \bar{a}^y$ take jobs in the import-competing sector when young and plan on doing so again when old. By the definition of $\bar{a}^o$ we know that workers born at $t = 0$ with $a > \bar{a}^o$ search for jobs in the export sector when young and plan on doing so again when old if their initial search proves fruitless. Workers with $a \in [\bar{a}^y, \bar{a}^o]$ search for export sector jobs when young

---

[15] It is straightforward to show that $\tilde{a}^y = \max\left[\dfrac{P_H + \pi_H P_L}{2\pi_H}, \dfrac{P_H}{\pi_H(2 - \pi_L)}\right]$.

[16] There is a third, less interesting case where $\tilde{a}^y < \bar{a}^y < a_1^o < \bar{a}^o$. In this case, the improvement in the terms of trade does not change behavior and does not induce regret.

and then, if their search is unsuccessful, plan on taking jobs in the import-competing sector when old. By the definition of a_1^o, when the terms of trade unexpectedly change, all old workers with $a > a_1^o$ who are not already employed in the export sector search for jobs in that sector. Thus, it is the old workers who are not already employed in sector X with $a \in [a_1^o, \bar{a}^o]$ who change their behavior—they had planned on taking jobs in the import-competing sector but now, because P has fallen, they search for export sector jobs instead. #

Lemma 2. *The old workers who regret the decisions they made when young are those with $a \in [\tilde{a}^y, \bar{a}^y]$. Instead of taking jobs in the import-competing sector they would have rather searched for jobs in the export sector.*

Proof. This follows directly from the definitions of $\tilde{a}^y$ and $\bar{a}^y$—if the workers who are born at $t = 0$ could anticipate the change in the terms of trade, then they would search when young if $a > \tilde{a}^y$ and then, if necessary, search again when old if $a > a_1^o$. However, since they do not anticipate the change in P, workers with $a \in [\tilde{a}^y, \bar{a}^y]$ take jobs in the import-competing sector when young instead. Note that a subset of these workers, those with $a \in [\tilde{a}^y, a_1^o]$, regret not having searched when young, yet do not change their behavior when old. #

Lemma 3. *The unexpected terms of trade improvement benefits the old workers who are employed in the export sector and harms those who are employed in the import-competing sector. Those who seek X-sector jobs could gain or lose—they are harmed by the reduction in the job acquisition rate in period 1 but benefit from the fall the consumer price index.*

Proof. Those employed in the export sector benefit from the fall in the consumer price index while those employed in the import-competing sector see their real incomes fall. #

Lemma 4. *If we compare the experience of the old workers in the current generation with the experience of the clones that replace them in future periods, there are two differences worth highlighting. First, the clones with $a \in [\tilde{a}^y, \bar{a}^y]$ are not surprised by the low price for good M and therefore search for export sector jobs when young. Second, by the time the clones age the congestion will have abated and the job acquisition rates will have returned to the relatively high value.*[17]

[17] For the sake of brevity, we have glossed over an important issue here—the economy does not reach the new steady state until $t = 3$. Thus, the low job acquisition rates faced by workers at $t = 1$ have effects on those workers born at $t = 2$ as well. While these workers are not surprised by the change in the terms of trade, the search pool that they are a part of may be larger than its steady-state value. As we show in the next subsection, a temporary

Proof. The first difference follows directly from the definitions of $\tilde{a}^y$ and $\bar{a}^y$. The second difference is due to the fact that we are focusing on the rational expectations equilibrium in which the job acquisition rate falls for only one period. #

With the aid of Lemmas 1–4, we are now in a position to examine the sort of equity considerations that the government might have in mind when instituting a temporary tariff on the import-competing good. If the decision is based on the welfare of the lowest ability workers, then the government must be primarily concerned with the old workers in this group—the temporary tariff keeps their real incomes from falling as far as they would without protection. Deardorff (1987), making use of Corden's social welfare function, suggests that this may be one reasonable equity-based explanation for temporary protection. He argues that the government's goal may be to prevent a significant fall in the real income of a significant sector of the economy. However, it should be clear that a temporary tariff could only achieve this goal for the old workers with low ability levels. For the young, a temporary tariff may *delay* the fall in real income, but it cannot *prevent* it. If the government truly wanted to use tariffs to prop up the wages of the young workers with low ability levels, it would have to institute a permanent tariff.

It is also unlikely that the government is concerned about the workers with the highest ability levels. While it is true that these workers are harmed by the fall in π when they are old, most of them will already have high-paying jobs in the export sector and will benefit from the lower consumer prices. In addition, these are the workers at the highest end of the income distribution.

This leaves us with the workers with $a \in [\bar{a}^y, \bar{a}^o]$.[18] Workers with ability levels in the low end of this range regret that they did not search when young (Lemma 2) and those with ability levels at the high end of this range are forced to change their behavior and search for export sector jobs when the prospects for finding such a job are relatively bleak (Lemma 1).[19] These are also the workers who are in a fundamentally different position than the clones that replace them because they were unable to anticipate the improvement in the terms of trade (Lemma 4). Of course, if the government tries to help these workers by instituting a temporary tariff, there are some additional benefits—the old workers

tariff is only effective at relieving congestion if it reduces S_1 below $\tilde{S}$ without increasing S_2 above this value. Thus, effective temporary protection cannot harm these workers.
[18] For the case in which $a_1^o < \tilde{a}^y < \bar{a}^y < a_1^o < \bar{a}^o$, this interval would be $[a_1^o, \bar{a}^o]$.
[19] For the case in which $a_1^o < \tilde{a}^y < \bar{a}^y < a_1^o < \bar{a}^o$, all workers in the interval change their behavior and search for export sector jobs (rather than take jobs in sector M) while only those in the middle of the range (with $a \in [\tilde{a}^y, \bar{a}^y]$) regret their behavior when young.

with the lowest ability levels have their wages propped up temporarily and those who are searching for export sector jobs face higher job acquisition rates if the tariff successfully reduces congestion. In addition, the young workers at $t = 1$, who are not surprised by the change in the terms of trade, benefit from the increase in π. These are the young workers we referred to in the introduction—government intervention can reduce or delay the adjustment costs imposed on them by instituting a temporary tariff. It is not clear, however, what the full welfare consequences of such an action would be since tariffs generate distortions as well. In the next subsection we demonstrate that a temporary tariff can alleviate the congestion. We defer the full welfare analysis to the subsequent section.

3.3 Temporary Protection

The existence of the congestion externality leaves open the possibility that government intervention could successfully increase economic welfare. The fact that the congestion is temporary suggests that the policy need not be permanent. While the best policies would be those that directly target the externality, they may not be feasible. We therefore explore the effects of a temporary import tariff.

Suppose that the government levies a specific import tariff (τ) during the first period, removing it for all subsequent periods. The purpose of the tariff is to keep enough workers from searching in the first period so that the congestion externality is averted. Since congestion is not a problem in the longer run, the tariff is not needed and is therefore removed.[20]

It will continue to be the case that the economy will be in the new steady state for $t \geq 3$ and therefore the measure of searchers in periods 3 and beyond (both young and old) will remain unchanged.[21] However, the measures of old and young searchers during the first period, and the measures of old searchers during the second period, are impacted by the tariff.[22] In figure 10.3, we show how S_1 and S_2 vary with τ, given a price P_L and

[20] It is possible to create numeric examples where a smaller tariff levied for two periods can also relieve the congestion externality. It is also conceivable that this could be a more efficient policy than the single-period tariff, since deadweight loss is proportional to the square of the tariff. However, our only purpose in this paper is to show that temporary protection can lead to welfare gains. Solving for the *optimal* policy is significantly more complex.

[21] This follows because the value of the tariff is zero and the price of the import-competing good is at its new steady-state value from period 2 on. It follows that all people born during period 2 make their steady-state choices, as do all people born in subsequent periods. Thus, those who are old in period 3 made their steady-state choices when they were young in period 2.

[22] As before, young searchers adjust instantly to any changes in the environment. Therefore the measure of young searchers attains its steady-state value starting in the second period.

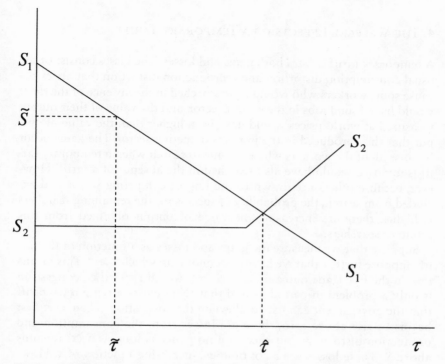

Figure 10.3. The measure of searchers per period as a function of the tariff.

assuming that $\pi_t = \pi_H$ for all t (the derivation of figure 10.3 is provided in the appendix). The measure of period-1 searchers is monotonically decreasing in the tariff. Higher tariff rates make the import-competing sector more attractive and fewer people search. By contrast, very small tariffs have no impact on the measure of searchers in the second period because all searchers who are old in period 2 also searched when young (in period 1). However, for high enough tariffs, some workers will choose to work in the import-competing sector in period 1 when they are young, but then search in the export sector when they become old and the tariff is removed. Higher tariffs increase the measure of these delayed searchers, implying that S_2 is increasing in the tariff rate.

From figure 10.3, there exists a tariff rate ($\hat{\tau}$) such that $S_1 = S_2$. It follows that if $S_1(\hat{\tau}) = S_2(\hat{\tau}) \leq \tilde{S}$, there exists a range of tariffs $\tau \in [\tilde{\tau}, \hat{\tau}]$ that can alleviate the congestion externality. Because any tariff is distortionary, the optimal tariff is either zero or $\tilde{\tau}$.

4. THE WELFARE EFFECTS OF A TEMPORARY TARIFF

A temporary tariff creates both gains and losses. The losses consist of the usual consumption distortion and a production distortion that arises because some workers who would have searched in the absence of the tariff would have found jobs in the export sector, and the value of their output measured at world prices would have been higher than the value of output that they produced in the import-competing sector. The gains occur because all of the workers who continue to search when a temporary tariff is imposed would have also searched in the absence of a tariff. However, because others are drawn to the import-competing sector and excluded from search, the probability of success for the remaining searchers is higher, therefore increasing the value of output obtained from this group of searchers.

Suppose that we measure the gains and losses as a function of the tariff. Suppose further that we have an economy in which $\hat{\tau} > \tilde{\tau}$. This means that in the free trade outcome $S_1 > \tilde{S} > S_t$ for all $t \neq 1$ (i.e., congestion is only a problem in period 1) and that there exists a temporary tariff that the government can use to alleviate the congestion. Then, as τ first begins to rise above zero, there are losses from the consumption and production distortions but there are no gains as long as $S_1(\tau)$ remains above $\tilde{S}$. These losses are a continuous, increasing function of τ. However, as the tariff continues to rise we eventually reach the point where $\tau = \tilde{\tau}$ and $S_1(\tau) = \tilde{S} > S_2(\tau)$.[23] At that point, a marginal increase in the tariff creates discrete gains as the job acquisition rate in period 1 jumps up from π_L to π_H. If these discrete gains dominate the losses accumulated by increasing τ from 0 to $\tilde{\tau}$, then the temporary tariff is welfare enhancing. It should be clear that this *must* be the case if the free trade value for S_1 is close to (but above) $\tilde{S}$. In that case, it takes only a very small tariff to alleviate congestion and boost job acquisition rates in the export sector. As for the gains and losses, the consumption distortion generated by such a small tariff is of second-order importance, as is the loss due to inducing a very small measure of workers to refrain from search. However, the discrete change from π_L to π_H applies to all of those workers who continue to search, which is nearly all of the workers who would have searched under free trade. Thus, the gains must dominate the losses.

---

[23] Since the increase in τ does not push S_2 above the threshold level (by the definition of $\hat{\tau}$), there are no spillover effects on period-2 searchers—although the search pool increases, it does not increase enough to lower job acquisition rates.

5. MULTIPLE EQUILIBRIA

Increasing the steady-state job acquisition rate in the export sector has two contradictory effects on the steady-state size of the search pool. First, for each generation the pool broadens to include workers of lesser ability. This effect tends to increase the steady-state measure of searchers. However, given the breadth of workers who prefer to search for a job in the export sector, a higher success rate leaves fewer old workers unemployed, thereby reducing the steady-state size of the pool. For values of π near 1, the second effect dominates and the steady-state measure of searchers is *decreasing* in the steady-state value of π. Formally:

$$\bar{S}(P,\pi) = \left\{1 - \frac{P}{\pi}\frac{1+\pi}{2}\right\} + (1-\pi)\left\{1 - \frac{P}{\pi}\right\} \tag{8}$$

where the first term on the right-hand side of (8) (representing the steady-state measure of young searchers) is strictly increasing in π, while the second term (representing the steady-state measure of old searchers) is first increasing and then decreasing in π. Differentiating (8) with respect to π reveals that $\bar{S}$ is decreasing in π if $\pi > \sqrt{3P/2}$.

Combining the fact that the steady-state measure of searchers may be decreasing in π with the existence of congestion externalities suggests that there are circumstances under which the economy has multiple steady states, with $\bar{S}(\pi_L) > \tilde{S} > \bar{S}(\pi_H)$. We illustrate this case in figure 10.4, where we are assuming that the economy is initially in a steady state with a low level of search ($\pi = \pi_H$). Suppose that the terms of trade unexpectedly improve and that workers correctly anticipate that this will lead to an immediate increase in the size of the search pool. Suppose further that workers expect the job acquisition rate to fall to π_L and remain there permanently. If this is the case, the permanent improvement in the terms of trade has pushed the economy into a new steady state with a permanently higher level of search and lower job acquisition rates in the export sector. This provides a new role for the government—it might be possible to use a temporary tariff to keep the economy from moving to the "bad" steady state. If so, the short-run loss associated with the temporary distorting effects of the tariff are likely to be more than offset by a perpetual stream of gains. This would be a situation in which *temporary* protection would lead to a *permanent* change in the allocation of resources.

To analyze this situation, we now assume that the probability of successfully finding a job in the export sector falls permanently to π_L concurrent with the improvement in the terms of trade. As before, young workers

$S^o + S^y$

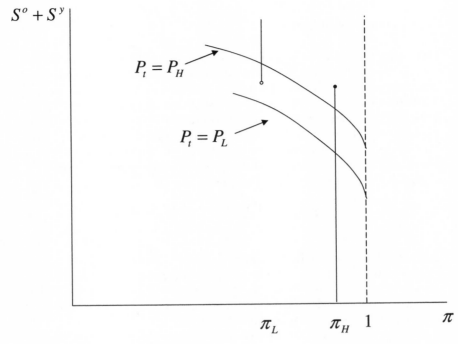

Figure 10.4. Multiple steady states.

adjust immediately to any change. Since there are no changes in the environment beyond the first period, the steady-state measure of young workers is reached immediately. Similarly, it only takes two periods for the measure of old workers to reach its new steady-state value. In figure 10.5 we show the total measure of searchers as a function of P_L (note that S_2 represents the size of the search pool in the new steady state since adjustment is complete after only two periods). If the terms of trade improve to a price within range I in figure 10.5, then our initial conjecture about the probability of success immediately falling to π_L and remaining there forever is validated. As drawn, this range of prices can be further divided into two subsections. For relatively high prices in range I, the measure of searchers monotonically approaches the new steady state. For lower prices in this range, the measure of searchers overshoots the new steady-state level.

   If there exists a steady state $\bar{S}(P_L, \pi_H) < \tilde{S}$, then a one-period tariff that holds the measure of searchers at $\tilde{S}$ during the first period of transition has *exactly the same effect* as in the case where the free trade measure of searchers would exceed $\tilde{S}$ in only the first period. In both cases, relieving

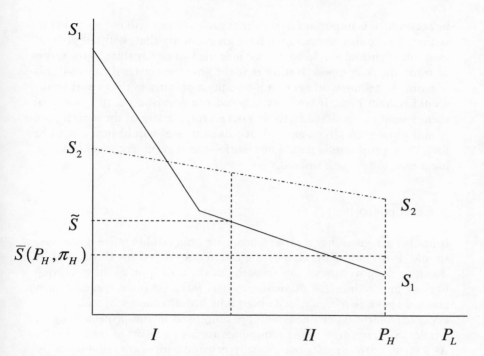

Figure 10.5. The measure of searchers per period as a function of price.

congestion in the first period has the beneficial impact of reducing the measure of workers who are old searchers in the second period.

Of course, we are not the first to point out that externalities in the search process can lead to multiple steady-state equilibria. Diamond (1982, 1984) and Diamond and Fudenberg (1989) provide models in which positive search externalities may generate this outcome. In their models, workers must search for a trading partner and the fact that more people are trading makes it easier to find a match. If people do not expect many others to search, then it is not in their interest to search and we get an equilibrium with a relatively low level of output. On the other hand, if people expect many others to be searching as well, then their own expected return to search will be high. In this case, we get an equilibrium with a high level of search activity and a relatively high level of output. Diamond and Fudenberg argue that there is a role in their model for the government to try and manipulate expectations in order to steer the economy away from the Pareto-inferior steady state. If, by telling workers to expect a bright future with high production, the government can convince workers to search, the government's projections will turn out to be accurate. It is important to note that such a policy will not work in our setting. To see this, suppose we have an economy that, without government intervention, would be pushed into the bad steady state by the terms of trade shock. Suppose further that the government tried to avoid this outcome by telling workers that job acquisition rates in the export sector would remain high. If workers believed the government, then more of them would be attracted to the export sector, the size of the search pool would grow even larger, and job acquisition rates would turn out to be low. Thus, propaganda would not work—the government would have to use a temporary tariff instead.

6. CONCLUSION

It has been argued that if governments are going to liberalize trade, they should do so gradually. One of the rationales offered for this is that by doing so the government can smooth out the transition to the new equilibrium and reduce the adjustment costs imposed on workers. Equity concerns have also been raised about how liberalization will affect workers, particularly older ones, who are employed in the protected sector. Similar concerns arise when economies are hit by terms of trade shocks. As a result, governments occasionally provide temporary relief to industries that have been injured by unexpected changes in world prices

In this paper we have presented an overlapping-generations model that highlights the manner in which current and future generations are affected by unexpected changes in the terms of trade. We have argued that if governments use *temporary* protection due to equity concerns, then their concerns cannot be about the welfare of those workers who remain trapped in the injured sector. Instead, governments must be concerned about two groups—the older workers who regret the decisions made when they were young or who change their labor market behavior as a result of the terms of trade shock and the young workers who would face low job acquisition rates in the export sector without protection. We have also shown how temporary protection affects the different groups of workers both in the current and future generations.

To capture the notion that adjustment is costly, we have assumed that workers must search for export sector jobs so it takes time for the economy to reach the new steady-state equilibrium. We have shown that if there are congestion externalities present in the search process, temporary protection may be welfare enhancing, reducing adjustment costs for young and old workers alike. This result is not new—it can be found in Karp and Paul (1994) or Gaisford and Leger (2000). However, a result that is new to this paper is that these congestion externalities can give rise to multiple steady-state equilibria. If this is the case, then a terms of trade shock can *permanently* push the economy from a "good" steady state with high job acquisition rates and high output to a "bad" steady state with lower job acquisition and output rates. Government intervention aimed at steering the economy back to the "good" equilibrium is then warranted. However, propaganda aimed at influencing expectations is not enough. The government must also provide some sort of tangible protection to the injured sector. We have shown that there are cases in which a temporary tariff will do the trick.

Appendix

The purpose of this appendix is to provide the detailed derivation of figures 10.2, 10.3, and 10.5. For figure 10.2, we begin by focusing on the younger generation. The measure of young searchers in the initial and terminal steady states, as well as those in the intervening period, are given in (A.1)–(A.3):

$$\bar{S}^y(P_H, \pi_H) = \left\{ 1 - \frac{P_H}{\pi_H} \frac{1 + \pi_H}{2} \right\} \tag{A.1}$$

$$S_1^y = \left\{ 1 - \frac{P_L}{\pi_L} \frac{1 + \pi_L}{2} \right\} \tag{A.2}$$

$$S_2^y = \bar{S}^y(P_L, \pi_H) = \left\{ 1 - \frac{P_L}{\pi_H} \frac{1 + \pi_H}{2} \right\} \tag{A.3}$$

Young workers adjust immediately to new circumstances. In particular, they adjust immediately to the simultaneous fall in P and π, and they immediately adjust one more time to the increase in π. This follows since the young workers make all of their decisions after the terms of trade improvement occurs.

In contrast, old workers can be surprised, since the change in price occurs in the middle of their life, after they have committed to a course of action based upon their expectations regarding future prices and labor market conditions. The measure of old searchers in the initial and terminal steady states, as well as those in the intervening period, are given in (A.4)–(A.7):

$$\bar{S}^o(P_H, \pi_H) = (1 - \pi_H) \left\{ 1 - \frac{P_H}{\pi_H} \right\} \tag{A.4}$$

$$S_1^o = (1 - \pi_H)\left\{1 - \frac{P_L}{\pi_L}\right\} + \pi_H \max\left\{0, \frac{P_H}{\pi_H}\frac{1+\pi_H}{2} - \frac{P_L}{\pi_L}\right\} \tag{A.5}$$

$$S_2^o = (1 - \pi_L)\left\{1 - \frac{P_L}{\pi_H}\right\} + \pi_L \max\left\{0, \frac{P_L}{\pi_L}\frac{1+\pi_L}{2} - \frac{P_L}{\pi_H}\right\} \tag{A.6}$$

$$S_3^o = \bar{S}^o(P_L, \pi_H) = (1 - \pi_H)\left\{1 - \frac{P_L}{\pi_H}\right\}$$
$$+ \pi_H \max\left\{0, \frac{P_L}{\pi_H}\frac{1+\pi_H}{2} - \frac{P_L}{\pi_H}\right\} \tag{A.7}$$

Combining (A.1)–(A.7), we obtain S_t as a function of P_L for $P_L \leq P_H$. These functions are depicted in figure 10.2. As discussed in the text, the curve $S_1 S_1$ is kinked because small deviations of P_L from P_H do not produce regret in old workers while large deviations induce some old workers to search for the first time. This can be seen by examining the second term on the right-hand side (rhs) in (A.5)—it is positive and decreasing in P_L for relatively small values of P_L, then turns to zero (and therefore becomes independent of P_L) once P_L surpasses a critical value.

Neither $S_2 S_2$ nor $S_3 S_3$ is kinked. The former is true because the value of P_L plays no role in determining whether the second rhs term in (A.6) is zero or positive. The latter is true because the second rhs term in (A.7) is always zero since the economy reaches the new steady state at time $t = 3$, and we have already shown that in any steady state there are no old searchers who were not also searchers when young.

As we noted in the text, it is region I of figure 10.2 that is of interest to us since this is the range of values for P_L such that $S_1 > \tilde{S} \geq S_2 \geq S_t$ for $t \geq 3$. The existence of range I is guaranteed if $S_1 > S_2$ when both are evaluated at $P_L = 0$. Using (A.1)–(A.7), this condition reduces to

$$\pi_L > \pi_H\left\{1 - \frac{P_H}{\pi_H}\frac{1+\pi_H}{2}\right\} \tag{A.8}$$

The incentive to search diminishes as π_L becomes smaller. If this probability is low enough, then the measure of searchers in period 1 is below the measure of searchers in subsequent periods, where the probability of success is higher. Thus, as long as π_L is not too low, a rational expectations equilibrium of the type we are seeking exists.

Turn next to figure 10.3. After the temporary tariff is imposed the measures of young and old searchers during periods 1 and 2 are now given by

$$S_1^y = \left\{ 1 - \frac{P_L + \tau}{\pi_H} \frac{1 + \pi_H}{2} \right\} \tag{A.9}$$

$$\begin{aligned} S_1^o = (1 - \pi_H) \left\{ 1 - \frac{P_L + \tau}{\pi_H} \right\} \\ + \pi_H \max \left\{ 0, \frac{P_H}{\pi_H} \frac{1 + \pi_H}{2} - \frac{P_L + \tau}{\pi_H} \right\} \end{aligned} \tag{A.10}$$

$$S_2^o = (1 - \pi_H) \left\{ 1 - \frac{P_L}{\pi_H} \right\} + \pi_H \max \left\{ 0, \frac{P_L + \tau}{\pi_H} \frac{1 + \pi_H}{2} - \frac{P_L}{\pi_H} \right\} \tag{A.11}$$

Combining (A.9)–(A.11) yields figure 10.3. Note the above three equations differ from their counterparts in two ways. Obviously, the relevant price in the first period is now the tariff-inclusive price. This also shows up in the equation for the measure of old searchers in period 2 because this measure is determined, in part, by the measure of young workers who searched in period 1. The second difference is that all of the probabilities now equal π_H under the assumption that $S_t \leq \tilde{S}$ for all t. Of course, this will not be true for very low values of the tariff. In particular, it will not be true when $\tau = 0$. However, assuming initially that it is true allows us to solve for the minimum tariff that is consistent with this assumption.

Finally, turn to figure 10.5. As before, the measures of young and old searchers in the initial steady state are given by (A.1) and (A.4). If the job acquisition rate falls to π_L and remains there permanently, then the measures of young and old searchers in subsequent periods are now given by (A.12) and (A.13):

$$S_1^y = \bar{S}^y(P_L, \pi_L) = \left\{ 1 - \frac{P_L}{\pi_L} \frac{1 + \pi_L}{2} \right\} \tag{A.12}$$

$$S_1^o = (1 - \pi_H) \left\{ 1 - \frac{P_L}{\pi_L} \right\} + \pi_H \max \left\{ 0, \frac{P_H}{\pi_H} \frac{1 + \pi_H}{2} - \frac{P_L}{\pi_L} \right\} \tag{A.13a}$$

$$S_2^o = \overline{S}^o(P_L, \pi_L) = (1 - \pi_L)\left\{1 - \frac{P_L}{\pi_L}\right\}$$

$$+ \pi_L \max\left\{0, \frac{P_L}{\pi_L}\frac{1 + \pi_L}{2} - \frac{P_L}{\pi_L}\right\} \quad \text{(A.13b)}$$

Combining (A.1), (A.4), (A.12), and (A.13) yields figure 10.5.

REFERENCES

Baldwin, Robert E. 1989. "The Political Economy of Trade Protection," *Journal of Economic Perspectives* 3(4): 119–35.

Baldwin, Robert E., John Mutti, and J. David Richardson. 1980. "Welfare Effects on the United States of a Significant Multilateral Tariff Reduction," *Journal of International Economics* 10(3): 405–23.

Bishop, William R. 2002. "Investigations Completed under Section 201 of the Trade Act of 1974," Unpublished, USITC, Washington, DC.

Cassing, James, and Jack Ochs. 1978. "International Trade, Factor Market Distortions, and the Optimal Dynamic Subsidy: Comment," *American Economic Review* 68(5): 950–55.

Cheh, John H. 1974. "United States Concessions in the Kennedy Round and Short-Run Labor Adjustment Costs," *Journal of International Economics* 4(4): 323–40.

Davidson, Carl, and Steven J. Matusz. 2001. "On Adjustment Costs," GEP Research Paper 2001/24, University of Notthingham.

Deardorff, Alan. 1987. "Safeguards Policy and the Conservative Social Welfare Function," In Henryk Kierzkowski (ed.), *Protection and Competition in International Trade: Essays in Honor of W. M. Corden*. Oxford: Basil Blackwell, pp. 22–40.

Diamond, Peter. 1981. "Mobility Costs, Frictional Unemployment and Efficiency," *Journal of Political Economy* 89(4): 798–812.

Diamond, Peter. 1982. "Aggregate Demand Management in Search Equilibrium," *Journal of Political Economy* 90(5): 881–94.

Diamond, Peter. 1984. *A Search-Equilibrium Approach to the Micro Foundations of Macroeconomics*. Cambridge: MIT Press.

Diamond, Peter, Fudenberg, Drew. 1989. "Rational Expectations Business Cycles in Search Equilibrium," *Journal of Political Economy* 97(3): 606–19.

Falvey, Rod, and Cha Dong Kim. 1992. "The Timing and Sequencing Issues in Trade Liberalization," *Economic Journal,* 102(413): 908–24.

Gaisford, James D., and Lawrence A. Leger. 2000. "Terms-of-Trade Shocks, Labor-Market Adjustment, and Safeguard Measures," *Review of International Economics* 8(1): 100–12.

Karp, Larry, and Thierry Paul. 1994. "Phasing in and Phasing Out Protectionism with Costly Adjustment of Labour," *Economic Journal* 104(427): 1379–92.

Karp, Larry, and Thierry Paul. 1998. "Labor Adjustment and Gradual Reform: When Is Commitment Important?" *Journal of International Economics* 46(2): 333–62.

Lapan, Harvey. 1976. "International Trade, Factor Market Distortions, and the Optimal Dynamic Subsidy," *American Economic Review* 66(3): 335–46.

Lapan, Harvey. 1978. "International Trade, Factor Market Distortions, and the Optimal Dynamic Subsidy: Reply," *American Economic Review* 68(5): 956–59.

Lapan, Harvey. 1979. "International Trade, Factor Market Distortions, and the Optimal Dynamic Subsidy: Reply," *American Economic Review* 69(4): 718–20.

Lavergne, Real. 1983. *The Political Economy of U.S. Tariffs: An Empirical Analysis*. New York: Academic Press.

Magee, Stephen. 1972. "The Welfare Effects of Restrictions on U.S. Trade," *Brookings Papers on Economic Activity* 3(3): 645–701.

Mayer, Wolfgang. 1974. "Short-Run and Long-Run Equilibrium for a Small Open Economy," *Journal of Political Economy* 82(5): 820–31.

Michealy, Michael. 1986. "The Timing and Sequencing of a Trade Liberalization Policy." In Armeane Choksi and Demetrios Papageorgiou (eds.), *Economic Liberalization in Developing Countries*. Oxford: Basil Blackwell.

Mortensen, Dale. 1982. "Property Rights and Efficiency in Mating, Racing and Related Games," *American Economic Review* 72(5): 968–79.

Mussa, Michael. 1974. "Tariffs and the Distribution of Income: The Importance of Factor Specificity, Substitutability and Intensity in the Short and Long Run," *Journal of Political Economy* 82(6): 1191–1203.

Mussa, Michael. 1978. "Dynamic Adjustment in the Heckscher-Ohlin-Samuelson Model," *Journal of Political Economy*, 86(5): 775–91.

Mussa Michael. 1986. "The Adjustment Process and the Timing of Trade Liberalization." In Armeane Choksi and Demetrios Papageorgiou (eds.), *Economic Liberalization in Developing Countries*. Oxford: Basil Blackwell.

Neary, Peter. 1978. "Short-Run Capital Specificity and the Pure Theory of International Trade," *Economic Journal* 88(351): 488–510.

Pissarides, Christopher. 1990. *Equilibrium Unemployment Theory*. Oxford: Basil Blackwell.

Ray, Edward. 1979. "Factor Market Distortions and Dynamic Optimal Intervention: Comment," *American Economic Review* 69(4): 715–17.

Sykes, Alan. 1991. "Protectionism as a 'Safeguard': A Positive Analysis of the GATT 'Escape Clause' with Normative Speculations," *University of Chicago Law Review* 58: 255–307.

Trefler, Daniel. 2001. "The Long and the Short of the Canada-U.S. Free Trade Agreement." Working Paper, University of Toronto.

United States International Trade Commission. 1998. "Summary of Statutory Provisions Related to Import Relief," USITC Publication 3125, Washington, DC.

Yashiv, Eran. 2000. "The Determinants of Equilibrium Unemployment," *American Economic Review* 90(5): 1297–1322.

Chapter 11

TRADE LIBERALIZATION AND COMPENSATION

CARL DAVIDSON AND STEVEN J. MATUSZ

1. INTRODUCTION

Two of the most generally accepted propositions in economics are that trade liberalization harms some groups but that it also generates aggregate net benefits. In fact, there are large literatures devoted to identifying the winners and losers from freer trade and measuring their gains and losses. Yet, there has been surprisingly little research aimed at investigating the best way to go about compensating those who lose. Using a traditional, full-employment model of trade Dixit and Norman (1980, 1986) have argued that it is possible to use commodity taxes to compensate the losers without exhausting the benefits from freer trade. This is an important finding since it indicates that with such a compensation scheme in place, trade liberalization would always lead to a Pareto improvement. Brecher and Choudhri (1994) have raised concerns about this result by showing that in the presence of unemployment this scheme may not work. They show that in such a setting, under reasonable conditions, fully compensating the losers may eat away all of the gains from trade. Feenstra and Lewis (1994) argue that similar problems arise when factors of production are imperfectly mobile. However, they demonstrate that the situation can be remedied by augmenting the Dixit-Norman scheme with policies aimed at enhancing factor mobility. In particular, they show that the use of commodity taxes *coupled* with trade adjustment assistance may be adequate to achieve true Pareto gains from liberalization. Freenstra and Lewis do not ask whether there is a superior way to achieve this goal.[1]

In contrast, the policy community has been interested in this question for quite some time. Much of the recent policy debate may have been triggered by findings that the *personal* cost of worker dislocation may be quite high. For example, Jacobson, LaLonde, and Sullivan (1993a, b) find

[1] In fact, the only other paper (that we know of) that addresses the issue of optimal compensation is Brander and Spencer (1994). See footnote 6 for a brief discussion of their approach and how it differs from ours.

that the average dislocated worker suffers a loss in lifetime earnings of $80,000! Kletzer (2001) also finds that the losses are nontrivial, but her estimates are less dramatic. Focusing on the reduction in wages that these workers eventually accept in order to find new jobs, she finds that the average dislocated worker accepts a 12% pay cut. The policy debate has centered on labor market policies that could be used to alleviate the burden placed on such workers.[2] Among the policies that have been considered are wage subsidies, employment subsidies (sometimes referred to as "reemployment bonuses"), trade adjustment assistance (usually in the guise of unemployment insurance), and training subsidies.[3] Many of the recent contributors to this debate have focused attention on wage subsidies largely because of their incentive effects—wage subsidies reward work and encourage dislocated workers to return to work quickly. In contrast, trade adjustment assistance lowers the opportunity cost of unemployment, resulting in longer spells of unemployment.

In this paper we compare a variety of labor market policies to determine the best way to compensate the groups that are harmed by liberalization.[4] We consider this to be an important question. The objections of those who will be harmed if trade barriers are removed create roadblocks that make freer trade difficult to achieve. Coupling liberalization with an adequate compensation scheme is one way to secure general agreement about trade policy.[5] However, compensating the losers distorts the economy and reduces welfare. Our goal is to find the labor market policy that

[2] For contributions to the debate, see Baily, Burtless, and Litan (1993), Burtless, Lawrence, Litan, and Shapiro (1998), Parsons (2000), Kletzer and Litan (2001), and Hufbauer and Goodrich (2001).

[3] In a recent policy brief that has generated much discussion, Kletzer and Litan (2001) argue that the best way to compensate dislocated workers is with "wage insurance," which is essentially a wage subsidy. See also Hufbauer and Goodrich (2001), who suggest a similar but more generous policy.

[4] We do not allow the government to redistribute income via commodity or income taxes. Thus, we rule out the type of compensation scheme envisioned by Dixit and Norman (1980, 1986). There are at least two reasons for this. First and foremost, we know of no government that has ever considered such a scheme to compensate workers harmed by changes in trade policies. In contrast, the labor market policies that we consider are at the center of the policy debate on dislocated workers. Second, some authors have raised concerns about the practicality of the Dixit-Norman scheme. As we mentioned above, Brecher and Choudhri (1994) argue that the scheme may not work in the presence of unemployment. Spector (2001) argues that the scheme may not work when borders are open. See also Kemp and Wan (1986, 1995), who raise concerns about the assumptions required to prove the Dixit-Norman result.

[5] This argument for compensation programs has been made by Lawrence and Litan (1986). We also note that recent survey evidence by Scheve and Slaughter (2001) indicates that a majority of American workers would be in favor of further liberalization *provided* that those who are harmed receive some sort of compensation or assistance.

fully compensates each group while imposing the smallest distortion on the economy.

To compare these policies, we develop a model of trade in which workers seeking employment must first complete costly training and search processes. The government can reduce the costs imposed on these workers by subsidizing training and/or offering unemployment benefits to searching workers. Alternatively, the government can augment the compensation received by employed workers through wage or employment subsidies.

There are two types of jobs in our economy. First, there are low-tech jobs that require few skills, are easy to find, pay low wages, and are not very durable. Second, there are high-tech jobs that require significant skills, are relatively difficult to obtain, pay high wages, and last for a long time. Workers differ in terms of ability with higher-ability workers producing more output in a given sector than their lower-ability counterparts. In equilibrium, workers separate with low-ability workers attracted to the low-tech sector and high-ability workers attracted to the high-tech sector. If we refer to the worker who is just indifferent between training for high- and low-tech jobs as the "marginal worker," then this implies that the average low-tech worker has lower ability than the marginal worker while the average high-tech worker has higher ability than the marginal worker. This distinction plays an important role in our policy analysis.

We assume that in the initial equilibrium the low-tech sector is protected by a tariff. As a result, some workers who, in terms of economic efficiency, should be employed in the high-tech sector are attracted to the low-tech sector instead. We then assume that the tariff is removed and allow the economy to move to the new equilibrium. The model is simple enough that we are able to solve for the adjustment path across steady states. This allows us to take the transition period into account when calculating welfare. We find that there are two groups of workers who are harmed by liberalization. First, there are the "stayers"—those workers who remain trapped in the low-tech sector because it would be too costly for them to acquire the skills required for high-tech jobs. Second, there are the "movers"—those workers who switch sectors after the tariff is removed. While the movers eventually gain by securing higher wages, they bear the burden of the adjustment costs imposed on the economy by liberalization. They must go through a costly training process to acquire high-tech skills and then engage in costly search in order to find new jobs. We find that for reasonable parameter values, these costs outweigh the long-term gains so that, as a group, the movers lose.

Removing the tariff and allowing the economy to adjust to the free trade equilibrium leads to the highest level of aggregate welfare. However, we assume instead that the government wants to compensate these two groups for their losses. Any attempt to do so creates a distortion, reducing

welfare. We compare wage subsidies, employment subsidies, trade adjustment assistance (i.e., unemployment benefits), and training subsidies to see
which policy achieves full compensation at the lowest cost to the economy.
We find that there are two rules that a compensation scheme should satisfy. The first rule is simple—any policy should be targeted. For example,
if a wage subsidy is to be used to compensate the movers, then it should
be offered only to those who switch sectors after the tariff is removed.

The second rule is more subtle and focuses on how the policies affect
the average and marginal workers in the targeted group. The policy's impact on the average targeted worker is important because it determines the
size of the program needed to compensate the group. If the average targeted worker's lifetime utility is highly sensitive to the policy parameter,
then only a modest sized program will be required to fully compensate the
group. The impact of a policy on the marginal worker determines the size
of the distortion that the compensation scheme imposes on the economy.
If the marginal worker's lifetime utility is highly sensitive to the policy parameter, then even a modest sized program may trigger a great deal of inefficient relocation by workers resulting in a large distortion. It follows
that the best policy will be one that has a large impact on the average
worker in the targeted group and a small impact on the marginal worker.

Applying these rules, we find that the best way to compensate the
movers is with a targeted wage subsidy. The subsidy is paid only to
those who switch sectors after liberalization. Under such a policy, high-
ability movers (who earn a higher wage) collect more compensation
than their low-ability counterparts. When compensating the movers,
this is a desirable feature—since the average mover has higher ability
than the marginal worker, a wage subsidy has a relatively larger impact
on the welfare of the average mover. As a result, it is possible to fully
compensate the movers with a modest sized program that creates only
a small distortion.

In contrast, the best way to compensate the stayers is with a targeted
employment subsidy. This subsidy, which would be independent of the
worker's wage, would be paid to workers holding low-tech jobs at the
time of liberalization and to any worker who obtains a job in that sector
shortly thereafter. This policy works better than a wage subsidy because
the average low-tech worker earns a lower wage than the marginal
worker. Thus, while the wage subsidy would be relatively more valuable
to the marginal worker, an employment subsidy affects the average stayer
and the marginal worker equally. It follows a wage subsidy would generate a larger distortion than an employment subsidy.[6]

---

[6] As far as we know, the only other paper that directly addresses the issue of optimal compensation is Brander and Spencer (1994). However, their focus is much narrower than ours.

The paper divides into four additional sections. In section 2, we introduce a simple two-sector full-employment model and use it to show that an optimal compensation scheme should be valued highly by the average worker in the targeted group while having a small impact on the welfare of the marginal worker. In section 3 we extend the model to allow for training and search-generated unemployment and show that a wage subsidy is the best way to compensate the movers while an employment subsidy works best for the stayers. In section 4, we calibrate the model and show that for reasonable parameter values, the cost of compensating either group is small relative to the gains from trade, provided that the right policy is used. However, if the wrong policy is used, particularly when trying to compensate the stayers, it is possible to almost completely wipe out all of the benefits from freer trade. We conclude the paper in section 5.

2. COMPENSATION WITH FULL EMPLOYMENT AND WITHOUT DYNAMICS

In this section, we build and analyze a parsimonious two-sector, full-employment model to highlight the fundamental differences between wage and employment subsidies. The central features of this model form the foundation for the more textured analysis that follows in the subsequent section.

We assume that labor is the only input. However, workers differ by ability, which we index by a. For simplicity, we assume that ability is uniformly distributed with $a \in [0,1]$.

Each worker is paid the value of her marginal product, which we assume is nondecreasing in ability and define $w_j(a)$ as the real wage rate earned by a worker with ability a employed in sector $j = 1,2$.

We wish to identify sector 1 as the "low-tech" sector, attracting relatively low-ability workers, and sector 2 as the "high-tech" sector, attracting relatively high-ability workers. To do so, we need to add a bit of structure to the wage functions. In particular, we assume that ability is more

---

To begin with, they are concerned only with the issue of how to compensate workers who lose their jobs and suffer wage losses due to changes in trade patterns and the only policy that they consider is a wage subsidy. To be precise, their goal is to determine whether the wage subsidy should be a decreasing, increasing, or constant function of the difference between the worker's old wage and his or her new wage. Moreover, since Brander and Spencer treat the wage offer distribution as fixed and exogenous, they do not use an equilibrium approach. This is not meant as a criticism—their paper is aimed at investigating a theory put forth by Lawrence and Litan (1986) that a tapered wage subsidy would be a good way to compensate dislocated workers. Brander and Spencer show that if a wage subsidy is to be used, then it should be tapered.

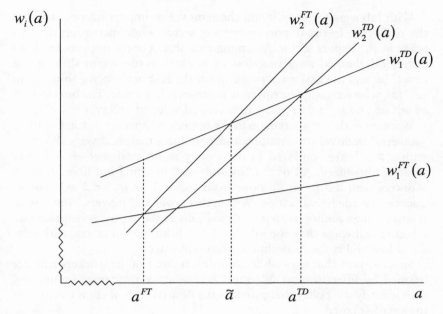

Figure 11.1.

important in the high-tech (knowledge-intensive) sector than in the low-tech sector—that is, $w_1'(a) < w_2'(a)$ with $w_1(0) > w_2(0)$ and $w_1(1) < w_2(1)$. If ability refers to intellectual capacity, then there is not much difference in the number of trucks that can be unloaded by a low-ability worker versus a high-ability worker, since this activity depends more on physical strength and endurance than on mental acuity. By contrast, a low-ability worker is unlikely to contribute much value to the development of software compared with her high-ability counterpart.

Two wage functions that satisfy these properties are illustrated by the curves $w_1^{TD}(a)$ and $w_2^{TD}(a)$ in figure 11.1, where the superscripts indicate the presence of a tariff distortion.[7] We follow Mayer (1984) by assuming that tariff revenue is distributed in lump-sum fashion in a way that leaves the overall distribution of income unchanged. As such, the *distribution* of tariff revenue does not distort decisions, and the two wage functions in figure 11.1 define a critical ability (a^{TD}) such that workers with $a < a^{TD}$ maximize their income by choosing to work in sector 1, and those with $a > a^{TD}$ maximize their income by choosing to work in sector 2.

[7] We have drawn these curves such that $w_1^{\cdot}(a) = w_2^{\cdot}(a) = 0$. This is for simplicity only; we discuss the general case below.

With labor as the only input, the removal of import barriers reduces the real wage in the import-competing sector while increasing the real wage in the export sector. Assuming that this country imports the low-tech good, the real wage function for workers in this sector shifts down to $w_1^{FT}(a)$ and the real wage function for the high-tech sector shifts up to $w_2^{FT}(a)$, where the superscript now represents free trade. The intersection of $w_1^{FT}(a)$ and $w_2^{FT}(a)$ defines a new critical value of ability $a^{FT} < a^{TD}$.

Workers with $a < a^{FT}$ remain in the import-competing sector. For these "stayers," trade reform unambiguously reduces their real wage. Workers with $a > a^{TD}$ are employed in the export sector both before and after trade is liberalized. All of the "incumbents" benefit from liberalization. Workers with $a \in [a^{FT}, a^{TD}]$ move from sector 1 to sector 2 as a consequence of trade liberalization. Within this group of "movers," those with relatively high ability (with $a > \tilde{a}$) find jobs in the export sector that pay a higher real wage than the job they leave behind, while those with relatively low ability face a decline in their real wage.

Suppose now that we wish to compensate some of the workers who are harmed by liberalization. We must first identify the target group, and then identify the policy that provides the desired level of compensation at the smallest cost.

We begin by assuming that we wish to compensate the movers for their losses. To minimize the cost of this program, it is obviously vital that compensation be offered to only those workers who actually switch sectors in response to trade reform. Even though we are interested in providing compensation to a group, it is analytically convenient to think about compensating a representative worker within that group. In the case of movers, we wish to design a policy that fully compensates the worker identified by $\hat{a} \in [a^{FT}, a^{TD}]$. It will shortly become evident that this choice implies that all movers with $a > \hat{a}$ are overcompensated, whereas those with $a < \hat{a}$ are undercompensated.

Focusing on a representative worker allows a wide range of possibilities. For example, if $\hat{a}$ corresponds to the average mover, then the scheme compensates the group of movers as a whole, with some overcompensated and others undercompensated. By contrast, all displaced workers are at least fully compensated if $\hat{a} = a^{FT}$. While we restrict attention to these two specific cases in sections 3 and 4, for now we allow $\hat{a}$ to take on any value between a^{FT} and a^{TD}.

Having identified the target worker, we illustrate in figure 11.2 the effects of two alternative compensation plans.[8] In one plan, compensation takes the form of an employment subsidy (η), which is independent of the

---

[8] In order to keep the diagram simple, we do not show the tariff-distorted curve for the high-tech sector.

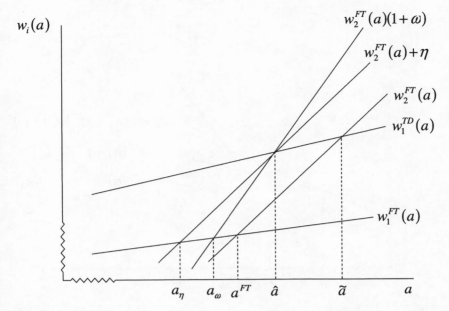

Figure 11.2.

wage rate. The other plan calls for a wage subsidy (ω) so that the amount of compensation received by any particular worker is increasing in the wage, which is itself increasing in ability. In this figure, the subsidies η and ω are chosen to satisfy $w_1^{TD}(\hat{a}) = w_2^{FT}(\hat{a}) + \eta = w_2^{FT}(\hat{a})(1 + \omega).$[9]

In figure 11.2, a_η and a_ω identify the worker who is just indifferent between remaining in sector 1 and moving to sector 2 if compensated by an employment subsidy or wage subsidy, respectively. These values are found as the solutions to $w_1^{FT}(a_\eta) = w_2^{FT}(a_\eta) + \eta$ and $w_1^{FT}(a_\omega) = w_2^{FT}(a_\omega)(1 + \omega)$. From the figure, it is clear that it will always be true that $a_\eta < a_\omega$. In turn, both of these values are less than a^{FT} since the subsidy induces workers to move who would have remained in sector 1 absent the compensation. Since allocative efficiency requires that all workers for whom $a < a^{FT}$ remain in sector 1, we conclude that the wage subsidy given only to displaced workers, by enticing a smaller magnitude of inefficient labor

---

[9] Lurking in the background is a constant marginal tax rate on all income (including subsidies) that is used to generate the revenues necessary to fund the subsidies. Since tax payments do not depend on choice of sector, they do not distort decisions and can be omitted from this diagram.

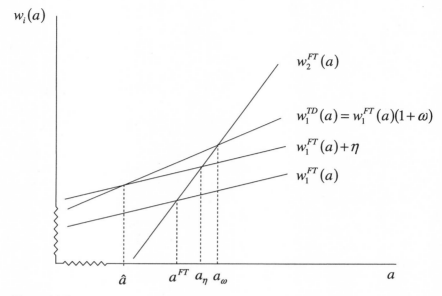

Figure 11.3.

movement, generates a higher level of social welfare than does the equivalent employment subsidy.[10]

Suppose now that we wish to compensate the group of stayers, so that $\hat{a}$ identifies a representative stayer who is targeted for compensation. Now the relative efficiency of the two policy instruments is reversed. We illustrate this result with the aid of figure 11.3. In this figure, the relevant subsidies affect the real wages of workers who stay in sector 1. We note that the curve labeled $w_1^{FT}(a)(1+\omega)$ coincides with the curve labeled $w_1^{TD}(a)$ since liberalization reduces the real wage for all stayers by the same percentage.

Since the employment subsidy is independent of the wage, it is relatively inconsequential for workers with higher ability, and therefore does not induce too many workers to forgo the higher earnings that can be had in sector 2. By contrast, the wage subsidy provides the same proportional benefit to high- and low-wage workers, and therefore leads to a larger number of workers who choose to remain in sector 1. We conclude that the employment subsidy is the preferred instrument when targeting those who are trapped in the import-competing sector.

[10] By "equivalent," we mean that the two policies target the same subset of movers for compensation.

Both of the examples illustrated here point to two simple rules for determining the welfare-maximizing compensation program. First, as we have already noted, compensation must be targeted. For example, in trying to compensate the movers, the program would be larger than necessary if the government were to subsidize all workers in sector 2. Rather, the government should only subsidize those workers who were employed in sector 1 prior to liberalization, and in sector 2 subsequently. Second, for a given targeted group, the welfare-maximizing compensation program is the one that generates the largest ratio of benefits for the average member of that group relative to the marginal worker, where the marginal worker is defined as the one who would be just indifferent between working in sector 1 or in sector 2 under a regime of free trade. Since all movers have higher abilities than the marginal worker, applying this latter rule implies that the program used to compensate the movers should provide a benefit that is increasing with ability—this is why a wage subsidy works better than an employment subsidy. In contrast, all stayers have lower ability than the marginal worker. It follows that when we are trying to compensate the stayers, an employment subsidy, which is valued equally by all stayers, is superior to a wage subsidy, which provides more compensation to the marginal worker than it provides to the average stayer in the targeted group. In each case, the welfare-maximizing program provides the desired amount of compensation while minimizing the amount of inefficient policy-induced labor misallocation.[11]

3. Unemployment and Training

3.1 The Assumptions and the Initial Steady State

We continue to assume that the wage earned by an employed worker depends on his ability, but we now extend the model to allow for training and unemployment. We do so in a relatively simple way so that we may keep the analysis tractable. As should be clear from what follows, our results should easily extend to more complex settings.[12]

In order to obtain a job we now assume that a worker must first acquire the appropriate skills and then search for suitable employment.

---

[11] Note that we only consider the case in which the low-tech good is imported. If, instead, a country that imports the high-tech good liberalizes trade, then our logic suggests that a wage subsidy should be used to compensate those who choose to remain in the high-tech sector, whereas an employment subsidy should be used to compensate those who move to the low-tech sector.

[12] We provide greater detail in Davidson and Matusz (2004b), where we derive solutions for the relevant differential equations and subject our calibration results to sensitivity analysis. This paper is available at www.msu.edu/~davidso4/currentnew.html.

Workers who are training for sector-j jobs exit the training process at rate τ_j, and the sector-j job acquisition rate is e_j. While training, each sector-j worker incurs a nominal flow training cost of $c_j p_j (1-\gamma_j)$, where p_j is the domestic (tariff-inclusive) price of the sector-j good (so that sector-j training costs are measured in terms of the sector-j good) and γ_j denotes the sector-j training subsidy (if there is one). Once suitable employment is found, a sector-j worker with ability a produces a flow of $q_j(a)$ units of output as long as the job lasts; and, since the worker is paid the value of her marginal product, the sector-j nominal wage is $p_j q_j(a)$. In addition to this wage, the worker may also receive an employment subsidy, denoted by η_j, or a wage subsidy, denoted by ω_j, so that total nominal compensation is given by $p_j q_j(a)(1 + \omega_j) + \eta_j$. Sector-$j$ jobs break up at rate b_j, and, once they do, workers must retrain if their skills are firm specific. If, however, their skills are sector specific, then the worker may immediately re-enter the search process (provided that she does not switch sectors). We use ϕ_j to denote the probability that a sector-j worker's skills transfer across sector-j jobs after termination and we use $\mu_j(a)$ to denote the unemployment insurance (UI) benefit offered to sector-j workers (μ_j varies with ability due to the fact that UI benefits are tied to the wage that the worker earned on her previous job). Given our assumptions about transitions across labor market states, it follows that the sector-j expected duration of training in sector j is $1/\tau_j$, the expected duration of unemployment is $1/e_j$, the expected duration of employment is $1/b_j$, and the probability that a worker will have to retrain after losing her job is $1 - \phi_j$.

In order to turn nominal terms into real values, we now specify a particular set of preferences. This is necessary because we want our compensation scheme to restore the lost welfare of the targeted group, and we cannot be precise about this magnitude without knowing preferences. Toward that end, we assume that all individuals have Cobb-Douglas preferences and that each individual spends half of her income on each good, so that real income is simply nominal income divided by $\sqrt{P_1 P_2}$.

We now assume that the compensation scheme is financed by taxing all earned income at a constant marginal rate of m and use $y_{ij}(a)$ to represent the flow of real income (inclusive of all subsidies and net of all taxes) earned by a sector-j worker who is currently in state i, where $i \in \{T,S,E\}$ represents training, searching, or employed, respectively; then we have

$$y_{Ej}(a) = \frac{\{p_j q_j(a)(1+\omega_j) + \eta_j\}(1-m)}{\sqrt{p_1 p_2}}, y_{Sj}(a) = \frac{\mu_j(a)}{\sqrt{p_1 p_2}}, \text{and } y_{Tj} = \frac{c_j p_j (1-\gamma_j)}{\sqrt{p_1 p_2}}$$

Workers choose an occupation based on expected income. If we represent the real expected lifetime income for a worker who is training, searching, or employed by V_{Tj}, V_{Sj}, and V_{Ej}, then we can derive these values by solving the following system of Bellman equations:

$$rV_{Tj}(a) = y_{Tj} + \tau_j \left\{ V_{Sj}(a) - V_{Tj}(a) \right\} + \dot{V}_{Tj}(a) \tag{1}$$

$$rV_{Sj}(a) = y_{Sj}(a) + e_j \left\{ V_{Ej}(a) - V_{Sj}(a) \right\} + \dot{V}_{Sj}(a) \tag{2}$$

$$rV_{Ej}(a) = y_{Ej}(a) + b_j \left\{ \phi_j V_{Sj}(a) + (1 - \phi_j)V_{Tj}(a) - V_{Ej}(a) \right\} + \dot{V}_{Ej}(a) \tag{3}$$

In these equations, r represents the discount rate and a dot over a variable represents the derivative of that variable with respect to time.[13] In each equation, the first term on the right-hand side represents current income. The second term on the right-hand side is the product of the capital gain (or loss) from changing labor market status and the rate at which such changes take place. For example, the flow rate from searching to employment in sector j is e_j while the capital gain associated with obtaining employment is $V_{Ej} - V_{Sj}$. Note that employed workers face two possibilities when they lose their job. Either they retain their skills and can begin to search for a new job immediately (this occurs with probability ϕ_j) or they must retrain before they can seek a new job. The last term on the right-hand side is the asset's rate of appreciation at time t. We include this term for completeness, but the structure of our model ensures that all changes in asset values that occur do so instantly, so that this term is always zero.

Jobless workers without skills train in the low-tech sector if $V_{T1}(a) \geq \max\{V_{T2}(a),0\}$ and they choose to train in the high-tech sector if $V_{T2}(a) \geq \max\{V_{T1}(a) 0\}$. Workers with ability such that $0 \geq \max\{V_{T1}(a), V_{T2}(a)\}$ stay out of the labor market since it is too costly for them to train for any job. These workers are effectively shut out of the labor market—there are no jobs available for them since their training costs exceed any income that they could expect to earn after finding employment. A sector-j searcher continues to search for a job if $V_{jS}(a) \geq V_{kT}(a)$; otherwise, she quits searching, switches sectors, and starts training in sector k. Finally, a sector-j worker quits her job and enters the sector-k training process if $V_{kT}(a) \geq V_{jE}(a)$; otherwise, she continues to work until an exogenous shock causes her job to dissolve.

This completes the description of the model. To characterize equilibrium we must place restrictions on the parameters. While we will be much more precise about the values of the parameters in the next section, it is

---

[13] In order to lighten the notation, we have not explicitly written expected lifetime incomes as functions time, though it should be clear that they are.

useful to sketch out the ideas that we are trying to capture in our model. We continue to characterize sector 1 as a low-tech sector that attracts low-ability workers and sector 2 as a high-tech sector that absorbs high-ability workers. What we have in mind is an economy in which high-ability workers are better suited to produce the high-tech good. We imagine that workers with high enough ability to choose between the two types of jobs know that they can find low-tech jobs without much effort and can master the skills they require rather easily.[14] However, they also know that these jobs do not pay well, do not last long, and require skills that are largely job-specific.[15] In contrast, we want high-tech jobs to require significant training and be relatively hard to find (because the matching problem is harder to solve) but durable. Moreover, high-tech skills are much more likely to transfer across jobs than low-tech skills.[16] We capture these ideas assuming that τ_1 is higher than τ_2, b_1 is higher than b_2 (low-tech training is quicker than high-tech training and low-tech jobs do not last as long as high-tech jobs), and by setting $e_1 = \infty$ and $c_1 = \phi_1 = 0$. Thus, low-tech jobs are obtained immediately after training, there is no resource cost to acquiring low-tech skills, and low-tech workers must always retrain after losing their jobs. The assumption that $c_1 = 0$ implies that $y_{T1} \geq 0$ so that $V_{T1}(a) \geq 0$ for all a, and therefore all workers enter the labor force. These assumptions, while admittedly extreme, greatly simplify our analysis.

Our final two assumptions are related to the relative importance of ability in the two sectors. to ensure that workers are properly sorted into sectors, we require that $V_{T1}^{TD}(a)$ and $V_{T2}^{TD}(a)$ have the qualitative properties represented in figure 11.4, which is analogous to figure 11.1, where the superscripts again denote the initial tariff-distorted equilibrium. If we set all time derivatives to zero and then solve (1)–(3) for V_{Tj}, we obtain

[14] Many low-ability workers face difficulties finding *any* job and therefore experience long spells of unemployment whenever they lose their job. We believe that this is largely due to their work history and overall lack of ability. By assuming that low-tech jobs are plentiful, we are trying to capture the idea that the *marginal* worker (who has the ability to train for a high-tech job) would be able to find menial employment easily if she chooses to do so.

[15] Consider, for example, a worker who moves from one low-tech job (working as a clerk in a department store) to a new one (working for a fast-food restaurant). While training as a clerk, the worker may need to learn the layout of the store, the procedures for opening and closing the store, how to handle the cash register, and so on. However, acquiring these skills will not shorten the time it takes to learn how to prepare fast food.

[16] High-tech workers (e.g., managers, accountants, lawyers) are often required to complete college and some may have a postgraduate education. If they lose their jobs, most of these workers will be able to find reemployment without retraining in the same field. Moreover, even if these workers change occupations, they will have acquired some general skills along the way that may help them land new jobs without acquiring new skills.

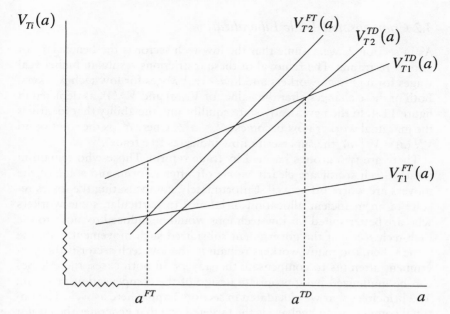

Figure 11.4.

$$V_{Tj}(a) = \frac{(r + e_j)(r + b_j) - \phi_j b_j e_j}{\Delta_j} y_{Tj} + \frac{\tau_j(r + b_j)}{\Delta_j} y_{S_j}(a) + \frac{\tau_j e_j}{\Delta_j} y_{E_j}(a) \quad (4)$$

where $\Delta_j = (r + b_j)(r + e_j)(r + \tau_j) - b_j e_j \tau_j$. Substituting our parametric assumptions into (4), the V_{Tj} curves will be consistent with figure 11.4 if $\tau_1 \Delta_2 y'_{E1}(a) < \tau_2 e_2 \Delta_1 y'_{E2}(a) + \tau_2 (r + b_2) \Delta_1 y'_{S2}(a)$.

Second, we want to assume that ability is more important in determining output in the high-tech sector than it is in the low-tech sector. The easiest way to capture this notion is to assume that if there are diminishing returns to ability, then returns diminish faster in the low-tech sector. In other words, if $q_j(a)$ is a concave function in both sectors, then we want to assume that $q_1(a)$ is more concave than $q_2(a)$ in the usual Rothschild-Stiglitz sense.

Returning to figure 11.4, the critical level of ability (a^{TD}) solves $V_{T1}^{TD}(a) = V_{T2}^{TD}(a)$. Thus, in the initial tariff-distorted steady state, all workers with $a < a^{TD}$ are attracted to the low-tech sector, whereas the remainder are attracted to the high-tech sector.

3.2 Compensated Trade Liberalization

As in section 2, we assume that the low-tech sector is the beneficiary of import restraints. The removal of these restrictions results in higher real wages for high-tech workers and lower real wages for low-tech workers. Both of these changes alter the values of $V_{T1}(a)$ and $V_{T2}(a)$, as depicted in figure 11.4. In the new steady-state equilibrium, the ability that identifies the marginal worker now becomes $a^{FT} < a^{TD}$, where a^{FT} is the solution to $V_{T1}^{FT}(a) = V_{T2}^{FT}(a)$ (the superscript now indicates free trade).[17]

There are two groups harmed by trade reform. Those who remain in the low-tech sector are clearly worse off after reform, and some of the movers are worse off as well. Unfortunately, compensating the losers results in an inefficient allocation of labor.[18] In particular, some workers who are better suited for low-tech jobs would be induced to move to the high-tech sector if the government subsidized such movement.[19] By the same token, too many workers remain in the low-tech sector if the government attempts to compensate the stayers. In both cases, these losses can be minimized by appropriate design of the compensation program. The principles that we elucidated in section 2 apply here as well. The optimal compensation package is the targeted one that generates the largest ratio of benefits for the average member of the targeted group relative to the marginal worker.

Now, suppose that the government wants to compensate those who are harmed by liberalization. In addition, let us assume, for now, that the movers lose as a whole when the tariff is removed. Then our first goal is to pin down the government's objective. As we pointed out in section 2, this is made nontrivial by the fact that ability varies across workers so that (a) the losses are not uniform within a group, and (b) different workers in the same group may differ in the values they place on the various compensation policies. We consider two alternatives. In the first, the government's goal is to fully compensate the group (i.e., the movers or the stayers) as a whole so that the average worker in the group is just indifferent between free trade with compensation and the original tariff-distorted outcome. In the second, the government fully compensates the worker in the group who suffers the largest losses (which, for both the movers and the stayers, is the worker with ability level a^{FT}). Note that in the first case, there will be some workers in the group who are undercompensated and these workers

---

[17] A detailed analysis of how the economy moves from the initial tariff-distorted steady-state equilibrium to the new, free trade steady-state equilibrium can be found in Davidson and Matusz (2004b).

[18] Because turnover rates are exogenous and there are no other distortions in our model, the laissez-faire equilibrium is efficient. See Davidson and Matusz (2004a).

[19] As always, we use world prices to value output and therefore gauge productivity.

will therefore still prefer the tariff, whereas in the second case, *all* workers in the compensated group are at least as well off after liberalization. Of course, compensation by the second criterion is more costly.

We begin by focusing on the movers and we assume that the government's objective is to fully compensate these workers as a group (the arguments easily generalize to the case in which the objective is to compensate the mover who suffers the largest loss). These workers can be compensated by offering wage or employment subsidies to those employed in the high-tech sector, or by offering training subsidies to those training for high-tech jobs, or by providing unemployment benefits to anyone searching for employment. Our first result is fairly obvious—any compensation offered should be targeted at only those workers who switch sectors as a result of liberalization. That is, if a wage subsidy is used, workers who were already employed in the high-tech sector at the time of liberalization should not be eligible for it. The reason is that the incumbents already gain as a result of liberalization and providing them with an additional benefit would needlessly add to the cost of the compensation program.

Turn next to the type of compensation that should be used. All four policies increase the expected lifetime income for a worker who switches sectors and starts to train for high-tech employment. Thus, the use of any one of these policies to compensate the movers would cause the V_{T2} curve in figure 11.4 to shift up, resulting in too much labor reallocation and deadweight loss. As we showed in section 2, the policy that allows the government to achieve its objective while generating the smallest deadweight loss is the one that is highly valued by the average worker in the targeted group relative to the value placed on that policy by the marginal worker. To see which policy works best, all that we need to do is compare the payments that the movers would receive from the government in each case. When the government uses a wage subsidy or unemployment insurance, the movers receive a payment that is increasing in ability. This follows from the fact that both payments are tied to the worker's wage (since unemployment benefits are always paid out as a fraction of the workers previous wage) and wages are increasing in ability. This means that compensating the movers with a wage subsidy or unemployment benefits shifts up the V_{T2} curve in a *nonparallel* fashion, with high-ability movers receiving larger payments than low-ability movers. In contrast, when the government uses employment or training subsidies, the payment received by the movers is independent of ability. As a result, the V_{T2} curve shifts up in *parallel* fashion.[20] This

---

[20] Note that if training costs decrease with ability, the V_{2T} curve would shift up in nonparallel fashion but in a way so that the average mover benefits *less* than the marginal worker. This would make training subsidies even worse.

difference is important because the average mover has higher ability than the marginal worker. This means that wage subsidies and UI both benefit the average mover more than the marginal worker, whereas training and employment subsidies benefit both the average mover and the marginal worker equally. As a result, wage subsidies and unemployment insurance programs are superior to training and employment subsidies—since the average mover benefits a great deal from these programs, a relatively small program can be used to compensate the movers as a group, and since the marginal worker does not benefit that greatly from these programs, a relatively small distortion will be imposed on the economy.

Finally, to distinguish between wage subsidies and UI, note that the former is tied to the mover's *new* wage, w_2, whereas the latter is tied to the mover's *previous* wage, w_1. And if high-tech wages are more sensitive to ability that low-tech wages (i.e., $q_1(a)$ is more concave than $q_2(a)$), then the spread between the benefit paid to the average mover and the marginal worker is greater with the wage subsidy. As a result, the wage subsidy is the best policy.

Turn now to the stayers. Since there is no low-tech unemployment in our model and since we have assumed away any resource cost associated with low-tech training, we cannot use UI or training subsidies to offset the stayers' losses. We therefore restrict attention to wage and employment subsidies. Comparing these programs, we again note that both increase expected lifetime incomes for trainers, shifting up the V_{T1} curve. However, as described earlier, an employment subsidy shifts this curve upward in a *parallel* fashion, whereas a wage subsidy increases the slope of the V_{T1} curve. In this case, the employment subsidy is worth the same to the average stayer as it is to the marginal worker, whereas the wage subsidy is worth relatively more to the marginal worker. Applying our earlier logic, a wage subsidy will therefore generate a larger misallocation of resources than the equivalent employment subsidy.[21] We conclude that the optimal policy for compensating stayers is a targeted employment subsidy.[22]

---

[21] If we were to allow for low-tech unemployment, the same argument would imply that employment subsidies dominate UI.

[22] It is worth noting that there are no current programs in the United States targeted at compensating those who remain in sectors that have been liberalized. There are programs designed to augment the incomes of low-wage workers with the most prominent one being the Earned Income Tax Credit (EITC). In our model, the EITC would be equivalent to a wage subsidy in which the level of the subsidy *decreases* with the worker's wage. This means that the EITC provides lower payments to high-wage workers than it provides to their low-wage counterparts. It should be clear that using such a program to compensate the stayers would be superior to an employment subsidy *if it could be targeted at the sector in question*, since the average stayer would receive a larger payment than the marginal worker. The problem is that, in practice, the EITC has always been a broad-based program that applies

4. QUANTIFYING THE COSTS OF COMPENSATION

How costly is compensation? Would a well-designed compensation program be nearly as distortive as the trade barrier that it replaces? In order to address these questions, we first describe how we measure welfare, and then we parameterize the model presented in section 3 to numerically compute this measure under the tariff-distorted steady state, the free trade equilibrium, and an equilibrium in which trade reform is accompanied by compensation.[23]

4.1 Measuring Welfare

As noted above, we assume that all workers have identical Cobb-Douglas utility functions, which implies that we can aggregate over groups of agents. In particular, if we define $C_j(t)$ as the aggregate consumption by a group of agents of good j at time t, then the instantaneous utility obtained by that group is $U(t) = \sqrt{C_1(t)C_2(t)}$. We measure the welfare for this group as the present discounted value of $U(t)$:

$$W = \int_0^\infty e^{-rt}U(t)dt \qquad (5)$$

When the group includes all agents in the economy, W represents social welfare.

We normalize quantities so that the world prices of both goods are unity. As before, good 1 is taken to be the import good, so that $p_1 \geq 1$, with equality under a regime of free trade. If we define $Q_j(t)$ as the quantity of good j produced at time t, balanced trade then implies that $Q_1(t) + Q_2(t) = C_1(t) + C_2(t)$. Moreover, preferences imply that $p_1 C_1(t) = C_2(t)$. From these two equations, we find that

$$C_1(t) = \frac{1}{1+p_1}\{Q_1(t) + Q_2(t)\} \qquad (6a)$$

$$C_2(t) = \frac{p_1}{1+p_1}\{Q_1(t) + Q_2(t)\} \qquad (6b)$$

---

to all low-wage workers. As we pointed out earlier, using a broad-based program adds unnecessarily to the program's cost. However, if a program like the EITC could be targeted to a specific sector, our analysis indicates that it might be the best way to compensate the stayers.
[23] The exercise carried out in this section is not intended as a serious calibration exercise (e.g., our assumption that ability is uniformly distributed is not realistic). Instead, it should be viewed as an expositional device that helps us understand and illustrate the effects at work in the model.

Output and prices differ across equilibria. Again, letting superscripts *TD* represent the tariff-distorted equilibrium, *FT* the free trade equilibrium, and *CFT* the compensated free trade equilibrium, we have social welfare in each case:

$$W^{TD} = \frac{\sqrt{p_1}}{1+p_1} \int_0^\infty e^{-rt} \left\{ Q_1^{TD}(t) + Q_2^{TD}(t) \right\} \tag{7a}$$

$$W^{FT} = \frac{1}{2} \int_0^\infty e^{-rt} \left\{ Q_1^{FT}(t) + Q_2^{FT}(t) \right\} \tag{7b}$$

$$W^{CFT} = \frac{1}{2} \int_0^\infty e^{-rt} \left\{ Q_1^{CFT}(t) + Q_2^{CFT}(t) \right\} \tag{7c}$$

Using (7), the welfare gain from uncompensated trade reform is measured as $W^{FT} - W^{TD}$. Compensating workers for their losses misallocates resources, generating a cost. We can compute Θ, the economic cost of the compensation policy as a percentage of the gains from trade:

$$\Theta = \frac{W^{FT} - W^{CFT}}{W^{FT} - W^{TD}} \times 100 \tag{8}$$

4.2 Parametric Assumptions

As noted above, we assume that jobs in the low-tech sector are available for the asking, meaning that duration of search in this sector $(1/e_1)$ is zero. In turn, this implies $e_1 = \infty$. By contrast, jobs in the high-tech sector do require search. For the United States, the average duration of unemployment fluctuates with the business cycle but is usually close to one quarter, rarely straying from that value by more than two weeks.[24] We assume that this is the average duration of unemployment in the high-tech sector in our model and correspondingly set $e_2 = 4$.

Data on the average duration of employment in U.S. manufacturing is available and can be used to pin down b_2. Davis, Haltiwanger, and Schuh (1996) provide data on annual rates of job destruction in U.S. manufacturing industries and report that the average annual rate was roughly 10% for the period 1973–88. This translates into an average duration of employment of 10 years. This value varies over the business cycle, reaching a peak in 1975 at 16.5% (implying an average duration of employment of six years).[25] Thus, we consider values for b_2, the separation rate

[24] See, for example, table B-44 of *The Economic Report of the President* (2001).
[25] See table 2.1 on p. 19 in Davis, Haltiwanger, and Schuh (1996).

in the high-tech sector, such that high-tech jobs last, on average, between 6 and 10 years.

Pinning down the separation rate in the low-tech sector is more complicated. We model these jobs as transitory, low-paying jobs that require few skills. While many of these jobs may be found in manufacturing, it is hard to know how to draw conclusions about the average length of the worst jobs in a sector from industrywide data. So, we follow a different approach. We think of our low-tech jobs as the types of jobs that many workers hold when they first enter the labor force. Data on jobs held over a lifetime indicate that up to the age of 24 workers start (roughly) one new job every two years.[26] Based on this evidence, we consider two cases—one in which low-tech jobs last one year ($b_1 = 1$) and one in which they last two years ($b_1 = 0.5$).

We assume that skills in the low-tech sector are relatively job specific, and therefore assume that $\phi_1 = 0$. From previous work with this model, we know that results are fairly insensitive to changes in r and ϕ_2.[27] For all empirically relevant values for the interest rate (below 20%) and for values of $\phi_2 \in [0.5, 0.9]$, our estimates of the adjustment costs triggered by trade reform vary only at the third decimal place. Since our results are insensitive to changes in these parameters, the only values that we consider are $r = 0.03$ and $\phi_2 = 0.8$.

The remaining parameters are tied to the training and production processes. Unfortunately, not much is known about the size and scope of training costs. For the low-tech sector, we want to choose a value for τ_1 that is consistent with the idea that low-tech skills are easy to master. Thus, we assume that the time costs are small by setting $\tau_1 = 52$ (so that it takes only one week to learn the skills required to perform low-tech jobs).

As for the high-tech sector, we turn to the limited information that is available on training costs. Hamermesh (1993) provides a survey of this evidence where the costs are assumed to include the costs of recruiting and training newly hired workers. He concludes that in some instances these costs may be quite high. For example, the cost of replacing a worker in a large firm in the pharmaceutical industry was pegged at roughly twice that worker's annual salary. In the trucking industry, the cost of replacing a driver was estimated to be slightly less than half the driver's annual salary.[28] Similar estimates can be found in Acemoglu and Pischke's

---

[26] See table 8.1 on p. 210 in Hamermesh and Rees (1998).

[27] See Davidson and Matusz (2002, 2004a).

[28] Of course, there are some industries in which these costs are quite low. The lowest estimate of turnover costs reported in Hamermesh's survey appears to be about three weeks worth of salary, although such a low figure appears to be an exception rather than the norm.

(1999) study of the German apprenticeship training system. They report estimates of training costs that vary from 6 to 15 months of the average worker's annual income. We capture this wide range of estimates by assuming that high-tech training lasts four months ($\tau_2 = 4$) and then vary the value of c_2 so that total training costs vary from a low of 1 month of pay for an average high-tech worker to a high of 15 months of pay. We also consider two intermediate values in which these costs are equal to 5 and 10 months of high-tech income.

This leaves only a description of the production process. We assume simple production functions, defining the marginal product of a sector-j worker as $q_j a$. We normalize q_2 and then vary q_1, which varies the attractiveness of sector 1. In particular, as q_1 increases, holding q_2 constant, sector 1 becomes more attractive relative to sector 2 and the ability index of the marginal worker (a^{TD} in the tariff-distorted equilibrium) increases. We consider three different values of q_1 for each combination of turnover rates. These values correspond to values of a^{TD} equal to 0.1, 0.2, and 0.33. Thus, we consider parameter values that imply that initially 10%, 20%, or 33% of the workforce is employed in the low-tech sector.

4.3 Methodology

We assume that this country initially protects the low-tech sector with a 5% ad valorem tariff. In addition, we maintain the assumption adopted in section 2 that tariff revenue is distributed to all agents in proportion to their income, therefore leaving the overall distribution of income unchanged. We solve for the equilibrium under these assumptions and calculate social welfare (W^{TD}). We then remove the import tariff and calculate social welfare under free trade (W^{FT}).

Finally, we turn to the issue central to this paper and calculate social welfare when we compensate the groups for their losses (W^{CFT}).[29] In order to do this, we choose the policy that minimizes the policy-induced labor misallocation, using a wage subsidy to compensate the movers and an employment subsidy to compensate the stayers. Moreover, we choose two different degrees of compensation. We first examine the effects of compensating the targeted group as a whole, implying that some members of that group are overcompensated while others are undercompensated. We then look at compensating the marginal worker, which effectively overcompensates every other member of the group.

[29] The detailed calculations of welfare in each of the three situations, along with a description of the transition path across steady states, can be found in Davidson and Matusz (2004b).

In conducting our experiment, we take care to implement a constant marginal income tax that generates enough revenue to balance the present discounted value of the cost of the compensation plans.

4.4 Results

For each set of parameters, the impact of liberalization varies across the groups with the low-ability movers and the high-ability stayers suffering the biggest losses (relative to the others in their group). In Davidson and Matusz (2004b), we examined the impact of trade reform on the movers as a group in some detail and found that, for all of the parameters discussed above, the group as a whole always loses when the tariff is removed. Even in the case in which high-tech training costs are extremely low and turnover is high (so that the transition to the new steady state is relatively quick) the adjustment costs imposed on this group always outweigh their long-term gains from higher wages and lower consumer prices. These losses vary from between 1.5% to 2.5%. Of course, the lowest ability movers suffer a much larger loss, usually around 4.5%, which is roughly the size of the loss suffered by the stayers. In each of our experiments, we solve for the value of the policy parameters required to offset these losses and then calculate the distortion imposed on the economy.

We report our results in tables 11.1–11.4. Since our main qualitative results are fairly insensitive to the turnover rates, we report them only for the two extreme cases—one in which the average high-tech job lasts 10 years while the average low-tech job lasts 1 year and one in which the average high-tech job lasts 6 years while the average low-tech job lasts 2 years. Tables 11.1 and 11.2 show the percentage of the net gain from trade reform that would be eaten away by a compensation plan targeted at the movers, while tables 11.3 and 11.4 do the same for the stayers. Tables 11.1 and 11.3 provide the results when the government uses correct policy, whereas Tables 11.2 and 11.4 provide the results when the government compensates the groups with an inferior policy.

The main entry in each cell refers to Θ, as defined in (8), when the government targets the average member of the group. The entries in parentheses show the same measure if the government targets the worker who suffers the largest losses (the worker with ability a^{FT}). For example, the efficient policy for compensating the movers is a wage subsidy. If we calibrate the policy based on the average mover, if training costs are 10 months of the average high-tech worker's income, if high-tech jobs last an average of 6 years, low-tech jobs last an average of 2 years, and if the initial equilibrium has 10% of the population in the low-tech sector, then table 11.1 indicates that using a wage subsidy to compensate the movers

TABLE 11.1
Deadweight Loss as a Percentage of the Net Gains from Trade when
Compensating the Average (Marginal) Mover Using a Wage Subsidy

	Percentage of Labor Initially in the Low-Tech Sector					
	Avg. Duration of Low-Tech Job = 2 yr Avg. Duration of High-Tech Job = 6 yr			Avg. Duration of Low-Tech Job = 1 yr Avg. Duration of high-Tech Job = 10 yr		
High-Tech Training Costs	10%	20%	33%	10%	20%	33%
1 month	0.75 (4.34)	0.25 (2.69)	0.02 (1.27)	0.51 (3.29)	0.14 (1.85)	0.01 (0.85)
5 months	2.18 (9.00)	3.91 (18.79)	1.97 (14.42)	2.27 (9.52)	3.08 (25.59)	1.30 (10.80)
10 months	1.15 (4.63)	5.40 (23.80)	4.71 (27.26)	1.58 (6.38)	5.13 (23.09)	3.68 (22.66)
15 months	0.43 (1.72)	4.90 (20.93)	6.27 (33.60)	0.83 (3.34)	5.30 (22.96)	5.40 (30.09)

costs approximately 1.15% of the net gains from trade. However, the cost rises to 4.63% when the policy is calibrated based on the marginal worker. Table 11.2 shows that these costs would increase to 1.30% and 5.24%, respectively, if an employment subsidy were used instead.[30]

Table 11.1 indicates that in all cases, the distortion created when compensating the the average mover is modest—generally less than 6% of the net gains from trade. There are two factors that contribute to this outcome. First, the movers in our model do not suffer huge losses from liberalization (as we noted above, the losses tend to be less than 2%). Second, liberalization does not trigger that much movement in our model. In the case in which 20% of the labor force is initially employed in the low-tech sector, only 4% of the labor force switches to the high-tech sector when the tariff is removed.[31] The fact that the cost imposed on the rest of the

---

[30] Bear in mind that in our model, unemployment compensation would generate the same costs as a wage subsidy while a training subsidy would generate the same cost as an employment subsidy.

[31] This fraction grows to 10% for the case in which 33% of the labor force starts out attached to sector 1 and shrinks to less than 0.5% for the case in which 10% begin in that sector.

TABLE 11.2
Deadweight Loss as a Percentage of the Net Gains from Trade when
Compensating the Average (Marginal) Mover Using an Employment Subsidy

	Percentage of Labor Initially in the Low-Tech Sector					
	Avg. Duration of Low-Tech Job = 2 yr Avg. Duration of High-Tech Job = 6 yr			Avg. Duration of Low-Tech Job = 1 yr Avg. Duration of High-Tech Job = 10 yr		
High-Tech Training Costs	10%	20%	33%	10%	20%	33%
1 month	2.49 (10.08)	1.52 (7.43)	0.21 (3.53)	2.02 (8.18)	1.05 (5.36)	0.07 (2.40)
5 months	2.99 (12.00)	7.14 (31.40)	4.71 (28.43)	3.39 (13.66)	6.41 (28.37)	3.63 (22.90)
10 months	1.30 (5.24)	7.38 (32.10)	7.73 (43.43)	1.90 (7.63)	7.65 (33.14)	6.79 (38.29)
15 months	0.47 (1.82)	5.94 (25.10)	8.76 (46.31)	0.92 (3.68)	6.83 (29.31)	8.26 (44.33)

economy is so modest makes these redistributional policies considerably attractive.

Not surprisingly, table 11.1 also indicates that the distortion created when fully compensating the marginal mover imposes a much greater burden on the economy. While there are many cases in which the cost remains small (below 10% of the net gains from trade), there are also cases in which up to 30% of the net gains from trade are eaten away by the compensation scheme.

The one curious result evident in table 11.1 is that the deadweight loss is often nonmonotonic in both the size of high-tech training costs and the size of the low-tech sector. This counterintuitive outcome emerges because of the manner in which we calibrate the model. First, hold constant the percentage of the labor force initially attached to the low-tech sector while reducing the training costs in the high-tech sector. The reduction in training costs makes the high-tech sector more appealing, putting downward pressure on the percentage of the workforce attracted to the low-tech sector. To hold this percentage constant, we must increase q_1, the sector-1 productivity parameter, thereby increasing the low-tech wage for all workers in that sector. This means that when a worker

TABLE 11.3
Deadweight Loss as a Percentage of the Net Gains from Trade when
Compensating the Average (Marginal) Stayer Using an Employment Subsidy

| | Percentage of Labor Initially in the Low-Tech Sector | | | | | |
| | Avg. Duration of Low-Tech Job = 2 yr Avg. Duration of High-Tech Job = 6 yr | | | Avg. Duration of Low-Tech Job = 1 yr Avg. Duration of High-Tech Job = 10 yr | | |
High-Tech Training Costs	10%	20%	33%	10%	20%	33%
1 month	0.16 (0.64)	0.12 (0.49)	0.06 (0.23)	0.08 (0.31)	0.05 (0.22)	0.03 (0.10)
5 months	0.19 (0.71)	0.60 (2.43)	0.61 (2.52)	0.13 (0.35)	0.34 (1.32)	0.33 (1.37)
10 months	0.09 (0.27)	0.70 (2.67)	1.22 (5.06)	0.07 (0.17)	0.48 (1.53)	0.78 (3.15)
15 months	0.03 (0.09)	0.60 (2.17)	1.60 (6.61)	0.04 (0.08)	0.47 (1.46)	1.12 (4.28)

TABLE 11.4
Deadweight Loss as a Percentage of the Net Gains from Trade when
Compensating the Average (Marginal) Stayer Using a Wage Subsidy

| | Percentage of Labor Initially in the Low-Tech Sector | | | | | |
| | Avg. Duration of Low-Tech Job = 2 yr Avg. Duration of High-Tech Job = 6 yr | | | Avg. Duration of Low-Tech Job = 1 yr Avg. Duration of High-Tech Job = 10 yr | | |
High-Tech Training Costs	10%	20%	33%	10%	20%	33%
1 month	41.49	61.82	37.79	43.15	72.43	31.01
5 months	16.09	56.50	61.40	20.45	59.56	58.90
10 months	5.78	41.73	62.35	8.90	47.57	62.30
15 months	1.87	29.66	59.36	3.93	36.64	61.13

moves to the high-tech sector, the amount of output forgone (and the corresponding wage) is larger than it would be if high-tech training costs were higher (and q_1 lower). Thus, when training costs are low the movers should require *more* compensation than when the training costs are high. On the other hand, the direct loss suffered by the movers due to the higher training costs increases with the magnitude of those costs. This suggests that when training costs are low the movers should require *less* compensation than when training costs are high. As a result of these two conflicting forces, this relationship can go in either direction. A similar argument explains the nonmonotonicity with respect to the initial size of the low-tech sector.[32]

Turn next to table 11.2, which shows how much the cost of compensation increases if the wrong policy is used. As the table clearly indicates, such a mistake can be quite costly. For example, when training costs are very low, choosing the wrong policy more than doubles the deadweight loss. At the other extreme, when training costs are high and the low-tech sector is small, such a policy mistake results in only a small increase in the cost of the program.

Turn now to tables 11.3 and 11.4, which report the cost of compensating the stayers. The employment subsidy that fully compensates the stayers is quite low for all of the parameter values that we considered. The reason for this is simple. These workers are quite poor and earn very low wages. While the losses that they suffer in percentage terms are larger than those suffered by the movers, in absolute magnitude they are quite small. Thus, it does not take much of an employment subsidy to make up for these small losses. This is particularly true for the average stayer, since this worker has a relatively low ability level. In contrast, such a small employment subsidy is not valued very highly by the marginal worker, since this worker has a considerably higher ability level and can earn much more than the average stayer by seeking a high-tech job. It follows that the small employment subsidy does not impose a large burden on the economy. This is clearly reflected by the main entries in table 11.3, where the

---

[32] When calibrating the model, to make the low-tech sector larger we must increase q_1. This increases the low-tech wage for all workers in that sector and means that when a worker moves to the high-tech sector, the amount of output forgone is larger than it would be if initial sector size were lower (and q_1 lower). Thus, when the low-tech sector is large the movers should require *more* compensation than when the low-tech sector is small. On the other hand, when the low-tech sector is large, the country produces more of the low-tech good domestically and imports less from the rest of the world. This means that the tariff is less distortionary and that the losses from removing the tariff will be smaller than they would be had the sector been smaller. As a consequence, when the low-tech sector is large the movers should require *less* compensation than when the low-tech sector is small. Since these two effects work in opposite directions, the relationship between the initial size of the low-tech sector and the level of compensation required can be nonmonotonic.

deadweight loss as a fraction of the net gains from trade is given for each of the parameter values when stayers are compensated as a group. With a single exception, this loss is well under 1% of the net gain from trade.

The second entry in each cell of table 11.3 shows the results when the policy is designed to fully compensate the stayer who is harmed the most by liberalization, therefore overcompensating all other stayers. In this case, deadweight loss due to compensation is higher, but it stills remains below 2% for almost all parameter values (rising to around 5% only when the low-tech sector initially accounts for one-third of all employment *and* training costs are high). This makes for a compelling argument in favor of providing such compensation.

We noted above that attempts to compensate the movers with the wrong policy could increase the deadweight loss by a large percentage. Mistakes are even more costly when attempting to compensate the stayers. Suppose, for example, that the government attempts to compensate the stayers with a wage subsidy. In our model, a wage subsidy acts much like a tariff in that it pushes up the wages of low-tech workers. In fact, the only difference is that consumer prices are not affected by the wage subsidy. It follows that the wage subsidy will have to be set a level slightly below the tariff in order to compensate the stayers. But such a high wage subsidy will cause almost as many low-tech workers to move to the high-tech sector as the tariff. As a result, the deadweight loss associated with a wage subsidy is quite high. These values are reported in table 11.4.[33] These results are striking for two reasons. First, the numbers can get quite high (in some cases the loss amounted to about 60% of the net gains from trade reform!). But, perhaps more important, they are striking when compared to the losses associated with the employment subsidy. Thus, if the government's goal is to compensate the stayers, choosing the right policy is vitally important.

5. CONCLUSIONS

This paper has been devoted to an important issue—what is the best way to compensate those who are harmed by trade liberalization? In addressing this question, we use a model that takes into account the training and search processes that workers must go through in order to find jobs. In the context of our model, we have argued that the optimal way to compensate the movers (who bear the adjustment costs imposed on the

---

[33] Note that when using a wage subsidy to compensate the stayers it does not matter whether the government attempts to fully compensate the group or the marginal stayer. This is evident from the fact that there is only one entry in each cell of table 11.4. This follows from the fact that a wage subsidy and the tariff both cause shift V_{T1} to shift up in the same manner.

economy by liberalization) is with a targeted wage subsidy. We have also argued that the optimal way to compensate the stayers (those who remain trapped in the low-tech sector because they find it too difficult to acquire the skills required for high-tech jobs) is with a targeted employment subisdy.

In order to keep our model tractable, we were required to make a number of simplifying assumptions. For example, we have assumed that labor is the only input, we have treated the steady-state labor market turnover rates as exogenous, we have assumed that these turnover rates do not vary with ability, and we have assumed that additional training does not increase productivity. The first assumption is particularly important since it gives us a model with a specific-factors flavor in that trade preferences split along industry lines. This has simplified our problem considerably by allowing us to design policies targeted at workers in previously protected industries. In a more complex model in which Stolper-Samuelson forces play a role, the problem will become more complex since the policies will have to be targeted, at least to some degree, toward factors as opposed to industries. In the future it will be vitally important to relax this and all other simplifying assumptions to see how our results must be modified. Our results should therefore be viewed as the first step in a long process of investigating optimal compensation schemes when labor markets are imperfect.

We close by pointing out that we take some comfort in our belief that our results should survive when the steady-state turnover rates are endogenized. The reason for this is that our optimal policies, wage and employment subisidies, should be even more appealing in such a setting. After all, they encourage workers to search harder for employment, resulting in lower average spells of unemployment. In contrast, if we compensate the losers by increasing unemployment benefits or by offering training subsidies, we would expect to see an increase in the average length of jobless spells. This follows from the fact that these two policies decrease the opportunity cost of unemployment.

REFERENCES

Baily, M. N., G., Burtless, and R. Litan. 1993. *Growth with Equity*. Washington, DC: Brookings Institution.

Brander, J., and B. Spencer. 1994. "Trade Adjustment Assistance: Welfare and Incentive Effects of Payments to Displaced Workers," *Journal of International Economics* 36(3–4): 239–62.

Brecher, R., and E. Choudhri. 1994. "Pareto Gains from Trade, Reconsidered: Compensating for Jobs Lost," *Journal of International Economics* 36(3–4): 223–38.

Burtless, G., Lawrence, R., Litan, R., and Shapiro, R. 1998. *Globaphobia: Confronting Fears about Open Trade*. Washington, DC: Brookings Institution.

Davidson, C., and S. J. Matusz. 2002. "Globalization, Employment and Income: Analyzing the Adjustment Process". In D. Greenaway and D. Nelson eds., *Globalization and Labor Markets*. New York: Palgrave Macmillan: 66–92.

Davidson, C., and S. J. Matusz. 2004a. "Should Policy Makers be Concerned about Adjustment Costs?" In D. Mitra and A. Panagariya eds., *The Political Economy of Trade, Aid and Foreign Investment Policies*. Amsterdam: Elsevier.

Davidson, C., and S. J. Matusz. 2004b. "Trade Liberalization and Compensation," working paper, Michigan State University. (Note: This paper is available at www.msu.edu/~davidso4/currentnew.html.)

Davis, S., J. Haltiwanger, and S. Schuh. 1996. *Job Creation and Destruction*. Cambridge: MIT Press.

Dixit, A., and V. Norman. 1980. *Theory of International Trade*. Cambridge: Cambridge University Press.

Dixit, A., and V. Norman. 1986. "Gains from Trade without Lump-Sum Compensation," *Journal of International Economics* 21(1–2): 111–22.

Feenstra, R., and T. Lewis. 1994. "Trade Adjustment Assistance and Pareto Gains from Trade," *Journal of International Economics* 36(3–4): 201–22.

Hamermesh, D. 1993. *Labor Demand*. Princeton: Princeton University Press.

Hamermesh, D., and A. Rees. 1998. *The Economics of Work and Pay*, 4th ed. New York: Harper and Row.

Hufbauer, G., and B. Goodrich. 2001. "Steel: Big Problems, Better Solutions." Policy Brief, Washington, DC: Institute for International Economics.

Jacobson, L., R. LaLonde, and D. Sullivan. 1993a. *The Costs of Worker Dislocation*. Kalamazoo, MI: W.E. Upjohn Institute for Employment Research.

Jacobson, L., R. LaLonde, and D. Sullivan. 1993b. "Earnings Losses of Displaced Workers," *American Economic Review* 83(4): 685–709.

Kemp, M., and H. Wan. 1986. "Gains from Trade without Lump-Sum Compensation," *Journal of International Economics* 21(1–2): 99–110.

Kemp, M., and H. Wan. 1995. "On Lump Sum Compensation." In M. Kemp, ed., *The Gains from Trade and the Gains from Aid: Essays in International Trade Theory*. London: Routledge: 296–316.

Kletzer, L. 2001. *What Are the Costs of Job Loss from Import-Competing Industries?* Washington, DC: Institute for International Economics.

Kletzer, L., and R. Litan. 2001. "A Prescription to Relieve Worker Anxiety," Policy Brief No. 73, Brookings Institution.

Lawrence, R., and R. Litan. 1986. *Saving Free Trade: A Pragmatic Approach*. Washington, DC: Brookings Institution.

Mayer, W. 1984. "Endogenous Tariff Formation," *American Economic Review* 74(5): 970–85.

Parsons, D. 2000. "Wage Insurance: A Policy Review," *Research in Employment Policy* 2: 119–40.

Scheve, F. K., and M. Slaughter. 2001. *Globalization and the Perception of American Workers*. Washington, DC: Institute for International Economics.

Spector, D. 2001. "Is It Possible to Redistribute the Gains from Trade Using Income Taxation?" *Journal of International Economics* 55(2): 441–60.

Chapter 12

CAN COMPENSATION SAVE FREE TRADE?

CARL DAVIDSON, STEVEN J. MATUSZ, AND DOUGLAS R. NELSON

1. INTRODUCTION

Welfare economics generally, and the welfare economics of international trade in particular, has long understood that there is a close connection between liberalization and the need for compensation. While liberalization generally implies gains, it also implies adjustment, and, loosely speaking, the bigger the gains, the bigger the adjustment. For a country unable to influence its terms of trade, we have a sizable number of results, under quite general conditions, showing that free trade dominates limited trade and, under more restricted conditions, that existing forms of protection could be liberalized in such a way as to produce an increase in aggregate economic welfare. These results, however, rely on two fundamental abstractions: first, these are long-run/comparative static results that do not consider the short-run costs of adjustment from the distorted to the undistorted equilibrium; and, second, these results implicitly or explicitly assume that compensation is carried out in such a way as to ensure that a potential welfare gain is made actual. While both sorts of questions have produced research seeking to evaluate the robustness of gains from trade results to their concerns, in this paper we are interested in the positive political economy of the second question.[1]

The great majority of research on the positive political economy of domestic trade policy can be seen as an attempt to answer the question: if protection is so bad, why is there so much of it? The key result, presented most clearly in Mayer's (1984) fundamental paper: under the assumptions of the two-good, two-factor small HOS model, with heterogeneity in household factor ownership, and determination of equilibrium policy

[1] See Davidson and Matusz (2004) for an overview and extension of research on the first question. Fundamental normative research on the second question goes back to debates on the status of potential gain criteria of the Kaldor-Hicks sort, eventually evolving into questions about the feasibility of, and limits to, various compensation schemes. Examples of this latter research include Dixit and Norman (1986), Kemp and Wan (1986), Brecher and Choudhri (1994), Feenstra and Lewis (1994), Hammond and Sempere (1995), Guesnerie (2001), and Spector (2001).

by simple referendum, except in the razor's edge case in which the median household factor ownership happens to be identical to that of the economy as a whole, free trade will not generally be an equilibrium policy.[2] This result, of course, relies on an assumption that the government does not possess a redistributive instrument (or does not choose to use it). Given the goals of that paper, and the plausible empirical claim that governments do not, in fact, seem to do much in the way of trade-contingent redistribution, this was an appropriate strategy.

In this paper, we follow Mayer's lead and adopt a referendum-based approach to the political economy of trade policy in which both protection and redistribution are essential components. Specifically, we construct a simple model in which a continuum of heterogeneous agents is inefficiently distributed between two industries due to protection. We assume that these agents face a choice between liberalization and protection, in which they will also choose whether to redistribute (some of) the gains from trade from (some of) the gainers to (some of) the losers. The particular institution involves three stages of voting. In the first stage, voters decide whether to liberalize trade. If liberalization is chosen, then in the second stage they vote on whether to provide compensation to the dislocated workers. Finally, if compensation is chosen, then in the third stage the workers vote on the method of compensation. We then compare the outcome of this political process with the outcome that would emerge if the only choices were uncompensated free trade or no liberalization. As in Mayer, the continuum assumption and the median voter framework allow us to focus on the fundamental question of policy choice/sustainability without getting bogged down in institutional details that have little claim to descriptive accuracy and even less claim to generating additional insight. That is, we can see the referendum as a reduced form for a more detailed representation of the political process.

In the context of this model, we address two interesting questions. First, would coupling trade liberalization measures with policies aimed at compensating dislocated workers increase the chances that free trade will emerge as the outcome of the political process? Many economists have argued that, in addition to moving trade liberalization in the direction of actual, as opposed to simply potential Pareto improvement, compensation makes liberalization politically more sustainable (Lawrence and Litan 1986). However, most attempts to evaluate this claim proceed under the assumption that the government seeks to maximize national welfare but is constrained politically in the pursuit of this goal (Feenstra and Bhagwati 1982; Magee 2003). Our approach proceeds by considering the

---

[2] For all of the massive boom in research on the political economy of trade policy, there is surprisingly little substantive content beyond this result.

simple referendum model in the institution described above.[3] Second, we ask whether or not the optimal compensation policy will be chosen if workers are allowed to vote on the design of that policy. In the context of our model, we consider three policies that have received some attention in the policy debates on compensation: unemployment compensation, wage subsidies, and employment subsidies. We show that in this model the wage subsidy is preferred to the other two policies on efficiency grounds and then ask whether the wage subsidy is preferred in the referendum.[4]

Our results offer much hope for those that favor compensating displaced workers, but they also raise one small concern. On the positive side, we find that in many instances allowing for compensation increases the likelihood that liberalization will emerge as the equilibrium outcome regardless of the order of the agenda. There does, however, exist a nontrivial portion of the parameter space for which the sequencing of decisions determines the outcome. In this portion of the parameter space, liberalization can be achieved if compensation is agreed upon beforehand, but not if the vote to compensate postdates the vote to liberalize. Finally, the one new concern that we uncover has to do with the choice of the compensation policy. We find that in some instances in which the agents vote in favor of liberalization with compensation, they also select an inefficient compensation policy.

2. THE MODEL

2.1 Overview

We assume that labor is the only input, but workers differ by ability (a). We assume that ability is uniformly distributed over the unit interval, implying that (with exceptions spelled out below) the worker for whom $a = \frac{1}{2}$ is the median voter and is therefore decisive.

Workers can produce one of two goods. We refer to the first good as the "low-skill" good and assume that each worker, regardless of ability, can produce 1 unit of this good. We call the other good the "high-skill" good and assume that a worker with ability a can produce a units of this good. Workers are perfectly mobile across sectors and can immediately find employment in the low-skill sector, but must search for a job in the high-skill sector. We assume that time is continuous and that job offers arrive according to a Poisson process in the high-skill sector, with e representing

---

[3] We return to a comparison of our results with those of Feenstra/Bhagwati and Magee in the conclusion.
[4] In a slightly more complex model, Davidson and Matusz (2006) provide a detailed analysis of the relative efficiency of all three instruments.

the rate at which unemployed workers find jobs. Moreover, jobs in the high-skill sector do not last forever, with involuntary separations also following a Poisson process. We use b to denote the rate of job separation.

We assume that all markets are perfectly competitive and choose the high-skill good to serve as numeraire. All employed workers are paid the value of their marginal product.[5]

We assume that the country under study has a comparative advantage in the high-skill good, and that the initial equilibrium (status quo) is distorted by a tariff levied on imports of the low-skill good. Following Mayer (1984), we assume that tariff revenue is neutral in that it is rebated to workers in proportion to their wage income. We describe below how the tariff rate is initially determined.

We only consider a subset of all possible parameterizations of the model. In particular, we are interested in exploring situations in which the median voter is initially employed in the protected low-skill sector and decides to switch sectors and search for a high-skill job in the event of liberalization. That is, we are interested in situations where the group of trade-displaced workers includes the median voter. It will become evident as we present the details of the model that other parameterizations are less interesting. For example, if the median voter is initially employed in the export sector, the status quo will be characterized by free trade (see below), and policies aimed at compensating trade-displaced workers cannot affect the political equilibrium if the median voter is trapped in the import-competing sector subsequent to liberalization.

To determine the status quo, we note that each worker has a most-preferred tariff. There are three groups that we must consider. First, there are those who would choose to work in the import-competing sector under free trade. For these workers, there exists a strictly positive tariff $\tilde{t}$ which leads to their globally optimal outcome. This is due to the fact that a tariff raises the wage of a worker in the import-competing sector and (to a point) increases tariff revenue. Thus, $\tilde{t}$ is higher than the tariff that maximizes tariff revenue. Indeed, the optimal tariff for these workers may be prohibitive, but need not be if tariff revenue constitutes a significant portion of income. Note that $\tilde{t}$ is independent of ability since the import-competing wage does not depend on ability.

The second group consists of the workers that would choose to seek employment in the export sector with $\tilde{t}$ in place. For this group, a zero tariff always leads to their most-preferred outcome.

---

[5] This assumption is used to ensure that the free trade equilibrium will be efficient. As is well known, search models are generally rife with externalities generated by the search process. We want to make sure that our results are not driven by how different compensation policies affect these search-related externalities.

This leaves us with the third group: those that would seek employment in the export sector under free trade but would work in the import-competing sector when the tariff is set at $\tilde{t}$. For these workers, preferences are not single-peaked and the optimal outcome is found by comparing utility with $\tilde{t}$ in place with utility under free trade.

To summarize to this point, $\tilde{t}$ and 0 are two obvious candidates for the status quo tariff. Since we are concerned with the problem of liberalization, we assume that the status quo tariff is $\tilde{t}$. With trade preferences determined by the median voter, this will in fact be the status quo tariff if the median worker prefers $\tilde{t}$ over free trade. In this case, a simple referendum on liberalization unaccompanied by any compensating policies is doomed to fail.

However, there are parameterizations of the model for which the globally optimal tariff for the median worker is zero. Consequently a referendum on liberalization will succeed even in the absence of compensating policies. In these cases, we can justify our assumption that the status quo tariff is $\tilde{t}$ in a variety of ways. For example, we could appeal to an unmodeled history where the initial distribution of ability may have been skewed in favor of low-skill workers, where import-competing workers may have had political power disproportionate to their numbers, or where the government may have had some noneconomic objective for protecting the low-skill sector. Alternatively, this could be viewed as a short cut to a more complicated problem in which the economy recently experienced a significant improvement in the terms of trade, causing the median worker to switch his preference in favor of uncompensated liberalization. In this latter case, the status quo tariff would differ slightly from the value of the status quo tariff modeled in this paper (in that it would depend on the initial terms of trade), but the substance of the analysis would not be affected.

Starting from the status quo, we consider a series of votes. The first vote is on the issue of trade liberalization, consisting of complete removal of the initial tariff. If the majority votes for liberalization, a second vote occurs. The issue addressed by the second referendum is whether displaced workers ought to be compensated for their losses. If the majority votes in favor of compensation, a final vote is held to select the instrument by which compensation is undertaken. As usual, the solution method requires us to start at the end of the process and work backwards. In most cases, the order of the vote is irrelevant. However, we highlight one case where the agenda does indeed matter.

2.2 Status Quo Equilibrium

Workers choose between finding a low-paying job with certainty in the low-skill sector or searching for a high-paying job in the high-skill sector.

Our assumption that tariff revenue is rebated to workers in proportion to their wage implies that the distribution of tariff revenue does not distort this decision, though the tariff itself clearly does create a distortion.

In order to determine the allocation of workers between sectors, we first begin by formulating the asset-value equations for each group of workers: those employed in a low-skill job (L), those who are unemployed and looking for a high-skill job (U), and those employed in a high-skill job (H). In doing so, we use $w_i(a)$ to denote the ability-specific wage, measured in terms of the numeraire, paid to a sector-i worker, where $i = L,H$, and we simplify the exposition by assuming that all workers have identical Cobb-Douglas preferences, spending a fraction of their income ($\beta \leq 1$) on the low-skill good and their remaining income on the high-skill good. Defining the discount rate as ρ, the asset-value equations are then written as

$$\rho V_L(a, P_{sq}) = w_L(a)(1 + r)P_{sq}^{-\beta} \tag{1a}$$

$$\rho V_U(a, P_{sq}) = e\left[V_H - V_U\right] \tag{2a}$$

$$\rho V_H(a, P_{sq}) = w_H(a)(1 + r)P_{sq}^{-\beta} - b\left[V_H - V_U\right] \tag{3a}$$

where P_{sq} is the status quo price (i.e., the domestic price inclusive of the tariff $\tilde{t}$), $P_{sq}^{-\beta}$ is the price index, and r is the ratio of tariff revenue to total wages. Each of the above equations is formulated in the standard way, namely the right-hand side of each represents the instantaneous real income earned by the worker adjusted for expected capital gains or losses.

The status quo tariff is implicitly defined by the difference between the status quo price and the free trade price (P_{ft}) of the low-skill good. Moreover, given the world price, r is clearly a function of the status quo price. For example, tariff revenue is zero (and therefore $r = 0$) if the status quo price equals the autarky price (a prohibitive tariff) or the world price (free trade).

Using the assumptions $w_L(a) = P_{sq}$ and $w_H(a) = a$, we can solve (1a)–(3a) to obtain

$$V_L(a, P_{sq}) = (1 + r)\frac{P_{sq}^{1-\beta}}{\rho} \tag{1b}$$

$$V_U(a, P_{sq}) = (1 + r)\frac{e}{\rho + b + e}\frac{aP_{sq}^{-\beta}}{\rho} \tag{2b}$$

$$V_H(a, P_{sq}) = (1+r)\frac{\rho + e}{\rho + b + e}\frac{aP_{sq}^{-\beta}}{\rho} \tag{3b}$$

Equating (1b) with (2b), we solve for the ability of the marginal worker who, given the status quo price, is just indifferent between working in the low-skill sector (earning V_L) or searching for a job in the high-skill sector (earning V_U). Defining this marginal worker's ability as a_{sq}, we have

$$a_{sq}(P_{sq}) = \frac{\rho + b + e}{e} P_{sq} \tag{4}$$

Workers with less ability choose to work in the low-skill sector, those with higher ability are either looking for a job in the high-skill sector or are actually employed in that sector. This outcome is illustrated in figure 12.1, where we graph (1b) and (2b) as functions of worker ability, taking as given the parameters of the model and the status quo price.

For purposes of numeric analysis, we set the status quo price equal to the price that would maximize present discounted utility for a low-skill worker. Our choice is based on the assumption that the median worker is employed in the low-skill sector in the status quo. That is, we only look at parameterizations such that $a_{sq} \geq \frac{1}{2}$. From (1b), it is clear that the real

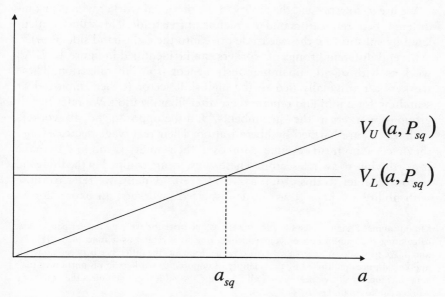

Figure 12.1. Determining the status quo distribution of workers.

wage of a low-skill worker is monotonically increasing in the status quo price, but the share of tariff revenue first increases and then decreases as the domestic price increases from equality with the world price to the autarky price. The status quo price therefore lies between the price that maximizes tariff revenue and the autarky price. While there is no closed-form solution for this price, it can be shown that the status quo price is implicitly a function of P_{ft} and β.[6] We lighten the notation by suppressing this functional dependence.

3. LIBERALIZATION AND COMPENSATION

Suppose that this economy now liberalizes trade, allowing the domestic relative price to fall to the exogenously given free trade price. We illustrate in figure 12.2 the resource-allocation and welfare effects of uncompensated liberalization. Clearly, low-skill employment now generates lower discounted utility than before since liberalization simultaneously reduces the real wage and removes any tariff revenue that low-skill workers might have been receiving in the status quo. In contrast, high-skill workers benefit from liberalization. This necessarily follows since liberalization benefits the economy as a whole (there are no distortions other than the tariff) and the only other group in the economy is harmed by liberalization.

We use a_{ft} to represent the ability of the marginal worker who is just indifferent between sectors under a regime of free trade. This value is calculated by substituting the free trade price into the right-hand side of (4).

Several different groups of workers can be identified in figure 12.2. All workers with $a > a_{sq}$ unambiguously benefit from liberalization. These workers are originally tied to the high-skill sector (either employed or searching for a job) and remain there after liberalization. We refer to this group of workers as the "incumbents." On the opposite end, all workers with $a < a_{ft}$ are harmed by liberalization. Their real wage decreases and they receive no tariff revenue. Moreover, their ability is too low to make it worthwhile to switch sectors. These workers are trapped in the low-skill sector. We refer to this group as the "stayers." Finally, we refer to those with ability $a \in [a_{ft}, a_{sq}]$ as "trade-displaced" workers, an expression in

[6] In our numeric analysis, we solve for the status quo price for every parameter pair by first calculating the equilibrium outcome (including tariff revenue) as a function of P_{sq}, P_{ft}, and β. We then allocate aggregate tariff revenue (found as the difference between domestic and world prices multiplied by the quantity of imports) to workers in proportion to their wage income. Finally, we search over all P_{sq} to find the value that maximizes the utility of a worker employed in the low-skill sector.

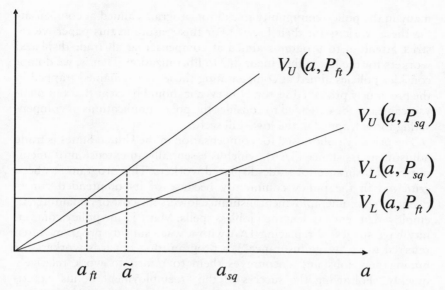

Figure 12.2. Effects of liberalization.

line with the terminology used by Jacobson, LaLonde, and Sullivan (1993), Kletzer (2001), and others who have attempted to measure the financial impact that globalization has had on this group of workers. Among trade-displaced workers, those with $a \in [a_{ft}, \tilde{a}_{sq}]$ are harmed by liberalization, while the remaining workers in this group benefit. That is, trade-displaced workers with lower ability can soften the blow of liberalization by switching sectors, but they cannot completely eliminate their losses. However, higher-ability trade-displaced workers actually benefit. This is entirely consistent with Kletzer's empirical findings.[7]

Some of the losses suffered by the trade-displaced workers are due to the adjustment costs that they must incur to switch occupations. We have chosen to model these adjustment costs in the form of search costs, but, in reality, these workers often face retraining and other costs as well. Recent research suggests that these costs may be significant. For example, Jacobson, LaLonde, and Sullivan (1993) find that the average dislocated worker suffers a loss in lifetime income of roughly $80,000 (see also Kletzer 2001). Concerns about the magnitude of these costs have led

[7] Kletzer (2001) reports that more than one-third of reemployed workers earn the same or higher wages at their new job compared with their predisplacement job.

many in the policy community to call for programs aimed at compensating these workers for their losses.[8] For this reason, in this paper we restrict attention to programs aimed at compensating all trade-displaced workers for the losses they incur due to liberalization. That is, we do not consider policies aimed at compensating those that remained trapped in the previously protected sector. However, it should be clear that our analysis can easily be extended to consider the policy implications of compensating those trapped in the low-skill sector.

The primary policy used for compensation in the United States is trade adjustment assistance (TAA), which is essentially an extension of unemployment insurance for trade-displaced workers. This program has been criticized in the policy community because of its unintended consequences: since unemployment insurance lowers the cost of remaining unemployed, it tends to lengthen jobless spells. Many in the policy community have suggested replacing TAA with a wage subsidy program (often referred to as "wage insurance"), a program that rewards workers for finding new jobs and encourages them to return to work relatively quickly.[9] Following the success of the "reemployment bonus experiments" sponsored by the federal government during the 1980s, others have argued in favor of employment subsidies (often referred to as "reemployment bonuses").[10] For example, a reemployment bonus program was included in President Bill Clinton's 1996 Workforce Investment Act and the George W. Bush administration introduced legislation (referred to as the "Growth and Jobs Plan") that included provisions for the establishment of "personal reemployment accounts" which would provide cash bonuses for unemployed workers who return to work within 13 weeks of losing their jobs.

The challenge for the government is to craft policies that fully compensate all trade-displaced workers and that can be implemented with minimal information.[11] In this paper we focus attention on the program currently in use (TAA) and the two types of programs that have been

[8] See, for example, Baily, Burtless, and Litan (1993), Jacobson, LaLonde, and Sullivan (1993), Brander and Spencer (1994), Brecher and Choudhri (1994), Feenstra and Lewis (1994), Burtless et al. (1998), Parsons (2000), Hufbauer and Goodrich (2001), Kletzer (2001), and Kletzer and Litan (2001).

[9] See the papers referenced in footnote 8.

[10] For more on the reemployment bonus experiments see Woodbury and Speigelman (1987) or Robins and Spiegelman (2001).

[11] In our simple two-sector model it would be fairly easy for a government to implement a Dixit-Norman (1986) type scheme whereby consumption taxes are levied so that consumers face preliberalization prices while producers face world prices. The resulting budget surplus could then be redistributed among all consumers to generate a Pareto gain. However, the complexity of this sort of scheme increases dramatically as the number of goods expands. By comparison, the complexity of a system of worker subsidies is relatively

suggested: wage subsidies and employment subsidies. Thus, we consider three distinct policies: unemployment compensation (μ), an employment subsidy (η), or a wage subsidy (ω). To the extent that unemployment benefits are based upon a worker's previous wage, they are, in this model, independent of the displaced worker's ability (all displaced workers earn the same wage in the status quo). Similarly, the magnitude of the employment subsidy is independent of ability. In this sense, the two policies are isomorphic. However, at least some workers have incentive to "cheat" with unemployment compensation. For example, unemployment compensation is likely to be higher than the value of the marginal product of labor for the lowest ability workers, suggesting a strong incentive to remain unemployed even when a job offer arrives. We therefore argue in the next section that unemployment compensation will never be the outcome of the political equilibrium and confine our analysis to a comparison of wage and employment subsidies.[12]

Policies can be either permanent or temporary. From the point of view of the recipient, all that matters is the expected discounted value of the subsidy, taking any expected termination into account. In the numeric examples constructed for this paper, we model policies as temporary. In particular, we assume that each subsidy (wage or employment) is given to a displaced worker only during his first spell of employment subsequent to liberalization. One can show that expected discounted utility for a displaced worker searching for his first job subsequent to liberalization is then[13]

$$V_{U\eta}(a,P_{ft}) = \left[\frac{\rho}{\rho+b}(a+\eta) + \frac{b}{\rho+b}\frac{e}{\rho+e+b}a\right]\left[\frac{e}{\rho+e}\right]\frac{P_{ft}^{-\alpha}}{\rho} \quad (5a)$$

$$V_{U\omega}(a,P_{ft}) = \left[\frac{\rho}{\rho+b}(1+\omega) + \frac{b}{\rho+b}\frac{e}{\rho+e+b}\right]\left[\frac{e}{\rho+e}\right]\frac{aP_{ft}^{-\alpha}}{\rho} \quad (5b)$$

where the subscript signifies either an employment subsidy (η) or wage subsidy (ω).

---

insensitive to the number of goods. The primary reason for the difference lies in the very demanding informational requirements for the former policy.

[12] Unemployment compensation would be isomorphic to a wage subsidy if the marginal product of workers varies with ability in both sectors and if unemployment compensation is related to a worker's wage prior to the spell of unemployment. This case was modeled in Davidson and Matusz (2006). It would still be the case, however, that some recipients of unemployment compensation would find it in their interest to cheat, suggesting that a majority would always prefer a wage subsidy to unemployment compensation in this case.

[13] See the appendix for details.

All trade-displaced workers are unemployed immediately subsequent to liberalization. All compensation packages work by increasing the discounted utility for unemployed workers. The idea is to choose the size of the policy parameter (e.g., the magnitude of η, the employment subsidy) such that the worker with ability a_{ft} is indifferent between searching for a high-skill job under free trade and being employed in the low-skill sector when that sector is protected by a tariff. The effects of the two compensating policies are illustrated in figure 12.3.

The employment subsidy results in a parallel upward shift of the curve representing the discounted utility earned by an unemployed worker. This follows from the observation noted above that the employment subsidy does not depend upon worker ability. In contrast, the wage subsidy shifts this curve up while simultaneously increasing its slope. In this case, the marginal trade-displaced worker earns a wage of $a_{ft}(1 + \omega)$ while the subsidy is in effect. Each displaced worker is subsidized by the same percentage, implying that the actual magnitude of the subsidy increases with ability.

We assume that compensation is calibrated to the marginal trade-displaced worker, but it is given to any worker who switches sectors subsequent to liberalization. This gives rise to a class of *policy-displaced* workers: that is, workers who would continue to maintain employment in the low-skill sector in the absence of compensation, but who find that searching for a job in the high-skill sector is more attractive if compensation is being offered.[14]

In terms of figure 12.3, all workers with ability $a \in [a_\omega, a_{ft}]$ are characterized as policy-displaced if a wage subsidy is used to compensate trade-displaced workers, while an employment subsidy expands this set to include all of those workers with $a \in [a_\eta, a_\omega]$.

The creation of policy-displaced workers distorts the equilibrium, partially offsetting the gross gain from liberalization. This raises two questions. First, what is the most efficient way to compensate displaced workers? That is, which policy creates the smallest distortion while fully compensating the marginal trade-displaced worker? Second, could the deadweight loss generated by the compensation policy outweigh the gains from freer trade? Both of these issues are addressed in Davidson in Matusz (2006). Regarding the second issue, while the question of whether the distortion is larger or smaller than the gross gain from liberalization is clearly empirical, Davidson and Matusz (2006) show that it is highly unlikely that the distortion can outweigh the gross gain. In any event, the net gain from liberalization is always positive for all of the parameterizations explored in this paper.

---

[14] Davidson and Matusz (2002) refer to these workers as "temporary movers" because they return to the low-skill sector once their initial spell of high-skill employment terminates.

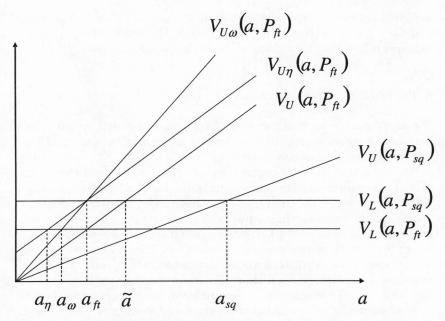

Figure 12.3. Liberalization with compensation.

As for the first issue, Davidson and Matusz (2006) show that a wage subsidy program is the most efficient way to compensate trade-displaced workers. While it is not quite this simple, the gist of the argument is as follows: since it is the creation of the policy-displaced workers that creates the distortion, then for any given compensation goal, the program that generates the smallest group of policy-displaced workers is the most efficient policy. Figure 12.3 shows that the wage subsidy is therefore superior to the employment subsidy, since it leads to a smaller set of policy-displaced workers.

Clearly, the compensation that we are analyzing has to be net of any taxes paid in order to effectively increase the discounted utility of trade-displaced workers. It is simplest, therefore, to assume that this group of workers is untaxed. Moreover, it seems unreasonable to tax stayers, who have lower income than trade-displaced workers. Therefore, all taxes used to pay for compensation come from the group of incumbents.[15] In essence, our tax scheme is a stylized progressive income tax where the

---

[15] This is an entirely innocuous assumption. We could assume instead, as we did in Davidson and Matusz (2006), that the compensation scheme is financed by taxing all workers at a constant marginal rate without altering our qualitative results.

marginal tax rate is zero for workers earning less than some critical wage and $t > 0$ for workers with higher income.[16] The results of our numeric example follow directly as long as the critical wage is below a_{sq}.[17]

4. PREFERENCES OVER POLICIES

We start by assuming that two votes have been completed, resulting in a majority of voters opting for compensated liberalization. The third vote determines the form of compensation.

We argue that unemployment compensation, which is currently the primary instrument used to compensate trade-displaced workers (through TAA), will never be the choice for the majority. Unemployment compensation and the employment subsidy both have the same effect on the utility of a trade-displaced worker; hence trade-displaced workers are indifferent between these two policies.[18] The two policies differ, however, for at least some policy-displaced workers. In instances in which the expected duration of unemployment is short relative to the expected duration of a high-skill job, the magnitude of the unemployment benefit necessary to fully compensate the marginal trade-displaced worker is likely higher than the wage that would be earned by a low-ability worker employed in a high-skill job. Indeed, this compensation may even be higher than the low-skill wage. As such, there may be some workers who would continue to collect unemployment benefits for as long as possible, refusing any job offers that might come their way. Unless the unemployment program is perfectly monitored, the ultimate cost of providing fully compensating unemployment benefits will exceed the cost of a fully compensating employment subsidy. By offering a slightly higher employment subsidy, incumbents can entice trade-displaced workers to vote for an employment subsidy over unemployment compensation. These two groups together

[16] A worker in the high-skill sector who faces the positive marginal tax rate has a net wage of $a(1 - t)$. Equations (2b) and (3b) are then simply modified by multiplying the right-hand side of each by $(1 - t)$.

[17] Workers with ability between a_{ft} and a_{sq} are net recipients of transfers, and therefore are unaffected by the tax structure. Those with ability below a_{ft} care about the tax structure, but the tax structure itself does not change their ranking of policy instruments, nor does it change their preferences regarding the status quo versus liberalization. Liberalization becomes more difficult if the critical value is above a_{sq}, since a smaller share of the population bears the burden of compensation. It is conceivable in this case that the magnitude of the transfer is larger than the gross gain from liberalization that is captured by this group of taxpayers, inducing them to vote against liberalization in instances where they foresee a majority in favor of compensation. We leave analysis of this case for future work.

[18] See Davidson and Matusz (2006) for a more discussion of the equivalency of various compensation policies.

constitute more than half of the population. As such, we eliminate unemployment compensation from further consideration, focusing instead on comparing the wage and employment subsidies.

We next observe that workers with $a \in [0, a_\eta]$ have no stake in the outcome of the political process. These workers do not pay taxes or receive compensation. Therefore the voting population consists only of workers with $a \in [a_\eta, 1]$. Trade-displaced workers clearly prefer the wage subsidy, since this generates a larger transfer than the fully compensating employment subsidy for all but the marginal trade-displaced worker. On the other side, workers with $a \in [a_\eta, a_{ft}]$ prefer the employment subsidy, since this policy generates for them a larger transfer than the equivalent wage subsidy (see figure 12.3). Incumbents prefer the policy that generates the smallest aggregate subsidy, since this generates the smallest tax burden. While the wage subsidy is more generous to trade-displaced workers, an employment subsidy creates more policy-displaced workers, raising the aggregate cost of the transfer. In the next section (and the appendix), we show that it is possible to divide the parameter space such that incumbents prefer the wage subsidy for one set of parameters, while preferring the employment subsidy for another set of parameters. Our numeric exercise indicates that none of the three groups form a majority on their own, therefore the preferences of incumbents are decisive in this vote.

We now back up to the vote on whether compensation should be offered, assuming that liberalization has been approved. Rational agents look forward to see the form of compensation that would be offered in the event that a majority favors compensation. If the perfect-foresight outcome is an employment subsidy, all workers with $a \in [a_\eta, a_{sq}]$ prefer compensation, while all incumbents oppose it. The remaining workers have no stake in the outcome, since they neither pay taxes nor receive compensation. The outcome is only modestly different if the perfect-foresight outcome is a wage subsidy, in which case all workers with $a \in [a_\omega, a_{sq}]$ prefer compensation, all incumbents continue to oppose it, and the remainder are indifferent.

Finally, consider the vote on whether or not to liberalize. Forward-looking agents anticipate whether or not compensation will be offered. They also anticipate the form that the compensation will take in the event that it is offered. Workers with $a \in [0, a_{ft}]$ lose relative to the status quo even when compensation is offered; therefore these workers always oppose liberalization. Workers with $a \in [a_{ft}, \bar{a}]$ join in the opposition in the event that compensation is not offered, while all remaining workers support liberalization. All trade-displaced workers with $a \in [a_{ft}, a_{sq}]$ support liberalization with compensation, regardless of the form that the compensation takes. Incumbents join in support for liberalization if the total transfer required under compensation is smaller than the gross gains from liberalization that accrue to them.

5. Constructing the Parameter Space

The nature of the political equilibrium depends on the parameters of the model. Taking labor market turnover rates and the discount rate as given, $a_\eta, a_\omega, a_{ft}, \tilde{a}$, and a_{sq} can all be written as functions of the free trade price (P_{ft}) and the preference parameter (β).

In order to focus on situations where the group of displaced workers contains $a = \frac{1}{2}$, we have to limit the range of P_{ft}. If P_{ft} is too high, the worker with $a = \frac{1}{2}$ would prefer to remain in the low-skill sector after liberalization, and if P_{ft} is too low, that worker would locate in the high-skill sector even under the status quo. Therefore, we assume that $P_{min} \le P_{ft} \le P_{max}$. The maximum price is the price at which the worker with $a = \frac{1}{2}$ is just indifferent between low-skill employment and searching for a high-skill job under free trade, and is found by replacing $a_{sq}(P_{sq})$ in equation (4) with $\frac{1}{2}$ and letting $P_{sq} = P_{max}$, so that

$$P_{max} = \frac{1}{2} \frac{e}{\rho + e + b} \qquad (6)$$

The minimum price is the price at which the worker with $a = \frac{1}{2}$ is just indifferent between low-skill employment and searching for a high-skill job assuming that this worker's most-preferred tariff is levied. To solve for this price, we first observe that if the autarky price (P_a) is too low, even a prohibitive tariff could not dissuade a worker with $a = \frac{1}{2}$ from seeking employment in the high-skill sector. We show in the appendix that

$$P_a(\beta) = \sqrt{\frac{e}{\rho + b + e}} \sqrt{\frac{\beta e}{(2 - \beta)(b + e) + \beta\rho}} \qquad (7)$$

so that the autarky price is increasing in the preference parameter. A minimum value of the autarky price therefore translates to a minimum bound on β, which can be found by replacing $a_{sq}(P_{sq})$ in (4) with $\frac{1}{2}$ and letting $P_{sq} = P_a(\beta)$. Doing so and solving for β, we obtain

$$\beta_{min} = \frac{2(b + e)}{3\rho + 5(b + e)} \qquad (8)$$

We can then use (4) to solve for P_{min} when $\beta > \beta_{min}$. To see this, first recall that P_{sq} depends upon P_{ft} and β. Then P_{min} is a function of β and is implicitly defined as the free trade price that solves (4) when $a_{sq} = \frac{1}{2}$.

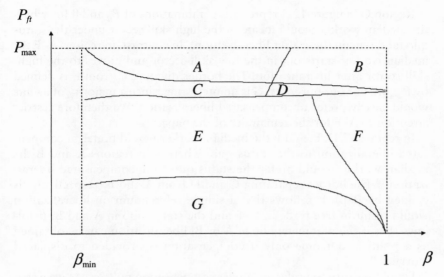

Figure 12.4. Division of the parameter space.

Note that $P_{max} = P_a(\beta_{min})$, from which it follows that $P_{max} \leq P_a(\beta)$ for all $\beta \geq \beta_{min}$ since the autarky price is increasing in β. Therefore, our restrictions guarantee that $P_{ft} \leq P_a(\beta)$ for all $\beta \geq \beta_{min}$ so that the economy has a comparative advantage in the high-skill good.

Finally, for every β there exists a free trade price at which the worker for whom $a = \frac{1}{2}$ is indifferent between the status quo and uncompensated free trade. Let $P_I(\beta)$ represent this price. Then $P_I(\beta)$ is implicitly defined as the solution to $V_U(a,P_{ft}) = V_L(a,P_{sq})$ evaluated at $a = \frac{1}{2}$, where we once again recognize that P_{sq} depends upon both P_{ft} and β. The median worker strictly prefers the status quo (uncompensated liberalization) for $P_{ft} >(<)P_I(\beta)$. This follows because the status quo price is chosen to maximize discounted utility, so a small change in the free trade price has only a second-order effect on discounted utility of a low-skill worker under the status quo, whereas the utility of a high-skill worker is strictly decreasing in P_{ft}.

We illustrate the relevant parameter space in figure 12.4, which we divide into seven regions. This figure was computer generated based on a particular parameterization of the model; however, experimentation with a wide range of parameters suggests that the qualitative features of the figure are not sensitive to the choice of parameters.[19]

---

[19] Specifically, we constructed this figure assuming that $\rho = 0.05$, $b = 0.1$, and $e = 4$. The parameter value for b implies that the expected duration of a high-skill job is 10 years, while the parameter for e suggests that the expected duration of a spell of unemployment is 3 months.

Region G in figure 12.4 represents combinations of P_{ft} and β for which the median worker would locate in the high-skill sector under the status quo (and remain there after liberalization). In contrast, in regions A–F the median worker starts out in the low-skill sector and moves to the high-skill sector after liberalization. The border dividing G from E is defined by $P_{min}(\beta)$. For our purposes, G is uninteresting, since a majority of agents would clearly prefer uncompensated liberalization. We therefore restrict attention to A–F for the remainder of the paper.

In regions C, D, E, and F the median worker would prefer uncompensated liberalization to the status quo, whereas in regions A and B the median worker would prefer the status quo to uncompensated liberalization.[20] The border separating C and D from A and B (respectively) is defined by $P_l(\beta)$. It follows that a simple referendum on liberalization would result in free trade in C–F and the status quo in A and B. It follows that if the parameters lie in A or B, liberalization can be obtained as a political outcome only if compensation is provided to displaced workers.[21]

Finally, we turn to preferences over compensation policies. As we noted in the previous section, we need to know how the magnitude of the aggregate transfer associated with an employment subsidy compares with that associated with a wage subsidy in order to determine the incumbents' preferences over the compensation programs. In contrast, we know that trade-displaced workers always prefer the wage subsidy, whereas policy-displaced workers always prefer the employment subsidy.

The border separating regions E and F from C and D (respectively) is defined as the set of parameters for which the two policies generate the same discounted value of the transfer.[22] The employment subsidy generates a smaller aggregate transfer for all parameter combinations lying above this border, with the wage subsidy generating the smaller transfer for all combinations lying below this border. Therefore, incumbents prefer the employment subsidy if parameters lie in regions A, B, C, or D, while they preferring the wage subsidy otherwise.

---

[20] Refer back to our discussion in section 2.a where we justify the initial tariff in C, D, E, and F as a legacy from past circumstances.

[21] The existence of regions A and B indicates that, as Mayer (1984) emphasized, free trade may not be the equilibrium outcome when the median voter's preferences determine trade policy. Our approach here is a bit different from Mayer's. In his model, agents have preferences over tariffs and he shows that the equilibrium tariff is the one preferred by the median voter. Since this tariff is zero only if the median voter's factor ownership is identical to that of the economy as a whole, his result is that free trade is not likely to be the outcome when agents vote on the level of protection. In contrast, we are assuming that protection is already in place and ask under what conditions society will choose to liberalize.

[22] In the appendix we show how to solve for this border.

6. The Political Equilibrium

We now combine information on policy preferences with information summarized in figure 12.4 to solve for the equilibrium outcome. As noted earlier, the solution technique is backwards induction.

Suppose that the majority has already voted in favor of compensated liberalization. All that remains is to determine the form of the compensation program. In describing policy preferences, we argued that all trade-displaced workers (of whom there are $a_{sq} - a_{ft}$) prefer the wage subsidy, while all policy-displaced workers (of whom there are $a_{ft} - a_\eta$) prefer the employment subsidy. Since those trapped in low-skill jobs are not affected by the form of compensation, they do not vote, implying that the voting population consists of $1 - a_\eta$ workers. In all of our numeric analysis, neither trade-displaced workers nor policy-displaced workers alone form a majority of this population. The policy that wins the majority is therefore the policy favored by the group of incumbents who align themselves with trade-displaced workers if parameters lie in regions E or F (where the wage subsidy is less costly to finance), or align themselves with policy-displaced workers if parameters fall into regions A, B, C, or D (where the employment subsidy is less costly).[23]

Knowing the outcome of the final stage of voting, we now step back to ask whether a majority would favor compensation in the event of liberalization. There are two cases to consider. Suppose first that parameters lie in A, B, C, or D, so that the final stage of voting results in an employment subsidy. In this case, workers with $a \in [a_\eta, a_{sq}]$ favor compensation, while those with $a > a_{sq}$ are opposed. Workers at the very bottom of the ability distribution have no stake in the outcome, since they would not be affected either way. The border in figure 12.4 that divides regions A and C from regions B and D (respectively) is defined as the set of parameters for which $1 - a_{sq} = a_{sq} - a_\eta$. If the parameters lie in B or D, displaced workers constitute a majority of the voting population and therefore compensation will be approved, whereas compensation will be defeated if the parameters lie in region A or C.

Similar reasoning separates E from F. The difference here is that the wage subsidy will carry the day in the event that compensation is approved. Under these circumstances, workers with $a < a_\omega$ have no stake in the outcome, so the voting population is smaller. The border between E and F is therefore the set of parameters for which $1 - a_{sq} = a_{sq} - a_\omega$.

---

[23] As already noted, region G will be associated with uncompensated liberalization since the median worker is an incumbent. We therefore need not consider choice of instrument in this region.

Displaced workers have a majority if parameters fall in F, whereas the incumbents are in the majority if the parameters fall in E.

To summarize to this point, no compensation will be offered if parameters lie in A, C, or E. If parameters lie in B or D, an employment subsidy will be used to compensate displaced workers, while a wage subsidy will be used to compensate these workers if parameters fall in F.

Turning to the initial vote, it is easy to see now that the status quo wins out if parameters fall in A. In this case, the median worker who opposes uncompensated liberalization recognizes that incumbents are strong enough to block all compensation if trade is liberalized. Therefore the median worker opposes liberalization.

If parameters lie in C or E, the median worker will vote to liberalize. Despite the recognition that there will ultimately be no compensation, the median worker prefers uncompensated liberalization to the status quo.

For parameters in A, C, or E, placing the issue of compensation on the table does not affect the outcome. However, the outcome *is* affected if parameters lie in B, D, or F. Compensation does buy liberalization in B, where the median worker opposes uncompensated liberalization but realizes that compensation will be forthcoming if trade is liberalized. Regions D and F will also result in liberalization, as they would in the absence of compensation; however, the outcome will not be a complete removal of all distortions. In these two cases, compensation will be offered, distorting the equilibrium by creating a class of policy-displaced workers. In all of our numeric analysis, however, the distortion created by offering compensation is smaller than the distortion generated by the status quo tariff. Hence, the net gain is positive.

We close this section by noting that the order of voting only matters in A. To see this, suppose that the economy first voted on compensation. This would be defeated in C and E, where incumbents hold a majority, but the median worker prefers uncompensated liberalization to the status quo, so liberalization would still occur. In B, D, and F, incumbents are in the minority, so compensation passes and liberalization occurs. Incumbents prefer compensated liberalization to the status quo; they would therefore find it in their interest to vote for compensation if parameters lie in A, since this is the only way to assure a favorable vote on liberalization.

7. Discussion

We see this paper as making two contributions. First, we have extended the standard referendum model of political economy of trade policy to incorporate compensation Second, our specific application considered the issue of whether compensation can "save free trade."

Our first contribution involves the extension of a Mayer-type referendum model to endogenize the compensation, as well as the trade policy, decision.[24] Although there is a sizable literature on the commonsense notion that compensation, in addition to moving a potentially Pareto-improving policy in the direction of an actual Pareto improvement, increases the political sustainability of trade liberalization, there is very little in the way of systematic political economic analysis on this question. Early work by Johnson and McCulloch (1973) argued that a welfare-maximizing government that was politically constrained to offer protection might gain relative to a tariff by using the distribution of quota revenues to support lower levels of protection. Feenstra and Bhagwati (1982) apply similar reasoning in a model in which a welfare-maximizing government uses tariff revenues to induce lower levels of lobbying on the part of a protection-seeking labor union. While Feenstra and Bhagwati do present an explicit model of political-economic interaction, the assumption of a welfare-maximizing government seems broadly inconsistent with the underlying goals of political economic analysis. More closely related to our work is Magee (2003). As with Feenstra and Bhagwati, in Magee's model the government is an active player, but unlike Feenstra and Bhagwati, instead of seeking purely to maximize welfare the government is of the Grossman-Helpman (1994) sort. Contrary to Feenstra and Bhagwati, Magee finds that, precisely because it lowers the cost of any given level of protection, the presence of compensation permits the government to offer more protection.[25] In particular, at low levels of protection (such as those currently applied in virtually all industrial countries) compensation may hinder further liberalization.[26]

There are two major differences between Magee's analysis and ours. First, where Magee's analysis evaluates the contribution of compensation to liberalization at the margin, our analysis focuses on the contribution of compensation to the overall sustainability of liberalization. That is, our model considers a choice between fixed, finite policy options. Second, and perhaps more important, Magee's analysis, like Feenstra and Bhagwati's, is really only indirectly about liberalization. As in Grossman and Helpman, what is really for sale is *protection*. In our analysis the issue on

---

[24] See Mayer (1984).

[25] This effect is particularly large in Magee's simulations because he takes the "result" of Golberg and Maggi (1999) that the government's weight on aggregate social welfare is 50 to 70 times the weight placed on contributions.

[26] This result is contrary to that obtained by Fung and Staiger (1996), who analyze compensation in a model without domestic political competition. Their model treats domestic compensation as part of the *international* political economy of trade policy. In their paper the implicit bribe is not directed to domestic factors of production but to one's negotiating partners in a trade agreement.

the agenda is liberalization. We think it is worth noting that trade policy in the post–Second World War era has been overwhelmingly about liberalization, and that arguments about compensation have been directly related to this policy and not to protection per se. Furthermore, this commitment to liberalization has been only very indirectly related to the sorts of forces modeled in standard work on political economy (Nelson 2003). Thus, while the details of intersectoral variation in protection may be well-modeled in something like a Grossman-Helpman framework, we believe that the issue of overall sustainability of a liberalization policy (adopted for some un-modeled reason) is more clearly treated in a framework such as that developed here.

Directly related to the last comment, our second contribution is an evaluation of claims that a well-constructed compensation program can help "save free trade" (Lawrence and Litan 1986). In the context of our model we find that allowing for the possibility of compensating trade-displaced workers does lead to liberalization in instances where it would have otherwise been blocked, but there are situations where compensation results in a distorted outcome when a Pareto-efficient outcome would have been obtained in the absence of compensation.

We close by offering some suggestions for extensions. With respect to the political economy model: first, it would be interesting to consider alternative structures of referendum; second, introducing an active government with alternative objectives would seem to be a useful extension; and third, it would seem important to consider the sustainability of compensation in the context of less robust information than considered here. Finally, with respect to the specific issue of "saving free trade," it would be interesting to bring more concrete structure to the analysis to permit some more specific evaluation of the role of compensation (i.e., what part of the parameter space do we find ourselves in?).

Appendix

A.1 Autarky

Let $\bar{a}$ represent the ability of the worker who is just indifferent between low-skill employment and searching for a job in the high-skill sector when the economy is in autarky. Given that ability is uniformly distributed over the unit interval, the allocation of labor implies that $\bar{a}$ is the fraction of workers employed in the low-skill sector with all remaining workers either employed in the high-skill sector or searching for a job in that sector. Of the $1 - \bar{a}$ workers affiliated with the high-skill sector, steady-state conditions imply that the fraction $b/(e + b)$ are unemployed, with the remaining $e/(e + b)$ employed. We can therefore solve for the supplies of the two goods as a function of relative price $(S_i(P), i = H, L)$:

$$S_L(P) = \int_0^{\bar{a}} da = \bar{a} \tag{A.1}$$

$$S_H(P) = \left(\frac{b}{e+b}\right)\int_{\bar{a}}^1 a\, da = \left(\frac{b}{e+b}\right)\left(\frac{1+\bar{a}}{2}\right)(1-\bar{a}) \tag{A.2}$$

Our assumption that all workers share the same Cobb-Douglas preferences implies that the demands for the two goods are related in the following way:

$$PD_L(P) = \frac{\beta}{1-\beta}D_H(P) \tag{A.3}$$

In the absence of trade, the demand for each good must equal its supply. We then use $(A.1) - (A.3)$ to obtain (7) in the text.

A.2 Tariff Revenue

Let R represent tariff revenue. Then

$$R(P_{sq}) = (P_{sq} - P_{ft})(D_L(P_{sq}) - S_L(P_{sq})) \tag{A.4}$$

The supply of the low-skill good is given in (A.1). Demand for the low-skill good has to satisfy (A.3) for $P = P_{sq}$ and the economywide budget constraint:

$$P_{ft}D_L(P_{sq}) + D_H(P_{sq}) = P_{ft}S_L(P_{sq}) + S_H(P_{sq}) \tag{A.5}$$

Therefore, demand for the low-skill good is

$$D_L(P_{sq}) = \frac{\beta(P_{ft}S_L(P_{sq}) + S_H(P_{sq}))}{\beta P_{ft} + (1-\beta)P_{sq}} \tag{A.6}$$

where we again note that P_{sq} is itself a function of P_{ft} and β.

Tariff revenue is distributed to each worker in proportion to the wage earned by the worker:

$$r(P_{sq}) = \frac{R(P_{sq})}{P_{sq}S_L(P_{sq}) + S_H(P_{sq})} \tag{A.7}$$

A.3 Discounted Utility with a Temporary Employment Subsidy

We assume that the employment subsidy is given to a displaced worker only during the duration of his first postliberalization job. The asset value equations are then as follows:

$$\rho V_H = aP_{ft}^{-\beta} - b[V_H - V_U] \tag{A.8}$$

$$\rho V_U = e[V_H - V_U] \tag{A.9}$$

$$\rho V_{H\eta} = (a + \eta)P_{ft}^{-\beta} - b[V_{H\eta} - V_U] \tag{A.10}$$

$$\rho V_{U\eta} = e[V_{H\eta} - V_{U\eta}] \tag{A.11}$$

where $V_{H\eta}$ represents discounted income for a displaced worker employed for the first time in the high-skill sector.

An analogous system can be written for a wage subsidy, replacing $(a + \eta)$ in (A.10) with $a(1 + \omega)$. The two systems can then be solved for (5a) and (5b) in the text.

A.4 Discounted Value of the Employment Subsidy

Everyone with ability $a \in [a_\eta, a_{sq}]$ receives the employment subsidy during the first spell of employment. Let $\Omega_{U\eta}$ represent the present discounted value of the employment subsidy received by a worker searching for his first job and let $\Omega_{H\eta}$ represent the present discounted value of the subsidy received by a worker in his first job. Then

$$\rho\Omega_{U\eta} = 0 + e[\Omega_{H\eta} - \Omega_{U\eta}] \tag{A.12}$$

$$\rho\Omega_{H\eta} = \eta - b\Omega_{H\eta} \tag{A.13}$$

Solving these two equations:

$$\Omega_{U\eta} = \frac{1}{\rho+b}\frac{e}{\rho+e}\eta \qquad (A.14)$$

so T_η, the total present discounted value of the transfer at the moment of liberalization, is

$$T_\eta = \left\{\frac{1}{\rho+b}\frac{e}{\rho+e}\eta\right\}\left\{a_{sq} - a_\eta\right\} \qquad (A.15)$$

Equations (A.16) and (A.17) are the analogues for a wage subsidy:

$$\Omega_{U\omega} = \frac{1}{\rho+b}\frac{e}{\rho+e}(1+\omega)P_{ft}a \qquad (A.16)$$

$$T_\omega = \frac{1}{\rho+b}\frac{e}{\rho+e}\frac{a_\omega^2 + a_{sq}^2}{2}(1+\omega)P_{ft} \qquad (A.17)$$

Setting $T_\eta = T_\omega$ provides the border dividing C and D from E and F in figure 12.4.

We can compare T_η and T_ω with the discounted value of the gains from liberalization that accrue to incumbents:

$$G = \frac{b}{e+b}\int_{a_{sq}}^1 \left\{V_H(P_{ft},a) - V_H(P_{sq},a)\right\}da$$

$$+ \frac{e}{e+b}\int_{a_{sq}}^1 \left\{V_U(P_{ft},a) - V_U(P_{sq},a)\right\}da \qquad (A.18)$$

In all of our numeric calculations, the discounted gain to the incumbents was larger in magnitude than the discounted value of either subsidy.

References

Baily, M. N., Burtless, G., Litan, R., 1993. *Growth with Equity*. Brookings Institution, Washington, DC.

Brander, J., Spencer, B. 1994. Trade adjustment assistance: Welfare and incentive effects of payments to displaced workers. *Journal of International Economics* 36(3–4): 239–61.

346 CHAPTER 12

Brecher, R., Choudhri, E. 1994. Pareto gains from trade, reconsidered: Compensating for jobs lost. *Journal of International Economics* 36(3–4): 223–38.

Burtless, G., Lawrence, R., Litan, R., Shapiro, R. 1998. *Globaphobia: Confronting Fears about Open Trade*. Brookings Institution, Washington, DC.

Davidson, C., Matusz, S. 2002. Trade liberalization and compensation. Working paper. Michigan State University.

Davidson, C., Matusz, S. J. 2004. *International Trade and Labor Markets: Theory, Evidence and Policy Implications*. W.E. Upjohn Institute for Employment Research, Kalamazoo, MI.

Davidson, C., Matusz, S. J. 2006. Trade liberalization and compensation. *International Economic Review* 47: 723–47.

Dixit, A., Norman, V. 1986. Gains from trade without lump-sum compensation. *Journal of International Economics* 21(1–2): 111–22.

Feenstra, R., Bhagwati, J. 1982. Tariff seeking and the efficient tariff. In Bhagwati, J. (Ed.), *Import Competition and Response*. University of Chicago Press/NBER, Chicago: 245–58.

Feenstra, R., Lewis, T. 1994. Trade adjustment assistance and Pareto gains from trade. *Journal of International Economics* 36(3–4): 201–22.

Fung, K. C., Staiger, R. 1996. Trade liberalization and trade adjustment assistance. In Canzoneri, M., Ethier, W., Grilli, V. (Eds.), *The New Transatlantic Economy*. Cambridge University Press/CEPR, Cambridge: 265–86.

Goldberg, P., Maggi, G. 1999. Protection for sale: An empirical investigation. *American Economic Review* 89(5): 1135–55.

Grossman, G., Helpman, E. 1994. Protection for sale. *American Economic Review* 84(4): 833–50.

Guesnerie, R. 2001. Second best redistributive policies: The case of international trade. *Journal of Public Economic Theory* 3(1): 15–25.

Hammond, P., Sempere, J. 1995. Limits to the potential gains from trade. *Economic Journal* 105(432): 1180–1204.

Hufbauer, G., Goodrich, B. 2001. Steel: Big Problems, Better Solutions. Policy Brief. Institute for International Economics, Washington, DC.

Jacobson, L, LaLonde, R., Sullivan, D. 1993. Earnings losses of displaced workers. *American Economic Review* 83(4): 685–709.

Johnson, H. G., McCulloch, R. 1973. A note on proportionally distributed quotas. *American Economic Review* 63(4): 726–32.

Kemp, M., Wan, H. 1986. Gains from trade with and without compensation. *Journal of International Economics* 21(1–2): 99–110.

Kletzer, L. 2001. *Job Loss from Imports: Measuring the Costs*. Institute for International Economics, Washington, DC.

Kletzer, L., Litan, R. 2001. A prescription to relieve worker anxiety. Policy Brief No. 73, Brookings Institution, Washington, DC.

Lawrence, R., Litan, R. 1986. *Saving Free Trade: A Pragmatic Approach*. Brookings Institution, Washington, DC.

Magee, C. 2003. Endogenous tariffs and trade adjustment assistance. *Journal of International Economics* 60(1): 203–22.

Mayer, W. 1984. Endogenous tariff formation. *American Economic Review* 74(5): 970–85.

Nelson, D. 2003. Political economy problems in the analysis of trade policy. Inaugural Lecture, University of Nottingham.

Parsons, D. 2000. Wage insurance: A policy review. *Research in Employment Policy* 2: 119–40.

Robins, P., Spiegelman, R. 2001. *Reemployment Bonuses in the Unemployment Insurance System*. W.E. Upjohn Institute for Employment Research, Kalamazoo.

Rosenthal, H. 1990. The setter model. In: Enelow J., and Hinich, M. (Eds.), *Advances in the Spatial Theory of Voting*. Cambridge University Press, Cambridge, pp. 199–234.

Shepsle, K. 1979. Institutional arrangements and equilibrium in multidimensional voting models. *American Journal of Political Science* 23: 27–58.

Shepsle, K. 1986. The positive theory of legislative institutions: An enrichment of social choice and spatial theory. *Public Choice* 50: 135–78.

Spector, D. 2001. Is it possible to redistribute the gains from trade using income taxation? *Journal of International Economics* 55(2): 441–60.

Woodbury, S., Spiegelman, R. 1987. Bonuses to workers and employers to reduce unemployment: Randomized trials in Illinois. *American Economic Review* 77(4): 513–30.

INTRODUCTION TO PART 5

In part 1 of this book we focused on the implications of adding labor market imperfections to the conventional Hechscher-Ohlin-Samuelson and Ricardian models of international trade. In both of these frameworks, the unit of analysis is the industry, with all firms within an industry assumed to be identical. These two models were the primary workhorses for the field as late as the mid-1980s, when this began to change as researchers borrowed modeling techniques from industrial organization, macroeconomics, and other areas to build richer models of product market interaction between firms in open economies. The once standard assumption of perfect competition in the product market was abandoned in favor of more sophisticated models of monopolistic competition in which firms produce varieties of goods that are imperfect substitutes for each other. As a result, a rich body of predictions linking globalization to price-cost markups, firm sizes, export behavior, and productivity (both at the firm and industry levels) has developed. Moreover, recent availability of new firm-level data sets has allowed for tests of these predictions as well as the establishment of a wide variety of new "stylized facts" concerning the evolution of industrial structures in dynamic open economies. Attempts to provide theoretical explanations for many of these stylized facts have forced trade theorists to extend their models of monopolistic competition in new directions with the introduction of firm-side heterogeneity (in terms of costs or productivity) now viewed as an essential component of many models. Thus the unit of analysis has changed and we now have a large, well-established literature that focuses on firm- and plant-level adjustment to globalization.

While "new" trade theory has both changed the way we model firms and given us a new set of facts regarding firm behavior, it has not changed the way in which we think about the labor market. The standard assumption of perfect competition, which implies flexible wages and full employment, is still used in most trade models, and it is certainly the common assumption in the "new" trade models. This is somewhat surprising, not only in light of the reasons highlighted in the introduction to this book, but because many of the new micro-level data sets match workers and firms so that there is now a rich source of information about the characteristics of the workers that firms employ. Thus it should be possible to derive a new set of stylized facts about the impact of openness on the labor market experiences of workers. In other words, it should be possible to do for the labor market what has already been done for the product market.

About the same time that the field of international trade began to change, the policy community began discussing the economic impact of worker dislocation. Studies by Jacobson, LaLonde, and Sullivan (1993a, b) and Kletzer (2001) indicated that the personal cost of worker dislocation is quite high, although the size of the loss depended heavily on worker characteristics such as age and skill level. Such findings have led some in the policy community to call for programs aimed at compensating dislocated workers for their losses (see, for example, Kletzer and Litan 2001). In addition, concerns have been raised about the fragmentation of production, and the perception that firms have begun to outsource high-skill jobs to low-wage foreign countries has grown. Controversy has swirled around stories of computer call centers located in India and Mexico and x-rays being sent abroad for analysis and whether such production decisions are good or bad for domestic workers. Many in the public seem convinced that as these high-skill jobs are shipped abroad, high-skilled domestic workers will be forced to take inferior jobs to remain employed. Thus the public seems to hold the view that in addition to causing unemployment, trade in services can cause "underemployment."

Around the turn of the century we began discussing ways to use new trade models to examine some of the emerging policy issues that were gaining a great deal of national attention, such as the outsourcing of high-skill service jobs. Some of these discussions included one of our junior colleagues, Andrei Shevchenko, a Randy Wright student well versed in general equilibrium search theory. The three of us were convinced that the appropriate way to examine such issues required a framework that would allow for firm heterogeneity in terms of technologies that were adopted, worker heterogeneity in terms of skills and imperfect labor markets that allowed for equilibrium unemployment, and the possible mismatch of workers and firms. By then, the Mortensen-Pissarides approach to labor market frictions had become standard in macroeconomics, so we knew that we wanted to adopt their framework. Andrei reminded us of a paper by Albrecht and Vroman which had recently appeared in the *IER* that offered an appealing model. In the Albrecht-Vroman model, initially identical firms choose between two technologies: a modern one that requires high-skill labor and a basic one that can be used by either high-skill or low-skill labor. Firms that adopt the modern technology may have to search longer for a worker and pay higher wages, but, once their vacancy is filled, their worker would be more productive. Firms that adopt the basic technology have an easier time filling their vacancy and pay lower wages, but they wind up with less productive workers. Thus in equilibrium it is possible to have both types of firms coexist in the same product market. In addition, if the revenues earned by the two types of firms are sufficiently close, high-skill workers randomly matched with low-tech firms might find it optimal to accept such jobs rather than continuing to search for a high-tech firm offering slightly higher wages. These workers would be underemployed since they would not be matched with firms offering the type of job that they are best suited for.

Our main goal was to focus on how changes in trade policy and/or gloabalization (modeled as falling trade costs) would affect the incentives faced by firms to create certain types of jobs (high-tech versus low-tech) and the incentives faced by workers to accept certain jobs. In other words, we wanted to examine how trade would affect the type of job matches that we would observe in equilibrium. As we began working on the project, we became aware almost immediately that the model was yielding predictions that were in accord with many of the recently established stylized facts linking openness, exporting behavior by firms, and measures of productivity at the firm and industry levels. The resulting paper, which appeared in the *Journal of International Economics* in July 2008, is presented in chapter 13.

In chapter 14 we use the model to investigate the manner in which the outsourcing of high-skill jobs affects the wages of low-skilled workers. Although this may be overly simplistic, a view that appears to be common among the public is as follows. Suppose that firms begin to outsource high-tech jobs to low-wage foreign countries; then the high-skilled workers displaced by outsourcing will be forced to take less appealing jobs at lower wages to find reemployment. These high-skilled workers will then, in turn, crowd out low-skilled workers from the labor market, resulting in lower wages for low-skilled workers as well. In the end, all domestic workers suffer with the only winners being the firms that now earn higher profits. A key feature of this scenario is that high-skill and low-skill workers are viewed as substitutes in the production process. The model introduced in chapter 14 adopts this assumption in an attempt to provide a framework that is consistent with publicly held views. We then use this framework to show that the wage effects are likely to be more complex than those described above, particularly for low-skilled workers. The reason for this is that the short-run increase in profits simulates new entry by domestic firms and this is likely to benefit low-skill domestic workers. We also show that although it is possible for high-skill outsourcing to lead to a reduction in domestic welfare, such a welfare loss can be averted by implementing a much-maligned policy, trade adjustment assistance, which provides unemployment benefits to high-skilled workers displaced by outsourcing.

We view the papers presented in chapters 13 and 14 as the starting point for a new research agenda. As we emphasize in chapter 13, this new framework that emphasizes both firm and worker heterogeneity yields a slew of testable hypotheses about the types of jobs that are created, the types of job matches that we should expect to observe, the equilibrium distribution of wages, and how all three of these are affected by openness. One of our future goals is to use micro-level data to test the predictions of this model.

However, our new research agenda is actually much broader than this. In particular, we plan to use the data that match workers with their employers to develop a better understanding of how trade and commercial policy affect job turnover. Our hope is that such an analysis will provide us with new micro-level insights into the incidence of worker dislocation, the manner in which openness affects the job search process, the pattern of worker turnover across industries, and the manner in which the gains and losses from freer trade are distributed across firms and their workers within industries.

REFERENCES

Jacobson, L., LaLonde, R., Sullivan, D. 1993a. Earnings losses of displaced workers. *American Economic Review* 83(4): 685–709.
Jacobson, L., LaLonde, R., Sullivan, D. 1993b. *The Costs of Worker Dislocation*. Kalamazoo, MI: W.E. Upjohn Institute for Employment Research.
Kletzer, L. 2001. *Job Loss from Imports: Measuring the Costs*. Washington, DC: Peterson Institute for International Economics.
Kletzer, L., Litan, R. 2001. A prescription to relieve worker anxiety. Policy Brief No. 73, Brookings Institution.

Chapter 13

GLOBALIZATION AND FIRM-LEVEL ADJUSTMENT WITH IMPERFECT LABOR MARKETS

CARL DAVIDSON, STEVEN J. MATUSZ, AND ANDREI SHEVCHENKO

1. INTRODUCTION

Even within narrowly defined industries, firms that produce similar products often use technologies with different levels of sophistication, employ different occupational mixes of workers, and pay different wages. If one looks for patterns across firms, then recent findings suggest that firms that adopt more modern technologies tend to employ more highly skilled workers and pay higher wages than their counterparts (Doms, Dunne, and Troske 1997). The purpose of this paper is to show that by combining this insight with the fact that unemployed workers must search for jobs, we are able to develop a simple model of a product market that is consistent with a large number of the stylized facts about industry dynamics in open economies and the impact of openness on productivity and wages.

The stylized facts of interest can be found in two related strands of the literature. One strand consists of firm- and plant-level studies that establish the existence of significant differences between firms that export and those that do not. Exporting firms are typically larger, more capital intensive, and more productive and pay higher wages than their counterparts (Bernard and Jensen 1999a). These studies also indicate that there is "imperfect persistence" in the export decision in that firms often change their export position from one period to the next (Roberts and Tybout 1997; Bernard and Jensen 1999a).[1]

Related studies have focused on the impact of openness on productivity at the firm and industry levels. One key finding in this strand of the literature is that openness tends to enhance productivity, although the

---

[1] These studies also find that firms typically export only a fraction of their output (Bernard and Jensen 1999a). As will become evident, this feature is absent from our model due to our assumption of perfect competition in the product market. We could generate this outcome by allowing for monopolistic competition, but have chosen not to do so in order to keep the analysis tractable.

mechanism is unclear.[2] At least three possible explanations have been offered. First, openness may allow exporting firms to take advantage of scale effects as they expand. Second, there may be increases in total factor productivity at the firm level, perhaps due to "learning-by-exporting." Third, since more efficient firms tend to export, liberalization may lead to a reallocation of market shares away from the least productive firms, resulting in higher aggregate productivity. Note that in the latter case, there are no within-firm productivity gains, only an increase in average productivity at the industry level.

Empirical studies do not offer much support for the scale-effect explanation (Tybout 2003) and provide mixed findings for the two other theories. Aggregate productivity gains in export-oriented industries are largely attributed to the fact that (a) it is the relatively efficient firms that choose to export; and (b) openness seems to trigger a reallocation in market shares in favor of these firms (Bernard and Jensen 1999b; Pavcnik 2002). It has been difficult to find evidence of within-firm productivity gains in export markets (Clerides, Lach, and Tybout 1998; Bernard and Jensen 1999a, b; Aw, Chung, and Roberts 2000).[3] On the other hand, there is evidence of within-firm productivity gains in *import-competing* markets (Pavcnik 2002; Fernandes 2007; Topalova 2007).

Motivated by these stylized facts, we develop a model where the product market is perfectly competitive but the labor market is beset by frictions. Specifically, our labor market is based on Albrecht and Vroman (2002), where workers with different skill levels search across firms for a job while initially identical firms must choose the type of technology to adopt. In equilibrium, some firms adopt a basic technology, employ relatively low-skilled workers, and pay low wages, whereas others adopt a more advanced technology, employ high-skilled workers, and pay high wages. One of the key features of the model is that if the revenues generated by the two different types of firms are sufficiently close, it is possible for underemployment to emerge in equilibrium. This occurs when high-skill workers, who are better suited for employment at high-tech firms, accept low-tech jobs because they happen to match with them first. Consistent with other models of firm heterogeneity, we show in the current

---

[2] For a survey of this literature see Tybout (2003).

[3] This is actually quite a complex issue. Many papers report increases in productivity just before a firm starts to export that persist and grow after exporting starts. Since the initial increase in productivity comes *before* the firm starts to export, papers such as those cited in the text view this as something other than "learning-by-exporting." However, others such as Castellani (2002), Baldwin and Gu (2003, 2004), Blalock and Gertler (2004), Girma, Greenaway, and Kellner (2004), Van Biesbroeck (2004), and Greenaway and Kellner (2005) point to the productivity gains *after* exporting begins and conclude that there evidence of learning-by-exporting.

setting that it is the largest, most productive firms paying the highest wages that face the strongest incentives to export. Moreover, we show that imperfect persistence may arise when equilibrium is characterized by underemployment. This occurs whenever low-tech firms that are matched with high-skill workers prefer to export their output while low-tech firms that are matched with low-skill workers prefer to sell their output domestically. Thus, our model predicts that the weakest firms in the industry may change their export position when the skill mix of its employee base changes.

When we turn to the impact of openness on productivity, we find that the relationship is complicated by the fact that there are two types of equilibria that are possible. Following Albrecht and Vroman, we define a "cross-skill matching" (CSM) equilibrium as one in which high-skill workers will accept low-tech jobs (i.e., they are mismatched) and an "ex-post segmentation" (EPS) equilibrium as one in which they are not willing to do so. If the economy starts in a CSM equilibrium and remains in one after liberalization, then we find that openness enhances productivity in export-oriented markets by reallocating market shares in favor of high-tech firms. However, within-firm productivity is unchanged. As for wages, since openness increases the surplus created by high-tech matches, high-skill workers employed by high-tech firms gain from liberalization. This increases the outside opportunities for high-skill workers with low-tech jobs, forcing the low-tech firms to increase the wages of these workers as well. On the other hand, since the number of low-tech firms shrinks, low-skill workers see their bargaining power eroded and may therefore lose from liberalization.

The fact that liberalization increases the spread between the revenues earned by the two types of firms opens up the possibility that it could cause the economy to move from a CSM equilibrium to an EPS equilibrium. When this occurs, liberalization's impact on productivity and wages is somewhat different. The main reason for this is that when high-skill workers start rejecting low-tech jobs, the number of low-tech firms falls dramatically. As a result, the aggregate productivity gains can be quite large and the wages of low-tech workers fall. In addition, since low-tech firms can now only attract low-skill workers, there are within-firm productivity *losses* for these firms. Thus, this case yields a surprising prediction: openness can dramatically increase aggregate productivity in export-oriented industries while generating within-firm productivity losses for the weakest firms.

In the latter part of the paper we examine the impact of openness on productivity in import-competing industries. Since import competition *reduces* the gap between the revenues earned by the two types of firms, it opens up the possibility that liberalization could shift the market from an

EPS equilibrium to a CSM equilibrium. If so, then the fact that high-skill workers start to accept low-tech jobs means that import competition will generate within-firm productivity gains for low-tech firms.

Our model can be viewed as a contribution along the lines of Melitz (2003), Bernard, Eaton, Jensen, and Kortum (2003), and Yeaple (2005). These papers attempt to explain why exporting firms are different from their counterparts, and generate aggregate productivity gains as the result of market share reallocations. In Melitz and Bernard et al., heterogeneity on the firm side is exogenous in that productivity is determined by a random draw. Firms make their exporting decision after learning their productivity, and, as in our setting, it is the high-productivity firms that choose to export. Openness then leads to a reallocation of market shares toward high-productivity firms and results in some low-productivity firms exiting the market. Yeaple generates endogenous heterogeneity across firms in the same manner that we do: initially identical firms make technology choices knowing that different choices allow them to employ different types of workers.[4] He shows that since the high-tech firms gain more from exporting, they have an easier time covering the costs associated with doing so. Consequently, just as in Melitz and Bernard et al., high-tech firms self-select into exporting.

While these papers model the relationship between liberalization and industrywide productivity, none are able to explain within-firm productivity gains due to changes in openness, nor do they address the issue of imperfect persistence.[5] In contrast, our model is able to generate both of these features due to the unique manner in which the labor market is modeled. In addition, due to our labor market structure, our model and Yeaple's generate different predictions about the impact of openness on industry wage profiles, an issue we discuss at greater length in the text.

After formulating the model in the following section, we rank order firms according to their incentive to export (section 3) and show how the

---

[4] In our opinion, Yeaple's approach is more satisfying since the firmside heterogeneity is a direct result of profit-maximizing decisions made by the firms.

[5] A small number of papers attempt to model within-firm productivity changes. Trindade (2004) explains the connection between openness and within-firm productivity gains as the result of a labor–leisure trade-off decision made by managers of monopolistically competitive firms. In his model, productivity is determined by managerial effort and managers, who are also consumers, value variety in consumption. By increasing the total variety of goods available, openness increases the rewards of working hard. As a result, liberalization inspires managers to work harder, resulting in higher productivity. Ederington and McCalman (2004) explain productivity gains in import-competing industries as the result of technology diffusion. The issue of persistence is taken up by Das, Roberts, and Tybout (2007), who focus on the trade-off between sunk costs that must be incurred each time a firm changes status from nonexporter to exporter, and the option value of a firm that continues to export.

decision to export impinges on domestic supply (section 4). Sections 5 and 6 illuminate the impact of liberalization on firms and the industry, respectively. We provide some numeric examples in section 7 to assist in cementing intuition, and briefly conclude in section 8.

2. THE MODEL

2.1 Technology

Our model is adapted from Albrecht and Vroman (2002), in which firms use capital and labor to produce a homogeneous good which is sold in a perfectly competitive product market with free entry. We assume that each firm requires a single manager to coordinate production and that the managerial labor market is characterized by frictions in that it takes time for unemployed managers and firms with vacancies to find each other. In this context, we use the term "manager" as a metaphor for all workers that cannot be found without search (this category would typically include nonproduction workers). By assuming one vacancy or manager per firm, as is standard in the search literature, we circumvent thorny issues dealing with returns to scale in the search process.

One of the key features of our model is that we allow for heterogeneity on both sides of the labor market. In this regard, we assume that there are two types of managers (high-skilled and low-skilled), where skills are assigned by nature. In contrast, firms are identical ex-ante, but make choices, described below, that result in ex-post heterogeneity.

We assume that firms undertake a series of decisions. The initial decision is whether to enter and create a vacancy and, if so, the type of technology to adopt. For simplicity, we assume that technology adoption is a binary choice, involving adoption of a basic (or "low-tech") technology or an advanced (or "high-tech") technology. The basic technology can be coordinated by managers of either skill level, whereas the advanced technology requires a high-skilled manager. Firms that adopt the advanced technology will pay higher wages and may end up searching longer for a manager, with these costs being offset by greater productivity once the vacancy is filled.

Once a vacancy is filled, the firm negotiates a wage with its manager, acquires all remaining inputs in perfectly competitive markets, and produces output. For simplicity, we treat all other inputs as a composite and call that composite capital.[6] As we show below, firms will also make heterogeneous

---

[6] The composite consists of land, intermediate inputs, and other categories of labor as well as capital.

choices regarding production levels and the market (domestic or foreign) in which to sell that output.[7]

We assume a continuum of risk-neutral managers with a total measure of 1. A fraction q of these managers have low skills, while the remainder have high skills.[8]

The set of assumptions sketched here results in three possible types of firms: low-tech firms that employ low-skilled managers, low-tech firms that employ high-skilled managers, and high-tech firms that employ high-skilled managers. Notationally, we refer to these firms types as L, M, and H and define y_{ij} as the amount of output produced by a type-i firm for sale in market j. The skill level of a type-i manager is denoted by s_i (e.g., s_M is the skill level of a high-skill manager employed by a low-tech firm).

For concreteness, we assume that

$$y_{ij} = k_{ij}^{\alpha} s_i, \ i = L, M, H \ j = d, f \tag{1}$$

where k_{ij} denotes the amount of capital rented by a type-i firm serving market j, d and f represent the domestic and foreign markets, $\alpha \in (0,1)$, and $s_H > s_M > s_L$.[9] Our assumption that $s_M > s_L$ indicates that a low-tech firm is more productive if coordinated by a high-skilled manager than it would be if coordinated by a low-skilled manager.[10] Assuming that $s_H > s_M$ indicates that a high-skilled manager is more productive when paired with a high-tech firm than when paired with a low-tech firm.

Once a firm hires a manager (and observes her skill), it rents capital in a perfectly competitive market. We choose capital as numeraire, so the profit-maximizing amount of capital is

$$k_{ij} = p_j \alpha y_{ij} \quad \text{for } i = L, M, H; j = d, f \tag{2}$$

where p_j is the price of the good in market j.

---

[7] Except for knife-edge cases, each firm will find one market or the other to be more profitable, and therefore will choose to sell all of its output in a single market.

[8] The exogeneity of the size and composition of the labor force greatly simplifies the analysis and can be justified on empirical grounds in the short to medium run. For example, see Currie and Harrison (1997), Revenga (1997), Harrison and Hanson (1999), Topalova (2007), Pavcnik et al. (2004), Attanasio, Goldberg, and Pavcnik (2004), and Warcziag and Seddon-Wallack (2004).

[9] We show below that a firm may be indifferent between serving the two markets. However, fixed costs rule out the possibility that a firm could earn higher profit from simultaneously serving both markets rather than concentrating on a single market.

[10] Albrecht and Vroman (2002) assume that $s_M = s_L$, which ensures uniqueness of a given type of equilibrium. Our assumption allows for a richer set of results but precludes us from making general statements about uniqueness.

For future reference, we define $R_{ij} = p_j y_{ij} - k_{ij} - c_v - c_j$, which is revenue net of nonmanagerial costs generated by a type-i firm serving market j. Here, c_v represents the cost of creating and maintaining a vacancy, and c_j represents a composite of costs associated with serving market j (this may include maintenance of a distribution network, market research, advertising, and so on).[11] We make the natural assumption that $c_f > c_d$. Using (2), we have $R_{ij} = (1 - \alpha) p_j y_{ij} - c_v - c_j$, which is the surplus that a type-i firm earns by serving market j. This is the surplus over which the manager and firm bargain.

2.2 Search and Matching

Unemployed managers and firms with vacancies are randomly matched. Firms observe the skill of the manager with whom they are matched, and managers observe the technology that the firm has adopted. Both the manager and the firm can look forward and know which market (domestic or foreign) generates the higher surplus, and therefore know which market will be served by the firm.[12] The firm and manager then negotiate a wage based on this set of information.

Matches are created according to a function, $m(u,v)$, that exhibits constant returns to scale in unemployment (u) and vacancies (v). Following the standard approach, we define $\theta = v/u$ as our measure of market tightness. Then, with random matching, the arrival rate of vacancies for any manager is given by the ratio of new matches to the total measure of job seekers, or $m(u, v)/u = m(\theta)$. By similar logic, the arrival rate of managers for any firm is $z(\theta) = m(u, v)/v = m(\theta)/\theta$. We assume that it becomes easier for managers to find a job and more difficult for firms to fill their vacancies as θ increases (i.e., $m'(\theta) > 0 > z'(\theta)$). Finally, we assume that jobs are destroyed at rate δ.[13]

2.3 Firms

As Albrecht and Vroman (2002) show, there are two types of equilibria in this model, depending on whether high-skill managers are willing to accept

---

[11] It is convenient to assume, as we do, that the cost of maintaining a vacancy is the same as the nonwage cost of employing a manager. Therefore c_v is a cost that firms carry even after the vacancy is filled. This assumption allows us to limit the number of parameters.

[12] The firm chooses to serve the market that generates the higher surplus. Both the manager and the firm have the same preferences concerning this decision since they split the surplus generated by the match.

[13] Of course, the job will also be destroyed if either party decides to voluntarily dissolve the match. This approach to modeling the labor market is due to Pissarides (2000) and Mortensen and Pissarides (1994).

jobs at low-tech firms. If they are, then we have a cross-skill-matching equilibrium (CSM), whereas if they are not, we have an ex-post segmentation equilibrium (EPS). A CSM equilibrium typically exists if the wages that high-skill managers can expect to earn on the two types of jobs are not too different. Thus, whether these equilibria exist depends upon parameter values and expectations.[14] In some instances, the equilibria coexist, whereas in other cases, the market equilibrium is unique. We provide more details on this issue below, but for now we assume that a CSM equilibrium exists. This means that high-skilled workers accept any job that is offered to them.

Continuing our description of firms, we use V_L to denote the expected value of present discounted income for a low-tech firm with a vacancy (the asset value of the firm), and V_H to denote the analogous value for a high-tech firm.[15] New firms enter the market as long as the expected discounted value of income is positive.[16] Moreover, entering firms choose the technology that generates the highest expected value of income. In this paper, we only consider steady-state equilibria where the economy is populated by low-tech *and* high-tech firms, implying the equilibrium condition $V_L = V_H = 0$. The first equality ensures that entering firms are indifferent with respect to the choice of technology, while the second equality ensures that the marginal firm is just indifferent with respect to the entry decision.

We use J_{ij} to represent a firm's expected value of present discounted income once it hires a manager. That is, J_{ij} denotes the asset value of a type-i firm that has filled its vacancy and chosen to serve market j for $i = L, M, H$ and $j = d, f$. Using the Bellman equation and the fact that

---

[14] As mentioned in footnote 10, Albrecht and Vroman (2002) assume $s_L = s_M$, which ensures that there exists at most one equilibrium of each type. Given our assumption that $s_L < s_M$, we cannot rule out the possibility that there might exist a multiplicity of CSM or EPS equilibria for a given set of parameters. Our results apply to all equilibria.

[15] The derivation of V_k is provided in the appendix.

[16] Our assumption that the firms make an irrevocable choice of technology implies, for example, that a low-tech firm cannot simply switch to the advanced technology if a shock pushes $V_L < 0 < V_H$. We could have alternatively assumed that an entering firm had to purchase some capital that was compatible with the initial choice of technology. A firm could then switch technology by switching the type of capital. However, this assumption adds complexity without insight. Firm exit is slightly more complicated. The discounted stream of income for a firm that has filled its vacancy is larger than a comparable firm with an open vacancy. A shock to the economy that pushes V_k below zero causes immediate exit of type-k firms with open vacancies. However, firms with filled vacancies have higher expected discounted income, and may therefore continue to produce if expected income remains above zero, only exiting after job separation. A sufficiently large shock can push expected income below zero even for firms with filled vacancies, in which case these firms exit immediately. These firm dynamics are standard in the search literature and consistent with Albrecht and Vroman (2002).

$V_k = 0$, we have (where r is the discount rate and w_{ij} is the wage paid by a type-i firm serving market j)

$$rJ_{ij} = \left\{ R_{ij} - w_{ij} \right\} - \delta J_{ij} \quad \text{for } i = L, M, H; j = d, f \tag{3}$$

The standard interpretation of (3) is that the flow value of the asset (rJ_{ij}) equals instantaneous profit ($R_{ij} - W_{ij}$) less the expected capital loss δJ_{ik}.

2.4 Managers

We now turn to the managers. Define N_{ij} to be the expected lifetime income earned by a manager who is currently employed by a type-i firm that sells its output in market j (for $i = L, M, H$ and $j = d, f$). We then have the following asset value equations for managers:

$$rN_{ij} = w_{ij} - \delta \left\{ N_{ij} - U_k \right\} \quad \text{for } i = L, M, H; j = d, f; k = L, H \tag{4}$$

and where the Bellman equations defining U_H and U_L are

$$rU_L = m(\theta) \phi_L \left\{ \max_j N_{Lj} - U_L \right\} \quad \text{for } j = d, f \tag{5}$$

$$rU_H = m(\theta) \left\{ \phi_L \max_j N_{Mj} + \left(1 - \phi_L \right) \max_j N_{Hj} - U_H \right\} \text{for } j = d, f \tag{6}$$

where ϕ_L represents the fraction of vacancies posted by low-tech firms. As with the firms, the right-hand side is the sum of flow income and the expected capital gain (or loss) from changing labor market status. Unemployed managers earn no flow income, whereas employed managers collect wages. In (5)–(6), note that the job acquisition rate for a high-skill manager is $m(\theta)$ (since they accept all jobs), whereas it is $\phi_L m(\theta)$ for low-skill managers (since they are only offered low-tech jobs). Moreover, an unemployed high-skill manager matches with a low-tech firm with probability $\phi_L m(\theta)$, in which case her capital gain is $\max_j N_{Mj} - U_H$; otherwise, she matches with a high-tech firm and gains $\max_j N_{Hj} - U_H$.

We assume that wages are negotiated with the outcome given by the generalized Nash bargaining solution. If β denotes the bargaining power of managers and U_i denotes the expected lifetime income of a type-i unemployed manager, then wages are given by (see Albrecht and Vroman 2002)

$$w_{ij} = \beta R_{ij} + (1 - \beta)rU_k \quad \text{for } i = L, M, H; j = d, f; k = L, H \qquad (7)$$

In equilibrium, high-skill managers will be willing to accept low-tech jobs only if they can be paid a wage in excess of the flow value of remaining unemployed. Using (7), this means that

$$\max_j R_{Mj} - rU_H > 0 \qquad (8)$$

which is the key condition that must be met for a CSM equilibrium to exist.

2.5 CSM Equilibria

As noted above, a steady-state equilibrium populated by both low-tech and high-tech firms must be characterized by $V_L = V_H = 0$. We derive the explicit functional forms for these variables in the appendix, where we also demonstrate that both can be reduced to functions of θ and γ_L, where γ_L represents the share of low-skilled managers in the pool of unemployed.

In the steady-state equilibrium, it must be the case that the flows into and out of each employment state must be equal. For low-skilled managers this condition is given by

$$\delta(q - \gamma_L u) = \phi_L m(\theta)\gamma_L u \qquad (9)$$

with the analogous condition for high-skilled managers:

$$\delta\{(1 - q) - (1 - \gamma_L)u\} = m(\theta)(1 - \gamma_L)u \qquad (10)$$

The key to understanding (9) and (10) is to recognize that there are $\gamma_L u$ unemployed low-skilled managers and $q - \gamma_L u$ low-skilled managers who are employed. Correspondingly, there are $(1 - \gamma_L)u$ unemployed high-skilled managers and $(1 - q) - (1 - \gamma_L)u$ high-skilled managers who are employed. All employed managers become unemployed at rate δ, whereas the arrival rate of suitable jobs varies by manager type, with the arrival rate of jobs suitable for low-skilled managers being $\phi_L m(\theta)$ and the arrival rate of jobs for which high-skilled managers are suited being simply $m(\theta)$.

Finally, it must be the case that the product market clears. If we use $D_j(p_j)$ and $S_j(p_d, p_f)$ to denote demand and supply in market j, then

$$D_j(p_j) = S_j(p_d, p_f) \quad \text{for } j = d, f \qquad (11)$$

This completes the description of the model when high-skill managers are willing to accept low-tech jobs.

2.6 EPS Equilibria

We close this section by describing how the model would be altered in an EPS equilibrium. For this to be the case, the wage paid by low-tech firms cannot exceed the flow utility of unemployment for high-skilled managers (the inequality in (8) is reversed). Since high-skill managers would be unwilling to accept low-tech jobs, there would be no type-M firms—thus (1)–(5) and (7) would only apply to type-L and type-H firms. In addition, (6) and (10) would have to be altered to reflect the fact that low-tech firms would be able to hire only low-skill workers. These equations would become

$$rU_H = m(\theta)(1 - \phi_L)\left\{\max_j N_{Hj} - U_H\right\} \quad \text{for } j = d, f \quad (6')$$

$$\delta\left\{(1 - q) - (1 - \gamma_L)u\right\} = m(\theta)(1 - \phi_L)(1 - \gamma_L)u \quad (10')$$

There are two factors that determine when CSM and EPS equilibria exist. First, a CSM equilibrium will not exist if low-tech firms cannot afford to pay high-skill managers enough to convince them to stop searching for a better job. This will occur if the revenue generated by a high-skilled manager at a low-tech firm *differs significantly* from the revenue generated if that manager were to be matched with a high-tech firm. This is important since, in the next section, we show that high-tech firms face a stronger incentive to export than low-tech firms. Thus, if liberalization results in high-tech firms exporting while low-tech firms do not, the increase in revenue generated when high-tech firms export can move the economy from a CSM equilibrium to an EPS equilibrium. The second important factor is expectations; and it is this factor that makes it possible to have CSM and EPS equilibria coexist. To see this, note that if high-skill managers are willing to accept low-tech jobs, then the value from adopting the basic technology will be high and a large number of firms do so. This would make it hard for high-skilled managers to find high-tech jobs, making them more willing to match with low-tech firms. Thus, there are some situations in which self-fulfilling expectations support equilibria of each type for given parameters.

3. THE EXPORT DECISION

We are now in position to discuss the firms' export decisions. Unless otherwise noted, we concentrate on CSM equilibria, although it should be clear that our basic message holds for all EPS equilibria as well. A type-i

firm will export if doing so maximizes its asset value—that is, if $J_{if} > J_{id}$. From (3), (6), and (7) we have

$$J_{if} - J_{id} = \frac{1-\beta}{r+\delta}(R_{if} - R_{id}) \quad \text{for } i = L, M, H \tag{12}$$

Substitute (2) into (1) to solve for y_{ij} and then substitute this result into the definition of R_{ij}, and then substitute back into (12). Doing so yields (with $A = (1-\alpha)\alpha^{\frac{\alpha}{1-\alpha}}$)

$$J_{if} - J_{id} = \frac{1-\beta}{r+\delta}\left(A\left[p_f^{\frac{1}{1-\alpha}} - p_d^{\frac{1}{1-\alpha}} \right]s_i^{\frac{1}{1-\alpha}} - \left[c_f - c_d \right] \right)$$
$$\text{for } i = L, M, H \tag{13}$$

Given our assumption that $c_f > c_d$, it is evident that a firm exports only if $p_f > p_d$. A more interesting finding is that (16) is increasing in s_i, our measure of managerial skill. Thus we have

Proposition 1. *If $p_f > p_d$ and $s_H > s_M > s_L$, then type-H firms face the strongest incentives to export while type-L firms face the weakest incentives to export. That is, $J_{Hf} - J_{Hd} > J_{Mf} - J_{Md} > J_{Lf} - J_{Ld}$.*

4. The Domestic Price

4.1 Autarky

We begin by assuming that the combination of p_f and c_f is such that $J_{if} < J_{id}$ for all firms, regardless of domestic price. A sufficient condition for this inequality to be satisfied can be obtained by evaluating (13) for a type-H firm when the domestic price is zero. The restriction on parameter values is then $c_f > A(p_f s_H)^{\frac{1}{1-\alpha}} + c_d$. In this case, no type-H firm would choose to export even if the domestic price were to fall to zero. Since type-M and type-L firms derive even less benefit from exporting, no firm will export. We can then solve for the autarkic domestic price.[17] After doing so, we can imagine that there is a reduction in the cost of serving the foreign market (or an increase in the foreign price) that is sufficient to

---

[17] Here we concentrate on the case where this industry would be a net exporter if the cost of serving the foreign market is sufficiently low. We defer discussion of the possibility of imports to a later section.

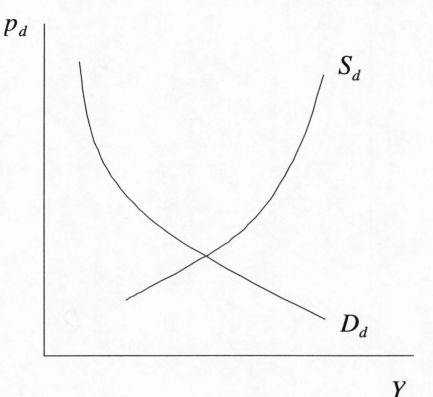

Figure 13.1a.

induce at least some firms to start exporting. It is this latter case that we explore in the next subsection.

Each firm serving a given market produces more as the price increases. This is easily seen by substituting (2) into (1):

$$y_{ij} = (\alpha p_j)^{\frac{\alpha}{1-\alpha}} s_i^{\frac{1}{1-\alpha}} \qquad \text{for } i = L, M, H \qquad (14)$$

Moreover, the higher price of output creates incentive for more entry, further expanding supply. The autarky equilibrium is illustrated in figure 13.1.a.

4.2 Trade

Now suppose that there is a reduction in c_f. In particular, assume that c_f now satisfies $A(p_f s_H)^{\frac{1}{1-\alpha}} + c_d > c_f > A(p_f s_M)^{\frac{1}{1-\alpha}} + c_d$. In this case, type-$H$

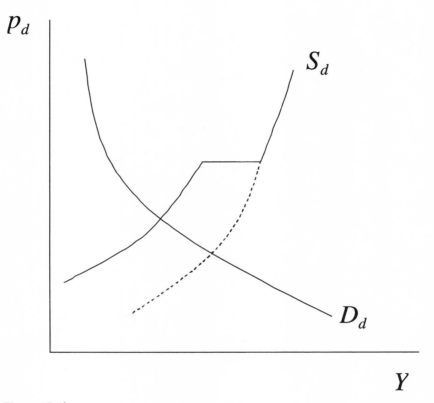

Figure 13.1b.

firms would export rather than serve the domestic market for sufficiently low domestic prices. However, all other firms would continue to serve the domestic market, shifting the relevant portion of the supply curve left-ward, as illustrated in figure 13.1.b.[18] The critical price below which type-H firms export is found by setting $J_{Hf} = J_{Hd}$:

$$p_d = \left(p_f^{\frac{1}{1-\alpha}} - \frac{c_f - c_d}{As_H} \right)^{1-\alpha} \tag{15}$$

If the domestic price happens to equal this critical value, type-H firms are indifferent between serving either market. This is not a knife-edge result,

---

[18] We are being somewhat informal here. Because of the fixed costs associated with creating and maintaining a vacancy, a sufficiently low domestic price will shut all firms out of the market, resulting in zero output.

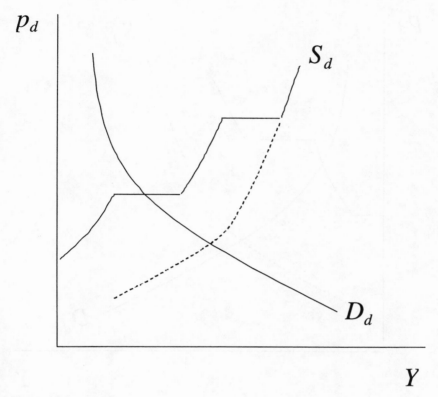

Figure 13.1c.

as there exists a wide range of demand for which this critical price could be the domestic equilibrium. In the event that the demand curve cuts the supply curve on the step, a portion of type-H firms will serve the domestic market with the remaining firms exporting.[19]

If we continue to let the cost of serving the foreign market fall, we find a range of prices where type-H and type-M firms both prefer exports to serving the domestic market, and the supply curve has two "steps," as in figure 13.1.c. Finally, if the cost of exporting and the domestic price are both sufficiently low, all three types of firms would prefer to serve the foreign market. This is the case in figure 13.1.d. Note that reducing c_f adds additional steps to the supply curve and raises the height of each existing step.

[19] Depending on parameter values, it is possible that these critical prices at which firms are indifferent between markets are lower than the minimum price consistent with a CSM equilibrium. In such situations, no firm would choose to export if a CSM equilibrium exists.

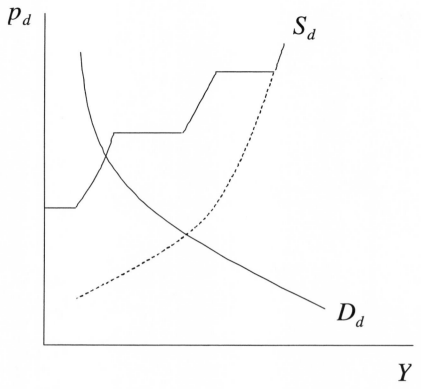

Figure 13.1d.

5. LIBERALIZATION AND FIRMS

A sufficiently large reduction in the cost of serving the foreign market induces some firms to start exporting. Our purpose in this section is to show how the characteristics of these firms change as they switch from serving the domestic market to serving the foreign market, and how these firms compare with those that continue to serve the domestic market.

For illustrative purposes, we consider the case depicted in figure 13.1.c, where costs have fallen low enough so that type-M firms are indifferent between serving the domestic and foreign markets. In this equilibrium, all type-H firms serve the foreign market, while all type-L firms serve the domestic market.

Proposition 2. *Assume a CSM equilibrium in which type-H firms strictly prefer to export, type-L firms strictly prefer to sell their output domesti-*

cally, and type-M firms are indifferent between exports and domestic sales. Compared with firms that serve the domestic market, exporting firms (a) are larger ($y_{Hf} > y_{Mf} > y_{Md} > y_{Ld}$); (b) employ more nonmanagerial inputs ($k_{Hf} > k_{Mf} > k_{Md} > k_{Ld}$); and (c) pay wages that are at least as high ($w_{Hf} > w_{Mf} = w_{Md} > w_{Ld}$).

Proof. Assuming, as we have, that $c_f > c_d$, it follows that $p_f > p_d$ is a necessary condition for any firm to export. Combined with the assumption that $s_H > s_M > s_L$, (a) follows directly from (17). Part (b) then follows from (2). To prove part (c), note from the definition of R_{ij} that $R_{Hf} > R_{Mf} = R_{Md} > R_{Ld}$. Then from (7), we have $w_{Hf} - w_{Mf} = \beta(R_{Hf} - R_{Mf}) > 0$ and $w_{Mf} - w_{Md} = \beta(R_{Mf} - R_{Md}) = 0$. Furthermore, $w_{Md} - w_{Ld} = \beta(R_{Md} - R_{Ld}) + (1 - \beta)(rU_H - rU_L)$, which is positive if $rU_H > rU_L$. We show in the appendix this last inequality holds, thereby completing the proof. #

Within firm type, exporters are larger than nonexporters because the price in the export market exceeds that in the domestic market. The higher price raises the value of the marginal product for variable inputs, so firms find it profitable to expand. Comparing different types of firms within the same market, type-*H* exporters are larger than type-*M* exporters because of superior technology, while type-*M* firms that serve the domestic market are larger than type-*L* firms (also serving the domestic market) because of more skilled management. Similarly, managers at type-*H* firms earn higher wages than those at type-*M* firms (regardless of export status) because of superior technology, while those at type-*M* firms (again regardless of export status) earn higher wages than those at type-*L* firms because they are more skilled.

We specified Proposition 2 for a particular equilibrium configuration, but applications to other equilibria are transparent. For example, the equilibrium illustrated in figure 13.1.b is such that only type-*H* firms export, with type-*M* and type-*L* firms strictly preferring to serve the domestic market. In this case, it follows directly that type-*H* firms are larger, hire more inputs, and pay higher wages than type-*M* firms, which in turn are larger, hire more variable inputs, and pay higher wages than type-*L* firms.

The results of Proposition 2 emerge from complementary models as well.[20] In addition, our model provides a theoretical basis for the stylized fact that firms often change their export decision from one period to the next. That is, the model provides an explanation for the observation of imperfect persistence in the decision to export (see Das, Roberts, and Tybout 2007 for an alternative explanation).

---

[20] For example, Bernard, Eaton, Jensen, and Kortum (2003), Melitz (2003), and Yeaple (2005).

To begin, we suppose that the equilibrium is qualitatively captured by figure 13.1.b, in which $J_{Hf} - J_{Hd} > 0 > J_{Mf} - J_{Md} > J_{Lf} - J_{Ld}$. In this case, all type-H firms export and all other firms serve the domestic market. In this case, there is perfect persistence—a firm that exports today always exports tomorrow, and no firm that serves the domestic market today exports tomorrow.[21]

We next turn to the case with $J_{Hf} - J_{Hd} > J_{Mf} - J_{Md} \geq 0 > J_{Lf} - J_{Ld}$. The subcase in which $J_{Mf} - J_{Md} = 0$ is depicted by figure 13.1.c, and the subcase with $J_{Mf} - J_{Md} > 0 > J_{Lf} - J_{Ld}$ in figure 13.1.d. In this case, type-H firms always export, and type-L firms always serve the domestic market. Some type-M firms export with the remainder serving the domestic market in the subcase $J_{Mf} - J_{Md} = 0$, otherwise all choose to export when $J_{Mf} - J_{Md} > 0$. But in the model, the distinguishing feature between type-L and type-M firms lies in the skill of the manager. A type-L firm that loses its low-skilled manager and finds a high-skilled replacement graduates to type-M status. Similarly, a type-M firm that finds only a low-skill manager to replace a lost high-skilled manager moves down to type-L status. In the context of the model, a change in export status is not driven by changes in market conditions, but by firm-level shocks.

If we use $\pi_s(i)$ to represent the "export survival rate" for a type-i firm (defined to be the probability that firm exports next period conditional on exporting today), then it follows that $\pi_s(H) = 1$ and $\pi_s(M) = (1 - \delta) + \delta(1 - \gamma_L)m(\theta)$.[22] Similarly, if we use $\pi_B(i)$ to denote the "export birth rate" for a type-i firm (defined to be the probability that a firm starts exporting tomorrow given that it is currently not exporting), then we have $\pi_B(L) = \delta(1 - \gamma_L)m(\theta)$[23]. Combining these results with Proposition 2, we have

Proposition 3. *In any cross-skill matching equilibrium with imperfect persistence, the export survival rate is positively correlated with the wage the firm pays. The export birth rate is positive only for firms that pay the lowest wages in the industry.*

Proposition 3 is consistent with Bernard and Jensen's (2004) finding that the probability of exporting in period t given that a firm was an exporter in $t - 1$ is increasing in the size and productivity of the firm.[24]

---

[21] Note that figure 13.1.a is also consistent with perfect persistence, as no firm would ever choose to export.

[22] Note that $\pi_s(L)$ is not defined.

[23] In this case, $\pi_B(H)$ and $\pi_B(M)$ are not defined.

[24] Using a different model of entry and exit behavior, Das, Roberts, and Tybout (2007) provide evidence for a sample of Colombian firms suggesting that the weakest firms within an industry are those that are most likely to be near the threshold of indifference between exporting or not.

6. Liberalization and the Industry

We now turn to a slightly different issue—what is the impact of liberalization on productivity and wages in export-oriented markets? To examine this, we begin by assuming that the cost of serving the foreign market is so high that no firms choose to export and equilibrium is characterized by figure 13.1.a. We then assume that the cost of serving the foreign market falls low enough so that type-H firms choose to export, while all other firms continue to serve the domestic market.[25] The latter equilibrium is illustrated in figure 13.1.b.

Clearly, the domestic price increases as the cost of exporting falls. Moreover, we must have $p_f > p_d$, otherwise no firms would export. Since all firms initially serve only the domestic market, we can conclude that type-H firms enjoy a larger increase in price compared with other firms. The price increase resulting from liberalization leads to expansion by existing firms and new entry. However, since type-H firms gain more than others, they expand by a greater amount and the overall fraction of firms using the advanced technology increases.

Since liberalization increases the prices received by firms, the surplus to be split between the firm and its worker increases. However, the increase in price is larger for firms that export; hence the increased surplus for type-H firms is higher than it is for others. The greater surplus induces new entry by both types of firms, with relatively more new entry by type-H firms. As a result, the share of vacancies posted by low-tech firms (ϕ_L) falls. Moreover, higher prices induce existing firms to expand by employing more nonmanagerial inputs, with type-H (exporting) firms expanding by a greater amount than those that serve only the domestic market. As a result of the reallocation of market shares toward type-H firms, measured productivity in the industry increases. But, at the firm level, all increased productivity can be fully attributed to the increased employment of nonmanagerial inputs, thus there are no within-firm increases in total factor productivity.[26]

As for wages, note that high-tech employees benefit from these changes since the surplus they share with their firm increases (p_f is larger than

---

[25] It is straightforward to extend the analysis to the case where type-M firms and then type-L firms choose to export.

[26] There is a bit of a semantic issue in our definition of a firm. For example, suppose that a low-tech firm exits and then chooses to reenter after having adopted the advanced technology. Based on our terminology, an old firm has exited and a new one has entered, with no change in firm-level productivity. In practice, this would show up as a within-firm productivity gain due to an improvement in technology. But this firm would then be reclassified as a high-tech firm.

the initial price) and their bargaining power increases (ϕ_L falls). Both effects work to increase w_H. The wages for low-skilled managers can rise or fall. On the one hand, the surplus created by low-tech firms increases (p_d is larger than the initial price), which works in favor of low-skilled managers. On the other hand, the fall in ϕ_L weakens their bargaining position, thereby putting downward pressure on their wage. Finally, consider the fate of high-skilled managers employed by low-tech firms. It should be clear that their wage, w_M, increases since the surplus created by these firms increases and the bargaining position improves for these workers. The latter is due to the decline in ϕ_L combined with better outside opportunities (i.e., the increase in w_H).

Of course, all of these results depend upon the assumption that high-skill managers are still willing to accept job offers from adopters of the basic technology—that is, we remain in a CSM equilibrium. We summarize these results in Proposition 4.

Proposition 4. *Suppose that the economy begins in a CSM equilibrium and that liberalization then results in a new CSM equilibrium. Then liberalization reallocates market shares in favor of type-H firms, thereby triggering an increase in productivity at the industry level. In addition, liberalization increases the wages earned by all high-skill managers, whereas the wages of low-skill managers might rise or fall. In either case, the gap in wages between what the highest paid and the lowest paid managers earn increases.*

Our predictions about the impact of openness on wage profiles differ significantly from Yeaple's (2005). Although both models predict gains for high-skill workers from liberalization, Yeaple's model predicts nominal wage losses for workers earning *moderate* wages and no change in the wages earned by the least skilled workers in the economy. In contrast, our model predicts gains for workers earning high and moderate wages, with possible losses for those at the low end of the skill distribution. Our results are therefore consistent with recent empirical findings that (a) exporting is associated with increases in wage inequality between high-skill and low-skill workers, and (b) wages of the least skilled workers have declined over the last 30 years as markets have become more open (see, for example, Bernard and Jensen 1997, Harrison and Hanson 1999; Baldwin and Cain 2000).

The fact that the wages paid by type-H firms rise faster than those paid by type-L firms opens up the possibility that after liberalization high-skill managers may no longer be willing to accept low-tech jobs. If this is the case, liberalization switches the economy to an EPS equilibrium. When this occurs, the wages of high-skill managers increase but the wages of low-skill managers fall. The reason for this is as follows. In the CSM equilibrium the wages of low-skill managers are propped up by the fact that high-skill managers are willing to match with low-tech firms. This means that it is easy for such firms to find a match and thus a large number of vacancies are created by low-tech firms. This gives the low-skilled managers bargaining power and allows them to earn a relatively high wage. But when liberalization causes the market to switch to an EPS equilibrium, it becomes much harder for low-tech firms to find a match, so fewer low-tech vacancies are created (or, alternatively, type-L and type-M firms exit upon loss of their manager). As a result, the bargaining power of low-skilled managers falls and so does their wage.

As for productivity, the reduction in the number of type-L and type-M firms coupled with the entry by new type-H firms results in a big reallocation of market shares in favor of type-H firms. This can result in large aggregate productivity gains. However, this gain would be somewhat moderated by within-firm productivity *losses* for low-tech firms. This follows from the fact that these firms would no longer be able to attract high-skilled managers and would have to rely on low-skilled managers.

7. NUMERIC EXAMPLES

We offer some examples to highlight the impact of openness on market shares and wages and to demonstrate the richness of the model. We follow Albrecht and Vroman (2002) and use a matching function that is Cobb-Douglas in u and v so that $m(\theta) = 2\sqrt{\theta}$. Our parameter values are specified in table 13.1. For purposes of our first example, we assume that c_f, the cost of serving the foreign market, is initially too high for any domestic firm to export.[27] We then allow c_f to fall, creating the potential for some domestic firms to start exporting. The actual set of firms that export depends on the endogenously determined domestic price compared with the exogenous foreign price and associated costs of serving the domestic and foreign markets. In turn, the endogenous p_d depends, in part, on domestic demand. We capture a range of cases by assuming that domestic demand is isoelastic such that

$$D_d(p_d) = (\Phi)(p_d)^{-\eta} \tag{16}$$

We vary Φ and η so that the demand curve rotates about an arbitrarily chosen point on the autarky supply curve. The trading equilibrium then

---

[27] This value was calculated based on the condition given in the first paragraph of section 4.1, which provides a sufficient condition for excluding domestic firms from foreign sales.

TABLE 13.1

Endogenous Variables	$c_f > 25$	$c_f = 2$		
		$\eta = \infty$	$13.3 < \eta < 46.9$	$\eta < 6.4$
P_d	0.939	0.939	0.949	0.959
W_L	11.35	11.30	11.61	11.92
W_M	15.66	16.22	16.21	16.50
W_H	17.75	18.59	18.58	18.69
ϕ_L	0.714	0.666	0.672	0.686
MS_H	0.134	0.157	0.154	0.147
u	0.049	0.052	0.051	0.049

Parameter values: $\alpha = 0.5, \beta = 0.5, \delta = 0.2, r = 0.05, q = 2/3, s_H = 10, s_M = 9,$
$s_L = 8, c_v = 2, c_d = 0, p_f = 1, c_f = 2.$

depends on the elasticity of demand (and the constant term), whereas the autarky equilibrium is independent of this elasticity. Key aspects of our example are displayed numerically in table 13.1 and visually in figure 13.2.

Using (13), we solve for values of p_d at which the three types of firms are indifferent between domestic and foreign sales. These prices form the perfectly elastic portions of the domestic supply curve. For example, type-H firms strictly prefer to export if $p_d < 0.959$ and strictly prefer to serve the domestic market if $p_d > 0.959$.

We arbitrarily choose autarky equilibrium such that $p_d = 0.939$. We then allow c_f to fall. In the first scenario, we assume that domestic demand is infinitely elastic, so that the equilibrium domestic price remains unchanged. In this case, both type-M and type-H firms choose to export, while type-L firms serve only the domestic market.

The consequences for the three wages are illustrated in table 13.1. The wage for low-skilled managers falls from 11.35 to 11.30, whereas w_M and w_H both increase, with the latter increasing proportionately more than the former. The wage falls for low-skilled managers because the surplus earned by their employing firms is unchanged (due to the unchanged market price) while their bargaining power erodes. The erosion of bargaining power follows from the fact that a smaller proportion of vacancies are created for low-skilled managers (ϕ_L falls). In turn, the reason that ϕ_L falls is that increased export opportunities for type-M and type-H firms causes these firms to expand while simultaneously providing stronger incentives for new entrants to adopt the advanced technology. The fall in ϕ_L is mirrored by an increase in MS_H, the market share of type-H firms.

Mismatched high-skilled managers see a small increase in their wage due to their increased bargaining strength as more type-H firms enter the

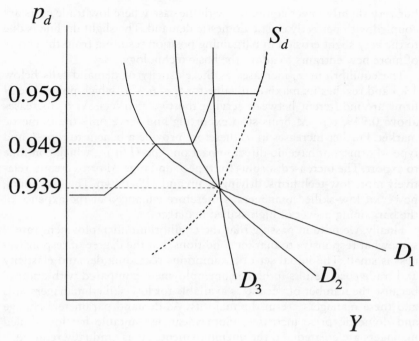

Figure 13.2.

market, and the fact that their outside options improve as w_H rises. Finally, high-skilled managers employed at type-H firms gain even more because of increased bargaining strength combined with the fact that the differential surplus earned by type-H firms vis-à-vis type-M firms is increasing in output price.

The reduction in c_f results in an increase in p_d for any finite elasticity of demand. The set of firms that choose to export is unchanged for any $\eta \in (46.9, \infty)$. Domestic price increases as demand becomes less elastic within this range. The higher domestic price increases the surplus earned by type-L firms without changing market conditions for type-M or type-H firms, both of which sell all output in the foreign market. More new entrants choose the basic technology, and existing type-L firms expand. Both effects reverse the initial fall (under an assumption of infinitely elastic demand) in ϕ_L. In turn, the wage for low-skilled managers begins to increase. For a sufficiently high domestic price, the wage for low-skilled managers surpasses its autarkic value.

For $\eta \in (13.3, 46.9)$, p_d equilibrates at the level for which type-M firms are indifferent between serving the two markets. Wages for high-skilled managers are higher at this equilibrium compared with autarky values, but very slightly lower compared with the case where low trade costs are coupled with perfectly elastic domestic demand. The slight decline is due to the very slight erosion in bargaining position resulting from the choice of more new entrants to adopt the basic technology.

The equilibrium p_d increases as the elasticity of demand falls below 13.3 and reaches its maximum value for $\eta < 6.4$, at which point type-H firms are indifferent between serving the two markets. As p_d increases above 0.949, type-M firms stop exporting and serve only the domestic market. Further increases in p_d therefore provide a benefit to type-L and type-M firms, but have no direct impact on type-H firms, which continue to export. The increased surplus for type-L and type-M firms creates relatively more low-tech firms, driving ϕ_L up and MS_H down. The bargaining power of low-skilled managers is therefore enhanced at the expense of the bargaining power of high-skilled managers.

Finally, we note in passing that the equilibrium unemployment rate is somewhat responsive to market conditions, but the degree of responsiveness is small. The initial set of assumptions regarding demand elasticity and trade costs results in higher unemployment compared with autarky because the number of vacancies available for low-skilled managers falls and these managers are in the majority. As demand parameters change and domestic price increases, more vacancies suitable for low-skilled managers are created and the unemployment rate is gradually reduced.

Table 13.2 shows what can happen when market conditions change sufficiently to push the economy from a CSM equilibrium to an EPS equilibrium. In constructing this example, we focus on the case where the elasticity of domestic demand is small enough so that it intersects with the top step of the domestic supply curve. All of the underlying parameters are the same as those used to generate table 13.1 except for p_f, which we initially set equal to 1.110, then allow to increase to 1.111. From (18), the equilibrium domestic prices for the two scenarios are 1.073 and 1.074. Given the other parameters of the model, it can be shown that 1.073 is the highest domestic price consistent with a CSM equilibrium. The thought experiment in which the foreign price increases by less than 0.01% therefore concludes with the economy switching from a CSM equilibrium to an EPS equilibrium. Even if a high-skilled manager were offered the entire surplus generated by a low-tech firm, she would find it in her interest to turn down the job offer and continue searching for a high-tech firm. As table 13.2 shows, the resulting equilibrium is dramatically different compared with the initial equilibrium. Because low-tech firms can no longer attract high-skilled managers, many fewer new entrants choose this route. This is seen by the significant reduction in ϕ_L. Because there are fewer vacancies for low-skilled managers, the bargaining power of this group erodes and their wage falls by

TABLE 13.2

Endogenous Variables	$p_f = 1.110$	$p_f = 1.111$
P_d	1.073	1.074
W_L	15.48	15.33
W_M	21.33	—
W_H	24.07	24.80
ϕ_L	0.66	0.528
MS_H	0.159	0.437
u	0.045	0.063

Parameter values: $\alpha = 0.5, \beta = 0.5, \delta = 0.2, r = 0.05, q = 2/3,$ $S_H = 10, S_M = 9, S_L = 8, C_v = 2, C_d = 0, C_f = 2.$

nearly 1%. In contrast, high-skilled managers have a stronger bargaining position. Consequently, their wages increase dramatically. Managers who might have formally been mismatched have a wage increase in excess of 15%. Even those who would have been properly matched in the CSM equilibrium find a wage increase of 3%. These large changes were triggered by a change in price that is less than 0.01%.

Two other numbers reported in table 13.2 deserve mention. First, the move to an EPS equilibrium results in a big increase in the market share of type-H firms. In turn, this triggers an increase in aggregate productivity despite the fact that low-tech firms become less productive. We note also that there is a fairly dramatic upswing in the unemployment rate. A small part of this change is due to the fact that there are fewer firms searching for low-skilled managers, and these managers are, in our parameterization, in the majority. The larger effect is that high-skill managers are now choosier about the jobs that they accept, therefore the average duration of unemployment increases for this group.

Although our main focus in this paper is on export-oriented industries, we close this section with a brief discussion of our model's predictions about the impact of openness on productivity in import-competing industries.[28] Our goal is to show that, consistent with the evidence, openness can increase within-firm measures of productivity by changing the job market preferences of high-skill workers.

[28] As suggested by an anonymous referee, our lack of a general equilibrium structure may overly simplify the analysis. In a multisector model where managers can flow between sectors, the degree of surplus in one sector may impinge on the type of equilibria possible in the other. While these concerns are certainly reasonable, refer back to footnote 8 where we provide references to recent evidence that between-sector flows in the short to medium run are quite small, suggesting that that our partial equilibrium approach has merit.

When the model applies to an import-competing industry, liberalization lowers the price received by all firms. This reduction in price causes all firms to contract by utilizing fewer variable inputs, and narrows the gap between the revenues generated by low-tech and high-tech firms. If high-skill managers are unwilling to accept low-tech jobs in the closed economy, then they may become willing to do so once trade is liberalized. If this occurs, then total factor productivity of the low-tech firms rises with liberalization.

Recall that Albrecht and Vroman showed that there exist parameterizations that could support both a CSM and an EPS equilibrium. In our model, our parameterizations are consistent with both types of equilibria for all $p_d \in (0.74, 1.11)$. We can then imagine that the economy begins at an EPS equilibrium at a price within this range, but then import competition pushes the domestic price lower. If the new price remains in this range, there are two possible outcomes. First, high-skilled managers may remain optimistic about finding jobs with high-tech firms, and these firms do not become worried that high-skilled managers will start to accept jobs at low-tech firms. Under these conditions, the economy will simply shift to a new EPS equilibrium at a lower output price.

However, it is perhaps easier to imagine newly unemployed high-skilled managers hearing news about an increase in import penetration in their industry and becoming pessimistic about their job prospects.[29] If so, they might begin to accept any job offer that comes along, and the economy could converge to a CSM equilibrium instead. This new equilibrium would then be characterized by low-tech firms that are, on average, more productive than they would have been in the closed economy. That is, type-M firms (which were nonexistent in the initial equilibrium) are more productive than type-L firms. Thus, our model yields a fairly sharp prediction concerning within-firm productivity gains from liberalization in import-competing industries: these gains should tend to occur at the weakest firms in the industry and they should be negatively correlated with the firm's wage (in that low-wage firms are more likely to gain by matching with higher-skilled managers).[30]

[29] Recent survey research suggests that such a scenario is highly credible. For example, Scheve and Slaughter (2004) find that a significant portion of the U.S. workforce fears that liberalization weakens job security.

[30] Fernandes (2007) finds that productivity gains due to liberalization are greater in larger plants, where larger plants are considered to be those with more than 50 employees prior to liberalization. According to note 30 in her paper, this correlation is robust to measuring plant size using market share. However, her explanation is that larger plants use more imported inputs (see her note 36). We do not consider this channel in our model. Using a sample of Indian firms, Topolova (2007) does not find any notable relationship between firm size and the effect of liberalization on productivity. In her analysis, large firms are in the top 1% of the sales distribution, medium firms have sales above the median (excluding firms

We close this section with a brief discussion of whether the within-firm productivity changes predicted by our model provide an explanation of the productivity changes that have been uncovered in the empirical literature. It is clear that the researchers in this area are looking for a link between openness and total factor productivity (TFP); that is, they are *not* looking for productivity changes that can be explained by changes in the factors used in the production process as a result of trade liberalization. In an attempt to avoid such confusion, most researchers attempt to control for the factors used in production. For example, Pavcnik (2002), who provides perhaps the most complete and careful approach to this issue, controls for the skill mix of labor used in each plant. Thus, if the plants in her sample responded to changes in openness by changing the skill intensity of the production process and if this led to changes in productivity, this would not show up in the data as a change in TFP.

In our model, within-firm productivity changes are driven by changes in the quality of workers that firms can attract. An econometrician who observes and controls for this quality change would therefore find that there is no change in TFP. One might be tempted to view this as just a change in the skill mix of labor and dismiss it as something already controlled for in Pavcnik's study. There is, however, a subtle but important distinction between the story that we are telling and one consistent with a change in the skill intensity of production in Pavcnik's model. To see this, note that in Pavcnik's model plants are assumed to use Cobb-Douglas technologies with unskilled labor, skilled labor, and capital as the primary inputs. So, for example, we can imagine a firm that combines nonproduction workers (managers, in our model) with production workers, capital, and raw materials (all part of the composite k in our model) to produce some final product. Suppose that liberalization leads the firm to substitute nonproduction workers for production workers and this substitution alters overall productivity. Pavcnik's approach would control for this change and would lead one to conclude that there is no change in TFP. Our story is somewhat different. In our model, there is heterogeneity in terms of ability within each skill class of workers and openness alters the *quality* of nonproduction workers that firms can attract. Thus, it is as if openness alters the *effective* units of labor generated by the average worker hired by the firm. As far as we know, no empirical study has controlled for this. It follows that if openness triggers the types of within-firm productivity changes predicted by our model, they would show up in the

---

already classified as large), and small firms are those with sales below the median. Topolova offers the suggestion that firm size may not be significant in her analysis because all firms in her sample (i.e., publicly listed firms) are substantially larger than the average Indian firm. Neither of these papers offers a clean test of our model.

residual in empirical studies—in other words, they would show up as changes in TFP.

8. CONCLUSION

We have presented a model based on Albrecht and Vroman (2002) in which managers differentiated by ability search over firms for jobs. Initially identical firms are ex-post heterogeneous as some adopt a basic technology and pay low wages, whereas others adopt a modern technology, employ high-skilled managers, and pay high wages. As in Melitz (2003), Bernard et al. (2003), and Yeaple (2005), we find that exporting firms are typically larger, more productive, and pay higher wages than their counterparts. In addition, as in Yeaple (2005), the firm-side heterogeneity in our model arises endogenously as a natural outcome of profit-maximizing decisions.

Our paper departs from previous work in the manner in which the labor market is modeled. Building on the insights of Albrecht and Vroman (2002), we have shown that industry dynamics are largely determined by two factors: the types of firms different managers are *willing* to match with and the types of matches that *actually* occur. In particular, we have shown that when high-skilled managers are willing to accept low-tech jobs, imperfect persistence in the decision to export is a natural feature of equilibrium in that these firms will export when matched with high-skilled managers and sell their output domestically when matched with low-skilled managers. Thus, our model yields strong predictions about how the export survival and birth rates will vary with firm-level measures of productivity and wages.

We have also shown that when high-skilled managers match with adopters of basic technology, openness enhances productivity in export markets by reallocating market shares in favor of the most productive firms. In this case, openness has no impact on within-firm measures of total factor productivity. While these two results can also be found in Melitz (2003), Bernard et al. (2003), and Yeaple (2005), a new possibility emerges in our model due to the fact that openness alters the spread between the revenues earned by firms that choose different technologies. In export markets, this spread is increased, causing the wages offered by the firms to diverge, whereas in import-competing markets the spread is decreased, causing the wage gap to contract. As a result, liberalization may alter the job-market preferences of the high-skilled managers. We have shown that in export markets, liberalization may cause high-skilled managers to reject job offers from firms that have adopted the basic technology. This then leads to large aggregate productivity gains due to market share reallocations and within-firm productivity *losses* for the weakest firms in the industry. In contrast, liberalization may cause high-skilled managers to start to accept these same jobs in import-competing industries. This would lead to within-firm productivity gains at this set of firms, an outcome that is consistent with recent empirical findings.

Our model also allows us to derive predictions that differ from Yeaple (2005) about the link between openness and the wage gap between skill groups. Since exporting increases the surplus generated by high-tech firms, high-skilled managers employed by these firms gain the most from liberalization. High-skilled managers employed by low-tech firms gain as well, since their outside opportunities are enhanced by the increase in wages paid by high-tech firms. Low-skilled managers, on the other hand, suffer nominal wage losses unless the domestic price rises sufficiently. The reason for this is that the shift in market shares away from low-tech firms (the only firms offering jobs to these workers) lowers the outside opportunities for low-skilled managers and weakens their bargaining power. These results are consistent with recent evidence that finds the wage gap between high-skilled and low-skilled rising as markets become more open.

There are a variety of ways to test the many predictions our model yields. We close by suggesting one test that we find particularly intriguing. In a paper closely related to Albrecht and Vroman (2002), Acemoglu (1999) presents a model of a labor market in which high-skilled and low-skilled workers search across (possibly) heterogeneous firms for jobs. He shows that two types of equilibria can exist. In the first, which he refers to as a "separating equilibrium," some firms create high-tech jobs and match only with high-skilled workers while other firms create low-tech jobs and match only with low-skilled workers (thus, this is similar to the EPS equilibrium in the Albrecht-Vroman model). In the other equilibrium, which he refers to as a "pooling equilibrium," all firms create the same type of jobs and match with both types of workers. Acemoglu refers to these jobs as "middling" and shows that middling jobs will be offered only when the relative productivity of high-skilled versus low-skilled workers is not too great; otherwise, equilibrium entails separation. In the latter part of his paper, Acemoglu offers a variety of evidence that in many industries middling jobs have been disappearing and have been replaced by the type of jobs that would be offered in a separating equilibrium. If we apply the logic presented in this paper to Acemoglu's model, the conclusion is that openness should cause middling jobs to *disappear* in export-oriented industries and *appear* in import-competing industries. This follows from the fact that exporting increases the spread between the revenues that the two types of workers can generate, while import competition decreases this spread. In his empirical analysis, Acemoglu does not separate his industries into groups based on their trade status. Our paper suggests that doing so might allow for a direct test of our model's prediction that openness can alter the nature of the labor market equilibrium.

APPENDIX

A.1 Solution Algorithm

The Bellman equations for unfilled vacancies can be written as

$$rV_L = -c_v + z(\theta)\left\{\gamma_L \max_j J_{Lj} + (1 - \gamma_L)\max_j J_{Mj} - V_L\right\}$$

for $j = d, f$ (A.1)

$$rV_H = -c_v + z(\theta)(1 - \gamma_L)\left\{\max_j J_{Hj} - V_H\right\} \quad \text{for } j = d, f \quad (A.2)$$

The right-hand sides of (A.1) and (A.2) both incorporate the instantaneous flow cost of maintaining the vacancy plus the expected capital gain earned in the event that a match is made. In both (A.1) and (A.2), the expected capital gain incorporates the firm's optimal export decision upon finding a match. Equation (A.1) takes into account that a low-tech firm can employ managers of either skill level, whereas (A.2) recognizes that the marginal product of a low-skilled manager is zero when employed by a high-tech firm.

In a steady state, $V_H = 0 = V_L$. Moreover, we can use the definition of R_{ij} and (3)–(7) to solve for J_{ij} a function of ϕ_L and θ. Therefore, we have

$$c_v = \frac{z(\theta)\left\{\gamma_L \max_j J_{Lj}(\phi_L, \theta) + (1 - \gamma_L)\max_j J_{Mj}(\phi_L, \theta)\right\}}{r + z(\theta)}$$

for $j = d, f$ (A.3)

$$c_v = \frac{(1 - \gamma_L)z(\theta)\max_j J_{Hj}(\phi_L, \theta)}{r + (1 - \gamma_L)z(\theta)} \quad \text{for } j = d, f \quad (A.4)$$

Equations (A.3) and (A.4) form a system of two equations in three unknown variables: θ, γ_L, and ϕ_L. We can use steady-state conditions (9) and (10) to solve for ϕ_L and u as functions of θ and γ_L. Substitution of $\phi_L(\theta, \gamma_L)$ allows us to then solve (A.3) and (A.4) for θ and γ_L.

A.2 *The Value of Search*

The validity of Proposition 2.c requires $rU_H > rU_L$. From (4)–(7):

$$rU_L = \frac{\beta\phi_L m(\theta)}{r + \delta + \beta\phi_L m(\theta)} R_{Lj} \quad \text{for } j = d, f \qquad (A.5)$$

$$rU_H = \frac{\beta m(\theta)}{r + \delta + \beta m(\theta)} \left\{ \phi_L R_{Mj} + (1 - \phi_L) R_{Hj} \right\} \quad \text{for } j = d, f \qquad (A.6)$$

From (A.6) and the requirement that $0 < \phi_L < 1$, we have

$$rU_H > \frac{\beta\phi_L m(\theta)}{r + \delta + \phi_L \beta m(\theta)} \left\{ \phi_L R_{Mj} + (1 - \phi_L) R_{Hj} \right\}$$
$$\text{for } j = d, f \qquad (A.7)$$

Comparing (A.7) with (A.5), it follows directly that $rU_H > rU_L$ if and only if

$$\phi_L R_{Mj} + (1 - \phi_L) R_{Hj} > \phi_L R_{Lj} \quad \text{for } j = d, f \qquad (A.8)$$

This last inequality is satisfied by the fact that $R_{Hj} \geq R_{Mj} \geq R_{Lj}$ for $j = d, f$.

REFERENCES

Acemoglu, Daron. 1999. Changes in unemployment and wage inequality: An alternative theory and some evidence. *American Economic Review* 89(5): 1259–78.

Albrecht, James, and Susan Vroman. 2002. A matching model with endogenous skill requirements. *International Economics Review* 43(1): 282–305.

Attanasio, Orazio, Pinelopi Goldberg, and Nina Pavcnik. 2004. Trade reforms and wage inequality in Colombia. *Journal of Development Economics* 74(2): 331–66.

Aw, Bee Yan, Sukkyun Chung, and Mark Roberts. 2004. Productivity and turnover in the export market: Micro evidence from Taiwan and South Korea. *World Bank Economic Review* 14(1): 65–90.

Baldwin, Robert, and Glen Cain. 2000. Shifts in US relative wages: The role of trade, technology, and factor endowments. *Review of Economics and Statistics* 82(4): 580–95.

Baldwin, John, and Wulong Gu. 2003. Export market participation and productivity performance in Canadian manufacturing. *Canadian Journal of Economics* 36(3): 634–57.

Baldwin, John, and Wulong Gu. 2004. Trade liberalization: Export-market participation, productivity growth and innovation. *Oxford Review of Economic Policy* 20(3): 372–92.

Bernard, Andrew, and J. Bradford Jensen. 1997. Exporters, skill upgrading, and the wage gap. *Journal of International Economics* 42(1–2): 3–31.

Bernard, Andrew, and J. Bradford Jensen. 1999a. Exceptional exporter performance: Cause, effect or both? *Journal of International Economics* 47(1): 1–25.

Bernard, Andrew, and J. Bradford Jensen. 1999b. Exporting and productivity. NBER Working Paper No. 7135.

Bernard, Andrew, and J. Bradford Jensen. 2004. Why some firms export. *Review of Economics and Statistics* 86(2): 561–69.

Bernard, Andrew, Jonathan Eaton, J. Bradford Jensen, and Samuel Kortum. 2003. Plants and productivity in international trade. *American Economic Review* 94(3): 1265–90.

Blalock, Garrick, and Paul Gertler. 2004. Learning from exporting revisited in less developed settings. *Journal of Development Economics* 75(2): 397–416.

Castellani, Davide. 2002. Export behavior and productivity growth: Evidence from Italian manufacturing firms. *Weltwirtschaftliches Archiv* 138(4): 605–28.

Clerides, Safronis, Saul Lach, and James Tybout. 1998. Is learning by exporting important? Microdynamic evidence from Columbia, Mexico, and Morocco. *Quarterly Journal of Economics* 113(3): 903–47.

Currie, Janet, and Ann Harrison. 1997. Trade reform and labor market adjustment in Morocco. *Journal of Labor Economics* 15(3): S44–71.

Das, Sanghamitra, Mark J. Roberts, and James R. Tybout. 2007. Market entry costs, producer heterogeneity, and export dynamics. *Econometrica* 75(3): 837–73.

Doms, Mark, Timothy Dunne, and Kenneth Troske. 1997. Wages, workers, and technology. *Quarterly Journal of Economics* 112(1): 252–90.

Ederington, Josh, and Phillip McCalman. 2008. Endogenous firm heterogeneity and the dynamics of trade liberalization. *Journal of International Economics* 74:422–40.

Fernandes, Ana. 2007. Trade policy, trade volumes and plant-level productivity in Columbian manufacturing industries. *Journal of International Economics* 71(1): 52–71.

Girma, Sourafel, David Greenaway, and Richard Kellner. 2004. Does exporting increase productivity? A microeconomic analysis of matched firms. *Review of International Economics* 12: 855–66.

Greenaway, David, and Richard Kellner. 2005. Exporting, productivity and agglomeration: A difference in difference analysis of matched firms. University of Nottingham Working Paper.

Hanson, Gordon, and Ann Harrison. 1999. Trade and wage inequality in Mexico. *Industrial and Labor Relations Review* 52(2): 271–88.

Harrison, Ann, and Gordon Hanson. 1999. Who gains from trade reform? Some remaining puzzles. *Journal of Development Economics* 59(1): 125–54.

Melitz, Mark. 2003. The impact of trade on intra-industry reallocations and aggregate industry performance. *Econometrica* 71(6): 1695–1726.

Mortensen, Dale, and Christopher Pissarides. 1994. Job creation and job destruction in the theory of unemployment. *Review of Economic Studies* 61(3): 397–415.

Pavcnik, Nina. 2002. Trade liberalization, exit, and productivity improvements: Evidence from Chilean plants. *Review of Economics Studies* 69(1): 245–76.

Pavcnik, Nina, Andreas Blom, Pinelopi Goldberg, and Norbert Schady. 2004. Trade policy and industry trade wage structure: Evidence from Brazil. *World Bank Economic Review* 18(3): 319–44.

Pissarides, Christopher. 2000. *Equilibrium Unemployment Theory*, 2nd ed., Cambridge, MA: MIT Press.

Revenga, Ana. 1997. Employment and wage effects of liberalization: The case of Mexican manufacturing. *Journal of Labor Economics* 15(3): S20–43.

Roberts, Mark, and James Tybout. 1997. The decision to export in Columbia: An empirical model of entry with sunk costs. *American Economic Review* 87(4): 545–64.

Scheve, Kenneth, and Matthew Slaughter. 2004. Economic insecurity and the globalization of production. *American Journal of Political Science* 48(4): 267–92.

Topalova, Petia. 2007. Trade liberalization and firm productivity: The case of India. IMF Working Paper.

Trindade, Vitor. 2004. Openness and productivity: A model of trade and firm-owners' effort. Syracuse University Working Paper.

Tybout, James. 2003. Plant- and firm-level evidence on "new" trade theories. In E. Kwan Choi and James Harrigan, eds., *Handbook of International Trade*. Malden, MA: Blackwell Publishers.

Van Biesebroeck, Johannes. 2005. Exporting raises productivity in Sub-Saharan African manufacturing firms. *Journal of International Economics* 67: 373–91.

Wacziarg, Romain, and Jessica Seddon-Wallack. 2004. Trade liberalization and intersectoral labor movements. *Journal of International Economics* 64(2): 411–39.

Yeaple, Stephen. 2005. A simple model of firm heterogeneity, international trade and wages. *Journal of International Economics* 65(1): 1–20.

Chapter 14

OUTSOURCING PETER TO PAY PAUL: HIGH-SKILL EXPECTATIONS AND LOW-SKILL WAGES WITH IMPERFECT LABOR MARKETS

CARL DAVIDSON, STEVEN J. MATUSZ, AND ANDREI SHEVCHENKO

1. INTRODUCTION

Over the past few decades many American companies have faced growing economic incentives to move certain productive activities abroad. Technological advances, improvements in telecommunications, and trade deregulation have made it very attractive to move some stages of the production process to foreign countries where labor can be hired at relatively low cost. Over the past few years, new concerns have arisen as firms have begun to outsource services that were typically performed by relatively high-skilled workers in the United States. The *New York Times* and other major publications have been filled with stories of computer companies staffing their call centers with workers located in foreign countries and hospitals sending their x-rays to be read by doctors overseas. The concern seems to be that now even high-skilled workers are losing their jobs to foreign competition and that this is a major problem because these are the very jobs that are the most desirable to keep.

Economists have responded to such concerns in a variety of ways. We have pointed out that the total number of jobs actually outsourced is rather small relative to production and employment (see, for example, a discussion pertaining to the U.S. economy in Bhagwati, Panagariya, and Srinivasan 2004) and that the process of outsourcing makes manufacturing firms more viable, leading to greater domestic job *creation* with the net effect on employment being positive (Slaughter 2004). However, many in the policy community remain skeptical that concerns about outsourcing can be dismissed so easily and point out that even though the size of the relocation activities is rather small now, there is no doubt that in the future these numbers will increase significantly. As a result, the impact of outsourcing on income distribution and living standards has become a major concern for the general public and policymakers. While there are long-held concerns that import competition from low-wage countries creates pressure on low-skill wages in manufacturing, the current concern seems to be that the outsourcing of high-tech services will reinforce the increase in income inequality.

The purpose of this paper is to investigate the impact of high-skill outsourcing on wages with a particular emphasis on its effect on low-skill wages. Our emphasis on the impact on low-skill workers follows from concerns that these workers are often hit the hardest by trade liberalization in industrialized economies. To investigate this issue, we think that it is essential to use a framework that captures many of the key features of the job dislocation process, as reported by Jacobson, LaLonde, and Sullivan (1993) and Kletzer (2001). In particular, we want to use a model in which high-skill workers, dislocated due to outsourcing, suffer nontrivial spells of unemployment before eventually finding a new job at a lower wage. Evidence suggests that these wage losses may be substantial, especially for older workers. For example, Jacobson, LaLonde, and Sullivan estimate that the average loss in lifetime earnings for a dislocated worker is roughly $80,000 with the bulk of this loss attributed to a reduction in the reemployment wage.

We also want to use a framework that captures one of the essential features of American manufacturing industries, as report by Doms, Dunne, and Troske (1997), which is that firms make heterogeneous technology choices with those using the more advanced technologies employing workers with higher skills and paying higher wages. Thus, we want a model in which workers differ in terms of their skills and firms endogenously choose to adopt technologies of different levels of sophistication. This results in a setting in which we have heterogeneity on both sides of the labor market.

We develop a model with these features by adopting a framework first suggested by Albrecht and Vroman (2002). The basic idea behind the model is really rather simple. There are two types of workers, high and low skilled, that must search for employment across firms that have chosen to adopt different technologies. The firms' technology choices are endogenous, with all firms starting out ex-ante identical. Those that choose the less sophisticated option, the "basic technology," can produce output using either high- or low-skilled labor and pay their workers relatively low wages. That is, for low-tech firms, high- and low-skilled workers are perfect substitutes in the production process. Firms that adopt the more sophisticated option, the "modern technology," can produce output using only high skilled workers and must pay these workers relatively high wages. However, the fact that these workers are using a more sophisticated technology implies that they will be more productive than if they had been employed by a low-tech firm.

When firms enter the market, they must first make their irreversible technology decision and then post a vacancy which will be filled as workers apply for the position. Entry occurs until the expected profit from posting a vacancy is driven to zero for both types of firms. Note that the two types of firms can coexist in equilibrium since the low-tech firms pay lower wages but employ less productive workers.

The most intriguing feature of this model is that for a wide variety of parameter values, two types of equilibria coexist. In one type of equilibrium, high-skill workers refuse to accept jobs at low-tech firms. Albrecht and Vroman refer to this as an "ex-post segmentation" (EPS) equilibrium since the market effectively separates with low-tech firms employing only low-skill workers and high-tech firms employing only high-skill workers. In the other type of equilibrium high-skill workers accept the first job offered to them. In this "cross-skill matching" equilibrium, the low-tech firms can afford to pay high-skill workers enough to entice them to stop searching before finding a high-tech job.

The type of equilibrium which emerges depends to a large extent on the labor market expectations of the high-skill workers. If these workers expect it to be relatively easy to find a high-tech job, they will refuse to accept low-tech jobs. This makes it harder for low-tech firms and easier for high-tech firms to fill their vacancies and leads to an equilibrium in which a greater proportion of firms choose to adopt the more sophisticated technology. As a result, the high-skilled workers' expectations that high-tech jobs will be easy to find are fulfilled.

Things are exactly reversed in the CSM equilibrium: high-skill workers take low-tech jobs because they expect high-tech jobs to be relatively hard to find. These expectations are then self-fulfilling as their willingness to accept such jobs leads to a greater proportion of firms adopting the less sophisticated technology. The implication is that the main differences between the two types of equilibria are the expectations of the high-skilled workers and the proportion of firms that adopt the two types of technologies.

To investigate the impact of high-skill outsourcing on wages we assume that firms are initially constrained to hire only domestic workers. We assume further that unemployed high-skill workers are optimistic about the chances of finding high-tech jobs, so that the initial equilibrium is of the EPS variety. Globalization then makes it possible for high-tech firms to find and employ high-skill foreign labor at a cost below the cost of searching for and employing domestic high-skill workers. In the short run, when new firms have not yet entered the market, some high-tech firms start to outsource their jobs. As fewer high-tech jobs are available for domestic high-skill workers, the domestic wage earned by these workers falls. Domestic high-skilled workers, now facing lower high-tech job opportunities *and* lower high-tech wages, start to accept low-tech jobs. In other words, in the short run outsourcing destroys the viability of the ex-post segmentation equilibrium. The economy therefore moves to the cross-skill matching equilibrium. High-skill workers lose, since they see their wages eroded by outsourcing. Low-skill workers also lose, since they faced increased competition for low-tech jobs from their high-skill counterparts. Firms are the only winners, now earning higher profits due to their ability to outsource and the across-the-board reduction in wages.

In the long run, these short-run profits induce new entry. As new firms enter, they make their technology choice based on the expectations of the high-skilled workers. If the high-skill workers who were dislocated by outsourcing in the short run continue to expect difficulty finding high-tech jobs (a reasonable assumption based on their most recent labor market experiences), then the economy will stay in the CSM equilibrium. And, since this CSM equilibrium is characterized by a greater proportion of firms using the less sophisticated technology than in the original (preglobalization) EPS equilibrium, this new long-run equilibrium is relatively more attractive for the low-skilled workers. In particular, once sufficient entry has occurred (particularly by low-tech firms), the low-skill workers find it easier to find employment and earn higher wages than they did in the initial long-run equilibrium. Thus, our main finding is that, under certain conditions, the outsourcing of high-skill jobs in a particular industry is likely to lead to wage gains for low-skill workers in that same industry. Note that this result follows directly from the impact of outsourcing on the labor market expectations of high-skill workers and the role these expectations play in shaping the structure of the industry.

After discussing the impact of high-skill outsourcing on wages, we go on to investigate its welfare implications. We find that when outsourcing alters the expectations of high-skill workers, globalization can lead to aggregate welfare losses. However, if the government offers trade adjustment assistance (TAA) to workers dislocated by globalization, such welfare losses can be averted. The reason for this is straightforward—TAA is effectively an increase in unemployment benefits, which lowers the cost of remaining unemployed for dislocated workers. Thus, by increasing unemployment benefits in the short run, the government can keep high-skill workers from accepting low-tech jobs and can ensure that their expectations do not change in a way that destroys the viability of the EPS equilibrium. These additional benefits can then be phased out in the long run as new high-tech firms enter the market to replace those that have engaged in outsourcing.

The remainder of the paper divides into four sections. In the next section, we describe the model when firms are constrained to employ only domestic workers, and in section 3 we extend the model to allow for outsourcing by high-tech firms. In section 4, we describe the short- and long-run adjustment in wages and profits to high-skill outsourcing. We discuss the policy implications of our results in the concluding section.

2. THE MODEL WITHOUT OUTSOURCING

We use a two-country version of the model developed in Albrecht and Vroman (2002). We refer to the more developed country as the North (N) and the less developed country as the South (S). In each country, there are two types of workers: low skilled and high skilled, with the proportion of the workforce that is high-skilled varying across the two countries. In particular, we assume that both countries are characterized by a continuum of risk-neutral workers of measure 1 with q_i denoting the fraction of workers in country i that are low skilled. By assumption, the North has a more productive labor force than the South in that $q_N < q_S$. In addition, we assume that firms in the North have access to two technologies: a basic (or low-tech) technology and a modern (or high-tech) technology, whereas firms in the South can only use the basic technology.

Our objective is to investigate the impact of high-skill outsourcing by Northern firms on Northern wages when labor markets are imperfect. This is accomplished by first assuming that Northern firms can only hire Northern workers. We then compare this outcome with the equilibrium that emerges when Northern high-tech firms can outsource production by hiring high-skilled Southern workers. In this section, we describe the model without outsourcing. Since the South plays no role in determining the Northern wages when outsourcing is not possible, we delay further discussion of the activities in the South until the next section.

Because workers differ by skill and Northern firms differ in the technologies that they adopt, the labor market in the North is characterized by heterogeneity on both sides of the market. The imperfection in the labor market is assumed to be generated by trading frictions that make it costly for unemployed workers and firms with vacancies to meet. This allows us to model the search process that dislocated workers in the North must go through in order to find reemployment after their jobs have been outsourced. Although some firms may use different technologies, we assume that all firms produce the identical product, which is then exported to a competitive world market. Both countries are assumed to be small, so that the price of this product is fixed exogenously at the world price and labor, which is the only input, is sector specific in both countries. The world price is normalized to 1.

As noted above, in this section we assume that, due to prohibitive costs associated with outsourcing, Northern firms employ only Northern workers. Each Northern firm that chooses to adopt the low-tech technology produces y_L units of output whenever its vacancy is filled *regardless* of the type of worker they hire. That is, for low-tech firms, high- and low-skill workers are perfect substitutes in production. A Northern firm that adopts the high-tech technology can only produce by hiring a high-skill worker and when their vacancy is filled they produce $y_H > y_L$ units of output.[1] Note that each firm employs at most one worker.

When a Northern firm first enters the market, it must commit to a technology and then post a vacancy. The flow cost of creating and maintaining a vacancy is c, regardless of which type of technology is adopted. After the risk-neutral firms post vacancies, unemployed workers and firms with vacancies are randomly matched. Once these two are matched, the firm reveals its technology choice to the worker. If the firm decides to hire the worker and the worker is interested in the job, the two agents then negotiate a wage rate with the outcome given by the generalized Nash bargaining solution. The matching function is given by $m(u, v)$ where u denotes unemployment and v denotes vacancies. We assume that $m(u, v)$ is characterized by constant returns to scale and define $\theta \equiv v/u$ as our measure of market tightness. Then, with random matching, the arrival rate of vacancies for a typical worker is given by $m(\theta)$, whereas the arrival rate of workers for a typical firm is given by $z(\theta) \equiv m(\theta)/\theta$. Following Albrecht and Vroman (2002) we assume that $m'(\theta) > 0$ and that $z'(\theta) < 0$. Finally, we assume that jobs are destroyed at rate δ.[2]

Albrecht and Vroman (2002) demonstrate that there are two types of equilibria in this model. Using Albrecht and Vroman's terminology, the economy is characterized by a "cross-skill-matching equilibrium" (CSM) if high-skill workers are willing to accept low-tech jobs. In contrast, the economy is characterized by an "ex-post segmentation equilibrium" (EPS) if high-skill workers refuse jobs at low-tech firms. A CSM typically exists if the wages that high-skill workers can expect to earn on the two types of jobs are not too different. Thus, the type of equilibrium that exists depends upon parameter values and the expectations of the high-skilled workers. At most, there can be only one CSM equilibrium and one EPS equilibrium. For some parameterizations, the two types of equilibria coexist, whereas in other cases, the market equilibrium is unique. We provide more details on this issue below, but for now we assume that a cross-skill-matching

---

[1] One can make more general technological assumptions allowing for both types of workers to perform any type of job with high-skill workers being more productive than low-skill ones. This would make presentation less tractable without adding new insights to the paper.

[2] Of course, the job will also be destroyed if either party decides to voluntarily dissolve the match. This approach to modeling the labor market is due to Pissarides (2000) and Mortensen and Pissarides (1994).

equilibrium exists. This means that high-skilled workers accept any job that is offered to them.

Under this assumption, the value functions for the firms' problem can be written as

$$rJ_i = \{y_i - w_i - c\} - \delta[J_i - V_i] \quad \text{for } i = L, H \tag{1}$$

$$rJ_U = \{y_L - w_U - c\} - \delta[J_U - V_L] \tag{2}$$

$$rV_L = -c + z(\theta)\{\gamma J_L + (1 - \gamma)J_U - V_L\} \tag{3}$$

$$rV_H = -c + z(\theta)(1 - \gamma)[J_H - V_H] \tag{4}$$

where J_i for $i = L, H$ is the value function for an active low- or high-tech Northern firm that employs a low- or high-skill worker correspondingly; J_U is the value function of an active Northern low-tech firm that employs a high-skill worker;[3] and V_i for $i = L, H$ is the value of an unmatched low- or high-tech Northern firm. In (1)–(4) we also use w_i with $i = L, H$ to denote the wage a low- or high-tech Northern firm pays to its low- or high-skill worker correspondingly; w_U to denote the wage paid by a low-tech Northern firm to a high-skill worker; r to denote the discount rate; and γ to denote the fraction of low-skill workers in the unemployment pool.

In (1)–(4), the first term on the right-hand side is the flow income earned by the firm. So, for example, an active type-i Northern firm earns a flow profit of $y_i - w_i - c$ when it sells its output, whereas a firm with a type-i vacancy earns no revenue and incurs a flow cost of c to maintain its vacancy. The second term on the right-hand side is the firm's expected capital gain (or loss) from changing its labor market status. For example, an active type-i Northern firm loses its worker at rate δ and when this occurs the firm's expected lifetime profits drop from J_i to V_i. On the other hand, low-tech Northern firms fill their vacancy at rate $z(\theta)$ and their expected lifetime profit jumps to J_L if they match with a low-skill worker (which happens with probability γ) or J_U if they match with a high-skill worker. Note that a high-tech Northern firm fills its vacancy at a lower rate of $(1 - \gamma)z(\theta)$ since it can employ only high-skill workers.

As we noted above, wages are negotiated by the firm and its worker with the solution given by the generalized Nash bargaining solution. If we use β to denote the bargaining power of the workers and use U_i to denote the expected lifetime income of an unemployed worker with skill level i, then Albrecht and Vroman show that the wages are given by

---

[3] The subscript U stands for underemployed.

$$w_i = \beta(y_i - c) + (1 - \beta)rU_i \quad \text{for } i = L, H \tag{5}$$

$$w_U = \beta(y_L - c) + (1 - \beta)rU_H \tag{6}$$

Note (5)–(6) implies that although high- and low-skill workers are perfect substitutes in production for low-tech firms, these workers do not receive the same wages in the North. In particular, since high-skill workers have better outside options, low-tech firms must pay them higher wages than they would pay to low-skill workers. Thus, in general, $w_U > w_L$. This implies that Northern low-tech firms prefer to hire low-skill workers.

We assume that in the long run there is free entry into the market. This implies that firms enter until the expected return from creating a type-i vacancy is zero, or

$$V_L = V_H = 0 \tag{7}$$

We are now ready to analyze the worker's problem. Let W_j denote the expected lifetime income for a worker with skill level j who is employed by a type-j firm (with $j = L, H$) and let W_U denote the expected lifetime income for a high-skill Northern worker who is employed by a low-tech firm. Then, using ϕ to denote the fraction of vacancies posted by low-tech firms in the North and b_N to denote unemployment benefits, we have the following value functions for the workers:

$$rU_L = b_N + \phi m(\theta)[W_L - U_L] \tag{8}$$

$$rU_H = b_N + m(\theta)[\phi W_U + (1 - \phi)W_H - U_H] \tag{9}$$

$$rW_j = w_j - \delta(W_j - U_j) \quad \text{for } j = L,H \tag{10}$$

$$rW_U = w_U - \delta(W_U - U_H) \tag{11}$$

As with the firms, the right-hand side is the sum of flow income and the expected capital gain (or loss) from changing labor market status. For unemployed workers, flow income is b_N, whereas employed workers collect wages. In (8)–(9), note that the job acquisition rate for a high-skill worker is $m(\theta)$ (since high-skill workers accept all jobs), whereas it is $\phi m(\theta)$ for low-skill workers (since they are only offered low-tech jobs). Moreover, an unemployed high-skill worker in the North matches with a low-tech firm with probability $\phi m(\theta)$, in which case the capital gain is $W_U - U_H$; otherwise, she matches with a high-tech firm and gains $W_H - U_H$.

In equilibrium, high-skill workers will be willing to accept low-tech jobs only if

$$y_L - c - rU_H > 0 \tag{12}$$

that is, if such a match creates positive surplus. Thus, this is the key condition that must be met for a CSM equilibrium to exist.

The remaining equilibrium conditions guarantee that we are in a steady state by ensuring that the flows into and out of each employment state are equal. For low-skilled workers this condition is given by

$$\delta E_L = (q - E_L)\phi m(\theta) \tag{13}$$

where $E_L \equiv q - \gamma u$ denotes low-skill employment. The analogous condition that must hold for high-skilled labor is

$$\delta E_H = (1 - q - E_H)m(\theta) \tag{14}$$

where $E_H \equiv 1 - q - (1 - \gamma)u$ denotes high-skill employment and where u is the measure of unemployment. In (13) and (14), the flow into unemployment is given on the left-hand side, whereas the flow out of unemployment is given on the right-hand side.

This completes the description of the model when high-skill workers are willing to accept low-tech jobs. Although the model may look complex, it is really rather simple. Firms have only two decisions to make: whether to enter and which type of technology to adopt. Low-tech workers simply search until finding a low-tech firm with a vacancy, whereas high-tech workers need to decide whether to accept low-tech jobs. Wages are negotiated at the time that the match occurs and jobs are destroyed randomly. Expected profits for the firms are given by (1)–(4), wages are given by (5)–(6), and the free entry conditions in (7)–(8) determine the measures of firms that enter. For the workers, expected lifetime income for different labor market states are determined by (8)–(11) and the steady-state conditions which ensure that employment is stable over time are given in (13)–(14). Finally, (12) ensures that high-skill workers make the right decision about accepting low-tech jobs.

Our next goal is to describe how the model would be altered in an EPS equilibrium. Since high-skill workers would be unwilling to accept low-tech jobs, (2), (6), and (11) would not apply. In addition, (3), (9), and (14) would have to be rewritten to take into account the fact that low-tech firms would be able to hire only low-skill workers. These equations would become

$$rV_L = -c + z(\theta)\gamma\{J_L - V_L\} \tag{3'}$$

$$rU_H = b_N + m(\theta)(1 - \phi)[W_H - U_H] \qquad (9')$$

$$\delta E_H = (1 - q - E_H)(1 - \phi)m(\theta) \qquad (14')$$

Such an equilibrium exists if (12) fails to hold when evaluated in equilibrium.

There are two key features that determine when CSM and EPS equilibria exist. First, a CSM equilibrium will not exist if low-tech firms cannot afford to pay high-skill workers enough to convince them to stop searching for a high-tech job. This will occur if the revenue generated by a low-tech firm that matches with a high-skill worker differs significantly from the revenue generated by a high-tech job. The second important factor is expectations, and it is this factor that makes it possible to have CSM and EPS equilibria both exist for the same underlying parameters. To see this, note that if high skill workers are willing to match with low-tech firms, then the value from creating a low-tech vacancy will be high and a large measure of such vacancies will be created. This would make it hard for high-skill workers to find high-tech jobs, making them more willing to match with low-tech firms. Thus, there are some situations in which self-fulfilling expectations can support equilibria of each type for a fixed set of parameters. And, when they do coexist, the main difference between the two equilibria rests with the technology choices made by firms. The EPS equilibrium is characterized by a greater fraction of the firms adopting the modern technology. This implies that high-skill workers typically prefer the EPS equilibrium, whereas low-skill workers are typically better off in the CSM equilibrium.

In terms of social welfare, as is well known, equilibria in search models are generally not efficient since decisions made by agents generate external effects. This is the case here as well. For example, the entry and technology decisions made by firms alter the match probabilities for other firms and workers. One way to correct for these external effects is to alter the wage setting mechanisms so that workers are paid their true dynamic marginal products (see Hosios 1990 for details). Since this issue has received ample attention in the literature, we will not deal with it in this paper. Instead, we focus on a welfare comparison of the CSM and EPS equilibria when they coexist.

Since high-skill workers are more productive when using the modern technology, the natural presumption would be that the EPS equilibrium generates greater aggregate income than the CSM equilibrium. However, since high-skill workers typically search longer in the EPS equilibrium (since they reject all low-tech job offers), the EPS equilibrium is characterized by higher unemployment than the CSM equilibrium. Moreover, since the high-skill workers' search decisions are generally suboptimal, it is possible for the CSM equilibrium to be the preferred outcome. For our purposes, the more interesting case is the one in which the natural presumption is accurate. Thus, for the remainder of the paper we focus on the case in which the EPS outcome yields higher aggregate income than the CSM outcome. We also assume that in the absence of outsourcing, the optimism of high-skill workers is sufficient to make the EPS equilibrium the initial outcome.

3. THE MODEL WITH OUTSOURCING

In the previous section we implicitly assumed that the cost of establishing and maintaining vacancies by Northern high-tech firms in the South was very high. One effect of globalization is that it becomes cheaper for firms to post vacancies abroad and outsource parts of the production process. In this section, we describe how our model works when Northern high-tech firms are able to post vacancies in the South and hire Southern high-skilled workers to produce their output. This requires us to now provide the details of the Southern economy.

As noted in the previous section, the Southern economy is quite similar to the Northern economy. The main differences are that the workforce is, on average, more productive in the North and that Southern firms do not have access to the modern technology. Since all active Southern firms must use the basic technology, this implies that before outsourcing becomes possible, all Southern workers hold low-tech jobs and receive the same wages. Southern firms enter until the expected profit from posting a low-tech vacancy is zero.

Once outsourcing is a viable option, Northern high-tech firms must decide whether to post a vacancy in the North or the South. If they post a vacancy in the South, they must go through the same type of search process that they would face in the North. For simplicity, we assume that the matching functions in the South and North are identical. Southern workers are assumed to be less productive than their counterparts in the North, and high-skill Southern workers employed by Northern high-tech firms are assumed to be more productive than they would be if employed by a low-tech firm. To be precise, if we let y_{LS} denote the output produced by any Southern worker employed by a low-tech firm and let y_{HS} denote the output produced by a high-skill Southern worker employed by a Northern high-tech firm, then we have $y_H > y_{HS} > y_L > y_{LS}$. Since we are interested in the impact of high-tech outsourcing, we assume that y_{LS} is low enough that it is never profitable for Northern low-tech firm to outsource production.

The value functions for Northern high-tech firms that outsource production are given by

$$rV_{HS} = -c^* + z(\theta_S)(1 - \gamma_S)[J_{HS} - V_{HS}] \tag{15}$$

$$rJ_{HS} = \{y_{HS} - w_{HS} - c^*\} - \delta[J_{HS} - V_{HS}] \tag{16}$$

where $c^* > c$ is the cost of posting and maintaining a vacancy in the South, J_{HS} is the value for an active Northern high-tech firm that has filled its vacancy with a Southern high-skill worker, V_{HS} is the value for an unmatched Northern high-tech firm that has outsourced production, w_{HS} is the wage paid to Southern high-skill workers employed by Northern high-tech firms, θ_S is the measure of labor market tightness in the South, and γ_S is the fraction of low-skill workers in the pool of unemployment in the South. The logic behind (15)–(16) is identical to that given for (1)–(4).

For simplicity, we assume that when outsourcing becomes viable for Northern firms, high-skill Southern workers stop accepting low-tech jobs. Thus, the South moves to an EPS equilibrium (the analysis is slightly more complicated but the qualitative results are unchanged if the Southern labor market exhibits cross-skill matching). This implies that the value functions for Southern firms are given by

$$rV_{LS} = -c + z(\theta_S)\gamma_S[J_{LS} - V_{LS}] \tag{17}$$

$$rJ_{LS} = \{y_{LS} - w_{LS} - c\} - \delta[J_{LS} - V_{LS}] \tag{18}$$

where c is the cost to a Southern firm of posting and maintaining a low-tech vacancy, J_{LS} is the value for an active low-tech Southern firm, V_{LS} is the value for an unmatched low-tech Southern firm, and w_{LS} is the wage that Southern firms pay their low-skill workers.

As in the North, Southern wages are negotiated with their values given by the generalized Nash bargaining solution. Thus, if we use U_{iS} to denote the expected lifetime income of an unemployed type-i Southern worker (for $i = L, H$), then w_{HS} and w_{LS} satisfy

$$w_{HS} = \beta(y_{HS} - c^*) + (1 - \beta)rU_{HS} \tag{19}$$

$$w_{LS} = \beta(y_{LS} - c) + (1 - \beta)rU_{LS} \tag{20}$$

As for Southern workers, their value functions are given by

$$rU_{LS} = b_S + \phi_S m(\theta_S)[W_{LS} - U_{HS}] \tag{21}$$

$$rU_{HS} = b_S + (1 - \phi_S)m(\theta_S)[W_{HS} - U_{HS}] \qquad (22)$$

$$rW_{iS} = w_{iS} - \delta(W_{iS} - U_{iS}) \qquad (23)$$

where W_{iS} denotes the value function for a type-i Southern worker employed in a type-i job (for $i = L, H$), b_S denotes unemployment benefits in the South, and ϕ_S denotes the proportion of vacancies in the South that are posted by low-tech firms. The logic for (21)–(23) is the same as that given for (8)–(11) above.

Finally, we turn to the steady-state and equilibrium conditions for the South. For employment to remain stable over time, the flows into and out of employment must be equal for both types of workers. Thus, we must have

$$\delta E_{LS} = (q_S - E_{LS})\, \phi_S m(\theta_S) \qquad (24)$$

$$\delta E_{HS} = (1 - q_S - E_{HS})\, (1 - \phi_S)m(\theta_S) \qquad (25)$$

where E_{iS} denotes the measure of employment for type-i Southern workers (for $i = L,H$). In equilibrium, all agents must be behaving optimally. High-skill Southern workers are behaving optimally when they reject low-tech jobs if

$$y_{LS} - c - rU_{HS} < 0 \qquad (26)$$

This completes the description of the Southern economy when outsourcing is a viable option for high-tech Northern firms. In the next section, we describe the short- and long-run adjustment of the North when globalization results in high-tech outsourcing.

4. Adjusting to Globalization

In this section, we assume that c^* is initially too high to justify outsourcing by high-tech Northern firms. Therefore, these firms hire only Northern workers. Northern high-skill workers, optimistic about the prospect of finding high-tech jobs, refuse to accept low-tech jobs and this decision results in the economy settling down in an EPS equilibrium. Globalization then causes c^* to fall, making outsourcing an attractive option. Our goal is to describe how the Northern economy adjusts in the short run, when new firms cannot enter the market, and the long run, when free entry drives the expected return from posting a vacancy back down to zero.

If c^* falls enough that V_{HS} becomes positive, unmatched Northern high-tech firms start posting vacancies in the South. Northern high-tech firms that are already producing must compare J_H, the value of continuing to produce using their Northern workers, and V_{HS}, the value obtained if the firm lays off its current employee and posts a vacancy in the South. If $J_H > V_{HS}$, the firm continues to produce in the North, whereas if $J_H < V_{HS}$, it lays off its worker and outsources production immediately.

As Northern firms start to outsource, the demand for high-skill Southern workers starts to rise, pushing up w_{HS}. For simplicity, we assume that this increase in the wage is sufficient to cause Southern high-skill workers to start rejecting low-tech jobs. In the North, as high-tech firms start shifting production to the South, the demand for high-skill labor falls, causing w_H to fall. As this wage falls, dislocated workers in the North start accepting low-tech jobs—that is, the EPS equilibrium is destroyed. For the high-tech firms, the increase in w_{HS} causes V_{HS} to fall, whereas the reduction in w_H causes V_H to rise. A short-run equilibrium is established when Northern high-tech firms are indifferent between posting vacancies in the North and South; that is, when $V_H = V_{HS}$. Note that since $V_{HS} = 0$ in the initial equilibrium and V_{HS} increases in the short run, outsourcing leads to positive profits for Northern high-tech firms.

Turn next to the impact of globalization on Northern low-skill workers and low-tech firms. As high-skill workers become dislocated, unemployment increases (altering θ, our measure of labor market tightness). Moreover, as high-tech workers start accepting low-tech jobs, low-skill workers face increased competition for employment. Both of these factors cause w_L to fall, harming Northern low-skill workers. This reduction in the low-skill wage and the fact that high-skill workers are now willing to work for low-tech firms implies that Northern low-tech firms benefit and start to earn positive profits.

In summary, the short-run impact of high-tech outsourcing is not all that different from the view commonly held in public arenas. High-skill workers become dislocated, see their bargaining power and wages eroded, and start to accept jobs for which they are overqualified. Low-skill workers are crowded out of the labor market as high-skill workers start competing with them for low-tech jobs. Thus, low-skill workers suffer wage losses as well. The big winners are the firms that all start to earn positive profits due to the reductions in wages and increased availability of workers.

These positive profits trigger entry by new firms in the long run, with the proportion of new firms that choose to adopt the high-tech technology depending upon the expectations of high-skill workers. Based on their most recent labor market experiences, it seems reasonable to assume that high-skill workers will continue to expect high-tech jobs to be difficult to acquire. As a result, the Northern economy will remain in a

CSM equilibrium, with the bulk of new firms that seek to hire Northern workers adopting the basic technology.[4] In fact, since the world price has not changed, entry by firms will continue until the North reaches the *original* (pre-outsourcing) CSM equilibrium.

The entry by new firms that employ Northern workers pushes Northern wages back up toward their old levels. However, since the new long-run equilibrium is identical to the original CSM equilibrium, we know that high-skill workers suffer long-run wage losses while low-skill workers benefit. That is, in the long run, outsourcing benefits low-skill workers at the expense of their high-skill counterparts. Given our assumption that aggregate income in the initial situation was higher in the EPS equilibrium, the total gains by the low-skill workers must be smaller than the total losses suffered by the high-skill workers, so that social welfare declines.

We close this section by providing a simple example to illustrate the short- and long-run effects of outsourcing described above. We follow the search literature in assuming that firms and workers have equal bargaining power ($\beta = 0.5$) and that the matching function is Cobb-Douglas $m(u,v) = 2\sqrt{uv}$. As for the parameters, we assume that jobs last, on average, 5 years so that $\delta = 0.2$; agents discount the future a rate such that $r = 0.05$; c, the cost of creating a vacancy in the North, is given by 0.1; and that b_i, $i = N,S$, unemployment benefits are equal to 0.5 and 0.3 correspondingly. As we will see below, this assumption about unemployment benefits implies a replacement rate in the North of about 30%, which is in line with most estimates of the effective replacement rate in the United States (see, for example, Millard and Mortensen 1997). The Northern economy is characterized by $y_H = 1.8$, $y_L = 1.6$, and $q_N = 0.6$, so that 40% of the Northern labor force is highly skilled. In the South, we have $y_{HS} = 1.7$, $y_{LS} = 0.6$, and $q_S = 0.8$.

It is straightforward to check that these parameter values satisfy all of our assumptions and guarantee that in the initial, preglobalization Northern economy both EPS and CSM equilibria exist. We assume that the North starts out in the EPS equilibria. The EPS equilibrium wages are $w_H = 1.611$ and $w_L = 1.433$. Social welfare, which we define as the sum of expected lifetime income across all Northern workers, is given by

$$\Omega_N^{EPS} = E_L W_L + E_H W_H + (q_N - E_L)U_L + (1 - q_N - E_H)U_H \qquad (27)$$

---

[4] A fraction of new high-tech entrants outsource production to the South. However, these firms do not hire Northern workers and therefore their entry has no impact on Northern wages.

which, in this case, is equal to 28.855. In this initial equilibrium, 57% of the firms that enter choose to adopt the basic technology.

Now, suppose that c^*, the cost to a Northern high-tech firm of posting a vacancy in the South, falls from some initial high level down to 0.2. At this value for c^*, it is now profitable for some high-tech firms to out-source. As they do so, the deterioration of high-tech job prospects forces high-skill workers in the North to start accepting low-tech jobs. That is, the EPS equilibrium is destroyed and the economy moves to a short-run CSM equilibrium. Calculating the short-run equilibrium is difficult, since it requires workers to forecast future entry and take this into consider-ation when negotiating wages with the firms.[5] However, we can obtain a back-of-the-envelope calculation if we assume that there is no future entry. This assumption would overstate the bargaining power of firms, therefore overstating the losses that workers are likely to suffer. Given that caveat, our numeric analysis (assuming no entry) suggests that the short-run equilibrium is reached when roughly 32% of the Northern high-tech firms outsource production. As we discussed above, both types of Northern workers are harmed by this. Indeed, the wage earned by an average high-skill worker falls from 1.611 to 1.030, whereas low-skill workers see their wages drop from 1.433 to 0.668.

Assuming that the economy remains in a CSM equilibrium, the short-run profits earned by firms leads to significant entry in the long run, with the measure of low-tech firms increasing by roughly 30%. These new low-tech entrants take advantage of the fact that high-skill workers now accept low-tech vacancies. When the Northern economy reaches its new long-run equilibrium, low-skill workers find that their wages have in-creased to a value above what they earned in the initial EPS equilibrium (from 1.433 to 1.45), whereas the high-skill workers suffer permanent wages losses (their wage drops from an initial value of 1.611 to an aver-age of 1.512). Aggregating expected lifetime income across workers gives social welfare in a CSM equilibrium, which is given by

$$\Omega_N^{CSM} = E_L W_L + E_H[\phi W_U + (1-\phi)W_H] + (q_N - E_L)U_L \\ + (1-q_N-E_H)U_H \tag{28}$$

In our example, $\Omega_N^{CSM} = 28.753$, so that globalization reduces welfare. This reduction in welfare is a direct result of the impact of globalization on the labor market expectations of high-skill workers in the North.

[5] The main difficulty caused by this is that the model would be characterized by nonstation-ary value functions.

5. DISCUSSION

The primary policy instrument used to compensate dislocated workers in the United States is unemployment insurance (through TAA). Because this policy discourages workers from finding new jobs quickly (by effectively rewarding them for remaining unemployed) it has been widely criticized as inefficient and many in the policy community have suggested replacing it with a wage subsidy program (see, for example, Parsons 2000, Kletzer and Litan 2001, and Hufbauer and Goodrich 2001). In our model, the disincentive effects of TAA that seem troubling in other contexts make unemployment insurance a relatively good way to compensate displaced workers. To see this, note that an increase in the unemployment benefit (b) results in an increase in U_H, which makes it easier to support the EPS equilibrium.[6] Thus, the government can keep the economy from moving to a CSM equilibrium in the short run by increasing the unemployment benefits offered to high-skill workers dislocated by outsourcing. These extra benefits could then be phased out in the long run. This follows from the fact that if high-skill workers do not change their expectations, entry by new high-tech firms will restore the initial EPS equilibrium in the long run.

In closing, it is worth emphasizing that our focus in this paper has been rather narrow. We have restricted attention to one aspect of globalization, the outsourcing of high-skill jobs. In particular, we have assumed away one of the main benefits of globalization, exploiting an economy's comparative advantage. It should be clear, however, that we could easily embed the economy studied in this paper in a simple general equilibrium model. We could expand our concept of globalization by assuming an initial protective tariff that is reduced at the same time that the cost of outsourcing falls. One of our main results would still go through in that the difference between high- and low-skill wages would decrease. However, distributional effects caused by a change in relative price could mitigate the potential increase in the wage earned by low-skill workers. This would be the case if, for example, the import-competing sector is also the sector for which outsourcing is an issue and if labor is specific to this sector.

We have also assumed that the types of production technologies used by firms are fixed. Our objective was to show that in this case low-skill workers may become better off if high-tech jobs are outsourced to low-cost labor markets. In reality, firms that enjoy high temporary profits do not rest on their laurels. Demand by consumers for new commodities and

[6] The EPS equilibrium exists when (12) does not hold. Increasing U_H makes this more likely.

product market competition between firms often force managers to reinvest their short-run profits in an attempt to develop new products, find new and better technologies, and start new businesses. All of these actions create new jobs and these activities are likely to take place in countries where the labor force is relatively more productive. As a result, workers face increased incentives to accumulate human capital. In such a setting, the impact of outsourcing on the development and adoption of new technologies can be ambiguous. It should depend on expectations of firms about the future distribution of skills in different countries and the expectations of workers about the availability of high-tech jobs (which would determine their willingness to invest in human capital). For now, we leave this as a topic for future research.

REFERENCES

Albrecht James, and Susan Vroman. 2002. A Matching Model with Endogenous Skill Requirements. *International Economics Review* 43(1): 282–305.

Antràs, Pol, and Elhanan Helpman. 2004. Global Sourcing. CEPR. Discussion Paper 4170.

Bhagwati, Jagdish N., Arvind Panagariya, and T.N. Srinivasan. 2004. The Muddles over Outsourcing. *Journal of Economic Perspectives* 18(4): 93–114.

Grossman, Gene M., and Elhanan Helpman. 2002. Integration vs. Outsourcing in Industry equilibrium. *Quarterly Journal of Economics* 117(1): 85–120.

Davidson, Carl, and Steven J. Matusz. 2006. Trade Liberalization and Compensation. *International Economic Review* 47: 723–47.

Doms, Mark, Timothy Dunne, and Kenneth R. Troske. 1997. Wages, Workers, and Technology. *Quarterly Journal of Economics* 112(1): 252–90.

Hosios, Arthur. 1990. On the Efficiency of Matching and Related Models of Search and Unemployment. *Review of Economic Studies* 57(2): 279–98.

Hufbauer, Gary Clyde, and Ben Goodrich. 2001. *Steel: Big Problems, Better Solutions*. Policy Brief. Washington, DC: Institute for International Economics.

Jacobson, Louis S., Robert J. LaLonde, and Daniel J. Sullivan. 1993. Earnings Losses of Displaced Workers. *American Economic Review* 83(4): 685–709.

Kletzer, Lori G. 2001. *What Are the Costs of Job Loss from Import-Competing Industries?* Washington, DC: Institute for International Economics.

Kletzer, Lori G., and Robert E. Litan. 2001. A Prescription to Relieve Worker Anxiety. Policy Brief No. 73. Washington, DC: Brookings Institution.

Millard, Stephen P., and Dale T. Mortensen. 1997. The Unemployment and Welfare Effects of Labor Market Policy: A Comparison of the USA and the UK. In D. J. Snower and G. de la Dehesa (eds.), *Unemployment Policy: Government Options for the Labor Market*. Cambridge: Cambridge University Press.

Mortensen, Dale T., and Christopher A. Pissarides. 1994. Job Creation and Job Destruction in the Theory of Unemployment. *Review of Economic Studies* 61(3): 397–415.

Pissarides, Christopher A. 2000. *Equilibrium Unemployment Theory*, 2nd ed. Cambridge, MA: MIT Press.

Parsons, Donald O. 2000. Wage Insurance: A Policy Review. *Research in Employment Policy* 2: 119–40.

Slaughter, Matthew J. 2004. Globalization and Employment by U.S. Multinationals: A Framework and Facts. Dartmouth College Working Paper. Available at http://mba.tuck.dartmouth.edu/pages/faculty/matthew.slaughter/MNE%20Outsourcing%200304.pdf.

Yeaple, Stephen R. 2005. A Simple Model of Firm Heterogeneity, International Trade and Wages. *Journal of International Economics* 65(1): 1–20.

INDEX